The Matrix
of Language

The Matrix of Language

Contemporary Linguistic Anthropology

edited by
Donald Brenneis and
Ronald K.S. Macaulay
PITZER COLLEGE

WestviewPress
A Division of HarperCollins*Publishers*

Copyright © 1996 by Westview Press, Inc., A Division of HarperCollins Publishers, Inc.

Published in 1996 in the United States of America by Westview Press, Inc., 5500 Central Avenue, Boulder, Colorado 80301-2877, and in the United Kingdom by Westview Press, 12 Hid's Copse Road, Cumnor Hill, Oxford OX2 9JJ

Library of Congress Cataloging-in-Publication Data
The matrix of language: contemporary linguistic anthropology / edited
by Donald Brenneis and Ronald K.S. Macaulay
    p. cm.
  Includes bibliographical references and index.
  ISBN 0-8133-2320-7. — ISBN 0-8133-2321-5 (pbk.)
    1. Anthropological linguistics.   I. Brenneis, Donald Lawrence,
1946–   . II. Macaulay, Ronald K.S.
P35.M29   1996
306.4'4'089—dc20   95-43947
                                                                                      CIP

The paper used in this publication meets the requirements of the American National Standard for Permanence of Paper for Printed Library Materials Z39.48-1984.

10   9   8   7   6   5   4   3   2   1

Dedicated to the memory of Ruth Borker,
colleague and friend

Contents

Part Four
Language as Social Practice

Acknowledgments

We would like to thank Michael Silverstein for suggesting our title, the contributors for the many ways in which they have stimulated our thinking, the readers for Westview Press for their helpful comments, and our students in Language in Culture for the delight, exasperation, and engagement they have shown over the years and the ways in which they have shaped this volume. Our thanks also go to Dean Birkenkamp and Jim Grode of Westview Press for their help and encouragement.

Donald Brenneis
Ronald K.S. Macaulay

1
Introduction

Since language enters into almost every facet of human experience, it is hardly surprising that it should be examined from a wide variety of perspectives. Philosophers, teachers, lawyers, advertisers, historians, politicians, comedians, and poets, to mention but a few, take a professional interest in language. Within the scientific study of language (linguistics) there is also great diversity, but the purpose of the present volume may best be clarified by contrasting four approaches to the study of language that are currently adopted by scholars.

The approach that is dominant in most U.S. university departments is that associated with the theories of Noam Chomsky. Starting with the publication of *Syntactic Structures* in 1957, Chomsky has placed the emphasis on studying "the system of knowledge attained and internally represented in the mind/brain" (1986:24). Central to Chomsky's purposes is a characterization of the universal qualities of language, that is, the features of language that make it possible for any normal infant to develop a knowledge of any human language, under widely varying conditions. Chomsky's approach requires a high degree of idealization: "Linguistic theory is concerned primarily with an ideal speaker-listener, in a completely homeogeneous speech community" (1965: 3). In contrast, the authors of the chapters in this book are concerned with the speech of imperfect human beings in communities in which there is great diversity of speech.

A second approach, which deals with the "investigation of language within the social context of the community in which it is spoken" (Labov 1966:3), is that of sociolinguists. Most sociolinguists follow Labov's example in using quantitative methods to study the correlation of linguistic features with social factors. Quantitative measures and the asterisks of statistical significance will be rare (but not totally absent) in the pages that follow. Sociolinguists have generally concentrated on phonological and morphological features, and the central focus of Labov's work has been tracking sound changes in progress. The chapters in the present volume are less concerned with linguistic form and more with how language is used. The empirical work of the scholars represented here relies more on observation and the qualitative analysis of texts than on counting occurrences of variables.

A third approach to language is that employed by the practitioners of Conversation Analysis. The conversation analysts examine the ways in which speakers accomplish the remarkable task of participating in the fluent exchange of utterances in a turn-taking schema that requires split-second timing and yet is accomplished without strain by almost every member of a speech community. The conversation analysts, however, for the most part deliberately ignore the social context in which the conversation takes place. In their own way, they are as concerned with abstract features as theoretical linguists, such as Chomsky.

The approach that characterizes the chapters in this volume sometimes falls under the rubric of ethnography of speaking (Hymes 1974) and sometimes under linguistic anthropology (Schieffelin 1993). Schieffelin summarized some of the interests of scholars in this discipline:

> In studies of language socialization, we look at how persons are socialized to use language(s) and socialized through language(s), throughout the life cycle, in households, workplaces and educational settings. How language is used in constituting power relationships, for example, in colonial and postcolonial contexts, in constructing ethnicity, gender and social class, are matters of concern. (1993:1)

Other areas of interest examined in this volume are verbal art and performance, including narrative, joking, and humor.

Theoretical linguists, taking physical science as the model for the scientific study of language, have, as it were, attempted to study language through a microscope, on the assumption that the universal structural characteristics of language can be identified in this way. Just as the specimen on the slide is often a fragment separated from a larger body, the forms of language studied by linguists using this approach are isolated from any actual situation in which they might have been used and examined as abstract, decontexualized, static examples. This approach emphasizes the importance of form over function.

An alternative scientific model for the description of language is that of the natural scientist studying animal behavior. In such an approach, the linguist observes how individuals in a society use language and attempts to create a coherent description of this usage. (The pioneer in this approach was Bronislaw Malinowski [1884–1942] whose work laid the foundations for anthropological linguistics.) Scholars working in this tradition take a dynamic view of language, seeing meaning, not in terms of dictionary definitions but as something socially negotiated. As M. M. Bakhtin pointed out, "it is not, after all, out of a dictionary that the speaker gets his words" rather he hears them "in other people's mouths, in other people's contexts, serving other people's intentions" (Bakhtin 1981:294).

The ethnography of speaking lies at the core of a range of perspectives often labeled *discourse analysis*. Characteristic of these perspectives is a commitment to the thoroughgoing analysis of talk—and other uses of language—as social practice. Language is taken to be firmly lodged not only in immediate contexts of performance and use but within broader relationships often characterized by disparities in and contests over power and inflected by past events.

In one sense discourse analysis denotes a cluster of related techniques for describing what goes on when people speak with or to each other. Transcripts of actual talk play an important role in such descriptions as they make the detailed consideration of the contents and styles of particular events. Several of the chapters in this book provide detailed examples of such transcript analysis, whether in dinner table conversations (Ochs, Smith, and Taylor) or gossip (Brenneis). Other pieces, for example, Silverstein's examination of the notion of "standard language" or Feld and Schieffelin's consideration of "hardness" in Kaluli culture highlight particular key terms within specific discourses. Although scholars in other fields such as cultural studies often use discourse analysis to convey primarily this latter, meaning-focused sense (see Williams 1976 for examples of this strategy at its best), the linguistic anthropological studies represented here suggest the value of a fuller picture in which both the content and conduct of communication figure significantly.

In addition to denoting a range of techniques, discourse analysis often connotes a theoretical orientation within which language is seen as both reflecting and consequential for relationships of conflict, cooperation, and dominance within society. The chapters in Part Two illuminate the complexities of these relationships—and of how they might be studied—in regard to the question of gender and power. Several of the chapters in Part Three are concerned, at least in part, with the political meanings and implications of particular genres, as in Limón's consideration of joking in south Texas. The political dimensions of discourse lie at the heart of Part Four, although the chapters are concerned with a wide range of points at which language and power intersect. Brenneis and Myers, for example, are concerned with the constitutive role of particular communicative events, that is, with how they weave an interactional web, making both specific relationships and broader sociability possible. Other pieces, for example, Hill's, consider the complex ties among economic and political position and history, consciousness, and identity. In all cases, however, the critical nexus is discourse, language as a social activity, both embodying old relationships and offering at times the possibilities of transformation.

Rather than trying to encompass the entire range of issues within linguistic anthropology, in this volume we have selected four general and intersecting topics as the organizational framework. We believe that these four clearly heuristic topics speak in useful ways to each other and intersect with other fields, for example, psychology, gender and feminist studies, literature and folklore, political theory, and sociocultural anthropology more generally. They provide a range of methodological models for students to consider and, perhaps, employ and help them to triangulate toward a better understanding of the interaction of language, culture, and social practice at the heart of linguistic anthropology as a field. We have not excerpted sections from the chapters, so that readers can have the chance to understand and evaluate the authors' strategies, arguments, and empirical data as fully as possible.

The first topical cluster deals with language socialization and the broader questions of social and cultural knowledge: How is learning language (and that cluster of local theories and social practices with which it is entangled) linked to becoming a member of a community? Given that children are innately endowed with a language acquisition capacity, what role do caregivers play in their language development? Is it possible that some forms of early language socialization are maladapted for the roles speakers will be asked to play in later life?

The second topical cluster has to do with issues of gender and language. Central to these pieces is an ongoing debate about the relationship between culture and power in explaining differences between men's and women's speech in various societies. The chapters in this part reflect a range of theoretical and methodological perspectives. One of our broader goals in Part Two is to help students engage in principled ways with contentious issues and to suggest some methods through which they can explore and add to the discussion. There are also enough cautionary examples in the published literature to discourage premature interpretive claims.

The third part, dealing with genre, style, and performance, draws primarily upon work in the ethnography of speaking. Central questions here focus on the role of verbal art and performance, including such critical genres as narrative, joking, and humor. The chapters illustrate the usefulness and complexity of understanding situated language through a genre-based approach. This part also raises methodological questions for social science more generally.

Finally, the fourth topic focuses on the relationship between language and social and political life. Several of the chapters deal with language and power in face-to-face communities, viewing language as both reflective of and active in constituting political relationships. The other chapters are concerned with the broader political economy of language, treating such issues as the economic implications of verbal skill, linguistic ideology, and code-switching as a nexus of identity and consciousness. Part Four comes closest to a classic focus of language and culture studies—the relationship between language and thought. These studies, however, locate such connections in the flow of everyday social life and interaction, and not in a more abstract and decontextualized notion of cognition.

It is our hope that those who use this reader will approach the chapters and the topics with a constructively critical frame of mind. There is much to be learned from these studies in terms of both the assumptions and methodologies employed and also from the conclusions of the investigations. But the study of language as a dynamic, contextualized social phenomenon is still in its infancy. There is much work to be done, but with help of pioneers like the scholars represented in this collection, anyone can take up the challenge set out by Edward Sapir sixty-six years ago: "Language is primarily a cultural or social product and must be understood as such. . . . It is peculiarly important that linguists, who are often accused, and accused justly, of failure to look beyond the pretty patterns of their subject matter, should become aware of what their science may mean for the interpretation of human conduct in general." (1929:214)

5

References

Bakhtin, M. M. 1981. *The Dialogic Imagination: Four Essays by M. M. Bakhtin,* ed. Michael Holquist, trans. Caryl Emerson and Michael Holquist. Austin: University of Texas Press.

Chomsky, Noam. 1965. *Aspects of the Theory of Syntax.* Cambridge, MA: MIT Press.

———. 1986. *Knowledge of Language.* New York: Praeger.

Hymes, Dell. 1974. *Foundations in Sociolinguistics: An Ethnographic Approach.* Philadelphia: University of Pennsylvania Press.

Labov, William. 1966. *The Social Stratification of English in New York City.* Washington, DC: Center for Applied Linguistics.

Sapir, Edward. 1929. "The status of linguistics as a science," *Language* 5:207–214.

Schieffelin, Bambi B. 1993. "The current state and fate of linguistic anthropology," *Anthropology Newsletter* 34(4): 1, 19–20.

Williams, Raymond. 1976. *Keywords: A Vocabulary of Culture and Society.* New York: Oxford University Press.

Part One
Learning Language,
Learning Culture

"Ethnocentrism is that state of mind in which the ways of one's own group seem natural and right for all human beings everywhere" (Brown and Lenneberg 1954:454). Nowhere is this more true than in the study of language development. Since the 1960s the study of how children develop the communication skills that distinguish human beings from other creatures has been a growth industry in the United States. The classic work is Roger Brown's study of three children in Cambridge, Massachusetts (Brown 1973). Through examining samples of speech from the children at regular intervals Brown was able to document their progress in developing certain skills in the use of language. Brown was influenced by the views of Noam Chomsky (1965) and consequently concentrated on the children's mastery of certain linguistic structures. There was no attempt to study the circumstances in which the children were developing these skills.

One linguistic anthropologist, Martha Ward, set out to explore the "real-life conditions under which children learn their language" (Ward 1971:2). She chose a plantation settlement, called Rosepoint in the study, west of New Orleans on the Mississippi River, with a predominantly English-speaking population. She found that the methodology that had proved so fruitful for Brown at Harvard was useless in Rosepoint:

> For the first two months of this project attempts to elicit spontaneous speech from the children met with defeat, with or without the tape recorder. The readiness to show off, the constant flow of speech, and the mother-child interaction so common in middle-class children were nowhere in evidence. The children appeared to speak as little to their parents as to the investigator. One twenty-eight-month male spoke three words in as many months. Meanwhile, the mothers complained that the verbal precocity of their children was driving them up the wall. (Ward 1971:15)

Despite this apparently unfavorable situation and the apparent contradiction between mothers' reports and Ward's own formal observations, the children succeeded in developing linguistic skills.

Shirley Brice Heath had the time in which to undertake a more extended ethnographic study in the Piedmont Carolinas communities she discusses. Heath devoted nine years to this study, which is fully reported in Heath 1983. Heath contrasts the language socialization of children in three communities: Maintown, a mainstream middle-class community, Roadville, a blue-collar white community, and Trackton, a poorer, working-class black community. Heath makes it quite clear that each of the three communities provides a locally appropriate and effective form of language socialization for their children—until the children enter the school system. Then it becomes clear that the Maintown children have a distinct advantage because their socialization has prepared them for the culture of the school. In interestingly different ways the children of Roadville and Trackton are less well-prepared for the situation they will encounter at school. Unfortunately, the teachers are equally less well-prepared to deal with the children from Roadville and Trackton. In her full-length account (1983:284–287) Heath describes how a dedicated and imaginative teacher succeeded with a group of black first-grade children who were deemed "potential failures" on the basis of their performance on reading readiness tests. But the success was short-lived because the children went on to "regular" classes in which the self-fulfilling prophecies of failure proved yet again to be justified. It is a further justification for Basil Bernstein's warning that we need to rethink the schools as if the middle-class child did not exist (Bernstein 1961:306).

Heath's chapter in the present volume draws attention to the kinds of activities that are taken as "normal" in mainstream U.S. middle-class families. She asks how the middle-class child is socialized into the analytical, field-independent learning style that is frequently presented as that which correlates with academic achievement and success in school. Manuel Ramírez and Alfredo Castañeda (1974) suggest that an important factor is a match between the teaching style of the teacher and the learning style of the child. They also draw attention to the mainstream bias in the use of the terms *field independent* and *field dependent*. They point out that the bias would be reversed if the term for field dependent were *field sensitive* and its contrary *field insensitive*. It is, of course, those who have been successful academically who chose the label field independent for their own learning style. Katherine Nelson (1973) draws attention to a similar possibility of match or mismatch between the very young child's learning style and the mother's expectations and practice. It is a cautionary reminder that not all differences of this kind can be related to social or cultural categories since Nelson's families were all mainstream middle-class white U.S. Americans.

One of the ironies that future historians will note is that Chomsky and his disciples have in theory emphasized the universal aspects of language acquisition but in practice they have tended to base their views on how middle-class U.S. Americans socialize their children. Heath shows the difference in the socialization of the children in Maintown, Roadville, and Trackton. Where the Maintown children are encouraged to be curious about the world around them, the Roadville children are expected to see the world very clearly in terms of true versus false, right versus wrong, and the Trackton children are rewarded for being entertaining, imaginative, and socially adept.

Steven Feld and Bambi Schieffelin describe a different kind of socialization among the Kaluli in Papua New Guinea. The Kaluli emphasize the need for the child to learn to use language for practical reasons, *to halaido,* "hard words." Kaluli adults train their children to do this by telling the child exactly what to say in a particular situation. Word play is considered "bird talk" and discouraged. The Kaluli adults place great importance on correct behavior and early language instruction is intended to reinforce this behavior. The four approaches to language socialization described in these two chapters are interesting for their similarities and differences:

1. In Maintown and Roadville and among the Kaluli the adults are very concerned about their children's language development and intervene to guide it in the right direction. Trackton adults assume that the children will learn from observation and example; they do not provide explicit instruction.
2. The Maintown and Roadville children are brought up in the relative isolation of single-family homes. The Trackton and Kaluli children spend most of their time in a wider social context, which includes adults who are not part of their immediate family.
3. Maintown and Roadville adults interpret very young children's unclear utterances. Trackton and Kaluli adults ignore or discourage such utterances.
4. Roadville and Kaluli adults give specific instructions to children on what to say in particular situations. Maintown adults are more likely to try to elicit the appropriate form from the child. Trackton adults are less concerned about encouraging language development.
5. Maintown and Trackton adults encourage their children to use language imaginatively and creatively. Roadville and Kaluli adults explicitly discourage this.
6. In all four communities the adults pay more attention to what the children are doing with language than to linguistic form.

These two chapters provide a window into the circumstances in which children develop linguistic skills. Chomsky has claimed that children are genetically endowed with a language acquisition device that enables them to develop these skills in a predictable manner regardless of the efforts of the adults around them. One of the questions that these chapters raise is: Do they support or refute Chomsky's view?

Language development does not cease at the age of three or four. In their chapter, Elinor Ochs, Ruth Smith, and Carolyn Taylor show how family members solve problems by discussing them in a narrative framework. Most accounts of narratives deal with the structure of narratives told by a single speaker (Bauman 1986; Johnstone 1990; Labov and Waletzky 1967; Labov 1981). Ochs et al., however, are concerned with co-narration in which the "story" is socially negotiated by the participants. They show how a story that starts out in one direction can end up with a rather different conclusion because of the contribution of other participants. The question of who is "entitled" to tell a particular story (Shuman 1986) thus becomes negotiable. In this chapter, Ochs et al. take the analysis of speech events (Hymes 1974) to a more refined level than Heath or Feld and Schieffelin do in theirs. Whereas the latter deal with "types" of interaction, Ochs et al. deal with two specific examples. As in all empirical work, there is a trade-off. Ochs et al. provide details of a kind that are glossed over in the other chapters, but they provide no comparative data. We do not know how typical their examples are or whether there are differences in family style that can be related to social categories.

Suggestions for Further Reading

The articles in *The Development of Language,* edited by J. B. Gleason, give a good overview of research in the area of children's language acquisition. C. Snow and C. Ferguson (eds.), *Talking to Children,* R. Scollon's *Conversations with a One-year-Old,* and L. Bloom, *The Transition from Infancy to Language* give good accounts of children's early language development. Chomsky's *Knowledge of Language* provides a comprehensive introduction to his views; see also his *Aspects of the Theory of Syntax.* Two other books that deal with children's early syntactic development are L. Bloom, *Language Development* and M. Bowerman, *Early Syntactic Development.* Children's later syntactic development is discussed in C. Chomsky, *Acquisition of Syntax from 5 to 10* and in S. Romaine, *The Language of Children and Adolescents.* D. Slobin (ed.), *A Cross-cultural Study of Language Acquisition,* provides a wide range of information on children learning languages other than English. E. Ochs's *Culture and Language Development: Language Acquisition and Language Socialization in a Samoan Village* and B. Schieffelin, *The Give and Take of Everyday Life: Language Socialization of Kaluli Children* give insightful accounts of language development in non-English-speaking communities.

References

Bauman, Richard. 1986. *Story, Performance, and Event: Contextual Studies of Oral Narrative.* Cambridge: Cambridge University Press.

Bernstein, Basil. 1961. "Social class and linguistic development: A theory of social learning." In A. H. Halsey, J. Floud, and A. Anderson, eds., *Education, Economy, and Society.* New York: Free Press, 288–314.

Bloom, Lois. 1970. *Language Development: Form and Function in Emerging Grammars.* Cambridge, MA: MIT Press.

———. 1993. *The Transition from Infancy to Language: Acquiring the Power of Expression.* Cambridge: Cambridge University Press.

Bowerman, Melissa. 1973. *Early Syntactic Development: A Cross-Linguistic Study with Special Reference to Finnish.* Cambridge: Cambridge University Press.

Brown, Roger. 1973. *A First Language: The Early Stages.* Cambridge, MA: Harvard University Press.

Brown, Roger, and Eric Lenneberg. 1954. "A study in language and cognition." *Journal of Abnormal and Social Psychology* 49:454–462.

Chomsky, Carol. 1969. *The Acquisition of Syntax in Children from 5 to 10*. Cambridge, MA: MIT Press.

Chomsky, Noam. 1965. *Aspects of the Theory of Syntax*. Cambridge, MA: MIT Press.

————. 1986. *Knowledge of Language: Its Nature, Origins, and Use*. Cambridge, MA: MIT Press.

Gleason, Jean Berko, ed. 1989. *The Development of Language* (2nd edition). Columbus, OH: Merrill.

Heath, Shirley Brice. 1983. *Ways with Words: Language, Life, and Work in Communities and Classrooms*. Cambridge, MA: Cambridge University Press.

Hymes, Dell. 1974. *Foundations in Sociolinguistics: An Ethnographic Approach*. Philadelphia: University of Pennsylvania Press.

Johnstone, Barbara. 1990. *Stories, Community, and Place: Narratives from Middle America*. Bloomington, IN: Indiana University Press.

Labov, William. 1981. "Speech actions and reactions in personal narrative." In Deborah Tannen, ed., *Analyzing Discourse: Text and Talk*. Washington, DC: Georgetown University Press: 219–247.

Labov, William, and Joshua Waletzky. 1967. "Narrative analysis: Oral versions of personal experience." In June Helm, ed., *Essays on the Verbal and Visual Arts*. Seattle: University of Washington Press: 12–44.

Nelson, Katherine E. 1973. *Structure and Strategy in Learning to Talk*. Monographs of the Society for Research in Child Development 39 (1–2) (Serial No. 149).

Ochs, Elinor. 1988. *Culture and Language Development: Language Acquisition and Language Socialization in a Samoan Village*. Cambridge: Cambridge University Press.

Ramírez III, Manuel, and Alfredo Castañeda. 1974. *Cultural Democracy, Bicognitive Development, and Education*. New York: Academic Press.

Romaine, Suzanne. 1984. *The Language of Children and Adolescents: The Acquisition of Communicative Competence*. Oxford: Blackwell.

Schieffelin, Bambi B. 1990. *The Give and Take of Everyday Life: Language Socialization of Kaluli Children*. Cambridge: Cambridge University Press.

Scollon, Ronald. 1976. *Conversations with a One-Year-Old*. Honolulu: University of Hawaii Press.

Shuman, Amy. 1986. *Story-telling Rights: The Uses of Oral and Written Texts by Urban Adolescents*. Cambridge: Cambridge University Press.

Slobin, Dan, ed. 1985. *A Cross-cultural Study of Language Acquisition*. Hillsdale, NJ: Erlbaum.

Snow, Catherine E., and Charles A. Ferguson, eds. 1977. *Talking to Children: Language Input and Acquisition*. Cambridge: Cambridge University Press.

Ward, Martha Coonfield. 1971. *Them Children: A Study in Language Learning*. New York: Holt, Rinehart, and Winston.

2

What No Bedtime Story Means: Narrative Skills at Home and School

SHIRLEY BRICE HEATH

In the preface to *S/Z*, Roland Barthes' work on ways in which readers read, Richard Howard writes: "We require an education in literature . . . in order to discover that *what we have assumed*—with the complicity of our teachers—*was nature is in fact culture, that what was given is no more than a way of taking*" (emphasis not in the original; Howard 1974:ix).[1] This statement reminds us that the *culture* children learn as they grow up is, in fact, "ways of taking" meaning from the environment around them. The means of making sense from books and relating their contents to knowledge about the real world is but one "way of taking" that is often interpreted as "natural" rather than learned. The quote also reminds us that teachers (and researchers alike) have not recognized that ways of taking from books are as much a part of learned behavior as are ways of eating, sitting, playing games, and building houses.

As school-oriented parents and their children interact in the pre-school years, adults give their children, through modeling and specific instruction, ways of taking from books which seem natural in school and in numerous institutional settings such as banks, post offices, businesses, or government offices. These *mainstream* ways exist in societies around the world that rely on formal educational systems to prepare children for participation in settings involving literacy. In some communities these ways of schools and institutions are very similar to the ways learned at home; in other communities the ways of school are merely an overlay on the home-taught ways and may be in conflict with them.[2]

Yet little is actually known about what goes on in story-reading and other literacy-related interactions between adults and preschoolers in communities around the world. Specifically, though there are numerous diary accounts and experimental studies of the preschool reading experiences of mainstream middle-class children, we know little about the specific literacy features of the environment upon which the school expects to draw. Just how does what is frequently termed "the literate tradition" envelope the child in knowledge about interrelationships between oral and written language, between knowing something and knowing ways of labeling and displaying it? We have even less information about the variety of ways children from *non-mainstream* homes learn about reading, writing, and using oral language to display knowledge in their preschool environment. The general view has been that whatever it is that mainstream school-oriented homes have, these other homes do not have it; thus these children are not from the literate tradition and are not likely to succeed in school.

A key concept for the empirical study of ways of taking meaning from written sources across communities is that of *literacy events:* occasions in which written language is integral to the nature of participants' interactions and their interpretive processes and strategies. Familiar literacy events for mainstream preschoolers are bedtime stories, reading cereal boxes, stop signs, and television ads, and interpreting instructions for commercial games and toys. In such literacy events, participants follow socially established rules for verbalizing what they know from and about the written material. Each community has rules for socially interacting and sharing knowledge in literacy events.

This paper briefly summarizes the ways of taking from printed stories families teach their preschoolers in a cluster of mainstream school-oriented neighborhoods of a city in the Southeastern region of the United States. We then describe two quite different ways of taking used in the homes of two English-speaking communities in the same region that do not follow the school-expected patterns of bookreading and reinforcement of these patterns in oral storytelling. Two assumptions underlie this paper and are treated in detail in the ethnography of these communities (Heath 1983): (1) Each community's ways of taking from the printed word and using this knowledge are interdependent with the ways children learn to talk in their social interactions with caregivers. (2) There is little or no validity to the time-honored dichotomy of "the literate tradition" and "the oral tradition." This paper suggests a frame of reference for both the community patterns and the paths of development children in different communities follow in their literacy orientations.

Mainstream School-Oriented Bookreading

Children growing up in mainstream communities are expected to develop habits and values which attest to their membership in a "literate society." Children learn certain customs, beliefs, and skills in early enculturation experiences with written materials: the bedtime story is a major literacy event which helps set patterns of behavior that recur repeatedly through the life of mainstream children and adults.

In both popular and scholarly literature, the "bedtime story" is widely accepted as a given—a natural way for parents to interact with their child at bedtime. Commercial publishing houses, television advertising, and children's magazines make much of this familiar ritual, and many of their sales pitches are based on the assumption that in spite of the intrusion of television into many patterns of interaction between parents and children, this ritual remains. Few parents are fully conscious of what bedtime storyreading means as preparation for the kinds of learning and displays of knowledge expected in school. Ninio and Bruner (1978), in their <u>longitudinal</u> study of one mainstream middle-class mother-infant dyad in joint picture-book reading, strongly suggest a universal role of bookreading in the achievement of labeling by children.

In a series of "reading cycles," mother and child alternate turns in a dialogue: the mother directs the child's attention to the book and/or asks what-questions and/or labels items on the page. The items to which the what-questions are directed and labels given are two-dimensional representations of three-dimensional objects, so that the child has to resolve the conflict between perceiving these as two-dimensional objects and as representations of a three-dimensional visual setting. The child does so "by assigning a privileged, autonomous status to pictures as visual objects" (1978: 5). The arbitrariness of the picture, its decontextualization, and its existence as something which cannot be grasped and manipulated like its "real" counterparts is learned through the routines of structured interactional dialogue in which mother and child take turns playing a labeling game. In a "scaffolding" dialogue (cf. Cazden 1979), the mother points and asks "What is x?" and the child vocalizes and/or gives a nonverbal signal of attention. The mother then provides verbal feedback and a label. Before the age of two, the child is socialized into the "initiation-reply-evaluation sequences" repeatedly described as the central structural feature of classroom lessons (e.g., Sinclair and Coulthard 1975; Griffin and Humphry 1978; Mehan 1979). Teachers ask their students questions which have answers prespecified in the mind of the teacher. Students respond, and teachers provide feedback, usually in the form of an evaluation. Training in ways of responding to this pattern begins very early in the labeling activities of mainstream parents and children.

Maintown Ways

This patterning of "<u>incipient literacy</u>" (Scollon and Scollon 1979) is similar in many ways to that of the families of fifteen primary-level school teachers in Maintown, a cluster of middle-class neighborhoods in a city of the Piedmont Carolinas. These families (all of whom identify themselves as "typical," "middle-class," or "mainstream,") had preschool children, and the mother in each family was either teaching in local public schools at the time of the study (early 1970s), or had taught in the academic year preceding participation in the study. Through a research dyad approach, using teacher-mothers as researchers with the ethnographer, the teacher-mothers audio-recorded their children's interactions in their primary network—mothers, fathers, grandparents, maids, siblings, and frequent visitors to the home. Children were expected to learn the following rules in literacy events in these nuclear households:

1. As early as six months of age, children *give attention to books and information derived from books.* Their rooms contain bookcases and are decorated

with murals, bedspreads, mobiles, and stuffed animals which represent characters found in books. Even when these characters have their origin in television programs, adults also provide books which either repeat or extend the characters' activities on television.

2. Children, from the age of six months, *acknowledge questions about books.* Adults expand nonverbal responses and vocalizations from infants into fully formed grammatical sentences. When children begin to verbalize about the contents of books, adults extend their questions from simple requests for labels (What's that? Who's that?) to ask about the attributes of these items (What does the doggie say? What color is the ball?)

3. From the time they start to talk, children *respond to conversational allusions to the content of books; they act as question-answerers who have a knowledge of books.* For example, a fuzzy black dog on the street is likened by an adult to Blackie in a child's book: "Look, there's a Blackie. Do you think *he's* looking for a boy?" Adults strive to maintain with children a running commentary on any event or object which can be book-related, thus modeling for them the extension of familiar items and events from books to new situational contexts.

4. Beyond two years of age, children *use their knowledge of what books do to legitimate their departures from "truth."* Adults encourage and reward "book talk," even when it is not directly relevant to an ongoing conversation. Children are allowed to suspend reality, to tell stories which are not true, to ascribe fiction-like features to everyday objects.

5. Preschool children *accept book and book-related activities as entertainment.* When preschoolers are "captive audiences" (e.g., waiting in a doctor's office, putting a toy together, or preparing for bed), adults reach for books. If there are no books present, they talk about other objects as though they were pictures in books. For example, adults point to items, and ask children to name, describe, and compare them to familiar objects in their environment. Adults often ask children to state their likes or dislikes, their view of events, and so forth, at the end of the captive audience period. These affective questions often take place while the next activity is already underway (e.g., moving toward the doctor's office, putting the new toy away, or being tucked into bed), and adults do not insist on answers.

6. Preschoolers *announce their own factual and fictive narratives* unless they are given in response to direct adult elicitation. Adults judge as most acceptable those narratives which open by orienting the listener to setting and main character. Narratives which are fictional are usually marked by formulaic openings, a particular prosody, or the borrowing of episodes in story books.

7. When children are about three years old, adults discourage the highly interactive participative role in bookreading children have hitherto played and children *listen and wait as an audience.* No longer does either adult or child repeatedly break into the story with questions and comments. Instead, chil-

dren must listen, store what they hear, and on cue from the adult, answer a question. Thus, children begin to formulate "practice" questions as they wait for the break and the expected formulaic-type questions from the adult. It is at this stage that children often choose to "read" to adults rather than to be read to.

A pervasive pattern of all these features is the authority which books and book-related activities have in the lives of both the preschoolers and members of their primary network. Any initiation of a literacy event by a preschooler makes an interruption, an untruth, a diverting of attention from the matter at hand (whether it be an uneaten plate of food, a messy room, or an avoidance of going to bed) acceptable. Adults jump at openings their children give them for pursuing talk about books and reading.

   In this study, writing was found to be somewhat less acceptable as an "any-time activity," since adults have rigid rules about times, places, and materials for writing. The only restrictions on bookreading concern taking good care of books: they should not be wet, torn, drawn on, or lost. In their talk to children about books, and in their explanations of why they buy children's books, adults link school success to "learning to love books," "learning what books can do for you," and "learning to entertain yourself and to work independently." Many of the adults also openly expressed a fascination with children's books "nowadays." They generally judged them as more diverse, wide-ranging, challenging, and exciting than books they had as children.

The Mainstream Pattern.   A close look at the way bedtime story routines in Maintown taught children how to take meaning from books raises a heavy sense of the familiar in all of us who have acquired mainstream habits and values. Throughout a lifetime, any school-successful individual moves through the same processes described above thousands of times. Reading for comprehension involves an internal replaying of the same types of questions adults ask children of bedtime stories. We seek *what-explanations*, asking what the topic is, establishing it as predictable and recognizing it in new situational contexts by classifying and categorizing it in our mind with other phenomena. The what-explanation is replayed in learning to pick out topic sentences, write outlines, and answer standardized tests which ask for the correct titles to stories, and so on. In learning to read in school, children move through a sequence of skills designed to teach what-explanations. There is a tight linear order of instruction which recapitulates the bedtime story pattern of breaking down the story into small bits of information and teaching children to handle sets of related skills in isolated sequential hierarchies.

   In each individual reading episode in the primary years of schooling, children must move through what-explanations before they can provide *reason-explanations* or *affective commentaries*. Questions about why a particular event occurred or why a specific action was right or wrong come at the end of primary-level reading lessons, just as they come at the end of bedtime stories. Throughout the primary grade levels, what-explanations predominate, reason-explanations come with increasing frequency in the upper grades, and affective comments most often come in the extra-credit portions of the reading workbook or at the end of the list of suggested activities in text books across grade levels. This sequence characterizes the total school career. High school freshmen who are judged poor in compositional and reading skills spend most of their time on what-explanations and practice in advanced versions of bedtime story questions and answers. They are given little or no chance to use reason-giving explanations or assessments of the actions of stories. Reason-explanations result in configurational rather than hierarchical skills, are not predictable, and thus do not present content with a high degree of redundancy. Reason-giving explanations tend to rely on detailed knowledge of a specific domain. This detail is often unpredictable to teachers, and is not as highly valued as is knowledge which covers a particular area of knowledge with less detail but offers opportunity for extending the knowledge to larger and related concerns. For example, a primary-level student whose father owns a turkey farm may respond with reason-explanations to a story about a turkey. His knowledge is intensive and covers details perhaps not known to the teacher and not judged as relevant to the story. The knowledge is unpredictable and questions about it do not continue to repeat the common core of content knowledge of the story. Thus such configured knowledge is encouraged only for the "extras" of reading—an extra-credit oral report or a creative picture and story about turkeys. This kind of knowledge is allowed to be used once the hierarchical what-explanations have been mastered and displayed in a particular situation and, in the course of one's academic career, only when one has shown full mastery of the hierarchical skills and subsets of related skills which underlie what-explanations. Thus, reliable and successful participation in the ways of taking from books that teachers view as natural must, in the usual school way of doing things, precede other ways of taking from books.

These various ways of taking are sometimes referred to as "cognitive styles" or "learning styles." It is generally accepted in the research literature that they are influenced by early socialization experiences and correlated with such features of the society in which the child is reared as social organization, reliance on authority, male-female roles, and so on. These styles are often seen as two contrasting types, most frequently termed "field independent-field dependent" (Witkin et al. 1966) or "analytic-relational" (Kagan, Sigel, and Moss 1963; Cohen 1968, 1969, 1971). The analytic field-independent style is generally presented as that which correlates positively with high achievement and general academic and social success in school. Several studies discuss ways in which this style is played out in school—in preferred ways of responding to pictures and written text and selecting from among a choice of answers to test items.

Yet, we know little about how behaviors associated with either of the dichotomized cognitive styles (field-dependent/relational and field-independent/

analytic) were learned in early patterns of socialization. To be sure, there are vast individual differences which may cause an individual to behave so as to be categorized as having one or the other of these learning styles. But much of the literature on learning styles suggests a preference for one or the other is learned in the social group in which the child is reared and in connection with other ways of behaving found in that culture. But how is a child socialized into an analytic/field-independent style? What kinds of interactions does he enter into with his parents and the stimuli of his environment which contribute to the development of such a style of learning? How do these interactions mold selective attention practices such as "sensitivity to parts of objects," "awareness of obscure, abstract, nonobvious features," and identification of "abstractions based on the features of items" (Cohen 1969: 844–45)? Since the predominant stimuli used in school to judge the presence and extent of these selective attention practices are written materials, it is clear that the literacy orientation of preschool children is central to these questions.

The foregoing descriptions of how Maintown parents socialize their children into a literacy orientation fit closely those provided by Scollon and Scollon for their own child Rachel. Through similar practices, Rachel was "literate before she learned to read" (1979: 6). She knew, before the age of two, how to focus on a book and not on herself. Even when she told a story about herself, she moved herself out of the text and saw herself as author, as someone different from the central character of her story. She learned to pay close attention to the parts of objects, to name them, and to provide a running commentary on features of her environment. She learned to manipulate the contexts of items, her own activities, and language to achieve book-like, decontextualized, repeatable effects (such as puns). Many references in her talk were from written sources; others were modeled on stories and questions about these stories. The substance of her knowledge, as well as her ways of framing knowledge orally, derived from her familiarity with books and bookreading. No doubt, this development began by labeling in the dialogue cycles of reading (Ninio and Bruner 1978), and it will continue for Rachel in her preschool years along many of the same patterns described by Cochran-Smith (1981) for a mainstream nursery school. There teacher and students negotiated story-reading through the scaffolding of teachers' questions and running commentaries which replayed the structure and sequence of story-reading learned in their mainstream homes.

Close analyses of how mainstream school-oriented children come to learn to take from books at home suggest that such children learn not only how to take meaning from books, but also how to talk about it. In doing the latter, they repeatedly practice routines which parallel those of classroom interaction. By the time they enter school, they have had continuous experience as information-givers; they have learned how to perform in those interactions which surround literate sources throughout school. They have had years of practice in interaction situations that are the heart of reading—both learning to read and reading to learn in school. They have developed habits of performing which enable them to run through the hierarchy of preferred knowledge about a literate source and the appropriate sequence of skills to be displayed in showing knowledge of a subject. They have developed ways of decontextualizing and surrounding with explanatory prose the knowledge gained from selective attention to objects.

They have learned to listen, waiting for the appropriate cue which signals it is their turn to show off this knowledge. They have learned the rules for getting certain services from parents (or teachers) in the reading interaction (Merritt 1979). In nursery school, they continue to practice these interaction patterns in a group rather than in a dyadic situation. There they learn additional signals and behaviors necessary for getting a turn in a group, and responding to a central reader and to a set of centrally defined reading tasks. In short, most of their waking hours during the preschool years have enculturated them into: (1) all those habits associated with what-explanations, (2) selective attention to items of the written text, *and* (3) appropriate interactional styles for orally displaying all the know-how of their literate orientation to the environment. This learning has been finely tuned and its habits are highly interdependent. Patterns of behaviors learned in one setting or at one stage reappear again and again as these children learn to use oral and written language in literacy events and to bring their knowledge to bear in school-acceptable ways.

Alternative Patterns of Literacy Events

But what corresponds to the mainstream pattern of learning in communities that do not have this finely tuned, consistent, repetitive, and continuous pattern of training? Are there ways of behaving which achieve other social and cognitive aims in other sociocultural groups?

The data below are summarized from an ethnography of two communities— Roadville and Trackton—located only a few miles from Maintown's neighborhoods in the Piedmont Carolinas. Roadville is a white working-class community of families steeped for four generations in the life of the textile mill. Trackton is a working-class black community whose older generations have been brought up on the land, either farming their own land or working for other landowners. However, in the past decade, they have found work in the textile mills. Children of both communities are unsuccessful in school; yet both communities place a high value on success in school, believing earnestly in the personal and vocational rewards school can bring and urging their children "to get ahead" by doing well in school. Both Roadville and Trackton are literate communities in the sense that the residents of each are able to read printed and written materials in their daily lives, and on occasion they produce written messages as part of the total pattern of communication in the community. In both communities, children go to school with certain expectancies of print and, in Trackton especially, children have a keen sense that reading is something one does to learn something one needs to know

(Heath 1980). In both groups, residents turn from spoken to written uses of language and vice versa as the occasion demands, and the two modes of expression seem to supplement and reinforce each other. Nonetheless there are radical differences between the two communities in the ways in which children and adults interact in the preschool years; each of the two communities also differs from Maintown. Roadville and Trackton view children's learning of language from two radically different perspectives: in Trackton, children "learn to talk," in Roadville, adults "teach them how to talk."

Roadville

In Roadville, babies are brought home from the hospital to rooms decorated with colorful, mechanical, musical, and literacy-based stimuli. The walls are decorated with pictures based on nursery rhymes, and from an early age, children are held and prompted to "see" the wall decorations. Adults recite nursery rhymes as they twirl the mobile made of nursery-rhyme characters. The items of the child's environment promote exploration of colors, shapes, and textures: a stuffed ball with sections of fabrics of different colors and textures is in the crib; stuffed animals vary in texture, size, and shape. Neighbors, friends from church, and relatives come to visit and talk to the baby, and about him to those who will listen. The baby is fictionalized in the talk to him: "But this baby wants to go to sleep, doesn't he? Yes, see those little eyes gettin' heavy." As the child grows older, adults pounce on word-like sounds and turn them into "words," repeating the "words," and expanding them into well-formed sentences. Before they can talk, children are introduced to visitors and prompted to provide all the expected politeness formulas, such as "Bye-bye," "Thank you," and so forth. As soon as they can talk, children are reminded about these formulas, and book or television characters known to be "polite" are involved as reinforcement.

In each Roadville home, preschoolers first have cloth books, featuring a single object on each page. They later acquire books which provide sounds, smells, and different textures or opportunities for practicing small motor skills (closing zippers, buttoning buttons, etc.). A typical collection for a two-year-old consisted of a dozen or so books—eight featured either the alphabet or numbers, others were books of nursery rhymes, simplified Bible stories, or "real-life" stories about boys and girls (usually taking care of their pets or exploring a particular feature of their environment). Books based on Sesame Street characters were favorite gifts for three- and four-year-olds.

Reading and reading-related activities occur most frequently before naps or at bedtime in the evening. Occasionally an adult or older child will read to a fussy child while the mother prepares dinner or changes a bed. On weekends, fathers sometimes read with their children for brief periods of time, but they generally prefer to play games or play with the children's toys in their interactions. The following episode illustrates the language and social interactional aspects of these bedtime events; the episode takes place between Wendy (2;3 at the time of this episode) and Aunt Sue who is putting her to bed.

[Aunt Sue (AS) picks up book, while Wendy (W) crawls about the floor, ostensibly looking for something]

W: uh uh

AS: Wendy, we're gonna read, uh, read this story, come on, hop up here on this bed.

[Wendy climbs up on the bed, sits on top of the pillow, and picks up her teddy bear]

[Aunt Sue opens book, points to puppy]

AS: Do you remember what this book is about? See the puppy? What does the puppy do?

[Wendy plays with the bear, glancing occasionally at pages of the book, as Aunt Sue turns. Wendy seems to be waiting for something in the book]

AS: See the puppy?

[Aunt Sue points to the puppy in the book and looks at Wendy to see if she is watching]

W: uh huh, yea, yes ma'am

AS: Puppy sees the ant, he's a li'l

[Wendy drops the bear and turns to book.]

fellow. Can you see that ant? Puppy has a little ball.

W: ant bite puppy

[Wendy points to ant, pushing hard on the book]

AS: No, the ant won't bite the puppy, the [turns page] puppy wants to play with the ant, see?

[Wendy tries to turn the page back; AS won't let her, and Wendy starts to squirm and fuss]

AS: Look here, here's someone else, the puppy

[Wendy climbs down off the bed and gets another book]

W: read this one

AS: Okay, you get back up here now. [Wendy gets back on bed]

AS: This book is your ABC book. See the A, look, here, on your spread, there's an A. You find the A. [The second book is a cloth book, old and tattered, and long a favorite of Wendy's. It features an apple on the cover, and its front page has an ABC block and ball. Through the book, there is a single item on each page, with a large representation of the first letter of the word commonly used to name the item. As AS turns the page, Wendy begins to crawl about on her quilt, which shows ABC blocks interspersed with balls and apples. Wendy points to each of the A's on the blanket and begins talking to herself. AS reads the book, looks up, and sees Wendy pointing to the A's in her quilt.]

AS: That's an A, can you find the A on your blanket?

W: there it is, this one, there's the hole too. [pokes her finger through a place
     where the threads have broken in the quilting]
AS: [AS points to ball in book] Stop that, find the ball, see, here's another ball.

This episode characterizes the early orientation of Roadville children to the
written word. Bookreading time focuses on letters of the alphabet, numbers,
names of basic items pictured in books, and simplified retellings of stories in the
words of the adult. If the content or story plot seems too complicated for the
child, the adult tells the story in short, simple sentences, frequently laced with requests that the child give what-explanations.

Wendy's favorite books are those with which she can participate: that is, those
to which she can answer, provide labels, point to items, give animal sounds, and
"read" the material back to anyone who will listen to her. She memorizes the passages and often knows when to turn the pages to show that she is "reading." She
holds the book in her lap, starts at the beginning, and often reads the title,
"Puppy."

Adults and children use either the title of the book or phrases such as "the book
about a puppy" to refer to reading material. When Wendy acquires a new book,
adults introduce the book with phrases such as "This is a book about a duck, a little yellow duck. See the duck. Duck goes quack quack." On introducing a book,
adults sometimes ask the child to recall when they have seen a "real" specimen
such as that one treated in the book: "Remember the duck on the College lake?"
The child often shows no sign of linking the yellow fluffy duck in the book with
the large brown and gray mallards on the lake, and the adult makes no efforts to
explain that two such disparate looking objects go by the same name.

As Wendy grows older, she wants to "talk" during the long stories, Bible stories,
and carry out the participation she so enjoyed with the alphabet books. However,
by the time she reaches three and a half, Wendy is restrained from such wide-ranging participation. When she interrupts, she is told:

Wendy, stop that, you be quiet when someone is reading to you. You listen; now sit still
and be quiet.

Often Wendy immediately gets down and runs away into the next room saying
"no, no." When this happens, her father goes to get her, pats her bottom, and puts
her down hard on the sofa beside him. "Now you're gonna learn to listen." During
the third and fourth years, this pattern occurs more and more frequently; only
when Wendy can capture an aunt who does not visit often does she bring out the
old books and participate with them. Otherwise, parents, Aunt Sue, and other
adults insist that she be read a story and that she "listen" quietly.

When Wendy and her parents watch television, eat cereal, visit the grocery
store, or go to church, adults point out and talk about many types of written material. On the way to the grocery, Wendy (3;8) sits in the backseat, and when her

mother stops at a corner, Wendy says "Stop." Her mother says "Yes, that's a stop sign." Wendy has, however, misread a yield sign as *stop*. Her mother offers no explanation of what the actual message on the sign is, yet when she comes to the sign, she stops to yield to an oncoming car. Her mother, when asked why she had not given Wendy the word "yield," said it was too hard, Wendy would not understand, and "it's not a word we use like *stop*."

Wendy recognized animal cracker boxes as early as 10 months, and later, as her mother began buying other varieties, Wendy would see the box in the grocery store and yell "Cook cook." Her mother would say, "Yes, those are cookies. Does Wendy want a cookie?" One day Wendy saw a new type of cracker box, and screeched "Cook cook." Her father opened the box and gave Wendy a cracker and waited for her reaction. She started the "cookie," then took it to her mother, saying "You eat." The mother joined in the game and said "Don't you want your *cookie*?" Wendy said "No cookie. You eat." "But Wendy, it's a cookie box, see?", and her mother pointed to the C of *crackers* on the box. Wendy paid no attention and ran off into another room.

In Roadville's literacy events, the rules for cooperative discourse around print are repeatedly practiced, coached, and rewarded in the preschool years. Adults in Roadville believe that instilling in children the proper use of words and understanding of the meaning of the written word are important for both their educational and religious success. Adults repeat aspects of the learning of literacy events they have known as children. In the words of one Roadville parent: "It was then that I began to learn . . . when my daddy kept insisting I *read* it, *say* it right. It was then that I *did* right, in his view."

The path of development for such performance can be described in three overlapping stages. In the first, children are introduced to discrete bits and pieces of books—separate items, letters of the alphabet, shapes, colors, and commonly represented items in books for children (apple, baby, ball, etc.). The latter are usually decontextualized, not pictured in their ordinary contexts, and they are represented in two-dimensional flat line drawings. During this stage, children must participate as predictable information-givers and respond to questions that ask for specific and discrete bits of information about the written matter. In these literacy events, specific features of the two-dimensional items in books which are different from their "real" counterparts are not pointed out. A ball in a book is flat; a duck in a book is yellow and fluffy; trucks, cars, dogs, and trees talk in books. No mention is made of the fact that such features do not fit these objects in reality. Children are not encouraged to move their understanding of books into other situational contexts or to apply it in their general knowledge of the world about them.

In the second stage, adults demand an acceptance of the power of print to entertain, inform, and instruct. When Wendy could no longer participate by contributing her knowledge at any point in the literacy event, she learned to recognize bookreading as a performance. The adult exhibited the book to Wendy: she was to be entertained, to learn from the information conveyed in the material, and to remember the book's content for the sequential followup questioning, as opposed to ongoing cooperative participatory questions.

In the third stage, Wendy was introduced to preschool workbooks which provided story information and was asked questions or provided exercises and games based on the content of the stories or pictures. Follow-the-number coloring books and preschool "push-out and paste" workbooks on shapes, colors, and letters of the alphabet reinforced repeatedly that the written word could be taken apart into small pieces and one item linked to another by following rules. She had practice in the linear, sequential nature of books: begin at the beginning, stay in the lines for coloring, draw straight lines to link one item to another, write your answers on lines, keep your letters straight, match the cutout letter to diagrams of letter shapes.

The differences between Roadville and Maintown are substantial. Roadville adults do not extend either the content or the habits of literacy events beyond bookreading. They do not, upon seeing an item or event in the real world, remind children of a similar event in a book and launch a running commentary on similarities and differences. When a game is played or a chore done, adults do not use literate sources. Mothers cook without written recipes most of the time; if they use a recipe from a written source, they do so usually only after confirmation and alteration by friends who have tried the recipe. Directions to games are read, but not carefully followed, and they are not talked about in a series of questions and answers which try to establish their meaning. Instead, in the putting together of toys or the playing of games, the abilities or preferences of one party prevail. For example, if an adult knows how to put a toy together, he does so; he does not talk about the process, refer to the written material and "translate" for the child, or try to sequence steps so the child can do it.[3] Adults do not talk about the steps and procedures of *how* to do things; if a father wants his preschooler to learn to hold a miniature bat or throw a ball, he says "Do it this way." He does not break up "this way" into such steps as "Put your fingers around here," "Keep your thumb in this position," "Never hold it above this line." Over and over again, adults do a task and children observe and try it, being reinforced only by commands such as "Do it like this," "Watch that thumb."

Adults at tasks do not provide a running verbal commentary on what they are doing. They do not draw the attention of the child to specific features of the sequences of skills or the attributes of items. They do not ask questions of the child, except questions which are directive or scolding in nature, ("Did you bring the ball?" "Didn't you hear what I said?"). Many of their commands contain idioms which are not explained: "Put it up," or "Put that away now" (meaning to put it in the place where it usually belongs), or "Loosen up," said to a four-year-old boy trying to learn to bat a ball. Explanations which move beyond the listing of names of items and their features are rarely offered by adults. Children do not ask questions of the type "But I don't understand. What is that?" They appear willing to keep trying, and if there is ambiguity in a set of commands, they ask a question such as "You want me to do this?" (demonstrating their current efforts), or they try to find a way of diverting attention from the task at hand.

Both boys and girls during their preschool years are included in many adult activities, ranging from going to church to fishing and camping. They spend a lot of time observing and asking for turns to try specific tasks, such as putting a worm on the hook or cutting cookies. Sometimes adults say "No, you're not old enough." But if they agree to the child's attempt at the task, they watch and give directives and evaluations: "That's right, don't twist the cutter." "Turn like this." "Don't try to scrape it up now, let me do that." Talk about the task does not segment its skills and identify them, nor does it link the particular task or item at hand to other tasks. Reason-explanations such as "If you twist the cutter, the cookies will be rough on the edge," are rarely given, or asked for.

Neither Roadville adults nor children shift the context of items in their talk. They do not tell stories which fictionalize themselves or familiar events. They reject Sunday School materials which attempt to translate Biblical events into a modern-day setting. In Roadville, a story must be invited or announced by someone other than the storyteller, and only certain community members are designated good storytellers. A story is recognized by the group as a story about one and all. It is a true story, an actual event which occurred to either the storyteller or to someone else present. The marked behavior of the storyteller and audience alike is seen as exemplifying the weaknesses of all and the need for persistence in overcoming such weaknesses. The sources of stories are personal experience. They are tales of transgressions which make the point of reiterating the expected norms of behavior of man, woman, fisherman, worker, and Christian. They are true to the facts of the event.

Roadville parents provide their children with books; they read to them and ask questions about the books' contents. They choose books which emphasize nursery rhymes, alphabet learning, animals, and simplified Bible stories, and they require their children to repeat from these books and to answer formulaic questions about their contents. Roadville adults also ask questions about oral stories which have a point relevant to some marked behavior of a child. They use proverbs and summary statements to remind their children of stories and to call on them for simple comparisons of the stories' contents to their own situations. Roadville parents coach children in their telling of a story, forcing them to tell about an incident as it has been pre-composed or pre-scripted in the head of the adult. Thus, in Roadville, children come to know a story as either an accounting from a book, or a factual account of a real event in which some type of marked behavior occurred and there is a lesson to be learned. Any fictionalized account of a real event is viewed as a *lie;* reality is better than fiction. Roadville's church and community life admit no story other than that which meets the definition internal to the group. Thus children cannot decontextualize their knowledge or fictionalize events known to them and shift them about into other frames.

When these children go to school they perform well in the initial stages of each of the three early grades. They often know portions of the alphabet, some colors and numbers, can recognize their names, and tell someone their address and their parents' names. They will sit still and listen to a story, and they know how to answer questions asking for what-explanations. They do well in reading workbook exercises which ask for identification of specific portions of words, items from the story, or the linking of two items, letters, or parts of words on the same page. When the teacher reaches the end of story-reading or the reading circle and asks questions such as "What did you like about the story?", relatively few Roadville children answer. If asked questions such as "What would you have done if you had been Billy [a story's main character]?", Roadville children most frequently say "I don't know" or shrug their shoulders.

Near the end of each year, and increasingly as they move through the early primary grades, Roadville children can handle successfully the initial stages of lessons. But when they move ahead to extra-credit items or to activities considered more advanced and requiring more independence, they are stumped. They turn frequently to teachers asking "Do you want me to do this? What do I do here?" If asked to write a creative story or tell it into a tape recorder, they retell stories from books; they do not create their own. They rarely provide emotional or personal commentary on their accounting of real events or book stories. They are rarely able to take knowledge learned in one context and shift it to another; they do not compare two items or events and point out similarities and differences. They find it difficult either to hold one feature of an event constant and shift all others or to hold all features constant but one. For example, they are puzzled by questions such as "What would have happened if Billy had not told the policemen what happened?" They do not know how to move events or items out of a given frame. To a question such as "What habits of the Hopi Indians might they be able to take with them when they move to a city?", they provide lists of features of life of the Hopi on the reservation. They do not take these items, consider their appropriateness in an urban setting, and evaluate the hypothetical outcome. In general, they find this type of question impossible to answer, and they do not know how to ask teachers to help them take apart the questions to figure out the answers. Thus their initial successes in reading, being good students, following orders, and adhering to school norms of participating in lessons begin to fall away rapidly about the time they enter the fourth grade. As the importance and frequency of questions and reading habits with which they are familiar decline in the higher grades, they have no way of keeping up or of seeking help in learning what it is they do not even know they don't know.

Trackton

Babies in Trackton come home from the hospital to an environment which is almost entirely human. There are no cribs, car beds, or car seats, and only an occasional high chair or infant seat. Infants are held during their waking hours, occasionally while they sleep, and they usually sleep in the bed with parents until they are about two years of age. They are held, their faces fondled, their cheeks pinched, and they eat and sleep in the midst of human talk and noise from the television, stereo, and radio. Encapsuled in an almost totally human world, they are in the midst of constant human communication, verbal and nonverbal. They literally feel the body signals of shifts in emotion of those who hold them almost continuously; they are talked about and kept in the midst of talk about topics that range over any subject. As children make cooing or babbling sounds, adults refer to this as "noise," and no attempt is made to interpret these sounds as words or communicative attempts on the part of the baby. Adults believe they should not have to depend on their babies to tell them what they need or when they are uncomfortable; adults know, children only "come to know."

When a child can crawl and move about on his own, he plays with the household objects deemed safe for him—pot lids, spoons, plastic food containers. Only at Christmas time are there special toys for very young children; these are usually trucks, balls, doll babies, or plastic cars, but rarely blocks, puzzles, or books. As children become completely mobile, they demand ride toys or electronic and mechanical toys they see on television. They never request nor do they receive manipulative toys, such as puzzles, blocks, take-apart toys or literacy-based items, such as books or letter games.

Adults read newspapers, mail, calendars, circulars (political and civic-events related), school materials sent home to parents, brochures advertising new cars, television sets, or other products, and the Bible and other church-related materials. There are no reading materials especially for children (with the exception of children's Sunday School materials), and adults do not sit and read to children. Since children are usually left to sleep whenever and wherever they fall asleep, there is no bedtime or naptime as such. At night, they are put to bed when adults go to bed or whenever the person holding them gets tired. Thus, going to bed is not framed in any special routine. Sometimes in a play activity during the day, an older sibling will read to a younger child, but the latter soon loses interest and squirms away to play. Older children often try to "play school" with younger children, reading to them from books and trying to ask questions about what they have read. Adults look on these efforts with amusement and do not try to convince the small child to sit still and listen.

Signs from very young children of attention to the nonverbal behaviors of others are rewarded by extra fondling, laughter, and cuddling from adults. For example, when an infant shows signs of recognizing a family member's voice on the phone by bouncing up and down in the arms of the adult who is talking on the phone, adults comment on this to others present and kiss and nudge the child. Yet when children utter sounds or combinations of sounds which could be interpreted as words, adults pay no attention. Often by the time they are twelve months old, children approximate words or phrases of adults' speech; adults respond by laughing or giving special attention to the child and crediting him with "sounding like" the person being imitated. When children learn to walk and imitate the walk of members of the community, they are rewarded by comments on their activities: "He walks just like Toby when he's tuckered out."

Children between the ages of twelve and twenty-four months often imitate the tune or "general Gestalt" (Peters 1977) of complete utterances they hear around them. They pick up and repeat chunks (usually the ends) of phrasal and clausal utterances of speakers around them. They seem to remember fragments of speech and repeat these without active production. In this first stage of language learning, the repetition stage, they imitate the intonation contours and general shaping of the utterances they repeat. Lem 1;2 in the following example illustrates this pattern.

Mother: [talking to neighbor on porch while Lem plays with a truck on
             the porch nearby] But they won't call back, won't happen =
Lem: =call back
Neighbor: Sam's going over there Saturday, he'll pick up a form=
Lem: =pick up on, pick up on [Lem here appears to have heard *form*
             as *on*]

The adults pay no attention to Lem's "talk," and their talk, in fact, often overlaps his repetitions.

In the second stage, repetition with variation, Trackton children manipulate pieces of conversation they pick up. They incorporate chunks of language from others into their own ongoing dialogue, applying productive rules, inserting new nouns and verbs for those used in the adults' chunks. They also play with rhyming patterns and varying intonation contours.

Mother: She went to the doctor again.
Lem (2;2):   [in a sing-song fashion] went to de doctor, doctor, tractor, dis my
               tractor, doctor on a tractor, went to de doctor.

Lem creates a monologue, incorporating the conversation about him into his own talk as he plays. Adults pay no attention to his chatter unless it gets so noisy as to interfere with their talk.

In the third stage, participation, children begin to enter the ongoing conversations about them. They do so by attracting the adult's attention with a tug on the arm or pant leg, and they help make themselves understood by providing nonverbal reinforcements to help recreate a scene they want the listener to remember. For example, if adults are talking, and a child interrupts with seemingly unintelligible utterances, the child will make gestures, extra sounds, or act out some outstanding features of the scene he is trying to get the adult to remember. Children try to create a context, a scene, for the understanding of their utterance.

This third stage illustrates a pattern in the children's response to their environment and their ways of letting others know their knowledge of the environment. Once they are in the third stage, their communicative efforts are accepted by community members, and adults respond directly to the child, instead of talking to others about the child's activities as they have done in the past. Children continue to practice for conversational participation by playing, when alone, both parts of dialogues, imitating gestures as well as intonation patterns of adults. By 2;6 all children in the community can imitate the walk and talk of others in the community, or frequent visitors such as the man who comes around to read the gas meters. They can feign anger, sadness, fussing, remorse, silliness, or any of a wide range of expressive behaviors. They often use the same chunks of language for varying effects, depending on nonverbal support to give the language different meanings or cast it in a different key (Hymes 1974). Girls between three and four years of age take part in extraordinarily complex stepping and clapping patterns and simple repetitions of hand clap games played by older girls. From the time they are old enough to stand alone, they are encouraged in their participation by siblings and older children in the community. These games require anticipation and recognition of cues for upcoming behaviors, and the young girls learn to watch for these cues and to come in with the appropriate words and movements at the right time.

Preschool children are not asked for what-explanations of their environment. Instead, they are asked a preponderance of analogical questions which call for non-specific comparisons of one item, event, or person with another: "What's that like?" Other types of questions ask for specific information known to the child but not the adults: "Where'd you get that from?" "What do you want?" "How come you did that?" (Heath 1982a). Adults explain their use of these types of questions by expressing their sense of children: they are "comers," coming into their learning by experiencing what knowing about things means. As one parent of a two-year-old boy put it: "Ain't no use me tellin' 'im: learn this, learn that, what's this, what's that? He just gotta learn, gotta know; he see one thing one place one time, he know how it go, see sump'n like it again, maybe it be the same, maybe it won't." Children are expected to learn how to know when the form belies the meaning, and to know contexts of items and to use their understanding of these contexts to draw parallels between items and events. Parents do not believe they have a tutoring role in this learning; they provide the experiences on which the child draws and reward signs of their successfully coming to know.

Trackton children's early stories illustrate how they respond to adult views of them as "comers." The children learn to tell stories by drawing heavily on their abilities to render a context, to set a stage, and to call on the audience's power to join in the imaginative creation of story. Between the ages of two and four years, the children, in a monologue-like fashion, tell stories about things in their lives, events they see and hear, and situations in which they have been involved. They produce these spontaneously during play with other children or in the presence of adults. Sometimes they make an effort to attract the attention of listeners before they begin the story, but often they do not. Lem, playing off the edge of the porch, when he was about two and a half years of age, heard a bell in the distance. He stopped, looked at Nellie and Benjy, his older siblings, who were nearby and said:

Way
Far
Now
It a church bell
Ringin'
Dey singin'
Ringin'
You hear it?
I hear it
Far
Now.

Lem had been taken to church the previous Sunday and had been much impressed by the church bell. He had sat on his mother's lap and joined in the singing, rocking to and fro on her lap, and clapping his hands. His story, which is like a poem in its imagery and line-like prosody, is in response to the current stimulus of a distant bell. As he tells the story, he sways back and forth.

This story, somewhat longer than those usually reported from other social groups for children as young as Lem,[4] has some features which have come to characterize fully-developed narratives or stories. It recapitulates in its verbal outline the sequence of events being recalled by the storyteller. At church, the bell rang while the people sang. In the line "It a church bell," Lem provides his story's topic, and a brief summary of what is to come. This line serves a function similar to the formulae often used by older children to open a story: "This is a story about (a church bell)." Lem gives only the slightest hint of story setting or orientation to the listener; where and when the story took place are capsuled in "Way, Far." Preschoolers in Trackton almost never hear "Once upon a time there was a ___" stories, and they rarely provide definitive orientations for their stories. They seem to assume listeners "know" the situation in which the narrative takes place. Similarly, preschoolers in Trackton do not close off their stories with formulaic endings. Lem poetically balances his opening and closing in an inclusion, beginning "Way, Far, Now." and ending "Far, Now.". The effect is one of closure, but there is no clearcut announcement of closure. Throughout the presentation of action and result of action in their stories, Trackton preschoolers invite the audience to respond or evaluate the story's actions. Lem asks "You hear it?" which may refer either to the current stimulus or to yesterday's bell, since Lem does not productively use past tense endings for any verbs at this stage in his language development.

Preschool storytellers have several ways of inviting audience evaluation and interest. They may themselves express an emotional response to the story's actions; they may have another character or narrator in the story do so often using alliterative language play; or they may detail actions and results through direct discourse or sound effects and gestures. All these methods of calling attention to the story and its telling distinguish the speech event as a story, an occasion for audience and storyteller to interact pleasantly, and not simply to hear an ordinary recounting of events or actions.

Trackton children must be aggressive in inserting their stories into an ongoing stream of discourse. Storytelling is highly competitive. Everyone in a conversation may want to tell a story, so only the most aggressive wins out. The content ranges widely, and there is "truth" only in the universals of human experience. Fact is often hard to find, though it is usually the seed of the story. Trackton stories often have no point—no obvious beginning or ending; they go on as long as the audience enjoys and tolerates the storyteller's entertainment.

Trackton adults do not separate out the elements of the environment around their children to tune their attentions selectively. They do not simplify their language, focus on single-word utterances by young children, label items or features of objects in either books or the environment at large. Instead, children are continuously contextualized, presented with almost continuous communication. From this ongoing, multiple-channeled stream of stimuli, they must themselves select, practice, and determine rules of production and structuring. For language, they do so by first repeating, catching chunks of sounds, intonation contours, and practicing these without specific reinforcement or evaluation. But practice material and models are continuously available. Next the children seem to begin to sort out the productive rules for speech and practice what they hear about them with variation. Finally, they work their way into conversations, hooking their meanings for listeners into a familiar context by recreating scenes through gestures, special sound effects, etc. These characteristics continue in their story-poems and their participation in jump-rope rhymes. Because adults do not select out, name, and describe features of the environment for the young, children must perceive situations, determine how units of the situations are related to each other, recognize these relations in other situations, and reason through what it will take to show their correlation of one situation with another. The children can answer questions such as "What's that like?" ["It's like Doug's car"] but they can rarely name the specific feature or features which make two items or events alike. For example, in the case of saying a car seen on the street is "like Doug's car," a child may be basing the analogy on the fact that this car has a flat tire and Doug's also had one last week. But the child does not name (and is not asked to name) what is alike between the two cars.

Children seem to develop connections between situations or items not by specification of labels and features in the situations, but by configuration links.

Recognition of similar general shapes or patterns of links seen in one situation and connected to another, seem to be the means by which children set scenes in their nonverbal representations of individuals, and later in their verbal chunking, then segmentation and production of rules for putting together isolated units. They do not decontextualize; instead they heavily contextualize nonverbal and verbal language. They fictionalize their "true stories," but they do so by asking the audience to identify with the story through making parallels from their own experiences. When adults read, they often do so in a group. One person, reading aloud, for example, from a brochure on a new car decodes the text, displays illustrations and photographs, and listeners relate the text's meaning to their experiences asking questions and expressing opinions. Finally, the group as a whole synthesizes the written text and the negotiated oral discourse to construct a meaning for the brochure (Heath 1982b).

When Trackton children go to school, they face unfamiliar types of questions which ask for what-explanations. They are asked as individuals to identify items by name, and to label features such as shape, color, size, number. The stimuli to which they are to give these responses are two-dimensional flat representations which are often highly stylized and bear little resemblance to the "real" items. Trackton children generally score in the lowest percentile range on the Metropolitan Reading Readiness tests. They do not sit at their desks and complete reading workbook pages; neither do they tolerate questions about reading materials which are structured along the usual lesson format. Their contributions are in the form of "I had a duck at my house one time." "Why'd he do that?" or they imitate the sound effects teachers may produce in stories they read to the children. By the end of the first three primary grades, their general language arts scores have been consistently low, except for those few who have begun to adapt to and adopt some of the behaviors they have had to learn in school. But the majority not only fail to learn the content of lessons, they also do not adopt the social interactional rules for school literacy events. Print in isolation bears little authority in their world. The kinds of questions asked of reading books are unfamiliar. The children's abilities to metaphorically link two events or situations and to recreate scenes are not tapped in the school; in fact, *these abilities often cause difficulties*, because they enable children to see parallels teachers did not intend, and indeed, may not recognize until the children point them out (Heath 1978).

By the end of the lessons or by the time in their total school career when reason-explanations and affective statements call for the creative comparison of two or more situations, it is too late for many Trackton children. They have not picked up along the way the composition and comprehension skills they need to translate their analogical skills into a channel teachers can accept. They seem not to know how to take meaning from reading; they do not observe the rules of linearity in writing, and their expression of themselves on paper is very limited. Orally taped stories are often much better, but these rarely count as much as written compositions. Thus, Trackton children continue to collect very low or failing grades, and many decide by the end of the sixth grade to stop trying and turn their attention to the heavy peer socialization which usually begins in these years.

From Community to Classroom

A recent review of trends in research on learning pointed out that "learning to read through using and learning from language has been less systematically studied than the decoding process" (Glaser 1979: 7). Put another way, how children learn to use language to read to learn has been less systematically studied than decoding skills. Learning how to take meaning from writing before one learns to read involves repeated practice in using and learning from language through appropriate participation in literacy events such as exhibitor/questioner and spectator/respondent dyads (Scollon and Scollon 1979) or group negotiation of the meaning of a written text. Children have to learn to select, hold, and retrieve content from books and other written or printed texts in accordance with their community's rules or "ways of taking," and the children's learning follows community paths of language socialization. In each society, certain kinds of childhood participation in literacy events may precede others, as the developmental sequence builds toward the whole complex of home and community behaviors characteristic of the society. The ways of taking employed in the school may in turn build directly on the preschool development, may require substantial adaptation on the part of the children, or may even run directly counter to aspects of the community's pattern.

At Home.   In *Maintown* homes, the construction of knowledge in the earliest preschool years depends in large part on labeling procedures and what-explanations. Maintown families, like other mainstream families, continue this kind of classification and knowledge construction throughout the child's environment and into the school years, calling it into play in response to new items in the environment and in running commentaries on old items as they compare to new ones. This pattern of linking old and new knowledge is reinforced in narrative tales which fictionalize the teller's events or recapitulate a story from a book. Thus for these children the bedtime story is simply an early link in a long chain of interrelated patterns of taking meaning from the environment. Moreover, along this chain, the focus is on the individual as respondent and cooperative negotiator of meaning from books. In particular, children learn that written language may represent not only descriptions of real events, but decontextualized logical propositions, and the occurrence of this kind of information in print or in writing legitimates a response in which one brings to the interpretation of written text selected knowledge from the real world. Moreover, readers must recognize how certain types of questions assert the priority of meanings in the written word over reality. The "real" comes into play only after prescribed decontextualized meanings; affective responses and reason-explanations follow conventional presuppositions which stand behind what-explanations.

Roadville also provides labels, features, and what-explanations, and prescribes listening and performing behaviors for preschoolers. However, Roadville adults do not carry on or sustain in continually overlapping and interdependent fashion the linking of ways of taking meaning from books to ways of relating that knowledge to other aspects of the environment. They do not encourage decontextualization; in fact, they proscribe it in their own stories about themselves and their requirements of stories from children. They do not themselves make analytic statements or assert universal truths, except those related to their religious faith. They lace their stories with synthetic (nonanalytic) statements which express, describe, and synthesize actual real-life materials. Things do not have to follow logically so long as they fit the past experience of individuals in the community. Thus children learn to look for a specific moral in stories and to expect that story to fit their facts of reality explicitly. When they themselves recount an event, they do the same, constructing the story of a real event according to coaching by adults who want to construct the story as they saw it.

Trackton is like neither Maintown nor Roadville. There are no bedtime stories; in fact, there are few occasions for reading to or with children specifically. Instead, during the time these activities would take place in mainstream and Roadville homes, Trackton children are enveloped in different kinds of social interactions. They are held, fed, talked about, and rewarded for nonverbal, and later verbal, renderings of events they witness. Trackton adults value and respond favorably when children show they have come to know how to use language to show correspondence in function, style, configuration, and positioning between two different things or situations. Analogical questions are asked of Trackton children, although the implicit questions of structure and function these embody are never made explicit. Children do not have labels or names of attributes of items and events pointed out for them, and they are asked for reason-explanations not what-explanations. Individuals express their personal responses and recreate corresponding situations with often only a minimal adherence to the germ of truth of a story. Children come to recognize similarities of patterning, though they do not name lines, points, or items which are similar between two items or situations. They are familiar with group literacy events in which several community members orally negotiate the meaning of a written text.

At School.   In the early reading stages, and in later requirements for reading to learn at more advanced stages, children from the three communities respond differently, because they have learned different methods and degrees of taking from books. In comparison to Maintown children, the habits Roadville children learned in bookreading and toy-related episodes have not continued for them through other activities and types of reinforcement in their environment. They have had less exposure to both the content of books and ways of learning from books than have mainstream children. Thus their need in schools is not necessarily for an intensification of presentation of labels, a slowing down of the sequence of introducing what-explanations in connection with bookreading. Instead they need extension of these habits to other domains and to opportunities for practicing habits such as producing running commentaries, creating exhibitor/questioner and spectator/respondent roles. Perhaps most important, Roadville children need to have articulated for them *distinctions in discourse strategies and structures.* Narratives of real events have certain strategies and structures; imaginary tales, flights of fantasy, and affective expressions have others. Their community's view of narrative discourse style is very narrow and demands a passive role in both creation of and response to the account of events. Moreover, these children have *to be reintroduced to a participant frame of reference to a book.* Though initially they were participants in bookreading, they have been trained into passive roles since the age of three years, and they must learn once again to be active information-givers, taking from books and linking that knowledge to other aspects of their environment.

Trackton students present an additional set of alternatives for procedures in the early primary grades. Since they usually have few of the expected "natural" skills of taking meaning from books, they must not only learn these, but also *retain their analogical reasoning practices* for use in some of the later stages of learning to read. They must *learn to adapt the creativity in language, metaphor, fictionalization, recreation of scenes and exploration of functions and settings of items they bring to school.* These children already use narrative skills highly rewarded in the upper primary grades. They distinguish a fictionalized story from a real-life narrative. They know that telling a story can be in many ways related to play; it suspends reality, and frames an old event in a new context; it calls on audience participation to recognize the setting and participants. They must now *learn as individuals to recount factual events in a straightforward way* and *recognize appropriate occasions for reason-explanations and affective expressions.* Trackton children seem to have skipped learning to label, list features, and give what-explanations. Thus they need to *have the mainstream or school habits presented in familiar activities with explanations related to their own habits of taking meaning* from the environment. Such "simple," "natural" things as distinctions between two-dimensional and three-dimensional objects may need to be explained to help Trackton children learn the stylization and decontextualization which characterizes books.

To lay out in more specific detail how Roadville and Trackton's ways of knowing can be used along with those of mainstreamers goes beyond the scope of this paper. However, it must be admitted that a range of alternatives to ways of learning and displaying knowledge characterizes all highly school-successful adults in the advanced stages of their careers. Knowing more about how these alternatives are learned at early ages in different sociocultural conditions can help the school to provide opportunities for *all* students to avail themselves of these alternatives early in their school careers. For example, mainstream children can benefit from early exposure to Trackton's creative, highly analogical styles of telling stories and giving explanations, and they can add the Roadville true story with strict chronicity and explicit moral to their repertoire of narrative types.

In conclusion, if we want to understand the place of literacy in human societies and ways children acquire the literacy orientations of their communities, we must recognize two postulates of literacy and language development.

1. Strict dichotomization between oral and literate traditions is a construct of researchers, not an accurate portrayal of reality across cultures.
2. A unilinear model of development in the acquisition of language structures and uses cannot adequately account for culturally diverse ways of acquiring knowledge or developing cognitive styles.

Roadville and Trackton tell us that the mainstream type of literacy orientation is not the only type even among Western societies. They also tell us that the mainstream ways of acquiring communicative competence do not offer a universally applicable model of development. They offer proof of Hymes' assertion a decade ago that "it is impossible to generalize validly about 'oral' vs. 'literate' cultures as uniform types" (Hymes 1973: 54).

Yet in spite of such warnings and analyses of the uses and functions of writing in the specific proposals for comparative development and organization of cultural systems (cf. Basso 1974: 432), the majority of research on literacy has focused on differences in class, amount of education, and level of civilization among groups having different literacy characteristics.

"We need, in short, a great deal of ethnography" (Hymes 1973: 57) to provide descriptions of the ways different social groups "take" knowledge from the environment. For written sources, these ways of taking may be analyzed in terms of *types of literacy events,* such as group negotiation of meaning from written texts, individual "looking things up" in reference books, writing family records in Bibles, and the dozens of other types of occasions when books or other written materials are integral to interpretation in an interaction. These must in turn be analyzed in terms of the specific *features of literacy events,* such as labeling, what-explanation, affective comments, reason-explanations, and many other possibilities. Literacy events must also be interpreted in relation to the *larger sociocultural patterns* which they may exemplify or reflect. For example, ethnography must describe literacy events in their sociocultural contexts, so we may come to understand how such patterns as time and space usage, caregiving roles, and age and sex segregation are interdependent with the types and features of literacy events a community develops. It is only on the basis of such thorough-going ethnography that further progress is possible toward understanding cross-cultural patterns of oral and written language uses and paths of development of communicative competence.

Notes

1. First presented at the Terman Conference on Teaching at Stanford University, 1980, this paper has benefitted from cooperation with M. Cochran-Smith of the University of Pennsylvania. She shares an appreciation of the relevance of Roland Barthes' work for stud-

ies of the socialization of young children into literacy; her research (1981) on the story-reading practices of a mainstream school-oriented nursery school provides a much needed detailed account of early school orientation to literacy.

2. Terms such as *mainstream* or *middle-class* cultures or social groups are frequently used in both popular and scholarly writings without careful definition. Moreover, numerous studies of behavioral phenomena (for example, mother-child interactions in language learning) either do not specify that the subjects being described are drawn from mainstream groups or do not recognize the importance of this limitation. As a result, findings from this group are often regarded as universal. For a discussion of this problem, see Chanan and Gilchrist 1974, Payne and Bennett 1977. In general, the literature characterizes this group as school-oriented, aspiring toward upward mobility through formal institutions, and providing enculturation which positively values routines of promptness, linearity (in habits ranging from furniture arrangement to entrance into a movie theater), and evaluative and judgmental responses to behaviors which deviate from their norms.

In the United States, mainstream families tend to locate in neighborhoods and suburbs around cities. Their social interactions center not in their immediate neighborhoods, but around voluntary associations across the city. Thus a cluster of mainstream families (and not a community—which usually implies a specific geographic territory as the locus of a majority of social interactions) is the unit of comparison used here with the Trackton and Roadville communities.

3. Behind this discussion are findings from cross-cultural psychologists who have studied the links between verbalization of task and demonstration of skills in a hierarchical sequence, e.g., Childs and Greenfield 1980; see Goody 1979 on the use of questions in learning tasks unrelated to a familiarity with books.

4. Cf. Umiker-Sebeok's (1979) descriptions of stories of mainstream middle-class children, ages 3–5 and Sutton-Smith 1981.

References

Basso, K. (1974). The ethonography of writing. In R. Bauman & J. Sherzer (eds.), *Explorations in the ethnography of speaking.* Cambridge University Press.

Cazden, C. B. (1979). Peekaboo as an instructional model: Discourse development at home and at school. *Papers and Reports in Child Language Development* 17: 1–29.

Chanan, G., & Gilchrist, L. (1974). *What school is for.* New York: Praeger.

Childs, C. P., & Greenfield, P. M. (1980). Informal modes of learning and teaching. In N. Warren (ed.), *Advances in cross-cultural psychology,* vol. 2. London: Academic Press.

Cochran-Smith, M. (1981). The making of a reader. Ph.D. dissertation. University of Pennsylvania.

Cohen, R. (1968). The relation between socio-conceptual styles and orientation to school requirements. *Sociology of Education* 41: 201–20.

———. (1969). Conceptual styles, culture conflict, and nonverbal tests of intelligence. *American Anthropologist* 71 (5): 828–56.

———. (1971). The influence of conceptual rule-sets on measures of learning ability. In C. L. Brace, G. Gamble, & J. Bond (eds.), *Race and intelligence.* (Anthropological Studies, No. 8, American Anthropological Association). 41–57.

Glaser, R. (1979). Trends and research questions in psychological research on learning and schooling. *Educational Researcher* 8 (10): 6–13.

Goody, E. (1979). Towards a theory of questions. In E. N. Goody (ed.), *Questions and politeness: Strategies in social interaction.* Cambridge University Press.

Griffin, P., & Humphrey, F. (1978). Task and talk. In *The study of children's functional language and education in the early years.* Final report to the Carnegie Corporation of New York. Arlington, Va.: Center for Applied Linguistics.

Heath, S. (1978). *Teacher talk: Language in the classroom.* (Language in Education 9.) Arlington. Va.: Center for Applied Linguistics.

———. (1980). The functions and uses of literacy. *Journal of Communication* **30** (1): 123–33.

———. (1982a). Questioning at home and at school: A comparative study. In G. Spindler (ed.), *Doing ethnography: Educational anthropology in action.* New York: Holt, Rinehart Winston.

———. (1982b). Protean shapes: Ever-shifting oral and literate traditions. To appear in D. Tannen (ed.), *Spoken and written language: Exploring orality and literacy.* Norwood. N.J.: Ablex, 91–117.

———. (1983). *Ways with words: Ethnography of communication in communities and classrooms.* Cambridge: Cambridge University Press

Howard, R. (1974). A note on S/Z. In R. Barthes, *Introduction to S/Z.* Trans. Richard Miller. New York: Hill and Wang. Cambridge: Cambridge University Press.

Hymes, D. H. (1973). On the origins and foundations of inequality among speakers. In E. Haugen & M. Bloomfield (eds.), *Language as a human problem.* New York: W. W. Norton & Co.

———. (1974). Models of the interaction of language and social life. In J. J. Gumperz & D. Hymes (eds.), *Directions in sociolinguistics.* New York: Holt, Rinehart and Winston.

Kagan, J., Sigel, I., & Moss, H. (1963). Psychological significance of styles of conceptualization. In J. Wright & J. Kagan (eds.), *Basic cognitive processes in children.* (Monographs of the society for research in child development.) 28 (2): 73–112.

Mehan, H. (1979). *Learning lessons.* Cambridge, Mass.: Harvard University Press.

Merritt, M. (1979). Service-like events during individual work time and their contribution to the nature of the rules for communication. NIE Report EP 78–0436.

Ninio, A., & Bruner, J. (1978). The achievement and antecedents of labeling. *Journal of Child Language* **5:** 1–15.

Payne, C., & Bennett, C. (1977). "Middle class aura" in public schools. *The Teacher Educator* **13** (1): 16–26.

Peters, A. (1977). Language learning strategies. *Language* **53**: 560–73.

Scollon, R., & Scollon, S. (1979). The literate two-year old: The fictionalization of self. *Working Papers in Sociolinguistics.* Austin, TX: Southwest Regional Laboratory.

Sinclair, J. M., & Coulthard, R. M. (1975). *Toward an analysis of discourse.* New York: Oxford University Press.

Sutton-Smith, B. (1981). *The folkstories of children.* Philadelphia: University of Pennsylvania Press.

Umiker-Sebeok, J. D. (1979). Preschool children's intraconversational narratives. *Journal of Child Language* **6** (1): 91–110.

Witkin, H., Faterson, F., Goodenough, R., & Birnbaum, J. (1966). Cognitive patterning in mildly retarded boys. *Child Development* **37** (2): 301–16.

3

Detective Stories at Dinnertime: Problem-Solving Through Co-Narration

ELINOR OCHS, RUTH SMITH, AND CAROLYN TAYLOR

I. Introduction

A. Goals

For over a year, our research group[1] has been going into homes in the early evening for several hours, video- and audio- recording families eating dinner, relaxing, and putting children to bed. We are analyzing ways in which white, English-speaking American families varying in social class solve problems through talk. The present analysis is based on over a hundred hours of recorded interactions, approximately eight hours for each of 14 families (8 high SES and 6 low SES) from our initial corpus.

In this paper, our focus is on narrative as a problem-solving discourse activity. Our concern is the interface of cognitive and social activity, as outlined in Vygotskian theory (Vygotsky 1978, 1981, Wertsch 1985, Rogoff Lave 1984). Our data indicate how problem-solving through story-telling is a socially-accomplished cognitive activity: family members articulate solutions to problems posed by narrated events and at times work together to articulate the narrative problem itself. Such joint cognizing can be seen as part of what families do—what makes a family an 'activity system' (Engeström, 1987, *to appear*). Thus, joint problem-solving through narrative gives structure to family roles, relationships, values, and world views.

B. The Activity of Dinner

1. Dinner as an Opportunity Space. While narratives are told among family members in numerous settings, dinnertime is a preferred moment for this activity in many American families. Dinnertime is a time when adults and children often come together after being apart throughout the day, a somewhat unique time period for many families wherein there is some assurance of a relatively captive audience for sounding things out. Dinnertime is thus an *opportunity space—*

a temporal, spatial, and social moment which provides for the possibility of joint activity among family members. Families use this opportunity space in different ways: some families talk more than others; some talk only about eating; others use the moment to make plans or recount the day's events. Whatever direction the talk takes, dinnertime is a potential forum for generating both knowledge and social order/disorder through interaction with other family members. Dinnertime thus provides a crystallization of family processes, what activity theorists (Leontyev 1981, Wertsch 1985) might call a 'genetically primary example' of family life.

2. Dinner Arrangements.   Physical arrangements for eating dinner vary across the households in our study and within households in the course of a single evening. As illustrated in Figure 3.1, dinner arrangements vary in terms of three dimensions: time, space, and activity focus. In terms of the temporal dimension, dinners may be staggered or synchronous. That is, family members may eat at different times or concurrently. In some families, children and adults eat when they are hungry and not necessarily at the same time. Families often do not eat at the same time every day of the week. Second, dinners may vary *spatially* in that family members may be dispersed or assembled while eating. Sometimes children eat in one room or one part of a room and one or more adults eat elsewhere. Third, dinners vary in terms of whether family members are overtly attending to different activities or share the same activity focus. For example, certain members may be watching television as they eat, while others are talking to one another. In other families, all members, at least on the surface, appear to be engaged in the same activity focus, either as ratified participants in the same conversation or as co-viewers of the same TV program.

Dinners characterized by features along the right side of Figure 3.1 (*i.e.* family members eating at same time and place and sharing activity focus) are more centralized and tend to be more formal and last longer than dinners characterized by features on the left side of Figure 3.1 (*i.e.* family members eating at different times and places and engaging in different activities).

3. Dinner and Talk.   These different dinner arrangements have implications for the amount and kind of talk that takes place at dinnertime (cf. Feiring and Lewis, 1987). The more centralized dinners promote more extensive problem-solving through talk. Family members who sit down together to eat appear to use a wider range of problem-solving genres—not only stories, but plans and arguments as well. With respect to stories, centralized dinners tend to promote longer stories,

Dimensions	Arrangement Types		
	Decentralized		Centralized
Temporal	Staggered	vs.	Synchronous
Spatial	Dispersed	vs.	Assembled
Activity focus	Diverse	vs.	Shared

Figure 3.1   Dinner Arrangements

with more audience involvement in sorting out problems, solutions and stances. Stories in the decentralized dinners tend to fill one page or less of transcript and do not significantly involve other interlocutors in problem-solving. In contrast, stories in centralized dinners can fill several pages; in one example, a narrative threads through 46 pages of a 64-page dinner transcript as family members work through unresolved aspects of a narrative situation over a 40-minute period.

In this sense, families who eat together exploit the opportunity space differently from families who decentralize dinnertime. Centralized dinners appear to provide an enduring moment in which family members can help one another to sort out problematic events in their lives through co-narration. The resulting narratives, as we shall see, differ markedly from narratives in which a story line is presented in an orderly fashion, where settings are fixed at the outset of the telling and events are chronologically and causally ordered.

Centralized dinner arrangements tend to promote more than co-narrated stories; they also promote opportunities for adults to exert power over children. Relative to decentralized dinner arrangements, centralized dinners appear more ritualized, entailing conformity to numerous eating conventions. Many dinners involve opening and closing rituals, such as saying grace and asking permission to be excused. Further conventions include where to sit, how to sit, which utensils to use, how close the serving dish should be from the plate, how much food one should serve oneself, how to request food, how to respond to offers of food, when to speak vis-à-vis eating, the order of eating different foods, which foods must be eaten, quantity of food which must be eaten off plate and so on. Each of these conventions may become a locus for compliance-gaining negotiation between adults and children. In this sense, centralized dinners provide a greater opportunity space for the exertion of social control over children. In contrast, decentralized dinners empower children to organize their own dinner activities. Decentralization seems to allow children greater freedom while exposing them less to adult narrative styles and problem-solving approaches.

II. Narratives

A. Approaches to Narrative

Studies of narrative tend to be either cognitive or sociological. Cognitive studies focus on stories as problem-solving genres. While definitions of what constitutes a story differ, most studies emphasize that stories contain one central problematic event—sometimes called 'an initiating event'—which precipitates a series of actions and reactions. The presentation of the core narrative problem and its resolution or non-resolution entails several story components, including: setting, initiating event, internal response, attempt, consequence, and reactions (Stein 1979, Stein & Policastro 1984, Trabasso *et al.* 1984). In these studies, a major interest is the cause-effect relations among components and their mental representation by children and adults.

Sociological studies focus on social consequences or social production of a story. For example, Labov and others have demonstrated how narrators restructure their biographies through careful reframing of past events (Labov, 1984; Fisher, 1985a, 1985b; Schiffrin; 1987). Other studies have emphasized the role of the audience as co-author of the narrative (Duranti 1986, Goodwin 1986a, 1986b, Haviland 1986, Jefferson 1978, Lerner 1987, Mandelbaum 1987a, 1987b, Sacks 1964–72). These studies look at the co-construction of stories and consider the impact of audience's (story recipients') participation on the telling of stories. In this framework, recipients as well as tellers impact the life of a story in various ways: they may derail a story, encourage its continuation and elaboration, or change its direction.

Our approach is synthetic, recognizing the importance of both cognitive and sociological approaches to narrative and their implications for each other. In particular, cognitive approaches tend to focus on *individual* tellings and retellings of stories without attending to the fact that stories are often if not typically collaboratively produced, *i.e. co-narrated*, by those participating in the social interaction. On the other hand, sociological approaches emphasize co-narration but do not link co-narration to *co-cognition*, specifically to the joint working out of problems. Our study will demonstrate both that narrative components are constituted, ordered, and clarified through social collaboration and that problem-solving motivates co-narration. We believe, in other words, that the activity of co-narration stimulates problem-solving, while the activity of problem-solving stimulates co-narration. To see how this mutual stimulation manifests itself, we turn to dinner narratives in American households.

B. Detective Stories

1. Introduction.   The stories in our corpus differ in the degree to which story problems are reformulated in the course of storytelling. Certain tellings involve extensive participation of other family members in a groping process to make sense out of the problem underlying the narrative's initiating event. We call such narratives 'detective stories' in the sense that there is missing information felt by some co-narrator(s) to be vital to understanding the problem that motivates actions and reactions of protagonists and others in the storytelling situation. Co-narrators return, sometimes again and again, like Lieutenant Columbo, to pieces of the narrative problem in an effort to find 'truth' through 'cross-examination' of the details, sometimes struggling for an illuminating shift in perspective.

The co-narrated detective stories in our corpus differ from stories in which a story problem is laid out by an authoritative teller whose perspective on the problem is relatively undisputed (cf Lerner 1987 and Mandelbaum 1987a and 1987b for extended discussion). In the latter cases, the perspective on a story problem, that is, the version of an initiating event presented by an authoritative teller, is more or less sustained throughout the telling. In detective stories, however, authority to define a narrative problem is not vested solely in a single knowing teller.

A story problem is scrutinized in the course of the telling: other co-present participants, even those who do not have direct knowledge of the narrated events, probe for or contribute information relevant to clarifying a narrative problem. This new information may or may not lead to a reformulated perspective on a narrative problem. When family co-narrators do overtly adopt a novel perspective on a narrative problem, we see evidence of a paradigm shift. Such cognitive shifts are socially engendered and have social implications, reaffirming the family as a dynamic activity system capable of working through problems.

Besides subverting the notion of one authoritative teller, detective stories also impact the organization of story components. In detective stories, there are at least two versions of a narrative problem that emerge. A story with a setting, an initiating event and subsequent responses is presented and could be treated by those co-present as complete; however, the mark of the detective story is that somebody persists in examining the narrative problem beyond this point, eliciting or introducing relevant information not provided in the initial version of the story. Sometimes the 'missing' information is presented immediately following the first version of a story, e.g. example (1) below. In other cases, the 'missing' information surfaces much later and, as we shall see in example (2), may be extracted from other stories that involve relevant characters or events. Turning two or more seemingly inconsequential stories, or bits and pieces, into one detective story requires someone who makes a commitment—someone who persists, who makes connections, who draws inferences. The information which surfaces may lead to a reanalysis of the earlier story's central problem. Such information thus recontextualizes the earlier story as not *the* story but a story, *i.e.* only one version of the narrated events.

We believe that talk which recontextualizes earlier storytelling is storytelling as well. Our analysis of detective storytelling illustrates our more general view that storytelling in conversation is dynamic and open-ended. Stories often do not come in neat packages. Recent research suggests that story beginnings are socially negotiated (Lerner 1987; Mandelbaum 1987a, 1987b). In detective stories, we see that 'the end' is also socially negotiated.

Our working hypothesis is that detective stories are typical of everyday narration. They grow out of the process of grappling with life's incomplete understandings. Initial narrators often seek the kind of co-narration that both helps further their own comprehension of their stories and give meaning to their stories and their lives.

2. The Role of Slow Disclosure.   The structure of detective stories in conversation parallels that of certain literary and cinematic tales. Such stories are particularly characterized by a strategy known as 'slow disclosure,' that is, the gradual emergence of relevant information or the "prolonged delay in giving away crucial facts in a story" (Sharff 1982: 119). For film directors and writers, slow disclosure is a conscious technique for drawing audiences into some unfolding problem; its strategic use creates rhetorical and powerful effects, such as heightened tension. In the narratives we are examining, slow disclosure does not appear to be a conscious technique but rather an outcome of problem-solving through co-narration. Critical elements of the narrated events are slowly disclosed through joint attention to particular parts of the narrative, especially through the probing contributions of intimates.

For example, the setting, which provides physical and psychological background to understanding the narrative problem, may be probed and subsequently elaborated or revised through further co-narration. Experiences and events critical to assessing the psychological setting—beliefs, values and attitudes—may not even be treated by initial tellers as relevant or desirable to reveal at the outset of the narrative. While family members can assume some of this information because of familiarity with the narrator and the narrative circumstances, they also depend on the talk itself to index parts of the psychological setting. These may prove critical to their assessments and thus to the evolution of the narrative itself. New settings present opportunities for co-narrators to recontextualize the initiating event and the responses and reactions it incurs. Thus, co-constructed, unfolding settings orient and re-orient a story throughout its telling.

Slow disclosure of elements such as psychological setting may result in part from a preference of initial tellers to present narrated events in a way that portrays themselves in the most complimentary light. We refer to this preference as the 'looking good' constraint on storytelling.

Example (1) is a relatively simple illustration of slow disclosure and the 'looking good' constraint operating in a detective story, showing how settings unfold through co-narration:

(1) Detention Narrative—Family B Dinner #2, p 12–14

Mother, Father, and two children—Lucy, 9 years and Chuck, 6 years—are seated around dinner table; they have been discussing degrees of familiarity a person can have with colleagues at work or school and Chuck has offered, as an example, that he knows Mrs. Arnold, the school principal, very well and Mother has commented that she is a good person to know.

Lucy:	I don't think Mrs. Arnold is being fair because um
Mother:	Bill?
Father:	(?)
Lucy:	When we were back in school um—this girl—she pulled um Valerie's dress up to here ((gestures with hand across chest)) in front of the boys
Mother:	mhm?
Lucy:	She only—all she did was get a day in detention
Mother:	mhm?—*You* think she should have gotten suspended? (pause)
Lucy:	at *least*—that's—

Mother:	mhm?
Lucy:	not allowed in *school*
	(pause)
Father:	((clears throat)) hm—(fortunately capital)
	punishment is still=
Chuck:	Was it a girl Lucy who did it or a boy=
	[
Father:	=beyond the (pri-/reach of) elementary
	school principals
Chuck:	=that did that
	[
Mother:	(?)
Chuck:	hm?
Mother:	(Lucy) was *really* embarrassed ((talking while
	eating)) (I mean you really) would have liked to
	kill the girl—huh? Cuz you were upset with her?
	But you were held back because you thought your
	school was goin to do it and the school didn't
	do it and you feel upset
	(pause)
Chuck:	I think she should be in there for a *whole* MONTH
	or so well maybe (pause) *each day* she have to go
	there—*each* day *each* day *each* day even if the—
	[
Lucy:	If you go to
	detention more than three times then you get
	suspended
Father:	((head leaning forward)) More than how many times?
Lucy:	Three
Father:	((nods))
	(pause)
Chuck:	Lucy—you only went to it *once*—right?
Father:	((clears throat))
	((Lucy arches her back, eyes open wide, looks at
	Chuck, shocked, starts shaking her head;
	father immediately looks up at her))
Father:	You can tell us can't you?
	[
Mother:	I'm listening
Lucy:	((low to Chuck)) (thanks)—((louder)) yeah—that
	was—
Mother:	was in detention once?—
Lucy:	once

Mother: in Mr. Dodge's year
Chuck: only once that's all
             [
Mother: (?   ) in the playground?
Father: hm
Chuck: Lucy if you get a second a third and a fourth that
             means you're out—*right?*
Mother: Well no honey not every year—(you're allowed) to
             start new every year
             (pause)
Father: like the statute of limitations
             (fairly long pause)
Mother: things run out after a while

In this narrative, the information that Lucy, the initial narrator, was once pun-
ished by Mrs. Arnold, the principal of her school, is a critical aspect of the setting,
because it illuminates Lucy's psychological stance towards the same principal's
punishment of another student's misdemeanor. Lucy at first does not present her
own past misdemeanor as part of the setting but simply situates the initiating
event in a physical setting ("When we were back in school . . . "). In line with the
'looking good' constraint, Lucy would probably never have disclosed this personally damaging critical background information.

Prior to this disclosure, family members had only Lucy's version of the narrated
problem as data for interpreting her reactions. Presumably Lucy felt the way she
did only because of the morally offensive nature of the misdemeanor. This is the
interpretation her mother promotes, co-constructing the telling of her daughter's
internal responses and emotional reactions. A joint sense of moral indignation
stimulates increasingly drastic proposals for punishment—from "suspension" to
"at least (suspension)" to "would have liked to kill the girl"—until Lucy's younger
brother elicits the crucial background information by asking his sister, "Lucy, you
only went to it [detention] once, right?" Lucy glares at her brother, mumbles to
her parents and grudgingly admits to going to detention.

This new co-authored setting recontextualizes both the narrative problem and
Lucy's reactions: Now the principal is not fair because the principal gave the same
punishment—one day's detention—to both Lucy *and* the horrid girl who committed a far more serious transgression than Lucy presumably had. Thus we see
how co-participants in the telling of a story "assist" one another in bringing a narrative problem into focus. Such assistance, however, is not always welcome: it may
subvert the initial narrator's attempt to look good. In this case, the narrative seems
to have backfired on Lucy and left her damaged by the account, further indexed
by her sudden inarticulateness after the revelation.

3. Paradigm-Shifting Detective Stories.   In the case of the Detention narrative,
there is no overt evidence that the family has in fact used the newly disclosed set-

ting to reanalyze the problem embedded in the initiating event, i.e. they do not overtly use the knowledge of Lucy's own misdemeanor and one day's detention to reframe the morally untenable misdemeanor (the pulling up of the dress) in a new context: It is more serious than the wrongdoing committed by Lucy in the past. The family's doubletake does lead to a softening of response towards transgressors, now that Lucy is included in this category, but then the topic is abruptly dropped.

In other narratives, however, co-tellers display through talk their realization that there is a problem with earlier framings of the problem. Attending to the unfolding disclosures, co-narrators negotiate and in some cases adopt an entirely new perspective, or even a new paradigm, for considering a narrated problem. The adoption of a new paradigm is akin to scientific paradigm shifts of the sort noted by Kuhn (1962, 1977).

Paradigm-shifting through co-narration is illustrated in example (2), a very complex detective story extending over 40 minutes of dinnertime talk and still going on during clean-up. The initial narrator of this story is Marie, the mother in the family being recorded and director of a day care center in their home. Her story grows out of an incident which has just occurred prior to dinner in which Bev, the mother of one of the day-care children, presents Marie with $320. The evolving issue which drives the narrative concerns the meaning of this act—the definition of the narrative problem. Is it payment for one month's child care? Or is it a penalty fee for pulling the child out of the school without two weeks' notice? As Marie first reports the incident, only the first of these questions arises between Marie and Bev:

(2-a) Bev Narrative–7:17 p.m., F Dinner #1, p 18–19

Mother (Marie), Father (Jon) and 3 children—Adam, 9, Julie, 5, and Eric. 3— seated around dinner table; food has been distributed, Jon has said grace, and a family friend has just left.

Marie:	Bev walked up and handed me three twenty
Jon:	mhm
Marie:	And I *thought* she only owed me eighty—and she said she didn't want a receipt and I went in and got the receipt book and she only owed me eighty ((Marie holds her corn, looks intently at Jon))
Jon:	mmhm
Marie:	n she was real happy about that (pause) ((Marie starts to eat corn, then stops)) She says "no no no no no, *I* don't need a receipt"—
Julie:	(Mom look/May I have the)
	[
Marie:	and just hands me three twenty (long pause)

                    ((sounds of eating corn on the cob))
Marie: I—took my book—out though cuz she hardly *ever*—
                    makes ((laughing)) mis*takes*—I thought maybe I
                    wrote it wrong but I went back and got three
                    receipts
Adam: (No::) ((to cat))
                        [
Marie: and they all were
Jon: mhm
Marie: in—you know—what do you call that?
Adam: Daddy, is the (pepper ?   )
                                             [
Jon: consecutive order?
Marie: Yeah—mhm
Jon: (Cat) are you hungry—Has he been (fed) today?

   In this initial version, Marie views the narrative problem as whether or not Bev
was in arrears. Her reported internal response was one of self-doubt, grounded in
the belief that Bev hardly ever makes mistakes. In keeping with the 'looking good'
constraint, this version reveals Marie as an honest businessperson. The telling thus
far provokes minimal involvement from Marie's husband, Jon.
   After a considerable interval—15 minutes of attention to eating, other narra-
tions, etc., alternate reformulations of the Bev-narrative problem emerge in piece-
meal fashion. The reformulations grow out of a second narrative about Bev, introduced by Marie, in which Bev is characterized as opportunistic. At this point,
Jon is drawn in as an active co-narrator.
   (2-b) Bev Narrative— 7:35 p.m., Bev/Family Dinner #1, p 43–45
   Wherein Jon is elaborating on the second narrative, equating Bev's receiving
unwarranted insurance benefits after an accident with the behavior of a customer
who gets excessive change back from a grocery clerk.

Jon: you're supposed to think "Hey, that's *great*" and walk
                    out the store ((laughing))—n she gave me back—
                    twenty dollars too much cuz she must've thought I
                    gave her a fifty
Marie: mhm
Jon: you know—
Marie: mm
Jon: and you're not supposed to consider yer—consider
                    whether or not that comes out of her pay if the
                    drawer doesn't balance at the end of the night or=
                                             [
Marie: (I know)

Jon: =whether it's the ethic—*RIGHT* thing to do is to say
              "Hey lady you—you:—gave me too much money"

Marie: ((pointing index finger to Jon, hand extended from
              elbow)) Well, you know what—you know what though=
                                                [
Jon: it's (*just*) not *in* anymore=

Marie: =I started questioning was the fact she gave me –
              [
Jon: =it's gone to even to the extreme?

Marie: *no*—*no*:tice—she just called up after the accident
              and said

Jon: Yeah "I'm not coming anymore"
                                    [
Marie: "That's it"—no—no two weeks' pay—not =
                                              [   ]
Jon: (Marie)

Marie: =no consideration—(without ever?   )
                                      [
Jon: ((wiping mouth))   She did *all that* when she paid
              you the three hundred and twenty dollars =
              ((Marie with hand to mouth, reflective; Julie gets up and goes
              to the kitchen))

Jon: =she didn't do that by mistake—she wanted to see how *you* felt
              about it and she felt she *owed* you
                                    [
Marie: No: way no no no no—no
              ((Marie shakes head and hand No as well))
                                              [
Jon: Oh no? You don't
              think so?

Marie: No
Jon: Oh
              [
Marie: *She* thought she had not paid me for the month of
              June—and she's paying me from—
              the *first* week of June=
              [
Jon: eh I would read it—Oh eh
Marie: =to:—the—the ending—the third of
                          [   ]
Adam?:   (?   )
                                  [
Jon: You had *said* that she never

```
                made a mistake in the past? though didn't you she was
                always very—good about that
Marie:          ((with index finger pointed out to Jon)) No—she she's
                made one mistake in the past—but=
                                                  [
Jon:                                              oh oh huhuh
Marie:          =her record i:s—very few mistakes?= ((moves raised
                finger horizontally to indicate passage of time))
Jon:            hmhm (okay)
```

In the height of portraying Bev as opportunistic, Marie suddenly brings up
'new' information relevant to the initiating event in the first story about Bev, *i.e.*
Bev's handing over $320 to Marie. Marie recalls Bev's failure to give two weeks'
notice before pulling her daughter out of child care. Jon and Marie now attribute
to Bev different intentions concerning the $320 in light of Bev's knowledge of the
two weeks' notice requirement. Their discussion prefaces a reconceptualization of
the problem embedded in the act of handing over $320.

(2-c) Bev Narrative—7:40 p.m., Bev/Family F dinner #1, p 55–58

The kids have just remembered that Dad had promised them ice cream if they ate
a good dinner, and Marie has encouraged them to chant "Haagen Dazs" over and
over until Jon submits to taking them to the ice cream store. In the throes of these
negotiations, Marie abruptly returns again to the unresolved narrative problem.

```
Marie:          ((head on hand, elbow on table)) You know Jon—I verbally
                did tell Bev two weeks' notice Do you think I shouldov
                stuck to that? or to have done what I did?
Jon:            When I say something I stick to it unless she:-
                s-brings it up. If I set a policy and I—and—they=
Jon:            ((Adam goes toward living room, bouncing a ball))
                =accept that policy—unless they have reason to
                change it and and say=
                                     [
Adam:           (Let's go outside and play)
Jon:            =something? I do not change it—I don't
                automatically assume "We:ll it's not the right thing to do"
                If I were to do that eh – I would be saying in the first place
                I should never have mentioned it=
                ((Julie and Eric leave table to join Adam))
Jon:            =I should never have set the policy if I didn't believe
                in it—If I thought it was—a hardship on people I
                shouldn'a brought it up?—shoulda kept my mouth shut
                —If I: say there's a two weeks' notice required—I
                automatically charge em for two weeks' notice without
```

thinking twice? about it—I say and it "You—you
need—Your pay will include till such and such a
date because of the two neek-weeks' notice that's
required." I:f *THE:Y* feel hardship it's on *thei:r*
part—*it's*—*THEIRS* to say "Marie—I really—you
know—I didn't expect this to happen 'n I'm sorry
((softly)) I didn't give you two weeks' notice but it
was really un-*avoid*able"—a:nd you can say "We:ll—
okay I'll split the difference with you—(it's har-)
a one week's notice"=
[

Marie: see you know in one way wi- in one (instance)
                    [

Jon: =and then they s- if they *push* it
Marie: ((pointing to Jon)) she owed me that money—but I just
    didn't feel right?=
    [

Jon: well you're—you
Marie: =taking it on that (principle) cuz she (wanted)—*She*
    thought she was paying for something that she didn't
                  [

Jon: You: give her the
    money and then you let it *bo*ther you then you –
    then you get all ups-set—You'll be upset for weeks
                [

Marie: no no no I'm *not* upset—it's just
    ((Marie says this calmly but waving of corn cob, then plops corn
    cob down and raps knuckles on table))
Adam: ((from outside)) *Julie*—go get Spirit [the dog] out
Julie: ((from living room)) Why:?
Marie: I guess I just wish I would have said—I'm not upset with
    what happened—I just wanted—I think I=
    [

Adam: ((from outside)) (?   )
Marie: =would feel better if I had said something

    In this passage, Marie and Jon take the reanalysis of the problem one step fur-
ther, a step we propose constitutes a paradigm shift. The paradigm shift is a result
of problem-solving enriched through co-narration. Jon and Marie's earlier dispute over Bev and the two weeks' notice sets in motion a shift in perspective. The
issue of the two weeks' notice has continued to haunt Marie, as indicated by her
abrupt re-introduction of the topic. Here Marie emphatically confirms that she
did indeed make the two-week rule very explicit to Bev prior to the initiating

event. Marie uses this new piece of the setting to reformulate the narrative problem in terms of a new dilemma, namely whether she should have insisted that Bev give her the $320 to compensate for the lack of a two-week notice or should have kept quiet. This reformulation evidences, for us, a paradigm shift, wherein the $320 is now rightfully Marie's and not Bev's. (Marie: "In one instance she owed me that money . . . "; Jon: "You give her the money . . . ") The reformulation casts Marie's way of responding to Bev's handing her $320 in a new light. Whereas Marie's action of taking out the receipt book and proving that Bev was not in arrears successfully resolved the first formulation of the narrated problem, the newly formulated definition of the problem makes that action seem inadequate. This inadequacy is articulated by both Marie ("I think I would feel better if I had said something") and Jon ("If *I:* say there's a two weeks' notice required—I automatically charge em for two weeks' notice without thinking twice") and leads to Jon's subsequently chiding Marie for feeling upset.

A critical factor in determining whether or not a detective story takes on the dimensions of a paradigm shift is the uptake of listeners and their willingness to actively enter the narrating process. Our data demonstrate that important missing information surfaces in the throes of collaborative narration. For example, Marie's rather sudden recall of the two-week notice in (2-b) overlaps with Jon's active involvement in assessing Bev's insurance dealings, as if inspired by the energy and support of the collaboration. When a new paradigm is internalized by a narrator, as Marie seems to have internalized the reconstituted problem, we see an exemplar of the Vygotskian passage from interpersonal to intrapersonal knowledge, through co-narration. The presence of family members, apparently facilitated in the more centralized family dinners around a common table, leads to socially accomplished problem-solving and thereby transports narrative co-construction into the arena of joint and individual cognition.

C. Social Consequences of Narrative Practices

It is widely recognized that narratives strengthen social relationships and a general sense of co-membership by providing a medium for illustrating common beliefs, values, and attitudes of tellers and audiences. Research on co-narration demonstrates further that beliefs, values, and attitudes are not so much transmitted from teller to audience as they are collectively and dialogically engendered (see Holquist 1983). Audiences are co-authors and as such co-owners of the narratives and the moral and other premises that these narratives illustrate. They co-own the narrative as an interactional product and more importantly share control over cognitive and verbal tools fundamental to problem-solving itself. Co-ownership is not a relationship that one enters into lightly as it involves sharing control and a commitment however temporary both to the activities of co-narration/co-problem-solving and to the product, *i.e.* the story. For this reason, interlocutors vary the extent and type of their narrative involvement.

Detective stories, particularly paradigm-shifting ones, display considerable cognitive, affective and linguistic involvement from interlocutors. Such extensive involvement structures and restructures social relationships among co-narrators and impacts the balance of power in the social unit. Interlocutors co-own the story in the sense that they participate in re-perspectizing the fundamental narrative problem. As such, they take on shared responsibility for the story as a product, with or without the invitation of the initial teller. Entitlement to tell a story is thus not the exclusive right of an initial teller (Lerner 1987, Mandelbaum 1987a, 1987b). Even those who have not directly experienced the narrative events can acquire entitlement through expanding, querying, correcting, or challenging existing formulations of the narrative problem.

This sharing of narrative 'rights' evidences a sharing of power. At the same time, such sharing makes participants' perceptions of the world vulnerable to co-authored change. In detective stories, the sharing of narrative rights empowers co-present interlocutors to co-author one another's biographies, *i.e.* to construct collectively one party's past experience through co-narration. Such reconstruction (or deconstruction) potentially threatens a teller's drive to 'look good'. It is our hypothesis that this vulnerability serves as a constraint on full-fledged participation in detective storytelling. Whether participants undertake extended 'detecting' appears to be a function of the participants' willingness to commit time and energy and of an initial teller's willingness to risk vulnerability. And that is where the prolonged, centralized dinner may be a last holdout for familial co-authorship. Through the activity of co-authoring detective stories, family members construct perspectives and evoke values. Each exercise of narrative rights and practices reconstitutes family relationships and the family itself as an activity system.

III. Concluding Remark

Collaboration in the form of detective storytelling is akin to scaffolding and joint problem-solving practices characteristic of American middle-class care-giver-child interactions (Ochs & Schieffelin 1984, Wertsch & Hickmann 1987). Such practices empower intimates to influence each other's perceptions of the world and, in so doing, to socialize one another. In our view, the co-narrated detective story is not only a vehicle for the socialization of family values and the family's sense of order/disorder in the world; it is also an object itself of socialization. Children and others sitting at dinner tables and participating in co-narration are being socialized into ways of articulating and solving problems through social construction of a genre. Families who sit together for the duration of a meal have a potential opportunity space for socializing this mode of problem solving—and certain families do just that, exploiting narratives to co-construct new paradigms which order and reorder their everyday lives.

Notes

This paper is the result of the equal work of the three authors.

1. This research project ("Discourse Processes in American Families") is funded by NICHD (grant no.1 ROH HD 20992-01A1). Members of the research team include E. Ochs and T. Weisner (co-P.I.'s), M. Bernstein, D. Rudolph, R. Smith, and C. Taylor (research assistants).

References

Duranti, A. 1986. "The Audience as Co-Author: an Introduction." In Duranti, A. and Brenneis. D. (Eds.), *Text,* Special Issue: *The Audience as Co-Author,* 6-3: 239–247.

Engeström, Y. 1987. *Learning by Expanding: An Activity-Theoretical Approach to Developmental Research.* Helsinki: Orienta-Konsultit.

———. *to appear.* "Developmental Studies of Work as a Testbench of Activity Theory." In Lave, J. and Chaiklin, S. (Eds.), *Situated Learning.* Cambridge: Cambridge University Press.

Feiring, C. and Lewis, M. 1987. "The Ecology of Some Middle Class Families at Dinner." *International Journal of Behavioral Development,* 10(3): 377–390.

Fisher, W. 1985a. "The Narrative Paradigm: In the Beginning." *Journal of Communication* 35(4): 75–89.

———. 1985b. "The Narrative Paradigm: An Elaboration." *Communication Monographs.* 52:347–367.

Goodwin, C. 1986a. "Notes on Story Structure and the Organization of Participation." In Atkinson J.M. & Heritage, J. (Eds.), *Structures of Social Action: Studies in Conversation Analysis.* Cambridge: Cambridge University Press, 225–246.

———. 1986b. "Audience Diversity, Participation, and Interpretation." In Duranti, A. and Brenneis, D. (Eds.) *Text,* Special Issue: *The Audience as Co-Author,* 6–3 283–316.

Haviland, J. 1986. " 'Con Buenos Chiles': Talk, Targets and Teasing in Zinacantan." In Duranti A. and Brenneis, D. (Eds.), *Text,* Special Issue: *The Audience as Co-Author* 6-3: 249–282.

Holquist, M. 1983. "The Politics of Representation." *The Quarterly Newsletter of the Laboratory of Comparative Human Cognition,* 5: 2–9.

Jefferson, G. 1978. "Some Sequential Aspects of Storytelling in Conversation." In Schenkein, J. (Ed) *Studies in the Organization of Conversational Interaction.* New York: Academic Press, 219–248.

Kuhn, T. 1962. *The Structure of Scientific Revolutions.* Chicago: University of Chicago Press.

———. 1977. *The Essential Tension.* Chicago: University of Chicago Press.

Labov, W. 1984. "Intensity." In Schiffrin, D. (Ed.), *Meaning, Form and Use in Context: Linguistic Applications.* Washington, D.C.: Georgetown University Press. 43–70.

Leontyev, A.N.I. 1981. *Problems of the Development of Mind.* Moscow: Progress Publishers.

Lerner, G. 1987. *Collaborative Turn Sequences: Sentence Construction and Social Action,* Unpublished Ph.D. Dissertation, University of California, Irvine.

Mandelbaum, J. 1987a. "Couples Sharing Stories." *Communication Quarterly:* 35(2), 144–170.

———. 1987b. *Recipient-Driven Storytelling in Conversation.* Unpublished Ph.D. Dissertation, University of Texas at Austin.

Ochs, E. and Schieffelin, B. 1984. "Language Acquisition and Socialization: Three Developmental Stories." In Schweder, R. and Le Vine, R. (Eds.), *Culture Theory: Essays on Mind, Self, and Emotion*. Cambridge: Cambridge University Press, 276–320.

Rogoff, B. & Lave, J. 1984. *Everyday Cognition*. Cambridge, Massachusetts: Harvard University Press.

Sacks, H. 1964–72. Unpublished Lecture Notes. University of California.

Schiffrin, D. 1987. *Discourse Markers*. Cambridge: Cambridge University Press.

Sharff, S. 1982. *The Elements of Cinema: Toward a Theory of Cinesthetic Impact*. New York: Columbia University Press.

Stein, N. 1979. "How Children Understand Stories: A Developmental Analysis." In Katz, L. (Ed.), *Current Topics in Early Childhood Education (vol. 2)*. Norwood, New Jersey: Ablex.

Stein, N. & Policastro, M. 1984. "The Concept of a Story: A Comparison Between Children's and Teacher's Viewpoints." In Mandl, H., Stein, N., Trabasso, T. (Eds.), *Learning and Comprehension of Text*. Hillsdale, New Jersey: Lawrence Erlbaum Associates, 113–158.

Trabasso, T., Secco, T. and Van Den Broek, P. 1984. "Causal Cohesion and Story Coherence." In Mandl, H., Stein, N. and Trabasso, T. (Eds.), *Learning and Comprehension of Text*. Hillsdale, New Jersey: Lawrence Erlbaum Associates, 83–112.

Vygotsky, L. 1978. *Mind in Society*. Cambridge, Massachusetts: Harvard University Press.

———. 1981. "The Genesis of Higher Mental Functions." In Wertsch, J. *The Concept of Activity in Soviet Psychology*. Armonk, New York: M.E. Sharpe, 144–188.

Wertsch, J. 1985. *Vygotsky and the Social Formation of Mind*. Cambridge, Massachusetts: Harvard University Press.

Wertsch, J. and Hickmann, M. 1987. "Problem-Solving in Social Interaction: A Microgenetic Approach." In Hickmann, M. (Ed.), *Social and Functional Approaches to Language and Thought*. New York: Academic Press, 151–165.

4

Hard Words: A Functional Basis for Kaluli Discourse

STEVEN FELD AND BAMBI B. SCHIEFFELIN

0. Introduction. This paper is concerned with cultural constructions that frame appropriate Kaluli discourse and with some kinds of discourse that operate within that frame. We begin with ethnographic and metalinguistic materials scaffolding the Kaluli notion of 'hardness', the Kaluli conception of language and speech, and the specific idea of 'hard words'. These constructs illustrate the pervasive character of a Kaluli distinction between 'langue' and 'parole'. Based on these systematic notions of language form, socialization, and behavior we analyze some situated discourse examples that indicate both how these cultural constructions are learned and how they operate in everyday interactions.

0.1 People and Place. The Kaluli people are part of a population of about 1,200 who live in several hundred square miles of tropical rain forest just north of the slopes of Mt. Bosavi, on the Great Papuan Plateau of Papua New Guinea (E. L. Schieffelin 1976). They are one of four culturally identical but dialectically different subgroups who collectively refer to themselves as *Bosavi kalu* 'Bosavi people'. The Kaluli reside in longhouse communities made up of about 15 families (60–90 people), separated by an hour or so walk over forest trails. Subsistence is organized around swidden horticulture, the processing of wild sago palm to make a staple starch, and hunting and fishing. In broad terms, Kaluli society is highly egalitarian, lacking in the 'big man' social organization characteristic of the Papua New Guinea Highlands. Men and women utilize extensive networks of obligation and reciprocity in the organization of work and sociable interaction.

Kaluli is one of four dialects of Bosavi, a non-Austronesian verb-final ergative language. Most speakers are monolingual. While Tok Pisin (Neo Melanesian), is known by some younger men, it is almost never heard in daily discourse. Recently introduced literacy programs have affected few people.

Kaluli everyday life is overtly focused around verbal interaction. Talk is thought of and used as a means of control, manipulation, expression, assertion, and appeal. It gets you what you want, need, or feel owed. Extensive demarcation of kinds of speaking and speech acts further substantiate the observation that Kaluli are energetically verbal; talk is a primary way to be social, and a primary indicator of social competence (B. B. Schieffelin 1979; B. B. Schieffelin and Feld 1979).

More generally, the realm of sound yields the most elaborated forms of Kaluli expression. In the tropical forest and village longhouse it is difficult to find auditory privacy or quiet. Greetings, comings and goings, announcements, arguments, meetings, and all soundings are projected into aurally public space. No comparable variety, salience, or exuberance exists for Kaluli visual or choreographic modes of expressions.

1. 'Hard', 'Words', 'Hard Words': Putting a Construction on Life and Language.

1.1 Halaido *'Hard'.* *Halaido* 'hard' is a pervasive Kaluli notion that applies broadly in three cultural-semantic domains. The first is growth and maturation, where the socializing interactions in the acquisition of language are what 'makes (it) hard' (*halaido dom\epsilonki*); the development of strong teeth and bones in the uncoordinated infant who is 'without understanding' (*asugo andoma*) is a process of 'hardening' (*halaidan*). In these cases, the process of becoming 'hard' is a literal and metaphoric construct for physical and mental development and for cultural socialization. A second domain for *halaido* is the fully adult consequence of this maturation process. A *kalu halaido* or 'hard man' is one who is strong, assertive, and not a witch; a major component in this person's projection of his 'hardness' is the acquisition and command of *to halaido* 'hard words', the fully developed capacity for language.[1] The final area in which *halaido* is prominent is dramatic style. In ceremonial performance, songs are intended to be evocative and make the audience weep. The climax in the development of aesthetic tension, where the manner of singing and the textual elements coalesce, is what promotes the 'hardening' (again, *halaido dom\epsilonki*) of a song. A performance that does not 'harden' will not move listeners to tears and will not be considered successful. Furthermore, the ability to 'harden' a song is an important compositional (particularly in textual craft) and performative skill.

The cultural construction and prominence of *halaido* in Kaluli growth, adulthood, and presentational style can in part be traced to an origin myth which tells how the world was once muddy and soft; a megapode and Goura pigeon together stamped on the ground to make it hard. Like the hardening of the land which symbolizes the necessity of physical and geographical formation, the hardening of body, language, character, and dramatic style symbolizes the necessity of human socialization in order to develop cultural competence.

One term used in opposition to *halaido* is *taiyo* 'soft'. Within this oppositional frame, *taiyo* is 'soft' in the senses of: mushy foods, things which decay and rot, or debilitation. It signifies a stage in the process of decay, and all connotations with this state are unpleasant. Food taboos constrain the eating of certain soft substances (such as eggs) while young lest one not 'harden'. Children, moreover, do not eat the meat of certain birds who have 'soft' voices or redundant and other-

wise strange calls, lest their language not harden and they grow up to speak unintelligible sounds. (On the topic of children's food taboos vis-à-vis hardness, see B.
B. Schieffelin 1979:62–65, and Feld 1982:Chapter 2.) Similarly tabooed are all animal and vegetable foods which are yellow; like the leaves of plants, things yellow
as they decay. Witches are said to have yellow soft hearts, while the hearts of 'hard
men' are dark and firm (E. L. Schieffelin 1976:79, 128). In short, the passage from
'hardness' to 'softness' is undesirable, synonymous with debilitation, vulnerability,
and decay, states which must be avoided. The desired progression in all things is
from softness (infant) to hardness (adult); once hard in body, language, and dramatic style, Kaluli must stay that way.

    Another term utilized in opposition to *halaido* is *halaidoma* 'unhard', 'without
hardness', formed by the word 'hard' plus the negative particle -*ma*. Something
which is potentially hard—or which should be, but is not—is 'unhard'. For instance, when one of us was learning the Bosavi language (SF), his verbal behavior
was judged as *to halaidoma* and his mistakes greeted assuringly with *towɔ
halaidɛsɛge* 'when your language has hardened'. Never was this speech ability referred to as **to taiyo* 'soft words', a construction which was laughed at when suggested. 'Soft words' is neither an appropriate nor utterable phrase; language is either 'hard' or 'unhard', i.e. in the process of hardening, or in the state of becoming
unhard, as in sickness or delirium.

1.2 To 'Words/language'.   Kaluli observe a langue/parole distinction. This is
marked by the distribution of the terms *to* and *tolɛma* 'words', 'language' and imperative 'talk words/language' (langue) and *sama* imperative 'speak' (parole).[2] *To*
and *tolɛma* refer to the systematic form of language or its capacity; in contrast,
sama refers to the manner or act of speaking. To illustrate langue we examine the
items in (1).

(1) Bosavi to   Bosavi language
    bali to   'turned over words' = systematic linguistic
                   irony/euphemism, metaphor, or obfuscation
    malolo to   'narrated/told words' (= myths and stories)
    mugu to   'taboo words'

    In these examples, the noun *to* refers to the system or form of talk. All of these
nominal forms can be followed by the habitual verbs *salan* 'one speaks/says', *asu-
lan* 'one understands', or *dadan* 'one hears'. These indicate that one may speak, understand, or hear any of these systems of talk or different languages. The use of
tolɛma contrasts with constructions using *sama* ('parole'), for instance; (here with
sama in the present habitual form *salan*).

(2) wɔnoli-salan   one speaks secretly, stealthily
    tɛde-salan   one speaks in a deep voice
    hala-salan   one speaks with mispronunciations

In these instances (and a multitude of similarly constructed ones), *salan* concerns
the behavior of speaking, or some description of how speaking is performed.

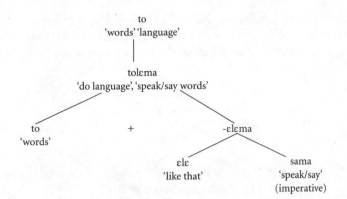

Figure 4.1

From our analysis the Kaluli theory of language and speech is one is which *to* 'words' are the prime substance of language; *tolɛma* is the doing or speaking of words.

As can be seen in Figure 4.1, *tolɛma* is formed by adding *to* 'words' and *-ɛlɛma*, imperative 'do/say/speak like that'. The item *ɛlɛma* is the contracted form of *ɛlɛsama*, 'like that' plus the imperative 'say/speak'. Many Kaluli verbs are formed in this way, by adding a substance or onomatopoeic root to *-ɛlɛma*. For instance, the verb for 'weep' is *yɛlɛma*, composed by contracting the onomatopoeic representation of the sound of weeping, *yɛ*, and the imperative 'say/speak like that' (Feld 1982:Chapters 3 and 4 contain materials on these formations in Kaluli metalinguistics; B. B. Schieffelin 1979:Chapter 3 contains materials on *ɛlɛma* and *ɛlɛsama* in interaction).

Everyday interactions make clear that the contrast between these two notions is salient for Kaluli. To take a simple instance, SF was once questioning some men about the fact that certain birds are claimed to speak some Bosavi words. He asked about *bɔlo*, the friarbird in the Kaluli myth about how birds received human tongues.

   (3a) Bɔlo-wɔ, Bosavi to salano?
      'As for *bɔlo*, does he speak Bosavi words/language?'

Two answers followed:

   (3b) Bosavi to salan.
      'He *speaks* Bosavi words/language.'

      Mugu tolan.
      'He *talks* taboo language.'

The first response is the usual specific one ('parole'), while the second was a response from a Christian referring to the way the systematic form of *bɔlo's* talk consists of words Christians consider taboo ('langue'). Yet in the context of listening to a tape recording of specific calls by *bɔlo*, the same man noted, *mugu to salab* 'he is speaking/saying taboo words/language', implying: in that specific instance.

In everyday talk the distribution of inflected verb forms for *sama* and *tolɛma* further exemplifies the importance of speaking as a situational act and language as a fundamental capacity. Part of the paradigm includes the items in (4).

(4) tolɛma   sama   imperative immediate
     tolɛbi   sɛlɛbi   imperative future
     tolomɛno   sɛlɛmɛno   future first person
     tolab   salab   present third person
     tolan   salan   habitual third person

but:

     *tolɔl   sɔlɔl   present first person
     *tolɔ   siyɔ   past

The fact that the present first person form and past form are blocked for *tolɛma* is consistent with the general nature of *to* as 'words/language' and *tolɛma* as 'talk'. Moreover, *tolɔl* contrasts with:

towɔ sɔlɔl 'I speak/say words/language'
towɔ mɔtolan 'It doesn't talk words/language' (can be said only about animals whose communication is assumed to be a system based upon a substance other than 'words'.)
*ɛlɛ tolɔ
*ɛlɛ tolɛma
ɛlɛ siyɔ 'said like that'
ɛlɛ sama 'say like that'

Use of 'like that' is also blocked with *to* and *tolɛma* because of lack of reference to a specific situation or context.

The metalinguistic area provides further examples of the distribution and further evidence for the cohesiveness of ways of describing related modalities of soundmaking. In one example across modalities, *gese*, the root of *gesema* 'make one feel sorrow or pity' is only blocked for *tolɛma* as illustrated in (5).

(5) gese-salan   one speaks sadly (plaintively; with descending intonation)
     gese-yɛlan   one weeps sadly (plaintively; with descending intonation)
     gese-holan   one whistles sadly (plaintively; with descending intonation)
     gese-molan   one sings sadly (plaintively; with descending intonation)

but:

*gese-tolan   inappropriate because gese describes the manner of speaking and is
                not applicable to the system or capacity of talk

In these cases the verbs deal with modes of soundmaking while the adverbs describe the manner of performance; like other verbs of soundmaking, *sama* refers to the behavioral aspect of speech; *to* and *tolɛma* refer to its form and capacity.

A major area of metalinguistic denomination is marked by use of *sa*. By itself, *sa* means 'waterfall'; the term also prefixes all verbs of soundmaking to indicate that the sound has an 'inside' or text. This usage derives from the metaphor that texts are composed 'like a waterfall flowing into a waterpool'; the sound is 'outside' and the text, like a waterfall, is the part that flows down and inside. Verbs of soundmaking turn into musical or compositional terms when prefixed by *sa* in this way, as in (6) (with verbs all in a present habitual form).

(6) salan   'one speaks'   sa-salan 'one speaks inside the words/one speak poetically'
    yɛlan   'one weeps'   sa-yɛlan 'one weeps with text'
    holan   'one whistles'   sa-holan 'one whistles with words in mind'
    molan   'one sings'   sa-molan 'one sings inside' i.e. 'one composes'

but:

    tolan   'one talks'   *sa-tolan inappropriate because one cannot have an
                                inner text to language capacity

Sa-salan, *sa-sama*, and *sa-siyo* all indicate an intention to mean more than what is said. *To* and *tolɛma* do not participate in this paradigm; *sa-to* and *sa-tolɛma* are blocked because there cannot be an 'inside' or inner text to the capacity or system of language. 'Insides' are specific and contextual, related to situated performances only.

1.3 To halaido, 'Hard Words/Talk/Language'.   Given the cultural importance and pervasiveness of 'hardness' as a construct underlying mature social process and capacity, and the role of 'hardness' in the distinction Kaluli observe between langue and parole, we turn to the specific importance of 'hard words'. In the most general sense, *to halaido* is the system of and capacity for grammatically well-formed and socially appropriate language. It is the substance of what Kaluli adults know and act upon in their verbal behaviors. It is what is normally acquired, the competence to perform, what Kaluli should 'have in mind' when they speak. The opposite of *to halaido* is not *to taiyo* 'soft words'; when language is in the process of forming, it is *to halaidoma* 'unhard words'.

Nevertheless, when asked if there is any language which is neither hard nor in the process of becoming hard, Kaluli indicate that such is the situation for the language of song.[3] This is a special poetic system called ɔbe gɔnɔ to 'bird sound words'. Songs are said to be composed and sung from a bird's point of view, and not a human one. They achieve their plaintive quality and ability to move people to tears in this way because birds are the spirit reflections of Kaluli dead. Song language is thus not human and hard, but birdlike, sad, sentimental, reflective.

The contrast between *to halaido* 'hard words' and ɔbɛ gɔnɔ to 'bird sound words' is basic. 'Hard words' are assertive and direct language forms which engage speakers in face-to-face talk that is interactive and mutual, and are intended to get speakers what they want or need out of social situations. On the other hand, 'bird sound words' are reflective and nostalgic, and are supposed to make a listener empathize with a speaker's message without necessarily or generally responding to it verbally. 'Bird sound words' involve linguistic means that communicate affect by revealing the speaker's state of mind and moving a listener to feel sympathy for that state.

It is not the case that the difference between these two constructs is simply one of referential/expressive or ordinary/nonordinary. Certain message forms and contents can appear in either; the different way that messages are interpreted depends on judgments about intention deriving from contextual constraints, as well as from placement in an ongoing textual chain. Consider example (7).

(7) Dowɔ ge oba hanaya?
    'Father, where are you going?'

There are numerous daily contexts in which this might be uttered by a person to someone called 'father'. Depending on the intonational contour, the utterance could be a request for information, a challenge, or a rhetorical question—all of which might be benign or threatening. However, when we shift from conversation to song usage, the implications shift radically and the audience immediately knows that the message is that a father has died and left someone behind. The person asking the question is in the resultant state of abandonment and appealing to the audience for sympathy. The form of the words is 'hard' in the sense that they are well formed and could be uttered in appropriate daily situations. However, in a song context the words show their 'inside', *sa*, and this is why they are 'bird sound words'. What is implied in the saying context and manner of saying is more important than the referential equivalents of the words which are said.

2. Learning and Speaking 'Hard Words'.

2.1 Imperatives.   To exemplify how the process of learning the model for discourse is the learning of 'speaking' and 'hard words', we turn to some discourse examples from tape-recorded family interactions. While these examples involve much adult-child speech, the same forms are used among adults (though perhaps not as frequently or with the same concentration in an episode, since child-adult speech involves more direction and repetition). Imperatives form an important class of examples since they provide major instances of learning by instruction. In addition to indicating specific rhetorical strategies for getting what one wants, imperatives teach directness, control, speaking out, sequencing, and cohesion in the flow of talk.[4] This is further strengthened by the unambiguous relation of speaker/addressee in imperatives, as evidenced by frequent deletion of the optional subject pronoun or a vocative. Moreover, imperatives are favored forms for requesting both actions and objects because Kaluli does not express requests indirectly with forms like 'would you, could you'. Additionally, language structure provides great flexibility, range, and specificity for imperatives. For example, Kaluli morphologically differentiates present and future imperative, marking iterative and punctual action, with various degrees of emphasis or seriousness, all of which can be indicated for single, dual, or plural subjects.

In the examples that follow, *sama*, *ɛlɛma*, and *to/tolɛma* clearly distribute according to whether specific instances of speaking or general prescriptions to talk are encouraged.

For the Kaluli infant, involvement in verbal interactions starts about a week after birth. A mother holds her infant so that it faces another child; she moves the infant as one might a ventriloquist's dummy, speaking for it in a nasalized falsetto voice. Her speech is well formed and clearly articulated, with the complexity of a 4-year-old's speech. The child to whom the baby is 'speaking' engages in conversation directed to the baby for as long as interest can be maintained. Through these verbal interactions the baby is presented as a person, an individual, and is made to appear more independent and mature than it actually is, largely through the mother's speech and her manipulation of the infant's body. These 'three-party' interactions, as well as the much less frequent direct talk between mother and infant, are said to 'give words/language understanding or meaning' (*to samiab*).

The use of language and rhetoric in interaction are the major means of social manipulation and control in Kaluli life. Thus, one of the most important achievements in childhood is to learn to speak Kaluli effectively to a variety of individuals with whom one participates in everyday activities. Kaluli say that language (*to*) has begun once the young child uses two critical words, *nɔ* 'mother' and *bo* 'breast'. Children who only name other people, animals, or objects are said to do so 'to no purpose' (*ba madali*); they are not considered to have begun to use language. This is evidence for the essentially social view of language taken by the Kaluli, a view which emphasizes not only the learning and using of words per se, but the use of specific words to express the first social relationship a person has, namely, the mother-child relationship mediated by food from the breast. This is a basic theme in Kaluli social life. The giving and receiving of food is a major way in which relationships are mediated and validated (E. L. Schieffelin 1976; Feld and B. B. Schieffelin 1980).

Once a child has begun to use the words 'mother' and 'breast', Kaluli begin to 'show language' (*to widan*). Kaluli say that children must be 'shown language' by other Kaluli speakers, principally by the mother. Kaluli use no baby talk lexicon as such, and claim that children must hear *to halaido* 'hard language', if they are to learn to speak correctly. When a Kaluli adult wants a child to say something in an ongoing interaction, a specific model is provided for what the child is to say, followed by the imperative 'say like that' *ɛlɛma*. The word *ɛlɛma* is a contraction of *ɛlɛ* 'like this/that' and *sama* 'say/speak' present imperative. While the adult occasionally asks the child to repeat utterances directly back to him or her, correcting the child's language or initiating a game, the vast majority of these directives to speak concern instructions to the child to say something to someone else.[5] An example of this type of interaction is given in (8).

(8) Mɛli (female, 25 months) and her mother are in the house. Mother has tried to get Mɛli into an ɛlɛma routine, and Mɛli has been distracted. Finally, she settles down. Grandfather is not in sight.[6]

1. *Mother*→Mɛli: Sit on this.   (Mɛli does)
   now speak words.
   ami *to ɛna sama*
2. *Mother*→Mɛli↠Grandfather:
   Grandfather! *ɛlɛma*
   (softly)   3. Grandfather/
4. *Mother*→Mɛli:
   speak more forcefully/loudly.
   ogole *sama*
   (louder)   5. Grandfather!/
6. *Mother*→Mɛli↠Grandfather:
   I'm hungry for meat! *ɛlɛma*

                                               7. I'm hungry for meat!/

(This continues for 14 turns, which consist of requests to grandfather to get different foods.)

In line 1, Mɛli's mother encourages her to 'speak words/language' (*to sama*), to engage verbally with someone. She has the addressee and utterances in mind, which she will provide followed by the imperative 'say like that' *ɛlɛma*. The addressee is named, but Meli does not call out loudly enough, and in line 4 her mother tells her how to speak, using *sama*. This is followed by a specific utterance, and another directive to speak, with which Mɛli complies. Thus, *to sama* refers to the activity of speaking and saying, where a sequence of utterances are followed by *ɛlɛma*. While in this episode the addressee, Grandfather, is not in the vicinity and therefore does not respond to Mɛli's requests, the majority of such episodes involve responses from a third person to the child's directed utterances. These sequences often involve extensive and cohesive turns of talk. This 'showing the language' helps the language 'harden' (*halaido domɛki*) and thus is consistent with the general goals of socialization and development: the achievement of 'hardening' which produces an individual who is in control of himself or herself, and who is capable of verbally controlling others.

Directives to speak, using the imperative, occur in a variety of speech situations, but are most frequent in those involving shaming, challenging, and teasing. The interactional sequence in (9) illustrates several of the rhetorical strategies used in such situations, and demonstrates the sensitivity young children develop about the consequences of what they say.

(9) Wanu (male, 27 months), his sister Binalia (5 years), cousin Mama (3½ years), and Mother are at home. The two girls (Mama and Binalia) are eating salt belonging to another child.

1. Mother → Wanu ↠ Mama:
                          Binalia

    Whose is it?! *ɛlɛma*

                                               2. Whose is it?!/

3. Is it yours?! *ɛlɛma*

                      4. is it yours?!/

5. Who are you?! *ɛlɛma*

                      6. who are you?!/

7. Binalia→Wanu⇢Mother:
Is it yours?! *ɛlɛma*

                      8. is it yours?!/

9. Mother → Wanu ⇢ Mama:
                          Binalia
It's mine! *ɛlɛma*

10. Mama→Binalia: Don't speak like that!
                       ɛlɛdo sɛlasabo!

Rhetorical questions, such as those found in lines 1, 3, 5, and 7 in example (9), are frequent in family interactions involving the use of *ɛlɛma*. They are intended to shame the addressee so that he or she will terminate undesirable behavior. Kaluli frequently utilize teasing, shaming, and other means of verbal confrontation that focus on an addressee who cannot answer rhetorical questions without the admission of fault. These strategies of confrontation and their component rhetorical skills set the tone of many interactions, while the use of directives (such as 'put the salt away') or physical intervention is much less common. Although children may challenge adults in certain situations (and are encouraged to do so), here Mama (age 3½) tells Binalia 'don't speak like that', referring to Binalia's attempt to get Wanu to challenge his mother. When asked about that utterance, Kaluli said that Mother could get angry and take the salt away. Thus, even children evidence a sensitivity to how language is being used in interactions, sensing the consequences of particular kinds of talk. This further serves the functional importance of directly putting the burden on the addressee.

The use of *ɛlɛma* in these interactions is consistent with the mother's treatment of her preverbal infant, in which she puts words into his mouth. She pushes her young language-learning child into social interaction, providing the words he cannot say or may not be interested in saying. This practice provides the opportunity for the child to acquire the verbal skills that are needed later on, when mother has her next baby and the child becomes part of a peer group. It is the ability not only to repeat rhetorical questions such as 'who are you?!' 'Is it yours?!' but to use them, spontaneously in the appropriate contexts, that lead Kaluli to comment about a young child, *to halaido momada salab* 'he/she is starting to speak hard language'.

It is important to note that throughout interactions using *ɛlɛma*, assertion prevails. In teaching language, mothers are teaching their small children assertion itself. For Kaluli this implies strength and independence. In interactional terms this means to request with imperatives, to challenge and confront, and to say something powerful so others will bend or give. Mothers never use *ɛlɛma* to instruct their children in begging, whining, or appealing to others for sympathy. In learning the types of things one says with *ɛlɛma*, Kaluli children are learning culturally specific ways in which to be tough, independent, and assertive, which reinforces the cultural value of acting in a direct, controlled manner.

In addition to the imperatives *sama* and *ɛlɛma*, the imperative *tolɛma* is also used in conversations. In contrast to the act of speaking (*sama*), use of *tolɛma* calls attention to the importance of verbal interaction as an activity in which children are encouraged to participate.

(10) Mɛli (female, 25 months) is with her father in the house. She is not involved in any activity. Mama is not in sight.

1. Father→Mɛli→Mama:
   Mama!   call out.
           holɛma

                                    2. Mama/

3. Come and talk together with
   me!   *ɛlɛma*
   nɛno to tomɛni mɛno!

                                    4. come and talk together with me/
(There is no response. Seeing another child)

5. Father→Mɛli: Now you and Babi go in order to talk.
           ami Babi gain tomɛ'hamana

6. (Mɛli puts marble in her mouth) Take out the marble!
   After taking it out with your hand, you will talk!
   to tolɛbi

In this episode, Father is trying to get Mɛli established in a verbal activity, made explicit in line 3 as a directive (*ɛlɛma*) to invite Mama to come and talk (*to tomɛni meno*). The word *ɛlɛma* marks what is specific to be said, and the concatenated form (*tomɛni* 'in order to talk' + *meno* 'come' imperative) marks the general activity to take place. A similar concatenated form is used in line 5, this time directing Mɛli to go in order to talk. And finally (line 6), *to tolɛbi* (future imperative) is used to indicate what Mɛli should do, but not what she will say.[7]

In this situation, talking is being established as a way to engage and be social. Parents assume the importance of integrating children into adult verbal activities and additionally encourage the organization and maintenance of verbal exchanges among children themselves. This establishes talk as a topic of talk, instructions to talk as instructions to be social, and talk as a modality that promotes social cohesion.

In addition to both the desire and the necessity to develop *to halaido*, children must learn to converse, *to kudan* 'one puts language/words together'. The expression *i kuduma* 'put wood together', is used to tell someone how to build a successful fire, by taking a stick with an ember, putting another stick to it to make contact and transferring the heat. Just as putting wood and sticks together makes a successful fire, talk must also be put together to be successful. Commenting on the language of a 2-year-old who wasn't collaborating with or building on the other's utterances, a Kaluli said, *to mɔkudab* 'he doesn't put language together'. The same expression was used with regard to a conversation between two adults, in which they had not agreed on what they were, in fact, talking about.

(11) As father is leaving Mɛli (age 25 months)
  my child! as for me, I'm going to converse.
          niyɔ to kudumɛni
  You stay here.
  ge ya tɛbi.

The use of *to kudan* in these contexts indicates the importance Kaluli attach to verbal interactions which are mutual, collaborative, and cohesive.

As has been seen, utterances directing a child to use language (*tolɛma*) and specifying what to say (*ɛlɛma*) and how to say it (*sama*) are used to promote and support young children's involvement with others in a variety of everyday interactions. The Kaluli say that without this kind of direction children would not learn what to say and how to say it. The idea is that after a child is 'shown' what to say, he or she will spontaneously use language to respond, to initiate, sustain, and control verbal interactions. However, children themselves initiate and participate in language interactions that are unlike any that their parents have shown them. Many of these exchanges are terminated by Kaluli mothers when they feel that these could impede language development or promote an undesirable effect. These situations provide an opportunity to examine what is and is not acceptable language behavior for small children, and the cultural reasons for these differences.

(12) Mɛli (30½ months) and her cousin Mama (45 months) are at home with Mɛli's mother, who is cooking and talking to several adults. Mama initiates a sequence of word play involving Mɛli which is marked by repetition, high pitch, staccato delivery, and exaggerated prosodic contours. After 10 turns this dissolves into sound play marked by overlap within turn pairs, higher pitch, vowel lengthening and shifting, and repetition. This continues for 15 more turns, at which point Mɛli's mother suddenly turns to the girls and says in a loud, authoritative voice:

Wai!   Try to speak good talk!   This is bird talk!
Wai!   *to nafa se sɛlɛiba!*   *ɔbɛ towɔ we!*

The girls suddenly become quiet.

The mother's abrupt termination of the children's verbal/vocal interaction was not due to mild irritation caused by the noise these girls were making, since similar sound levels caused by other kinds of verbal activity would never have prompted this reaction. Her response, which was consistent with that of other Kaluli mothers in similar situations, grows out of Kaluli ideas about language development and the broader notion of taboo.

As mentioned earlier, Kaluli have very definite ideas about appropriate verbal behavior for language learning children. When asked about this word/sound play, Kaluli said it had no name and was 'to no purpose'. Purposive language is encouraged in interactions and the vocalizations between Mɛli and Mama violated these cultural expectations.

However, in addition to their ideas about how a young child's language should sound, Kaluli say that children and birds are connected in a number of complex ways (Feld 1982:Chapter 2). In addition to prohibiting young children from eating certain birds lest they, too, only 'coo' and never develop hard language, children must not sound like birds, even in play. Thus, in order to insure that 'hard language' develops, the mother prevents a dangerous association by terminating this vocal activity. Furthermore, she makes it explicit to the children and to the others around them, that children are to speak 'good talk', not 'bird talk'. It is important to emphasize that Mother does not want them to stop speaking, but to speak properly.

Another form of verbal behavior that is not tolerated by Kaluli mothers is the imitation and distortion of a younger child's speech by an older child. It is important that older children do not engage in language interactions with younger children that are contradictory to the efforts made by adults to ensure 'good talk' and 'hard talk'. Consider example (13).

(13) Abi (27½ months) and his sister Yogodo (5½ years) are alone in the house, as Mother has gone out to get wood. Following Abi's utterances, Yogodo repeats what he says, phonologically distorting his words to tease him. When mother returns, Yogodo continues to repeat everything Abi says to her, leaving him very confused and frustrated. After hearing eight turns of this, mother turns to Yogodo and says:

speak words/language!
to sama

Mothers see this type of activity as not only mocking or teasing the young child's not as yet well-formed language, but as confusing the younger child about language, its correct form and appropriate use. Thus, an undesirable language interaction is terminated with the explicit directive to 'speak language' (*to sama*). By focusing on the form of talk rather than its specific content, the children are not discouraged from speaking to one another but encouraged to do it properly, on the model of 'hard words'.

By the time a child is about 3½ years old, and ɛlɛma directives have stopped, that child's language is considered sufficiently hard so that the playing of word and sound games with peers is acceptable. While closely timed, repetitive, formulaic utterances involving teasing and challenging are appropriate for older children, mothers do not want these children negatively influencing younger ones whose speech is not yet well developed.

(14) A mother, her son (28 months), and three siblings (ages 5–8), are sitting around a fire cooking bits of food. The three siblings are playing a teasing game about who

will and will not eat, which involves speaking rapidly and distorting words. After watching this for 16 turns, the little boy attempts to join the interaction by interjecting nonsense syllables. The mother turns to the older children saying:

speak hard!!
halaido sama!

to which one of the older children responds (teasing): huh?, followed by the mother's repetition with emphasis:

speak hard!!
halaido samɛ!!

'Speak hard' implies that until this point, speech has been 'unhard'. Such a reference is always to speech in an ongoing context. In this situation, as in many others like it, mothers are careful that their young children do not sound less mature than they actually are in their speaking. This is consistent with the goals of language socialization: to enable children to be independent and assertive by the time that they are 3–3½ years old. Independence and assertion in speech and action are functionally valued in this egalitarian society; ability to speak out is one important way to get what one needs.

Next, we examine situations with negative imperatives, where *sɛlɛsabo (sama)* and *tolɛsabo (tolɛma)* are used. The use of *sɛlɛsabo* 'don't say (that/it)' (parole) implies that one knows or suspects what is about to be said, and is telling another not to say that thing. It is also used with reference to a specific body of knowledge or secrets. One may say 'don't say that' or 'don't tell them' with reference to specific information. Note example (15).

(15) A number of people are socializing and eating in the longhouse. A guest enters, having walked through the muddy jungle paths; leeches have attached themselves to his ankles. A child runs up to alert the guest to this fact, and an adult intervenes, saying: *sɛlɛsabo!* 'don't say it!', thus directing the child not to say the speech specific word 'leech' while others are enjoying their meal. Kaluli etiquette strongly prohibits the saying of this word while people are eating.

The use of *sɛlɛsabo* contrasts with the use of *tolɛsabo*. *Tolɛsabo* means 'don't talk' in the sense, 'be quiet', 'shut up', or 'don't engage in language' (langue). The meaning is 'stop talking' or 'do something else besides engage in language'.

(16) Isa (age 8) is teasing her brother Wanu (32 months) about who will be his wife. Father tells him to counter her teasing with:

1. Father→Wanu→Isa:
   no! *ɛlɛma*

                      2. no!/

3. that's mother! *ɛlɛma*

4. that's mother!/

5. One doesn't speak/say like
   that! ɛlɛma
   ɛlɛdo mɔsalano!

6. One doesn't speak/say like that!/

7. Father→Isa: girl, Isa, you . . .
   that's being bad.
   Shut up! Shut up!
   tolɛsabowo!

In this sequence, an adult uses ɛlɛma to instruct a young child in how to provide an appropriate response to his sister's teasing. In addition, in line 5 the child is directed to say 'one doesn't say that', calling attention to the inappropriateness of what is being said. This response is yet another way to counter teasing. In such interactions the conventions of language use are made explicit to younger members who may not as yet know them or may need to be reminded of them. This sequence ends when the father, being angry at his daughter, tells her to 'stop talking'. This instructs the children as to what is and is not out of bounds and further draws attention to the social need to control the flow of talk by forcefully ending undesirable speech.

A final example completes the point that in some interactions the issue is not to say what you want to say better, but to stop talking completely.

(17) A group of children are loudly talking and playing, and mother turns to them:

Sosas,   shut up!
     tolɛsabo!

Sosas is the name of a very noisy bird, one whose sounds are considered unpleasant. By comparing the children to *sosas* birds, the mother emphasizes the irritating nature of the group noise, further marking the general injunction to stop the annoying verbal activity and do something else. *Tolɛsabo* is used here quite in contrast to *sɛlɛsabo;* the children are being told to stop the activity of talking, not to stop saying specific things.

In these examples of learning and speaking 'hard words', children are provided both with an explicit cultural model of the importance of verbal activity, and with the importance of saying or not saying the right thing. Functionally, such a model promotes social integration into a coherent world constructed upon the importance of direct, controlled, forceful face-to-face communication. Kaluli children learn to focus upon what they want and need, even when this requires challenge or confrontation. They learn that discourse is a means to social ends, and they openly utilize sequential talk following that model. Imperatives are often heard in the language of adults to children and adults to each other, and the ability to utilize language in interaction requires an understanding of when to demand specific speech and when to demand verbal closure.

When something has been said or done, or might be said or done, the ability to refer appropriately, report, or challenge is one consequence of the way Kaluli learn 'hard words'. Such situations continually reflect the choice of formulations about what has been said in order to focus the specifics of the situation. If one reports benignly to another that 'someone said something to me . . .', and the listener immediately wants to challenge the substance of the remarks, a common interruption at this point would be *ba madali siyɔ* 'it was said for no reason'. Remarks on the truth or intentions of what was said are very commonly the subject of initial interruptions in conversation, immediately letting the speaker know the listener's point of view on the reported speech. Remarks about the circumstances of what has been said must be formulated with *siyɔ* 'said', or *ɛlɛ siyɔ*, 'said like that'; these refer to a specific instance of speech or the 'said' of a report in a certain context. *Tolɔ* can never appear in these situations because one cannot have the capacity or system of language in the past; in fact, the construction is inappropriate in any utterance about the language of deceased persons.

More pointed rhetorical strategies for dealing with the reports or references of speakers are formulated with two common phrases: *ge siyɔwɔ dadaye?!* 'Did you hear what I said?!' and *ge oba siyɔwɔ?* 'What did you say?' While these can be requests for information, confirmation, or acknowledgment, they are often found breaking into or responding to the stream of discourse in order to focus reaction and challenge what is being said. Neither construction can be formulated with *to* and *tolɛma*, as both exemplify the necessity of controlling a specific instance of speaking.

Rhetorical challenge can be pushed a degree farther; escalation to threat is an important way not just to register response but to prohibit or shame someone who is doing something that is inappropriate or not approved of. In such cases the threat is registered simply with: *sameib!* 'someone will say (something)!' The implicit threat is that someone will say 'who are you?!', 'is it yours?!', or other pointed rhetorical questions that shame the addressee. Use of *sameib!* to control interactions that may get out of hand, rather than use of physical control, emphasizes the concern Kaluli exhibit about speaking as an instrument of social action and accomplishment. Such a threat cannot be formulated with *tolomeib!* because it is the implied 'something' that will be said that is so important to shaming as a regulatory action.

In these examples of learning, speaking, and controlling 'hard words', it is clear that Kaluli must understand when it is appropriate to talk about language, and when it is appropriate to talk about speaking. Kaluli discourse then is taught and utilized as an integration of linguistic and metalinguistic practice which is shaped and scaffolded by having a place in a culturally coherent world of beliefs about 'hardness', control, direct action, and assertion. Kaluli discourse must be analyzed in relation to the belief system that constructs its organization and goals, as well as the social ends which it accomplishes for participants. Cultural analysis then is an explicit manner of connecting form and function. We have found that constructing an analysis from the bottom up satisfies both the demands of ethno-graphically situated explications and the demands of explaining the ordinary and routine ways that Kaluli interactions actualize cultural expectations about language use and meaningful social behavior.

3. *Closure.* To close a story, a speech (or, in a recent adaptation among the few literate Kaluli, a letter), Kaluli utilize the phrase *ni towɔ kɔm* 'my talk/words/language are finished'. It is fitting that we close this paper by explicating why this phrase is appropriate and why the contrasting **ni siyɔwɔ kɔm* 'what I have said is finished' is inappropriate and not utterable.

For Kaluli, verbal closure implies directly that there is nothing left to talk about, at least for the moment. What is finished is the action of language, the invocation of words, the activity of talk. No such boundary is appropriately imposed upon the 'said' of speaking in a specific setting, which is always open-ended and ongoing. Verbal activities are closed by a boundary on talk, not a boundary on what has been said. The function of reaching closure, again, underscores the direct manner in which Kaluli control situations and behaviors by viewing talk as a socially organized and goal-directed actualization of the capacity for language, 'hard words'. *Ni towɔ kɔm.*

Notes

Fieldwork in Bosavi during 1975–1977 was supported by the National Science Foundation, the Wenner-Gren Foundation for Anthropological Research, the Archives of Traditional Music, and the Institute of Papua New Guinea Studies. We gratefully acknowledge their assistance. Detailed reports of our separate work are Feld (1982) and B. B. Schieffelin (1979). The order of author's names was determined by geomancy.

1. *Kalu* specifically means 'man' (opposing *kesale* 'women') but can generally refer to 'person' or 'people'. Kaluli see the ideal form of 'hardness' modeled on maleness; women, however, are clearly supposed to be competent language users. Sex role socialization is clear in the speech of mothers to children; little boys are encouraged to use language to be demanding, while little girls are encouraged to use language to be more complacent. These issues are addressed in detail in B. B. Schieffelin (1979: Chapter 2).

2. It is worth noting that, in contrast to some aspects of metalinguistics, Kaluli do not directly verbalize about the importance of a distinction between *to* and *sama*. The clear langue/parole distinction is consistent, however, in all of our elicited or tape-recorded naturally occurring data. Further discussion of how this distinction affects Kaluli poetic concepts can be found in Feld (1982:Chapter 4).

3. There is one additional context where the term *to halaido* or *halaido to* is found. This is in the talk of debate, heated discourse, anger, dispute, or confrontation (as, for example, in a bridewealth negotiation). This sense of *to halaido* is far less prominent than the broader usage. The morphological marking *-ait* is used only to indicate anger; it is not prominent in our sample of recorded speech (83 hours of family interactions, 50 hours of song, myth, texted weeping, and more formal modes).

4. We are speaking here about interactions in an assertive frame. These characterizations do not apply equally to frames of appeal. On Kaluli assertion and appeal, see E. L. Schieffelin (1976:117–134) and B. B. Schieffelin (1979:Chapters 3 and 4).

5. In casual adult interactions, εlεma may be used to direct a response to a speaker who is slow to respond to teasing or joking. A more marked and deliberate adult usage occurs in funerary weeping, where women improvise sung-wept texts to a deceased person lying before them. Often these texts contain lines like, 'Look up to the treetops, εlεma . . . ', indicating that the weeper is telling the deceased to say these words back to her. The grammaticality and pragmatics here rest on the notion that while the deceased is next to the woman in body, he or she is going elsewhere in spirit, in the form of a bird. The commanded words marked with εlεma must therefore be in the form of an appropriate utterance to a living person from one who is now a bird. 'Look up to the treetops' is such a line because it indicates that from then on the weeper will only see the deceased as a bird in the treetops. Feld (1982:Chapter 3) contains an analysis of εlεma in sung-texted-weeping.

6. Transcription conventions are described in B. B. Schieffelin (1979). Child speech is on the right and the speech of others plus contextual notes are on the left. Single arrow indicates speaker to addressee; double arrow indicates speaker to addressee who is to address a third party. Kaluli glosses are provided only where to, tolεma, εlεma, and sama, or other forms of these verbs, are used. Full transcripts of all examples with morpheme by morpheme glosses can be obtained by writing to the authors.

7. The use of concatenated forms also appears with sama, particularly in interactions with elema, where the child is too far from the intended addressee and is told to 'go in order to speak', sεmεni hamana.

References

Feld, Steven. 1982. Sound and sentiment: Birds, weeping, poetics and song in Kaluli expression. Philadelphia: University of Pennsylvania Press.

Feld, Steven, and Bambi B. Schieffelin. 1980. Sociolinguistic dimensions of Kaluli relationship terms. Paper presented at the Annual Meeting, American Anthropological Association.

Schieffelin, Bambi B. 1979. How Kaluli children learn what to say, what to do, and how to feel: An ethnographic study of the development of communicative competence. Unpublished Ph.D. dissertation. Department of Anthropology, Columbia University. [To appear: Cambridge University Press.]

Schieffelin, Bambi B., and Steven Feld. 1979. Modes across codes and codes within modes: A sociolinguistic analysis of conversation, sung-texted-weeping, and stories in Bosavi, Papua New Guinea. Paper presented at the Annual Meeting, American Anthropological Association.

Schieffelin, Edward L. 1976. The sorrow of the lonely and the burning of the dancers. New York: St. Martins Press.

Part Two
Gender, Power, and Discourse

Our sex is identified at birth (if not before) and whatever happens to us afterward, whatever we achieve through our own efforts or with the assistance of others, will be affected by this initial identification. It is therefore not surprising that there should be constant speculation about the contribution of this labeling to our lives. After Lazarus, perhaps the person we most want to question is Tiresias: What is the difference between being male or female? It is a question that has attracted the attention of scholars in many fields, including those interested in language. The question presupposes that there are differences, and as a result many scholars have been so preoccupied with locating differences that they have sometimes exaggerated the importance of the differences they have found and ignored the similarities (Macaulay 1978). In the reporting of sex differences, no news is not good news; it is not news of any kind, and neither tenure nor promotion will follow from the reporting of negative results. With such a bias in the system for rewarding positive results reporting sex differences, it is necessary to scrutinize any such claims very carefully. In particular, it is essential to examine the methodology employed, especially the form of data collection. This is critical in all attempts to study language use, but it is particularly problematic in looking at possible differences between males and females because the investigator may have preconceptions of the situation. Two recent reviews of conflicting claims, one dealing with whether men or women interrupt each other more (James and Clarke 1993) and the other with whether there are gender differences in the amount of talk (James and Drakich 1993), show how generalizing from a single context can provide misleading results.

It is generally accepted that the language speakers have acquired and use will have been affected by their experience: geographical location, family background, education, and occupation are all significant. To the extent that the lives of males and females differ, it is to be expected that the forms of language they use will also differ. In societies where males and females are largely segregated or where there are significant differences in their exposure to education, it might be expected that the linguistic differences will be great. In the United States, however, where equal opportunity is the slogan, expectations of differences might be lower. This was the current view in anthropology until twenty years ago. Dell Hymes (1971:69) commented: "If one were to examine the literature on 'men's and women's speech,' one would conclude that it was rare phenomenon, found mostly among extinct American Indian tribes."

Robin Lakoff changed that with an essay (Lakoff 1973), later expanded into a book (Lakoff 1975), in which she argued not only that there were characteristic forms of "women's language" (see pp. 8–19) but that these forms of language were the result of the subordinate situation of women in the United States. Lakoff's evidence was perfectly legitimate. She reported as a participant observer on the behavior of the women she knew through firsthand contacts. This is exactly the methodology adopted by Elinor Keenan (Ochs) in her study of a Malagasy community. In her chapter in this volume Ochs does not explain how she collected her evidence but reports the results of her investigations. Similarly, Lakoff does not explain her methods. An important difference, however, is that few U.S. scholars will visit Madagascar to verify Ochs's findings, which will stand unchallenged until someone goes there and produces a contrary report. By contrast, Lakoff's observations were immediately disputed.

Scholars did not attempt to refute Lakoff's claims just by appealing to their own observations. Instead, they used "objective" empirical methods. Where Lakoff (1973:53) had simply asserted that there is "at least one [syntactic] rule that a woman will use in more conversational situations than a man. . . . This is the rule of tag-question formation," Betty Lou Dubois and Isabel Crouch (1975) examined the tapes of the sessions of a small professional meeting and found that all thirty-three instances of tag questions were used by men. Although this could not refute Lakoff's claim about the use of tag questions in "more conversational situations," it did provide evidence that "in at least one genuine social context, men did, and women did not, use tag questions" (Dubois and Crouch 1975:294). The reference to a "genuine" social context emphasizes that the speech recorded had not been part of an artificially contrived experimental situation.

William O'Barr and Bowman Atkins (1980) also looked at a "genuine" social context—the speech of witnesses in a superior criminal court. O'Barr and Atkins argued that the features Lakoff found characteristic of "women's language" were instead features of "powerless" language. Since women have traditionally been in a subordinate situation, it would not be surprising if they should show more features associated with lack of power. O'Barr and Atkins based their conclusions on counting instances of the features Lakoff had cited. They found that both men and women, as witnesses, varied in the extent to which they used these features, and they attributed the greater frequency of use to lower status.

Counting instances of a feature requires a decision about what is important. For example, O'Barr and Atkins chose to count the use of "Sir" as an address form as "an indication of more polite speech," and consequently as an example of "powerless" language. Although this may be a justifiable assumption, it is important to emphasize that features do not come labeled as "powerless" or "powerful"; that is a judgment of the investigator. It is also likely that any single form will be used in several functions. For example, Janet Holmes (1984), in her study of tag questions, distinguished between their use as (1) expressing uncertainty, (2) being facilitative (positively polite), and (3) softening negative comments. She found that in her New Zealand sample women used tag questions more frequently than men in the facilitative function, whereas men used tag questions more often than women to express uncertainty or to soften a negative comment. It is, consequently, not enough simply to count instances of the occurrence of a form; it is also necessary to look at the context in which the form is used and the function it performs.

Another example of looking at function as well as form is Daniel Maltz and Ruth Borker's claim (this volume) that "minimal responses such as nods and comments like 'yes' and 'mm hmm'" may indicate something different when used by men and women. They suggested that women may use such minimal responses simply to indicate that they are listening, whereas men are more likely to indicate agreement in this way. Maltz and Borker argue that differences of this kind can lead to "massive miscommunication" between men and women. They also suggest that the source of this miscommunication lies in the different kinds of socialization that boys and girls receive from their peer groups in the period, roughly age 5 to 15, "when boys and girls interact socially primarily with members of their own sex." Maltz and Borker claimed that "women and men have different cultural rules for friendly conversation" as a result of these early experiences.

Maltz and Borker do not provide any original research findings to support their view of cross-cultural miscommunication between men and women, though they refer to some examples in the work of other scholars and suggest important areas for future research. Aki Uchida (1992) criticizes Maltz and Borker's approach for assuming "that same-sex rules will directly be carried over to mixed-sex interaction." She also argues that Maltz and Borker ignore the dimension of power, which is intertwined with the relationships between men and women. Uchida believes that "the problem of how to conceptualize gender has so far been dealt with in most language research in a too simplistic way."

Penelope Eckert (this volume) observes that "like age, sex is a biological category that serves as a fundamental basis for the differentiation of roles, norms, and expectations in all societies. It is these roles, norms, and expectations that constitute gender, the social construction of sex." She pointed out that "when people do compete in the role domain of the other sex, it is specifically their gender identity that gets called into question." She gives the example that "in the upper class, what is called effeminacy may be seen as the conscientious rejection of physical power by those who exercise real global power by appropriating the physical power of others." Eckert examines the "general misconception" that women's speech is more conservative than men's. By looking at an actual situation of two social categories in a Detroit high school, Eckert was able to show how the girls take the lead in certain linguistic changes because they are the ones "who must rely more on symbolic manifestations of social membership than boys." In her investigation,

Eckert combined the methods of participant observation with the collection of tape-recorded individual sociolinguistic interviews. Accordingly, she has quantitative data on the use of certain linguistic features and at the same time she has been able to observe the dynamics of social interaction.

Uchida (1992) notes that "it is very often the case that whenever a framework for analysis is presented using American examples, it is assumed to be universal until proven otherwise." Ochs's account of women's language in a Malagasy community provides evidence contradictory to any claim that women are universally "more polite" in their use of language than men. It was the Malagasy men who were more conservative in their speech and who preferred indirectness to directness. Keenan (Ochs)'s chapter in this volume provides a warning for those who wish to make universal claims about gender roles from sex differences.

The chapters in this part, dealing with gender differences in the use of language, thus raise some fundamental points about the study of language variation:

1. There are fashions in research, as in most social activities. This can be helpful in focusing attention on certain kinds of questions but can also lead to the neglect of other aspects of the situation. In any investigation it is important to consider what other factors than those being studied might affect the situation.
2. It is normal for an investigator to bring preconceptions to the study of any topic. Random searching for patterns is unlikely to be very productive. Although these preconceptions are useful in focusing attention on potentially interesting factors, they should be examined for possible bias that might distort the research.
3. Different kinds of methodology are appropriate for investigating certain situations. The trade-off is roughly the richness of firsthand observation versus the "objectivity" of large-scale surveys. Even a small-scale study can provide valuable results if carried out carefully.
4. Where quantitative methods are employed it is essential to look closely at which items are being counted, how and why they are selected, and whether the items have been correctly identified. In choosing which items to count, preference should be given (other things being equal) to those items that can be identified clearly by different investigators. This reduces the danger of subjective bias in counting instances.
5. A major problem for all linguistic investigation lies in the distinction between form and function. All forms have several functions. It is relatively easy to count forms; it is much harder to identify (and justify the identification of) functions. However, the trade-off is that accounts of functional differences are often more interesting than descriptions of formal differences.
6. Social categories are not given. They must be justified with reference to the particular situation. Members of a society belong to several social categories simultaneously and the effect of their membership in any one category can-

not be totally separated from the effects of their membership in any other categories.

7. Claims made on the evidence from one particular situation may not be valid in other situations even when they appear to be similar.

8. Scholars can differ in their interpretation of the results from an investigation.

Suggestions for Further Reading

There are a number of useful textbooks and collections of articles: J. Coates, *Women, Men, and Language*; J. Coates and D. Cameron (eds.), *Women in their Speech Communities*; D. Graddol and J. Swann, *Gender Voices*; M. R. Key, *Male/Female Language*; S. McConnell-Ginet, R. Borker, and N. Furman (eds.), *Women and Language in Literature and Society*; S. U. Philips, S. Steele, and C. Tanz (eds.), *Language, Gender, and Sex in Comparative Perspective*; D. Tannen (ed.), *Gender and Conversational Interaction*; B. Thorne and N. Henley (eds.), *Language and Sex*; and B. Thorne, C. Kramarae, and N. Henley (eds.), *Language, Gender and Society*. A good example of a carefully controlled study is B. Preisler, *Linguistic Sex Roles in Conversation*. P. Eckert and S. McConnell-Ginet provide a different perspective in "Think practically and look locally: Language and gender as community-based practice."

References

Coates, Jennifer. 1986. *Women, Men, and Language: A Sociolinguistic Account of Sex.* London: Longman.

Coates, Jennifer, and Deborah Cameron, eds. 1989. *Women in their Speech Communities: New Perspectives on Language and Sex.* London: Longman.

Dubois, Betty Lou, and Isabel Crouch. 1975. "The question of tag questions in women's speech: They don't really use more of them, do they?" *Language in Society* 4:289–294.

Eckert, Penelope, and Sally McConnell-Ginet. 1992. "Think practically and look locally: Language and gender as community-based practice." *Annual Review of Anthropology* 21:461–490.

Graddol, David, and Joan Swann. 1989. *Gender Voices.* Oxford: Blackwell.

Holmes, Janet. 1984. "Hedging your bets and sitting on the fence: some evidence for hedges as support structures." *Te Reo* 27:47–62.

Hymes, Dell. 1971. "Sociolinguistics and the ethnography of speaking." In Edwin Ardener, ed., *Social Anthropology and Language*, London: Tavistock: 47–93.

James, Deborah, and Sandra Clarke. 1993. "Women, men, and interruptions: A critical overview." In Deborah Tannen, ed., *Gender and Conversational Interaction.* New York: Oxford University Press: 231–280.

James, Deborah, and Janice Drakich. 1993. "Understanding gender differences in amount of talk: A critical review." In Deborah Tannen, ed., *Gender and Conversational Interaction.* New York: Oxford University Press: 281–312.

Key, Mary Ritchie. 1975. *Male/Female Language.* Metuchen, NJ: The Scarecrow Press.

Lakoff, Robin. 1973. "Language and woman's place." *Language in Society* 2:45–80.

———. 1975. *Language and Woman's Place.* New York: Harper.

Macaulay, Ronald K. S. 1978. "The myth of female superiority in language." *Journal of Child Language* 5:353–363.

McConnell-Ginet, Sally, Ruth Borker, and Nelly Furman, eds. 1980. *Women and Language in Literature and Society.* New York: Praeger.

O'Barr, William M., and Bowman K. Atkins. 1980. " 'Women's language' or 'powerless language'?" In Sally McConnell-Ginet, Ruth Borker, and Nelly Furman, eds. *Women and Language in Literature and Society.* New York: Praeger, 93–110.

Philips, Susan U., Susan Steele, and Christine Tanz, eds. 1987. *Language, Gender, and Sex in Comparative Perspective.* Cambridge: Cambridge University Press.

Preisler, Bent. 1986. *Linguistic Sex Roles in Conversation: Social Variation in the Expression of Tentativeness in English.* Berlin: Mouton de Gruyter.

Tannen, Deborah, ed. 1993. *Gender and Conversational Interaction.* New York: Oxford University Press.

Thorne, Barrie, and Nancy Henley, eds. 1975. *Language and Sex: Difference and Dominance.* Rowley, MA: Newbury House.

Thorne, Barrie, Cheris Kramarae, and Nancy Henley, eds. 1983. *Language, Gender, and Society.* Rowley, MA: Newbury House.

Uchida, Aki. 1992. "When 'difference' is 'dominance': a critique of the 'anti-power-based' cultural approach to sex differences." *Language in Society* 21:547–568.

5

A Cultural Approach to Male–Female Miscommunication

DANIEL N. MALTZ AND RUTH A. BORKER

Introduction

This chapter presents what we believe to be a useful new framework for examining differences in the speaking patterns of American men and women. It is based not on new data, but on a reexamination of a wide variety of material already available in the scholarly literature. Our starting problem is the nature of the different roles of male and female speakers in informal cross-sex conversations in American English. Our attempts to think about this problem have taken us to preliminary examination of a wide variety of fields often on or beyond the margins of our present competencies: children's speech, children's play, styles and patterns of friendship, conversational turn-taking, discourse analysis, and interethnic communication. The research which most influenced the development of our present model includes John Gumperz's work on problems in interethnic communication (1982) and Marjorie Goodwin's study of the linguistic aspects of play among black children in Philadelphia (1978, 1980a, 1980b).

Our major argument is that the general approach recently developed for the study of difficulties in cross-ethnic communication can be applied to cross-sex communication as well. We prefer to think of the difficulties in both cross-sex and cross-ethnic communication as two examples of the same larger phenomenon: cultural difference and miscommunication.

The Problem of Cross-Sex Conversation

Study after study has shown that when men and women attempt to interact as equals in friendly cross-sex conversations they do not play the same role in interaction, even when there is no apparent element of flirting. We hope to explore some of these differences, examine the explanations that have been offered, and provide an alternative explanation for them.

The primary data on cross-sex conversations come from two general sources: social psychology studies from the 1950s such as Soskin and John's (1963) research on two young married couples and Strodbeck and Mann's (1956) research on jury deliberations, and more recent sociolinguistic studies from the University of California at Santa Barbara and the University of Pennsylvania by Candace West (Zimmerman and West 1975; West and Zimmerman 1977; West 1979), Pamela Fishman (1978), and Lynette Hirschman (1973).

Women's Features

Several striking differences in male and female contributions to cross-sex conversation have been noticed in these studies.

First, women display a greater tendency to ask questions. Fishman (1978:400) comments that "at times I felt that all women did was ask questions," and Hirschman (1973:10) notes that "several of the female-male conversations fell into a question-answer pattern with the females asking the males questions."

Fishman (1978:408) sees this question-asking tendency as an example of a second, more general characteristic of women's speech, doing more of the routine "shitwork" involved in maintaining routine social interaction, doing more to facilitate the flow of conversation (Hirschman 1973:3). Women are more likely than men to make utterances that demand or encourage responses from their fellow speakers and are therefore, in Fishman's words, "more actively engaged in insuring interaction than the men" (1978:404). In the earlier social psychology studies, these features have been coded under the general category of "positive reactions" including solidarity, tension release, and agreeing (Strodbeck and Mann 1956).

Third, women show a greater tendency to make use of positive minimal responses, especially "mm hmm" (Hirschman 1973:8), and are more likely to insert "such comments throughout streams of talk rather than [simply] at the end" (Fishman 1978:402).

Fourth, women are more likely to adopt a strategy of "silent protest" after they have been interrupted or have received a delayed minimal response (Zimmerman and West 1975; West and Zimmerman 1977:524).

Fifth, women show a greater tendency to use the pronouns "you" and "we," which explicitly acknowledge the existence of the other speaker (Hirschman 1973:6).

Men's Features

Contrasting contributions to cross-sex conversations have been observed and described for men.

First, men are more likely to interrupt the speech of their conversational partners, that is, to interrupt the speech of women (Zimmerman and West 1975; West and Zimmerman 1977; West 1979).

Second, they are more likely to challenge or dispute their partners' utterances (Hirschman 1973:11).

Third, they are more likely to ignore the comments of the other speaker, that is, to offer no response or acknowledgment at all (Hirschman 1973:11), to respond slowly in what has been described as a "delayed minimal response" (Zimmerman and West 1975:118), or to respond unenthusiastically (Fishman 1978).

Fourth, men use more mechanisms for controlling the topic of conversation, including both topic development and the introduction of new topics, than do women (Zimmerman and West 1975).

Finally, men make more direct declarations of fact or opinion than do women (Fishman 1978:402), including suggestions, opinions, and "statements of orientation" as Strodbeck and Mann (1956) describe them, or "statements of focus and directives" as they are described by Soskin and John (1963).

Explanations Offered

Most explanations for these features have focused on differences in the social power or in the personalities of men and women. One variant of the social power argument, presented by West (Zimmerman and West 1975; West and Zimmerman 1977), is that men's dominance in conversation parallels their dominance in society. Men enjoy power in society and also in conversation. The two levels are seen as part of a single social-political system. West sees interruptions and topic control as male displays of power—a power based in the larger social order but reinforced and expressed in face-to-face interaction with women. A second variant of this argument, stated by Fishman (1978), is that while the differential power of men and women is crucial, the specific mechanism through which it enters conversation is sex-role definition. Sex roles serve to obscure the issue of power for participants, but the fact is, Fishman argues, that norms of appropriate behavior for women and men serve to give power and interactional control to men while keeping it from women. To be socially acceptable as women, women cannot exert control and must actually support men in their control. In this casting of the social power argument, men are not necessarily seen to be consciously flaunting power, but simply reaping the rewards given them by the social system. In both variants, the link between macro and micro levels of social life is seen as direct and unproblematic, and the focus of explanation is the general social order.

Sex roles have also been central in psychological explanations. The primary advocate of the psychological position has been Robin Lakoff (1975). Basically, Lakoff asserts that, having been taught to speak and act like 'ladies,' women become as unassertive and insecure as they have been made to sound. The impossible task of trying to be both women and adults, which Lakoff sees as culturally incompatible, saps women of confidence and strength. As a result, they come to produce the speech they do, not just because it is how women are supposed to speak, but because it fits with the personalities they develop as a consequence of sex-role requirements.

The problem with these explanations is that they do not provide a means of explaining why these specific features appear as opposed to any number of others, nor do they allow us to differentiate between various types of male-female interaction. They do not really tell us why and how these specific interactional phenomena are linked to the general fact that men dominate within our social system.

An Alternative Explanation: Sociolinguistic Subcultures

Our approach to cross-sex communication patterns is somewhat different from those that have been previously proposed. We place the stress not on psychological differences or power differentials, although these may make some contribution, but rather on a notion of cultural differences between men and women in their conceptions of friendly conversation, their rules for engaging in it, and, probably most important, their rules for interpreting it. We argue that American men and women come from different sociolinguistic subcultures, having learned to do different things with words in a conversation, so that when they attempt to carry on conversations with one another, even if both parties are attempting to treat one another as equals, cultural miscommunication results.

The idea of distinct male and female subcultures is not a new one for anthropology. It has been persuasively argued again and again for those parts of the world such as the Middle East and southern Europe in which men and women spend most of their lives spatially and interactionally segregated. The strongest case for sociolinguistic subcultures has been made by Susan Harding from her research in rural Spain (1975).

The major premise on which Harding builds her argument is that speech is a means for dealing with social and psychological situations. When men and women have different experiences and operate in different social contexts, they tend to develop different genres of speech and different skills for doing things with words. In the Spanish village in which she worked, the sexual division of labor was strong, with men involved in agricultural tasks and public politics while women were involved in a series of networks of personal relations with their children, their husbands, and their female neighbors. While men developed their verbal skills in economic negotiations and public political argument, women became more verbally adept at a quite different mode of interactional manipulation with words: gossip, social analysis, subtle information gathering through a carefully developed technique of verbal prying, and a kind of second-guessing the thoughts of others (commonly known as 'women's intuition') through a skillful monitoring of the speech of others. The different social needs of men and women, she argues, have led them to sexually differentiated communicative cultures, with each sex learning a different set of skills for manipulating words effectively.

The question that Harding does not ask, however, is, if men and women possess different subcultural rules for speaking, what happens if and when they try to interact with each other? It is here that we turn to the research on interethnic miscommunication.

Interethnic Communication

Recent research (Gumperz 1977, 1978a, 1978b, 1979; Gumperz and Tannen 1979) has shown that systematic problems develop in communication when speakers of different speech cultures interact and that these problems are the result of differences in systems of conversational inference and the cues for signalling speech acts and speaker's intent. Conversation is a negotiated activity. It progresses in large part because of shared assumptions about what is going on.

Examining interactions between English-English and Indian-English speakers in Britain (Gumperz 1977, 1978a, 1979; Gumperz et al. 1977), Gumperz found that differences in cues resulted in systematic miscommunication over whether a question was being asked, whether an argument was being made, whether a person was being rude or polite, whether a speaker was relinquishing the floor or interrupting, whether and what a speaker was emphasizing, whether interactants were angry, concerned, or indifferent. Rather than being seen as problems in communication, the frustrating encounters that resulted were usually chalked up as personality clashes or interpreted in the light of racial stereotypes which tended to exacerbate already bad relations.

To take a simple case, Gumperz (1977) reports that Indian women working at a cafeteria, when offering food, used a falling intonation, e.g. "gravy," which to them indicated a question, something like "do you want gravy?" Both Indian and English workers saw a question as an appropriate polite form, but to English-English speakers a falling intonation signalled not a question, which for them is signalled by a rising intonation such as "gravy," but a declarative statement, which was both inappropriate and extremely rude.

A major advantage of Gumperz's framework is that it does not assume that problems are the result of bad faith, but rather sees them as the result of individuals wrongly interpreting cues according to their own rules.

The Interpretation of Minimal Responses

How might Gumperz's approach to the study of conflicting rules for interpreting conversation be applied to the communication between men and women? A simple example will illustrate our basic approach: the case of positive minimal responses. Minimal responses such as nods and comments like "yes" and "mm hmm" are common features of conversational interaction. Our claim, based on our attempts to understand personal experience, is that these minimal responses have significantly different meanings for men and women, leading to occasionally serious miscommunication.

We hypothesize that for women a minimal response of this type means simply something like "I'm listening to you; please continue," and that for men it has a somewhat stronger meaning such as "I agree with you" or at least "I follow your argument so far." The fact that women use these responses more often than men is in part simply that women are listening more often than men are agreeing.

But our hypothesis explains more than simple differential frequency of usage. Different rules can lead to repeated misunderstandings. Imagine a male speaker who is receiving repeated nods or "mm hmm"s from the woman he is speaking to. She is merely indicating that she is listening, but he thinks she is agreeing with everything he says. Now imagine a female speaker who is receiving only occasional nods and "mm hmm"s from the man she is speaking to. He is indicating that he doesn't always agree; she thinks he isn't always listening.

What is appealing about this short example is that it seems to explain two of the most common complaints in male-female interaction: (1) men who think that women are always agreeing with them and then conclude that it's impossible to tell what a woman really thinks, and (2) women who get upset with men who never seem to be listening. What we think we have here are two separate rules for conversational maintenance which come into conflict and cause massive miscommunication.

Sources of Different Cultures

A probable objection that many people will have to our discussion so far is that American men and women interact with one another far too often to possess different subcultures. What we need to explain is how it is that men and women can come to possess different cultural assumptions about friendly conversation.

Our explanation is really quite simple. It is based on the idea that by the time we have become adults we possess a wide variety of rules for interacting in different situations. Different sets of these rules were learned at different times and in different contexts. We have rules for dealing with people in dominant or subordinate social positions, rules which we first learned as young children interacting with our parents and teachers. We have rules for flirting and other sexual encounters which we probably started learning at or near adolescence. We have rules for dealing with service personnel and bureaucrats, rules we began learning when we first ventured into the public domain. Finally, we have rules for friendly interaction, for carrying on friendly conversation. What is striking about these last rules is that they were learned not from adults but from peers, and that they were learned during precisely that time period, approximately age 5 to 15, when boys and girls interact socially primarily with members of their own sex.

The idea that girls and boys in contemporary America learn different ways of speaking by the age of five or earlier has been postulated by Robin Lakoff (1975), demonstrated by Andrea Meditch (1975), and more fully explored by Adelaide Haas (1979). Haas's research on school-age children shows the early appearance of important male-female differences in patterns of language use, including a male tendency toward direct requests and information giving and a female tendency toward compliance (1979:107).

But the process of acquiring gender-specific speech and behavior patterns by school-age children is more complex than the simple copying of adult "gender-lects" by preschoolers. Psychologists Brooks-Gunn and Matthews (1979) have labeled this process the "consolidation of sex roles"; we call it learning of gender-specific 'cultures.'

Among school-age children, patterns of friendly social interaction are learned not so much from adults as from members of one's peer group, and a major feature of most middle-childhood peer groups is homogeneity; "they are either all-boy or all-girl" (Brooks-Gunn and Matthews 1979). Members of each sex are learning self-consciously to differentiate their behavior from that of the other sex and to exaggerate these differences. The process can be profitably compared to accent divergence in which members of two groups that wish to become clearly distinguished from one another socially acquire increasingly divergent ways of speaking.[1]

Because they learn these gender-specific cultures from their age-mates, children tend to develop stereotypes and extreme versions of adult behavior patterns. For a boy learning to behave in a masculine way, for example, Ruth Hartley (1959, quoted in Brooks-Gunn and Matthews 1979:203) argues that:

> both the information and the practice he gets are distorted. Since his peers have no better sources of information than he has, all they can do is pool the impressions and anxieties they derived from their early training. Thus, the picture they draw is oversimplified and overemphasized. It is a picture drawn in black and white, with little or no modulation and it is incomplete, including a few of the many elements that go to make up the role of the mature male.

What we hope to argue is that boys and girls learn to use language in different ways because of the very different social contexts in which they learn how to carry on friendly conversation. Almost anyone who remembers being a child, has worked with school-age children, or has had an opportunity to observe school-age children can vouch for the fact that groups of girls and groups of boys interact and play in different ways. Systematic observations of children's play have tended to confirm these well-known differences in the ways girls and boys learn to interact with their friends.

In a major study of sex differences in the play of school-age children, for example, sociologist Janet Lever (1976) observed the following six differences between the play of boys and that of girls: (1) girls more often play indoors; (2) boys tend to play in larger groups; (3) boys' play groups tend to include a wider age range of participants; (4) girls play in predominantly male games more often than vice versa; (5) boys more often play competitive games, and (6) girls' games tend to last a shorter period of time than boys' games.

It is by examining these differences in the social organization of play and the accompanying differences in the patterns of social interaction they entail, we argue, that we can learn about the sources of male-female differences in patterns of language use. And it is these same patterns, learned in childhood and carried over into adulthood as the bases for patterns of single-sex friendship relations, we contend, that are potential sources of miscommunication in cross-sex interaction.

The World of Girls

Our own experience and studies such as Goodwin's (1980b) of black children and Lever's (1976, 1978) of white children suggest a complex of features of girls' play and the speech within it. Girls play in small groups, most often in pairs (Lever 1976; Eder and Hallinan 1978; Brooks-Gunn and Matthews 1979), and their play groups tend to be remarkably homogeneous in terms of age. Their play is often in private or semi-private settings that require participants be invited in. Play is co-operative and activities are usually organized in noncompetitive ways (Lever 1976; Goodwin 1980b). Differentiation between girls is not made in terms of power, but relative closeness. Friendship is seen by girls as involving intimacy, equality, mutual commitment, and loyalty. The idea of 'best friend' is central for girls. Relationships between girls are to some extent in opposition to one another, and new relationships are often formed at the expense of old ones. As Brooks-Gunn and Matthews (1979:280) observe, "friendships tend to be exclusive, with a few girls being exceptionally close to one another. Because of this breakups tend to be highly emotional," and Goodwin (1980a:172) notes that "the non-hierarchical framework of the girls provides a fertile ground for rather intricate processes of alliance formation between equals against some other party."

There is a basic contradiction in the structure of girls' social relationships. Friends are supposed to be equal and everyone is supposed to get along, but in fact they don't always. Conflict must be resolved, but a girl cannot assert social power or superiority as an individual to resolve it. Lever (1976), studying fifth-graders, found that girls simply could not deal with quarrels and that when conflict arose they made no attempt to settle it; the group just broke up. What girls learn to do with speech is cope with the contradiction created by an ideology of equality and cooperation and a social reality that includes difference and conflict. As they grow up they learn increasingly subtle ways of balancing the conflicting pressures created by a female social world and a female friendship ideology.

Basically girls learn to do three things with words: (1) to create and maintain relationships of closeness and equality, (2) to criticize others in acceptable ways, and (3) to interpret accurately the speech of other girls.

To a large extent friendships among girls are formed through talk. Girls need to learn to give support, to recognize the speech rights of others, to let others speak, and to acknowledge what they say in order to establish and maintain relationships of equality and closeness. In activities they need to learn to create cooperation through speech. Goodwin (1980a) found that inclusive forms such as "let's," "we gonna," "we could," and "we gotta" predominated in task-oriented activities. Furthermore, she found that most girls in the group she studied made suggestions and that the other girls usually agreed to them. But girls also learn to exchange in-formation and confidences to create and maintain relationships of closeness. The exchange of personal thoughts not only expresses closeness but mutual commit-ment as well. Brooks-Gunn and Matthews (1979:280) note of adolescent girls:

> much time is spent talking, reflecting, and sharing intimate thought. Loyalty is of cen-tral concern to the 12- to 14-year old girl, presumably because, if innermost secrets are shared, the friend may have 'dangerous knowledge' at her disposal.

Friendships are not only formed through particular types of talk, but are ended through talk as well. As Lever (1976:4) says of 'best friends,' "sharing secrets binds the union together, and 'telling' the secrets to outsiders is symbolic of the 'break-up.'"

Secondly, girls learn to criticize and argue with other girls without seeming overly aggressive, without being perceived as either 'bossy' or 'mean,' terms girls use to evaluate one another's speech and actions. Bossiness, ordering others around, is not legitimate because it denies equality. Goodwin (1980a) points out that girls talked very negatively about the use of commands to equals, seeing it as appropriate only in role play or in unequal relationships such as those with younger siblings. Girls learn to direct things without seeming bossy, or they learn not to direct. While disputes are common, girls learn to phrase their arguments in terms of group needs and situational requirements rather than personal power or desire (Goodwin 1980a). Meanness is used by girls to describe nonlegitimate acts of exclusion, turning on someone, or withholding friendship. Excluding is a fre-quent occurrence (Eder and Hallinan 1978), but girls learn over time to discour-age or even drive away other girls in ways that don't seem to be just personal whim. Cutting someone is justified in terms of the target's failure to meet group norms and a girl often rejects another using speech that is seemingly supportive on the surface. Conflict and criticism are risky in the world of girls because they can both rebound against the critic and can threaten social relationships. Girls learn to hide the source of criticism; they present it as coming from someone else or make it indirectly through a third party (Goodwin 1980a, 1980b).

Finally, girls must learn to decipher the degree of closeness being offered by other girls, to recognize what is being withheld, and to recognize criticism. Girls who don't actually read these cues run the risk of public censure or ridicule (Goodwin 1980). Since the currency of closeness is the exchange of secrets which can be used against a girl, she must learn to read the intent and loyalty of others and to do so continuously, given the system of shifting alliances and indirect ex-pressions of conflict. Girls must become increasingly sophisticated in reading the motives of others, in determining when closeness is real, when conventional, and when false, and to respond appropriately. They must learn who to confide in, what to confide, and who not to approach. Given the indirect expression of conflict, girls must learn to read relationships and situations sensitively. Learning to get things right is a fundamental skill for social success, if not just social survival.

The World of Boys

Boys play in larger, more hierarchically organized groups than do girls. Relative status in this ever-fluctuating hierarchy is the main thing that boys learn to manipulate in their interactions with their peers. Nondominant boys are rarely excluded from play but are made to feel the inferiority of their status positions in no uncertain terms. And since hierarchies fluctuate over time and over situation, every boy gets his chance to be victimized and must learn to take it. The social world of boys is one of posturing and counterposturing. In this world, speech is used in three major ways: (1) to assert one's position of dominance, (2) to attract and maintain an audience, and (3) to assert oneself when other speakers have the floor.

The use of speech for the expression of dominance is the most straightforward and probably the best-documented sociolinguistic pattern in boys' peer groups. Even ethological studies of human dominance patterns have made extensive use of various speech behaviors as indices of dominance. Richard Savin-Williams (1976), for example, in his study of dominance patterns among boys in a summer camp uses the following speech interactions as measures of dominance: (1) giving of verbal commands or orders, such as "Get up," "Give it to me," or "You go over there"; (2) name calling and other forms of verbal ridicule, such as "You're a dolt"; (3) verbal threats or boasts of authority, such as "If you don't shut up, I'm gonna come over and bust your teeth in"; (4) refusals to obey orders; and (5) winning a verbal argument as in the sequence: "I was here first" / "Tough," or in more elaborate forms of verbal dueling such as the 'dozens.'[2]

The same patterns of verbally asserting one's dominance and challenging the dominance claims of others form the central element in Goodwin's (1980a) observations of boys' play in Philadelphia. What is easy to forget in thinking about this use of words as weapons, however, is that the most successful boy in such interaction is not the one who is most aggressive and uses the most power-wielding forms of speech, but the boy who uses these forms most successfully. The simple use of assertiveness and aggression in boys' play is the sign not of a leader but of a bully. The skillful speaker in a boys' group is considerably more likable and better liked by his peers than is a simple bully. Social success among boys is based on knowing both how and when to use words to express power as well as knowing when not to use them. A successful leader will use speech to put challengers in their place and to remind followers periodically of their nondominant position, but will not browbeat unnecessarily and will therefore gain the respect rather than the fear of less dominant boys.

A second sociolinguistic aspect of friendly interaction between boys is using words to gain and maintain an audience. Storytelling, joke telling, and other narrative performance events are common features of the social interaction of boys. But actual transcripts of such storytelling events collected by Harvey Sacks (Sacks 1974; Jefferson 1978) and Goodwin (1980a), as opposed to stories told directly to interviewers, reveal a suggestive feature of storytelling activities among boys: audience behavior is not overtly supportive. The storyteller is frequently faced with mockery, challenges and side comments on his story. A major sociolinguistic skill which a boy must apparently learn in interacting with his peers is to ride out this series of challenges, maintain his audience, and successfully get to the end of his story. In Sacks's account (1974) of some teenage boys involved in the telling of a dirty joke, for example, the narrator is challenged for his taste in jokes (an implication that he doesn't know a dirty joke from a non-dirty one) and for the potential ambiguity of his opening line "Three brothers married three sisters," not, as Sacks seems to imply, because audience members are really confused, but just to hassle the speaker. Through catches,[3] put-downs, the building of suspense, or other interest-grabbing devices, the speaker learns to control his audience. He also learns to continue when he gets no encouragement whatever, pausing slightly at various points for possible audience response but going on if there is nothing but silence.

A final sociolinguistic skill which boys must learn from interacting with other boys is how to act as audience members in the types of storytelling situations just discussed. As audience member as well as storyteller, a boy must learn to assert himself and his opinions. Boys seem to respond to the storytelling of other boys not so much with questions on deeper implications or with minimal response encouragement as with side comments and challenges. These are not meant primarily to interrupt, to change topic, or to change the direction of the narrative itself, but to assert the identity of the individual audience member.

Women's Speech

The structures and strategies in women's conversation show a marked continuity with the talk of girls. The key logic suggested by Kalčik's (1975) study of women's rap groups, Hirschman's (1973) study of students and Abrahams's (1975) work on black women is that women's conversation is interactional. In friendly talk, women are negotiating and expressing a relationship, one that should be in the form of support and closeness, but which may also involve criticism and distance. Women orient themselves to the person they are talking to and expect such orientation in return. As interaction, conversation requires participation from those involved and back-and-forth movement between participants. Getting the floor is not seen as particularly problematic; that should come about automatically. What is problematic is getting people engaged and keeping them engaged—maintaining the conversation and the interaction.

This conception of conversation leads to a number of characteristic speech strategies and gives a particular dynamic to women's talk. First, women tend to use personal and inclusive pronouns, such as 'you' and 'we' (Hirschman 1973). Second, women give off and look for signs of engagement such as nods and minimal response (Kalčik 1975; Hirschman 1973). Third, women give more extended signs of interest and attention, such as interjecting comments or questions during a speaker's discourse. These sometimes take the form of interruptions. In fact, both Hirschman (1973) and Kalčik (1975) found that interruptions were extremely common, despite women's concern with politeness and decorum (Kalčik 1975). Kalčik (1975) comments that women often asked permission to speak but were concerned that each speaker be allowed to finish and that all present got a chance to speak. These interruptions were clearly not seen as attempts to grab the floor but as calls for elaboration and development, and were taken as signs of support and interest. Fourth, women at the beginning of their utterances explicitly acknowledge and respond to what has been said by others. Fifth, women attempt to link their utterance to the one preceding it by building on the previous utterance or talking about something parallel or related to it. Kalčik (1975) talks about strategies of tying together, filling in, and serializing as signs of women's desire to create continuity in conversation, and Hirschman (1973) describes elaboration as a key dynamic of women's talk.

While the idiom of much of women's friendly talk is that of support, the elements of criticism, competition, and conflict do occur in it. But as with girls, these tend to take forms that fit the friendship idiom. Abrahams (1975) points out that while 'talking smart' is clearly one way women talk to women as well as to men, between women it tends to take a more playful form, to be more indirect and metaphoric in its phrasing and less prolonged than similar talk between men. Smartness, as he points out, puts distance in a relationship (Abrahams 1975). The target of criticism, whether present or not, is made out to be the one violating group norms and values (Abrahams 1975). Overt competitiveness is also disguised. As Kalčik (1975) points out, some stories that build on preceding ones are attempts to cap the original speaker, but they tend to have a form similar to supportive ones. It is the intent more than the form that differs. Intent is a central element in the concept of 'bitchiness,' one of women's terms for evaluating their talk, and it relates to this contradiction between form and intent, whether putting negative messages in overtly positive forms or acting supportive face to face while not being so elsewhere.

These strategies and the interactional orientation of women's talk give their conversation a particular dynamic. While there is often an unfinished quality to particular utterances. (Kalčik 1975), there is a progressive development to the overall conversation. The conversation grows out of the interaction of its participants, rather than being directed by a single individual or series of individuals. In her very stimulating discussion, Kalčik (1975) argues that this is true as well for many of the narratives women tell in conversation. She shows how narrative "kernels" serve as conversational resources for individual women and the group as a whole. How and if a "kernel story" is developed by the narrator and/or audience on a particular occasion is a function of the conversational context from which it emerges (Kalčik 1975:8), and it takes very different forms at different tellings. Not only is the dynamic of women's conversation one of elaboration and continuity, but the idiom of support can give it a distinctive tone as well. Hannerz (1969:96), for example, contrasts the "tone of relaxed sweetness, sometimes bordering on the saccharine," that characterizes approving talk between women, to the heated argument found among men. Kalčik (1975:6) even goes so far as to suggest that there is an "underlying esthetic or organizing principle" of "harmony" being expressed in women's friendly talk.

Men's Speech

The speaking patterns of men, and of women for that matter, vary greatly from one North American subculture to another. As Gerry Philipsen (1975:13) summarizes it, "talk is not everywhere valued equally; nor is it anywhere valued equally in all social contexts." There are striking cultural variations between subcultures in whether men consider certain modes of speech appropriate for dealing with women, children, authority figures, or strangers; there are differences in performance rules for storytelling and joke telling; there are differences in the context of men's speech; and there are differences in the rules for distinguishing aggressive joking from true aggression.

But more surprising than these differences are the apparent similarities across subcultures in the patterns of friendly interaction between men and the resemblances between these patterns and those observed for boys. Research reports on the speaking patterns of men among urban blacks (Hannerz 1969), rural Newfoundlanders (Faris 1966; Bauman 1972), and urban blue-collar whites (Philipsen 1975; LeMasters 1975) point again and again to the same three features: storytelling, arguing and verbal posturing.

Narratives such as jokes and stories are highly valued, especially when they are well performed for an audience. In Newfoundland, for example, Faris (1966:242) comments that "the reason 'news' is rarely passed between two men meeting in the road—it is simply not to one's advantage to relay information to such a small audience." Loud and aggressive argument is a second common feature of male-male speech. Such arguments, which may include shouting, wagering, name-calling, and verbal threats (Faris 1966:245), are often, as Hannerz (1969:86) describes them, "debates over minor questions of little direct import to anyone," enjoyed for their own sake and not taken as signs of real conflict. Practical jokes, challenges, put-downs, insults, and other forms of verbal aggression are a third feature of men's speech, accepted as normal among friends. LeMasters (1975:140), for example, describes life in a working-class tavern in the Midwest as follows:

> It seems clear that status at the Oasis is related to the ability to "dish it out" in the rapid-fire exchange called "joshing": you have to have a quick retort, and preferably one that puts you "one up" on your opponent. People who can't compete in the game lose status.

Thus challenges rather than statements of support are a typical way for men to respond to the speech of other men.

What Is Happening in Cross-Sex Conversation

What we are suggesting is that women and men have different cultural rules for friendly conversation and that these rules come into conflict when women and men attempt to talk to each other as friends and equals in casual conversation. We can think of at least five areas, in addition to that of minimal responses already discussed, in which men and women probably possess different conversational rules, so that miscommunication is likely to occur in cross-sex interaction.

1. There are two interpretations of the meaning of questions. Women seem to see questions as a part of conversational maintenance, while men seem to view them primarily as requests for information.
2. There are two conventions for beginning an utterance and linking it to the preceding utterance. Women's rules seem to call for an explicit acknowledgment of what has been said and making a connection to it. Men seem to have no such rule and in fact some male strategies call for ignoring the preceding comments.
3. There are different interpretations of displays of verbal aggressiveness. Women seem to interpret overt aggressiveness as personally directed, negative, and disruptive. Men seem to view it as one conventional organizing structure for conversational flow.
4. There are two understandings of topic flow and topic shift. The literature on storytelling in particular seems to indicate that men operate with a system in which topic is fairly narrowly defined and adhered to until finished and in which shifts between topics are abrupt, while women have a system in which topic is developed progressively and shifts gradually. These two systems imply very different rules for and interpretations of side comments, with major potential for miscommunication.
5. There appear to be two different attitudes towards problem sharing and advice giving. Women tend to discuss problems with one another, sharing experiences and offering reassurances. Men, in contrast, tend to hear women, and other men, who present them with problems as making explicit requests for solutions. They respond by giving advice, by acting as experts, lecturing to their audiences.[4]

Conclusions

Our purpose in this paper has been to present a framework for thinking about and tying together a number of strands in the analysis of differences between male and female conversational styles. We hope to prove the intellectual value of this framework by demonstrating its ability to do two things: to serve as a model both of and for sociolinguistic research.

As a model *of* past research findings, the power of our approach lies in its ability to suggest new explanations of previous findings on cross-sex communication while linking these findings to a wide range of other fields, including the study of language acquisition, of play, of friendship, of storytelling, of cross-cultural miscommunication, and of discourse analysis. Differences in the social interaction patterns of boys and girls appear to be widely known but rarely utilized in examinations of sociolinguistic acquisition or in explanations of observed gender differences in patterns of adult speech. Our proposed framework should serve to link together these and other known facts in new ways.

As a model *for* future research, we hope our framework will be even more promising. It suggests to us a number of potential research problems which remain to be investigated. Sociolinguistic studies of school-age children, especially studies of the use of speech in informal peer interaction, appear to be much rarer than studies of young children, although such studies may be of greater relevance for the understanding of adult patterns, particularly those related to gender. Our framework also suggests the need for many more studies of single-sex conversations among adults, trying to make more explicit some of the differences in conversational rules suggested by present research. Finally, the argument we have been making suggests a number of specific problems that appear to be highly promising lines for future research:

1. A study of the sociolinguistic socialization of 'tomboys' to see how they combine male and female patterns of speech and interaction;
2. An examination of the conversational patterns of lesbians and gay men to see how these relate to the sex-related patterns of the dominant culture;
3. An examination of the conversational patterns of the elderly to see to what extent speech differences persist after power differences have become insignificant;
4. A study of children's cultural concepts for talking about speech and the ways these shape the acquisition of speech styles (for example, how does the concept of 'bossiness' define a form of behavior which little girls must learn to recognize, then censure, and finally avoid?);
5. An examination of 'assertiveness training' programs for women to see whether they are really teaching women the speaking skills that politically skillful men learn in boyhood or are merely teaching women how to act like bossy little girls or bullying little boys and not feel guilty about it.

We conclude this paper by reemphasizing three of the major ways in which we feel that an anthropological perspective on culture and social organization can prove useful for further research on differences between men's and women's speech.

First, an anthropological approach to culture and cultural rules forces us to re-examine the way we interpret what is going on in conversations. The rules for interpreting conversation are, after all, culturally determined. There may be more than one way of understanding what is happening in a particular conversation and we must be careful about the rules we use for interpreting cross-sex conversations, in which the two participants may not fully share their rules of conversational inference.

Second, a concern with the relation between cultural rules and their social contexts leads us to think seriously about differences in different kinds of talk, ways of categorizing interactional situations, and ways in which conversational patterns may function as strategies for dealing with specific aspects of one's social world. Different types of interaction lead to different ways of speaking. The rules for friendly conversation between equals are different from those for service encounters, for flirting, for teaching, or for polite formal interaction. And even within the apparently uniform domain of friendly interaction, we argue that there are systematic differences between men and women in the way friendship is defined and thus in the conversational strategies that result.

Third and finally, our analysis suggests a different way of thinking about the connection between the gender-related behavior of children and that of adults. Most discussions of sex-role socialization have been based on the premise that gender differences are greatest for adults and that these adult differences are learned gradually throughout childhood. Our analysis, on the other hand, would suggest that at least some aspects of behavior are most strongly gender-differentiated during childhood and that adult patterns of friendly interaction, for example, involve learning to overcome at least partially some of the gender-specific cultural patterns typical of childhood.

Notes

1. The analogy between the sociolinguistic processes of dialect divergence and genderlect divergence was pointed out to us by Ron Macaulay.

2. In the strict sense the term, 'dozens' refers to a culturally specific form of stylized argument through the exchange of insults that has been extensively documented by a variety of students of American black culture and is most frequently practiced by boys in their teens and pre-teens. Recently folklorist Simon Bronner (1978) has made a convincing case for the existence of a highly similar but independently derived form of insult exchange known as 'ranking', 'mocks', or 'cutting' among white American adolescents. What we find striking and worthy of note is the tendency for both black and white versions of the dozens to be practiced primarily by boys.

3. 'Catches' are a form of verbal play in which the main speaker ends up tricking a member of his or her audience into a vulnerable or ridiculous position. In an article on the folklore of black children in South Philadelphia, Roger Abrahams (1963) distinguishes between catches which are purely verbal and tricks in which the second player is forced into a position of being not only verbally but also physically abused as in the following example of a catch which is also a trick:

A: Adam and Eve and Pinch-Me-Tight
   Went up the hill to spend the night.
   Adam and Eve came down the hill.
   Who was left?

B: Pinch-Me-Tight
[A pinches B]

What is significant about both catches and tricks is that they allow for the expression of playful aggression and that they produce a temporary hierarchical relation between a winner and loser, but invite the loser to attempt to get revenge by responding with a counter-trick.

4. We thank Kitty Julien for first pointing out to us the tendency of male friends to give advice to women who are not necessarily seeking it and Niyi Akinnaso for pointing out that the sex difference among Yoruba speakers in Nigeria in the way people respond verbally to the problems of others is similar to that among English speakers in the U.S.

References

Abrahams, R. D. 1963. "The 'Catch' in Negro Philadelphia." *Keystone Folklore Quarterly* 8(3):107–111.

———. 1975. "Negotiating respect: Patterns of presentation among black women." In C. R. Farrar, ed., *Women in Folklore*. Austin, TX: University of Texas Press.

Bauman, R. 1972. "The LaHave Island General Store: Sociability and verbal art in a Nova Scotia community." *Journal of American Folklore* 85:330–343.

Bronner, S. J. 1978. "A re-examining of white dozens." *Western Folklore* 37(2):118–128.

Brooks-Gunn, J., and W. S. Matthews. 1979. *He and She: How Children Develop Their Sex-Role Identity*. Englewood Cliffs, NJ: Prentice-Hall.

Eder, D., and M. T. Hallinan. 1978. "Sex differences in children's friendships." *American Sociological Review* 43:237–250.

Faris, J. C. 1966. "The dynamics of verbal exchange: A Newfoundland example." *Anthropologica* 8(2):235–248.

Fishman, P. M. 1978. "Interaction: The work women do." *Social Problems* 25(4):397–406.

Goodwin, M. H. 1978. "Conversational practices in a peer group of urban black children." Doctoral dissertation. University of Pennsylvania, Philadelphia.

———. 1980a. "Directive-response speech sequences in girls' and boys' task activities." In S. McConnell-Ginet, R. Borker, and N. Furman, eds., *Women and Language in Literature and Society*. New York: Praeger.

———. 1980b. "He-said-she-said: Formal cultural procedures of a gossip dispute activity." *American Ethnologist* 7(4):674–695.

Gumperz, J. J. 1977. "Sociocultural knowledge in conversational inference." In M. Saville-Troike, ed., *Linguistics and Anthropology*. Washington, DC: Georgetown University Press.

———. 1978a. "The conversational analysis of interethnic communication. In E. Lamar Ross, ed., *Interethnic Communication*. Athens: University of Georgia Press.

———. 1978b. "Dialect and conversational inference in urban communication." *Language in Society* 7(3):393–409.

———. 1979. "The sociolinguistic basis of speech act theory." In J. Boyd and S. Ferrara, eds., *Speech Act Ten Years After*. Milan: Versus.

———. 1982. *Discourse Strategies*. New York: Cambridge University Press.

Gumperz, J. J., and D. Tannen. 1979. "Individual and social differences in language use." In W. Wang and C. Fillmore, eds., *Individual Differences in Language Ability and Language Behavior*. New York: Academic Press.

Gumperz, J. J., A. Agrawal, and G. Aulakh. 1977. "Prosody, paralinguistics and contextual-ization in Indian English." Language Behavior Research Laboratory, typescript. University of California, Berkeley.

Haas, A. 1979. "The acquisition of genderlect." In J. Orasanu, M. Slater, and L. Adler, eds., *Language, Sex and Gender: Does* La Différence *Make a Difference? Annals of the New York Academy of Sciences* 327:101–113.

Hannerz, U. 1969. *Soulside.* New York: Columbia University Press.

Harding, S. 1975. "Women and words in a Spanish village." In R. Reiter, ed., *Towards an Anthropology of Women.* New York: Monthly Review Press.

Hirschman, L. 1973. "Female-male differences in conversational interaction." Paper pre-sented at Linguistic Society of America, San Diego.

Jefferson, G. 1978. "Sequential aspects of storytelling in conversation." In J. Schenker, ed., *Studies in the Organization of Conversational Interaction.* New York: Academic Press.

Kalčik, S. 1975. " '. . . Like Anne's gynecologist or the time I was almost raped': personal narratives in women's rap groups." In C. R. Farrar, ed., *Women and Folklore.* Austin, TX: University of Texas Press.

Lakoff, R. 1975. *Language and Women's Place.* New York: Harper and Row.

LeMasters, E. E. 1975. *Blue Collar Aristocrats: Life-Styles at a Working-Class Tavern.* Madison, WI: University of Wisconsin Press.

Lever, J. 1976. "Sex differences in the games children play." *Social Problems* 23:478–483.

———. 1978. "Sex differences in the complexity of children's play and games." *American Sociological Review* 43:471–483.

Meditch, A. 1975. "The development of sex-specific speech patterns in young children." *Anthropological Linguistics* 17:421–433.

Philipsen, G. 1975. "Speaking 'like a man' in Teamsterville: Cultural patterns of role enact-ment in an urban neighborhood." *Quarterly Journal of Speech* 61:13–22.

Sacks, H. 1974. "An analysis of the course of a joke's telling in conversation." In R. Bauman and J. Sherzer, eds., *Explorations in the Ethnography of Speaking.* Cambridge: Cambridge University Press.

Savin-Williams, R. C. 1976. "The ethological study of dominance formation and mainte-nance in a group of human adolescents." *Child Development* 47:972–979.

Soskin, W. F., and V. P. John. 1963. "The study of spontaneous talk." In R.G. Barker, ed., *The Stream of Behavior.* New York: Appleton-Century-Croft.

Strodtbeck, F. L., and R. D. Mann. 1956. "Sex role differentiation in jury deliberations." *Sociometry* 19:3–11.

West, C. 1979. "Against our will: Male interruptions of females in cross-sex conversation." In J. Orasanu, M. Slater, and L. Adler, eds., *Language, Sex and Gender: Does* La Différence *make a difference? Annals of the New York Academy of Sciences* 327:81–100.

West, C., and D. H. Zimmerman. 1977. "Women's place in everyday talk: Reflections of par-ent-child interaction." *Social Problems* 24(5):521–529.

Zimmerman, D. H., and C. West. 1975. "Sex roles, interruptions and silences in conversa-tion." In B. Thorne and N. Henley, eds., *Language and Sex: Differences and Dominance.* Rowley, MA: Newbury House.

6

Norm-Makers, Norm-Breakers: Uses of Speech by Men and Women in a Malagasy Community

ELINOR KEENAN (OCHS)

The Community

Namoizamanga is a hamlet composed of twenty-four households, situated in the southern central plateau of Madagascar. This area is generally referred to as *Vakinankaratra*,[1] meaning 'broken by the Ankaratra.' The Ankaratra Mountains do in fact form a natural boundary in the north. They separate this area somewhat from other parts of the central plateau area. This separation has sociological significance in that the people of this community and communities nearby identify themselves as Vakinankaratra. The present generation recognize an historical link with the dominant plateau group, the Merina, but choose a separate social identity.

A partial explanation for this parochialism lies in the nature of the ties which brought these people formerly in contact. In the late eighteenth century and into the nineteenth century, people of the Vakinankaratra were conquered by the Merina and brought north as slaves. When the French abolished ownership of slaves and the existence of a slave class (*andevo*), many slaves moved back into the traditional homeland of their ancestors. A villager speaks of this time with great difficulty and embarrassment. The people know themselves to be former *andevo* and are known by others to be such, but the term itself is almost never used. To address or refer to someone as *andevo* is a grave insult. Genealogical reckoning is shallow, typically going back two to three generations. With some exceptions, local histories begin with the settling of ancestors into these villages in the early part of this century.

Within the village, fixed distinctions in social status are few. All members of a community (who are part of a household) are considered *havana* (kinsmen). Those outside the community are *vahiny* (guests, strangers). Within the *havana* group, those adults who have taken a spouse, especially those with children, are considered to be *ray-aman-dreny* (elders; literally 'father-and mother') of the community. A respected adult without spouse or children can be a *ray-aman-dreny*, but the status typically implies these qualifications. Decisions which affect a family or the community are usually handled by these *ray-aman-dreny*. Traditionally, village leadership is not fixed with any one particular individual.

Superimposed on this communal framework is a hierarchy of government officials who represent the national political party in power. These officials collect taxes, regulate elections, and act as general liaisons between the government and the people in their sphere of authority. These officials are referred to by French terms: *chef d'hameau* (head of a hamlet), *chef de village* (head of those hamlets which compose an official village), *chef de quartier* (head of those villages which compose a quartier) and so on.

Linguistic Repertoire of the Community

The language spoken throughout Madagascar, in various dialects, is Malagasy. It is a verb-first, subject-final language belonging to the Western Malayo-Polynesian subfamily of languages. The people of Namoizamanga speak the major dialect of the island, *Merina*. French is taught in local schools but few villagers, and no adults, speak fluently. Nonetheless sets of French terms may be employed to communicate specific information in particular activities. For example, French directional terms are used almost exclusively in giving orders to cows (see Bloch MS.). We will see below that this specific use of French can be understood in terms of the speech norms we shall present.

There are two major modes of speech use distinguished by the villagers. First, there is *resaka*. This term refers to *teny-an-dava'andro* (everyday speaking). *Resaka* is also characterized as *teny tsotra* (simple talk). The specific kinds of speech behavior covered by the term *reseka* are numerous. *Tafatafa* (gossip), *fiarahabana* (greetings), *fangatahana* (requests), *fiantsoana* (calling out), *fierana* (consultations), *dinika* (discussion), *mitapatap'ahitra* (examine closely; literally 'to break grass'), for example, are *resaka*.

Resaka contrasts with *kabary*, which refers both to ceremonial speech situations and to the highly stylized mode of speech which characterizes such situations. *Kabary* speech is governed by a series of well known rules which concern the sequencing and content of particular speeches. *Kabary* is characteristic of formal speech situations. *Fanambadiana* (marriages), *fandevenana* (burials), *famadihana* (ancestral bone-turnings), *famorana* (circumcisions), for example, use a specific *kabary* as part of the ritual. But any situation can become 'ceremonial' if one chooses to use the *kabary* format, as in for example the expression of gratitude by guest to host, or in the expression of sympathy in visiting mourners or the ill.

We consider *resaka* and *kabary* to be contrastive speech uses of the same generality. This consideration is based on comparison of these terms in unsolicited speech of the villagers themselves. In particular, these two modes of speech usage are frequently contrasted with each other by speechmakers. The contrast appears in that part of a *kabary* in which the speechmaker is expected to convey his inability, unworthiness as a speechmaker. He does this frequently by claiming that his words are not *kabary* but *resaka*.

Avoidance of Direct Affront as a Social Norm

Status as a Norm

Particular uses of speech by a villager are constrained to some extent by notions of what is expected behavior in particular situations. For example, in the Vakinankaratra, one is expected (in many social situations) to avoid open and direct confrontation with another. One is expected not to affront another, not to put an individual in an uncomfortable or unpleasant situation. It is this sort of expected behavior which I am considering as a behavioral norm, relative to particular situations.

When one conducts oneself in violation of these expectations, as in directly confronting another, the action is censured by other villagers. For example, children who confront strangers (*vahiny*) by making direct demands of them are reprimanded by their mothers or elder siblings. An adult who insults (*manevateva*) another openly is ignored by those sympathetic to the injured party. In one case for example, a family who had offended other members of the village with direct insults was physically cut off from most village social life. The footpath running between their house and the rest of the village was blocked. Sisal shrubs were placed across the passage. No member of the village helped the family with rice-planting, whereas normally groups of men and groups of women from each household cooperatively worked each other's fields.

Another form of public censure is to speak of offensive conduct as causing *henatra* (shame). One who has caused *henatra* is thought to *mangala-baraka* (to steal honor) from one's family or community. One who has caused *henatra* is the center of much gossip (*tafatafa*). One strives not to bring *henatra* upon himself or other individuals, and one way to reduce the risk of *henatra* is to act in ways which support the norm of non-confrontation.

Expression of the Non-Confrontation Norm in Speech Interaction

Affront can result from a number of interpersonal actions: catching an individual off-guard, unexpectedly, is an affronting action, for example. Thus, in Namoizamanga, to enter another's house without any warning is always inappropriate. If the callers are *havana* (kinsmen or neighbors), they shout *haody*, which signals to those inside the house that they are about to receive visitors. Those inside respond to this signal by saying *mandrosoa* (enter!). This exchange confirms that those inside the house are, in principle, ready to receive the callers. Such an exchange allows those inside the house a moment of preparation to rise from their beds, dress, stop eating, or the like. On the other hand, if the guests are not *havana*, they may in addition send a messenger ahead to ascertain whether or not these others can receive them. It is highly offensive then to catch one unawares, as this may put him in a disadvantaged position.

Equally inappropriate is an open and direct expression of anger or disagreement. Physical fighting among adults is almost non-existent. Small boys have mock fights, but these are always playful, never angry. Typically anger or disapproval is not directed toward the relevant person or persons. Rather, each side tells sympathetic associates of their sentiments, and these sentiments are then made known to the other side by intermediaries. Disputes then are often resolved by intermediaries, such as local elders or persons in the area known to be *mpanao fihavanana* (restorers of relationships). These persons are invited by some person associated with both sides to resolve the dispute.

We should note also that the censuring behavior referred to above is subject to the norm of non-confrontation. Thus, with one important exception to be discussed below, censure is not communicated directly and openly to an adult violator of a norm.

Similarly criticism leveled by speechmakers at each other during *kabary* performances is also subject to the nonconfrontation norm. Many *kabary* performances involve at least two speechmakers (*mpikabary*) who engage in a ritualized dialogue which varies according to the nature of the occasion. Usually the second speaker or group of speakers represents the listener group to whom the first speaker addresses himself. The second speaker normally affirms his (his group's) support for and solidarity with the first speaker and his group. However, there are occasions when the second speechmaker wishes to criticize the first one. For example, if the first has made some error in the sequence of speech acts which constitute the *kabary* or has given some incorrect information, the second speechmaker will usually point this out. In so doing he enhances his status as one knowledgeable in matters of the *kabary*. Thus the *kabary* functions on two levels at once. On one level, it is concerned with the ritual at hand: marriage request, funeral, circumcision. And on a second level it is a forum displaying the skill and knowledge of the speakers. An able speechmaker excels by revealing an intimate acquaintance with *kabary* format and with the range of proverbs (*ohabolana*) and traditional sayings (*hainteny*) associated with the particular event.

One way of expressing expertise is to dispute some aspect of the *kabary* handled by the other speechmaker. But the expression of disagreement must be done delicately. It must be shown that an error has been made, but it must not be shown too bluntly or explicitly. The second speechmaker must avoid confronting the first with explicit criticism. In fact, if the second speechmaker were to directly confront the first he would bring *henatra* upon himself and his group. On the other hand, the more subtly the criticism is couched, the greater his status as speechmaker becomes. So, rather than making explicit verbal attacks, the speechmaker makes use of a number of stylistic techniques. First, he softens the negative intent of his remarks by prefacing them with compliments. For example:

Thank you very much, sir. The first part of your talk has already been received in peace
and happiness. I am in accordance and agreement with you on this, sir. You were given
permission to speak and what you said gave me courage and strength. You said things
skillfully but not pretentiously. You originate words but also recognize what is traditional. But as for myself I am not an originator of words at all but a borrower. I am more
comfortable carrying the spade and basket. You, on the other hand, have smoothed out
all faults in the speech; you have woven the holes together. You have shown respect to
the elders and respect to the young as well. This is finished. But . . . (Criticism begins.)

Second, criticisms are usually not simply stated but rather alluded to. Proverbs,
poetry, traditional expressions are all brought in to reveal bit by bit the direction
of the utterance. The same kind of proverbs, poetry, and traditional expressions
are used over and over again for these purposes, so that the other speechmaker
knows exactly what is being implied by each stylistic device. For example, a criticism might typically begin with the proverb *Atao hady voamangan'Ikirijavola ka
potsika amin'ny amboamasony* (Done like Ikirijavola digging sweet potatoes: the
digging stick jabbed straight into a potato eye). This proverb refers to a similar behavior performed by the other speaker. It implies that the other speaker has
rushed into the *kabary* too swiftly and too abruptly. Like Ikirijavola who has
spoiled the sweet potato, the other speaker has mishandled some part of the
kabary. The proper way of digging sweet potatoes calls for a careful loosening of
the earth which surrounds the root. And the proper way of performing a *kabary*
calls for a careful treatment of each *kabary* segment. If such a criticism were uttered in all its explicitness the other speechmaker and his group would take of-
fense. They might choose to leave rather than bear this loss of face. In making use
of a more allusive frame, the speechmaker not only displays his knowledge and
skill, he also allows the *kabary* to continue and maintains the flow of communication between the two groups.

Accusations (*fiampangana*, or more usually *manome tsiny* [give guilt]) are another form of speech behavior subject to this norm in that they are rarely made in
an explicit and open manner. Typically suspicions are communicated in conversation and gossip, but explicit accusations are rare. One is not even directly accused when, as they say, one is caught *tratra am-body omby* (caught in the act; LIT
'caught on the back of the cow'). Thus one is rarely held accountable for having
done something wrong as others hesitate to confront that person with that information.

The hesitation to commit oneself explicitly to an idea or opinion is itself an important behavioral norm in this community. One is noncommittal for fear that an
action openly advocated might have consequences that would have to be borne
alone. One avoids accusation because one does not wish to be responsible for providing that information. If the wrongdoer is to be pointed out, the rest of the community must share the responsibility for the act, and they must share any guilt that
may result. One speechmaker gave this account of what occurs in such situations:

Even if someone was caught in the act of doing something wrong, then you cannot directly point at this person to dishonor him directly. You must use special expressions or go about it in a roundabout way. But if by chance there are people who demand that this wrongdoer be pointed out directly, then the speaker must say directly in the *kabary* who the person is. But because he must speak directly the speaker must ask the people to lift all guilt from him (*aza tsiny*). If there is someone in the audience who wants to know more, who doesn't understand, then he may respond during a break in the talk, 'It is not clear to us, sir. It is hard to distinguish the domestic cat from the wild cat. They are the same whether calico or yellow or grey. And if it is the wild cat who steals the chicken, we cannot tell him from the others. The wild cat steals the chicken but the domestic cat gets its tail cut off. So point directly to the wild cat.'

In general then one avoids confronting another with negative or unpleasant information. Disputes, criticisms, accusations are typically not straightforward. Disputes are often carried through mediators. Criticisms are veiled in metaphor. Accusations are left imprecise, unless the group is willing to share responsibility for the act of accusation. Direct affront indicates a lowering or absence of respect on the part of the affronter. In public situations, however, show of respect is expected. And, in formal public situations such as the *kabary* performance, it is obligatory. Every speechmaker interviewed stressed the importance of respect:

- In the *kabary*, it is not good to speak directly. If you speak directly the *kabary* is a *kabarin-jaza* (child's *kabary*) and there is no respect and honor.
- Speakers are not afraid to explain to one another, to answer with wisdom. But the censurer must be careful not to dishonor or mock or lower in public that speaker, because this was *fady* (taboo) for our ancestors.
- A *kabary* which blames, disgraces is not a *kabary fankasitrahana* (*kabary* of agreement) but a *kabary fankahalana* (*kabary* of hatred). And the audience leaves. 'This is a *kabary ratsy* (bad *kabary*),' they say.

Direct affront, then, risks censure of others. Directness is associated with the ways of children and with things contrary to tradition. A speechmaker who affronts may be left without an audience. His status as speechmaker is lowered. Direct affront can bring *henatra* and possibly *tsiny* (guilt). These considerations help to explain the general hesitation to openly accuse, criticize, or dispute.

The norm of avoidance of explicit and direct affront underlies other speech acts as well. The speech acts of *fandidiana* (ordering) and *fangatahana* (asking), for example, are affected. These speech acts are particular sorts of interpersonal directives (my terminology): they are used to get someone to do something. The use of an interpersonal directive creates an active confrontation situation. The person directed (ordered, asked) is confronted with having to comply with the directive or with having to reject it. And the director (orderer, asker) is confronted with the possibility that his authority to direct will not be acknowledged. A directive which is too explicit may affront the person directed. An explicit rejection of the directive may affront the director.

We consider *fandidiana* (ordering) and the ways the possibility of affront can be reduced.

First, the order is typically softened by a number of verbal niceties. The order is typically preceded by the word *mba* (please). It is typically followed by the word *kely*, usually translated as 'small' but here just a softening word which reduces the harshness of the speech act. These verbal softeners convey respect to the person ordered. In so doing, they transform the order into a more egalitarian type of encounter where personal affront is less likely.

A more important way in which the orderer shapes the speech act of *fandidiana* is in the handling of imperatives. Orders are frequently formed by imperatives. What is interesting is that the speaker has a choice of three distinct forms of imperative to use: the active imperative, the passive imperative, and the circumstantial imperative.

These imperative forms correspond to the three verb voices in Malagasy. The active and passive voices operate much the same as in Indo-European languages. The passive voice takes some object of the active sentence and makes it a superficial subject. The third verb voice, the circumstantial, operates in much the same way. The circumstantial voice makes a superficial subject out of a constituent which refers to some circumstance—place, time, instrument, etc.—of the action. Thus, the active declarative sentence:

Manasa ny lamba amin'ny savony <u>Rasoa.</u>
'Rasoa is washing the clothes with the soap.'
(LIT washes the clothes with the soap Rasoa.)

becomes in the passive voice:

Sasan-dRasoa amin'ny savony ny <u>lamba.</u>
'The clothes are washed by Rasoa with the soap.'
(LIT washed by Rasoa with the soap the clothes.)

The direct object of the active sentence is moved to subject position (indicated by underlining), and the verb form is modified. In the circumstantial voice, the instrumental constituent of the active is moved to subject position, and its case marker (*amin'ny*) is dropped. Again the verb form is modified:

Anasan-dRasoa ny lamba ny <u>savony.</u>
'The soap is used by Rasoa to wash the clothes.'
(LIT washes Rasoa the clothes the soap.)

The three forms of imperative operate in a similar fashion. In the active imperative:

Manasá ny lamba amin'ny savony.
'Wash the clothes with the soap.'

the person addressed ('you' in this example) is the subject. In the passive imperative:

Sasao ny lamba amin'ny savony.
'Have the clothes washed with the soap.'
(LIT have washed the clothes with the soap.)

it is the object of the active order 'the clothes' which is the subject. Likewise, the circumstantial imperative makes the instrumental complement 'the soap' the subject of the order:

Anasao lamba ny savony.
'The soap is to be used to wash clothes.'
(LIT have-washed-with clothes the soap.)

But although these three forms of imperative are available to the speaker, they are not used with equal ease in ordering. In cases where all three are grammatically possible, the speaker prefers to use the passive or the circumstantial voice. (This preference holds for declaratives as well.) The active imperative differs from both the passive and circumstantial in that the person ordered is the subject of the utterance. In the passive and circumstantial imperative, on the other hand, emphasis is withdrawn from the person ordered by making some other aspect of the order the subject. Thus the passive imperative topicalizes the object of the action—*what* is to be done rather than *who* is to do it. And the circumstantial imperative stresses the instrument or place or person for whom the action is to be accomplished rather than who is to accomplish the action.

To use the active imperative where it is grammatically possible to use the passive or circumstantial causes affront. The active imperative is considered harsh and abrupt, without respect. It is the socially marked form of imperative. The passive and circumstantial forms of imperative convey greater deference and are normally more appropriate in giving orders to persons. They avoid stressing the person ordered and, in so doing, reduce the risk of an unsuccessful, unpleasant social encounter.

A third way of mitigating an order lies in the interesting syntactic possibility Malagasy affords of focusing on some particular part of the action ordered. Syntactically the focus operation relates (1) and (2) below:

(1) *Narian'i John   ny fotsy.*
    'The white ones were   thrown out by John.'
    (LIT: thrown out by John the white.)

(2) *Ny fotsy   no narian' i John.*
    'It was the white   (ones) that were thrown out by John.'

The semantic effect of moving the constituent *ny fotsy* (the white ones) to the front and inserting the abstract particle *no* is exactly that indicated by its English translation. That is, in the focused sentence, (2), it is the information in the phrase 'the white ones' which is most prominent; it is only that information which can be naturally questioned or denied. That is, the question *Ny fotsy ve no narian 'i John?* (Was it the white ones that John threw out?) questions only the identity of the objects thrown out, not whether there were any. Similarly *Tsy ny fotsy no narian'i John* (It wasn't the white ones that were thrown out by John) still implies that John threw out something—it only denies that the things thrown out were the white ones. Notice however that if we question or deny sentence (1) we are not permitted to infer that John threw out something. For example *Tsy narian'i John ny fotsy* (The white ones were not thrown out by John) leaves open the possibility that John did not throw out anything at all. Thus focusing on a part of a sentence raises that information to the level of explicit assertion and relegates the rest to the level of presupposition, a level which is much less accessible to questioning and denial.

What is interesting in Malagasy is that this focus operation applies also to imperatives. Thus in addition to the unmarked passive imperative *ario ny fotsy* (roughly: have the white ones thrown out) we find *Ny fotsy no ario* (roughly: it's the white ones which are to be thrown out [by you]). The latter order differs in meaning from the former in essentially the same way as the focused declarative (2) differs from the unfocused one (1). Specifically the focused order basically presupposes that something is to be thrown out and asserts that it is the white things.

Thus in focused orders, the speaker focuses on some aspect of the action ordered—such as the object which will be affected by the order or some circumstance of the ordered action—rather than the order itself. The order is taken for granted, that is, presupposed, and the immediate issue in the utterance is the identity of the objects affected by the order. In this way, the speaker can give an order with minimum stress on the fact that it is an order which he is giving. Through the use of the focus operation the speaker is able to shift the attention of the listeners away from the fact that the utterance is an order. This provides the addressee with the option of failing to execute the order by calling into question the identity of the objects rather than by refusing to execute the order. That is, one might naturally respond to *Ny fotsy no ario* (it's the white ones you're to throw out) by questioning *Ny fotsy sa ny mainty?* (The white ones, or the black ones?). Thus, since the identity of the object to be thrown out has been made the issue, it is possible to 'disagree' with an order without actually refusing to execute it—and thus without directly challenging the authority of the orderer or explicitly asserting one's own power.

The risk of affront through direct confrontation is minimized in *fangatahana* (askings) as well. To understand the operation of this norm in this speech act, we must break it down into at least two unnamed modes of use. These two modes are distinguished on the basis of the social category of the asker and the one asked and on the nature of the service or property asked for. One mode of asking applies to situations in which the asker and one asked are *havana* (kinsmen) and in which what is being asked for is some ordinary minor service (expected of *havana*) or some ordinary, not uncommon piece of property, such as tobacco or hair grease. Let us call this category of things asked for category A. A second mode of asking applies to more than one social category and to more than one goods and services category. First of all, it applies to all *fangatahana* in which the asker and asked are *vahiny* (non-kinsmen) regardless of the goods and services asked for. Secondly, it applies to *fangatahana* between *havana* where the good or service asked for is not minor or ordinary or automatically expected of *havana*. Let us call this category of things category B. For example, a *havana* asking to borrow another's plough or wagon would use this mode of *fangatahana*. This second mode of use then applies to *vahiny* for category A or B things and to *havana* for category B things only.

	vahiny	havana
Mode 1	—	A
Mode 2	A or B	B

These two modes of use differ in the degree to which the one asked is obligated to comply with the directive. *Havana* asked for category A goods and services are obligated to comply. They must provide these goods and services, provided they are in a position to. This obligation is a basic behavioral expression of the *havana* relationship. Another verbal expression of the *havana* relationship is the greeting which one *havana* gives another when entering his or her house: *Inona no masaka?* (What's cooking?) This expression is taken as a demand for a cooked meal, in particular, for rice. Close *havana* have the right to this food. Many times there is no cooked food in the house, and the visitor does not really expect to eat. He demands just out of form, to emphasize the kind of tie which exists between them. Similarly, a *havana* expects another *havana* to provide him or her with tobacco or sweets or other goods which belong to this category. This kind of obligation is not expected among *vahiny*, however, nor among *havana* for category B goods and services.

Where a strong obligation to comply with the directive does not exist, the person asked is thought to be in a superior position relative to the asker; the one asked has the right to refuse the asker. This difference in status is well understood by speechmakers, who are often put in the position of asking for things in public *kabary*. In every *kabary*, the speechmaker asks for the blessing and support of the audience, permission to speak, guilt to be lifted, and so on. And in these parts of every *kabary*, the speechmaker stresses his inferiority in an elaborate manner.

> When I ask for the guilt and blame to be lifted from me (for standing here before you), I am not an originator of words but a preserver only of tradition, a successor to my father by accident. And not only this, I am like a small cricket, not master of the tall plant or able to perch on the tip of the tall plant like the *sopanga* cricket, but my destiny is to stay on the ground because I am the *tsimbotry* cricket, an orphan with no ancestors. I am not the prince of birds, the *railovy*, but the *tsikirity* bird who trails behind in the flock, for I am not an originator of words but a borrower and a preserver of tradition and by accident replace others. So I ask for the guilt and taboo to be lifted, respected gentlemen and all those facing (me) at this moment.

One *kabary* is a *fangatahana* in itself. That is the *kabary vody ondry*, the marriage request. The askers are the boy's family and those asked are the girl's family, and the marriage of the girl to the boy is what is asked for. The *kabary* itself is an elaborate expression of the second mode of *fangatahana*, where the speaker for the boy's family is considered to be much lower than that of the speaker for the girl's family. A speechmaker made these comments to me concerning this relationship:

> You should use *teny malemy* (soft words) when you make requests. You shouldn't be like a boaster or person on the same level as the other. It is our *fomba*, custom, to think of requesters, in this case, the boy's family, as lower than the requested, for example, the elders of the girl's family. Even if the girl's speaker is unskilled, you must put yourself in a lower position and appear to lose the *kabary* (that is, to appear less knowledgeable) to give honor to the girl's side of the family.

In the second mode of *fangatahana*, then, the one asked has in principle the option of refusing to comply. In the first mode, the one asked is rather obligated to comply. The risk of affront to the asker is much higher in the second mode than in the first because of this option. That is, a *havana* who asks another *havana* for a category A item is not risking loss of face. He knows the other must comply if possible. On the other hand, where rejection is a possibility as in the second mode of *fangatahana*, affront is also a possibility. Given this, the asker acts in ways which minimize the risk of personal affront. In particular, the asker avoids directly confronting the one asked with having to comply with the directive or having to reject it. He avoids putting the one asked on the spot.

First, direct affront is avoided in this mode of *fangatahana*, which I shall call the request mode, in that the request is often not presented by the actual requester(s) but by a stand-in who represents the actual requester(s). This is formalized in request *kabary* where speechmakers are employed to represent others. This arrangement does not place the actual requester and the one requested in a direct relationship. The actual requester is saved from any possible affront which could result from the request.

Second, the request mode is typically formulated and presented in a veiled manner. The asker does not make it explicit that he is requesting some object or service from the other. Rather, that which is desired is alluded to in the conversational context. Often a request is signaled by an abrupt change in conversational topic. The new topic moves the speaker or speakers to make reference to what is desired from the listener(s). Young boys suddenly speak of a journey to be made that evening and describe the blackness of the night and their lack of candles. Women will chatter about the poor quality of Malagasy soap in relation to European soap in my presence. Men will moan over the shortage of funds for a particular project. The host or listener is expected to pick up these cues and satisfy the request.

A consequence of this format is that neither the requester nor the requestee is committed to a particular action. That is, in alluding to, rather than openly specifying the thing requested, the requester does not commit himself to making the request and is not so open to the rebuff of having the request denied. He may intend the utterance to be taken as a request, but he does not make this explicit.

This lack of commitment, of course, allows the person requested the same option. He is not obligated to recognize the utterance as a request. He may choose just how he wishes to define the activity and need not commit himself to any response at all. Thus the party to whom the request is directed is not forced to deny the request (if that is his intention) and, in so doing, cause great loss of face on both sides. The allusive format, then, enables the one requested to deny the request (by 'misinterpreting' it) without affront.

Where the risk of affront is minimal, as in the first mode of *fangatahana*, these constraints do not exist. The asking is relatively direct and explicit, and there are no stand-in requesters. *Havana* are able to ask for category A items in this manner because compliance, if possible, is assured. The asker is not faced with a possible loss of face or rebuff. The one asked may only grudgingly give up tobacco from the market but he does give in to the *fangatahana*. Where affront is a risk, then, *fangatahana* are inexplicit and indirectly presented (mode 2). Where affront is not a risk or is a minimal risk, *fangatahana* are straightforward.

Women as Norm-Breakers

According to the norm, one avoids putting another individual in an uncomfortable or unpleasant position, where loss of face could result. One shows respect to the other by avoiding this type of confrontation. Women, however, do not appear to operate according to these community ground rules for speaking. In particular they are associated with the direct and open expression of anger towards others. Their social behavior contrasts sharply with men in this respect. Men tend not to express their sentiments openly. They admire others who use language subtly. They behave in public in such a way as to promote interpersonal ease. In short, they avoid creating unpleasant face-to-face encounters. Women, on the other hand, tend to speak in a more straightforward manner. They express feelings of anger or criticism directly to the relevant party. Both men and women agree that women have *lavalela*, a long tongue.

Men acknowledge this difference in the speechways of men and women. They consider the use of speech by men to be more skillful than that by women. What is not acknowledged is that men often make use of this difference. In other words, men often use women to confront others with some unpleasant information. Women communicate sentiments which men share but dislike expressing. Men are associated with the maintenance of good communication in a relationship, and women are associated with the expression of socially damaging information. In one instance, for example, the young boys of the village played ball against the side of a newly whitewashed house. They chipped off patches of color. The landlord returned, observed this situation but after an entire day in the village, said only, 'If you don't patch that, things might not go well between us.' The next day he returned with his wife. As she approached the village, she accosted the first person she saw (which happened to be the eldest man in the village) with accusations. She told everyone within hearing range of their anger and just what must be done to repair the wall. This outburst caused a great deal of grumbling and unpleasant feelings among the villagers. But the outburst was almost expected. It was not a shocking encounter as it came from the wife and not the landlord himself. Such a display of anger is permissible, perhaps even appropriate, because it is initiated by a woman.

In another instance, the oldest man in the village acquired a wife without consulting other kinsmen in his village. Without a word, the old man conducted the woman into his house. A week went by and no one said anything to him or his woman. Then, as the old man passed in front of a gathering of women one morning, they let loose their criticism of his behavior. He looked down, made excuses, and exhibited signs of discomfort. Then, one of the other village men approached and began to talk of some trivial topic, as if he had been totally unaware of the scene which had just passed. The other man marked his entrance with a change of topic. He refused to be associated with the behavior of the women, even though he agreed with their opinions. Women relieve some social pressure in this way, for after these episodes generally nothing more is said. But women can never be *mpanao fihavanana* (restorers of relationships) because they are thought to lack subtlety and sensitivity and because they are associated with communication of negative information.

In fact, women are associated with direct speech, and they are used by men wherever this manner is useful. A man and woman are walking along the side of a road. It is the woman who waves down our car and asks if they might have a ride. And it is the woman who asks for information such as: Where are you going? Where have you been? How much did that cost? All of these speech acts put the addressee on the spot. All are potentially affronting situations.

It is in part because women are more straightforward that they are the ones who sell village produce in the markets, and the ones who buy the everyday necessities in the markets. Buying and selling is a confrontation situation as bargaining is the norm and as the seller has to declare an initial price. The seller commits himself to wanting to sell by virtue of his position. Women are not afraid to confront the buyer or seller with their opinions as to what the price ought to be. They bargain in an expeditious and straightforward manner. Men bargain as well, but their manner is more subtle and ornate. The encounter is much more elaborate; it can sometimes be a show, where others gather round to watch the proceedings. And, rather than lose face, the buyer will frequently walk away from the last given price and later send a young boy back to buy the item. In this way, both the buyer and seller have avoided an unpleasant confrontation. This kind of bargaining is typical of that between men. But this kind of bargaining does not put as many coins in the pocket as do the more rapid transactions between women.

Men sell typically those items which have a more or less fixed price. For example, they sell all the meat in the market. Women tend to sell the more bargainable items such as vegetables and fruit. Sometimes these stalls are manned by a husband and wife. But it is typically the wife who bargains and the man who weighs the items and collects the money. Men pride themselves on their ability to bargain skillfully, but they leave the majority of bargaining encounters to their women.

Women use one kind of power and men another. Women initiate speech encounters which men shy away from. They are the ones who primarily reprimand children. They discuss in detail the shameful behavior of others in daily gossip and speak openly of those who *mangala-baraka*, steal honor away from the family. They are associated with direct criticism and haggling in markets. They are able to put others on the spot, to confront others with possibly offensive information where men cannot or prefer not. Women tend to be direct and open in manner. Men tend to conduct themselves with discretion and subtlety. Women dominate situations where directness is called for. Men, on the other hand, dominate situations where indirectness is desirable.

Indirectness as Ideal Style

Indirectness is desirable wherever respect is called for, and affront is to be avoided. In particular, it is desirable in all *kabary* (ceremonial speech situations). As mentioned before, the *kabary* performance is a formal dialogue between speechmakers representing different groups, for example, the hosts of a particular ceremony and those who have come to participate, or, as in the marriage request, the family of the girl and the family of the boy. Each speechmaker answers the other. That is, the first speechmaker completes one part of the *kabary* and the second speechmaker responds. The first speechmaker does not proceed without the support of the second speechmaker and the group he represents. Thus, a good deal of the *kabary* is spent eliciting the approval and support of the other group and affirming this support. For example, in the opening parts of a major *kabary*, the speechmaker asks for the blessing of the audience and they answer:

> *Mahaleova! Mahazaka! Andriamatoa o! Tsy ho solafaka, tsy ho tafintohina fa dia: mahavita soa aman-tsara.*
> Go ahead! Be able! Not to slip, not to bump into things, but to finish good and well.

Furthermore, the speechmaker stresses unity of both groups by making frequent reference to *isika mianankavy* (we family [inclusive of addressee]). Often reference to the inclusive *isika* will occur two or three times in one passage:

> *Dia misaotra an'Andriamanitra isika mianankavy, nohon'ny fanomezany tombon'andro antsika rehetra izao, ka tratry izao fotoana anankiray izay nokendrentsika mianankavy izao.*
> Then *we family* thank God for the gift of a tranquil day for *us all* at this time so one time has arrived now which was envisioned by *us family*.

Support and unity cannot be achieved where respect is not shown by the speech-maker. And the major way in which respect is expressed is by using indirect speech. A speechmaker who speaks directly, bluntly, affronts his audience. This effect is recognized by speechmakers, and they often make use of traditional sayings relevant to this behavior in the *kabary* itself. For example:

> *Tonga eto aminareo mianankavy izahay. Tsy mirodorodo toa omby manga, fa mitaitsika toa vorom-potsy, mandeha mora toa akanga diso an'Andringitra, ary mandeha miandana toy ny akoho hamonjy lapa.*
>
> We come here to you family. Not stampeding like wild bulls but approaching softly like a white bird and slowly, proceeding carefully like a lost pigeon and proceeding slowly like a chicken to reach the palace.

To speak indirectly is to speak with skill. Men and women alike consider indirect speech to be more difficult to produce than direct speech. Most villagers can tell you that one who speaks well *manolana teny* (twists words.) In *kabary*, a good speechmaker *miolaka* (winds in and out). The meaning of the utterance becomes clear gradually as the speaker alludes to the intent in a number of ways. This style of speech use is referred to in a number of proverbs often used by the villagers, for example:

> *Toy ny manoto, ka mamerina in-droa manan'antitra.*
> Like paint, one returns twice and makes it darker.

Each time a speechmaker alludes to the subject matter, the richer the meaning of that subject becomes. A good speechmaker can return to a subject in many ways. He is able to use proverbs (*ohabolana*), traditional sayings (*hainteny*), and elaborate metaphors to this end. One measures his ability in terms of this kind of richness. Speech which is used in this manner is *tsara lahatra* (well arranged). Speech which is simple and direct is *teny bango tokana* (speech of a single braid), that is, unsophisticated speech.

Men alone are considered to be able speechmakers. Even in everyday *resaka*, they are associated with the style of speaking required for the *kabary*: their requests are typically delayed and inexplicit, accusations imprecise, and criticisms subtle. They conduct themselves so as to minimize loss of face in a social situation. As women are associated with quite the opposite kind of behavior, they are in general considered unsuitable as speechmakers. The one exception to this is the *kabary* given by a woman of a boy's family to women of a girl's family in arranging for a marriage. The *kabary* is short and relatively simple, however, and many times it is replaced by simple *resaka*. Furthermore, it is a *kabary* to be heard by women only: 'When the mother of the boy speaks, it is only the women who listen. It is not right if there are men there,' commented one speechmaker.

Woman are considered able in handling everyday interactions within the village. The people with whom they interact most frequently are other women of the village and children. In fact, women with their young children form a semi-autonomous group within the village. They work together in the fields, and they relax together around the rice-mortars in the village courtyards. They have a more intimate relationship with one another than do men with each other or do men with women. (An exception to this generalization is the intimacy shown in joking relationships such as those which obtain between brothers-in-law, brother-and sister-in-law, and so on (M. Bloch, personal communication)). They use intimate terms of address and talk about intimate subjects: dysentery, intestinal worms, menstruation, malformed babies, sexual relations outside marriage. They are able to invade each other's personal space (Goffman 1971) in a way that would be taboo among most adult men. They dig into each other's hair looking for fleas. They look underneath a pregnant woman's dress to peek at the bands applied by the midwife to her womb. They bathe together in streams. Within this group, intimacy and directness is the norm.

Kabary, on the other hand, typically involve more than one village. They establish settings where people *tsy mifankazatra* (not accustomed to one another) interact—distant *havana* (kinsmen) and *vahiny* (strangers). Within this group, respect and indirectness are the norms.

We have, then, on the one hand, directness associated with women and children, and on the other hand, indirectness associated with men and intervillage situations. But directness and indirectness have further association. Indirectness is considered to be *fomban'ny ntaolo* (the way of one's ancestors). The use of *teny miolaka* (winding speech) represents to the villager a set of social attitudes held in the past, where respect and love for one another were always displayed. It is the traditional Malagasy speech-way. The use of direct speech, such as that of women and that of 'askings' between kinsmen, is associated with a loss of tradition, with contemporary mores. It is felt that today people speak directly because they do not value interpersonal relationships:

> The people today speak more directly than the ancestors. The people before took care to preserve relationships. Today people just say directly the faults of others, challenge the other. The ancestors could not answer like that. They made circles around the idea. Today few young people like the *kabary* and proverbs and traditional sayings. They don't like Malagasy language but foreign languages. Children are afraid of being beneath another child in knowledge of French or math. It is like our speechways were lost. . . . The government should give an examination, make everyone learn these Malagasy ways and the ways of mutual respect (speech-maker at Loharano).

As indicated in this quote, the change in speech use is thought to be due in part to the influence of European languages, in particular of French. Children learn foreign languages in school and they forget traditional speechways—this sentiment is expressed by many elders. The contrast in speech use for Europeans and for Malagasy is evident in urban contexts, where both interact in commercial settings. In these settings, the Malagasy must conform to the more direct, European-style service encounters. For the average villager from the countryside, these encounters are not always successful. For the European or European-trained Malagasy, these encounters are irritating and time-consuming. Some large business firms, in fact, recognize the difference in interactional style to the extent that particular employees are delegated to handle encounters with rural Malagasy. But further, Malagasy are expected to handle service encounters with Europeans in town markets, where *they* are the venders and Europeans form part of the clientele. It is appropriate, then, that women rather than men are recruited from the village to confront the European buyer. Directness and matter-of-factness are characteristic of both.

This final association of directness with the use of European languages helps to explain an important exception in the use of speech by men. There is one consistent situation in which men do not conform to the ideal style of indirect speech. When giving orders to cows, men speak in a terse and abrupt manner (Bloch MS.) But what is interesting is that these orders are couched in French rather than Malagasy. In particular, the French directional terms *à gauche!* and *à droite!* are used. There exists an equivalent set of directional terms in Malagasy. We must ask, then, why French is selected. At least a partial answer can be gained from this analysis, for the contexts in which men address cows necessitate immediate and direct action. For example, many tasks in cultivation are accomplished with cows. And in these contexts allusive speech is not effective. It is consistent with this analysis that men should choose to use French in such moments. Furthermore, animals occupy a low status. They are not approached with respect. The direct use of speech by men expresses this relationship (see also Bloch MS.)

INDIRECTNESS	DIRECTNESS
Men	*Women*
Skilled speech	*Unsophisticated speech*
Traditional speech ways	*Contemporary speech ways*
Malagasy language	*European languages*

We have presented a norm and an ideal speech style. Men tend to conduct themselves in public in accordance with the norm. Women tend to operate outside this norm. Further, the speech of men is thought (by men and women) to come closer to the ideal use of speech than the speech of women. Where subtlety and delicacy are required in social situations, men are recruited—witness the *kabary*. Where directness and explicitness are desirable in social situations, women are recruited.

Notes

1. Native terms and transcriptions from the native language follow the established conventions for written Malagasy.

References

Bloch, M. (MS.). *Why do Malagasy cows speak French?*
Goffman, E. (1971). *Relations in public.* New York: Harper & Row.

7

The Whole Woman: Sex and Gender Differences in Variation

PENELOPE ECKERT

The tradition of large-scale survey methodology in the study of variation has left a gap between the linguistic data and the social practice that yields these data. Since sociolinguistic surveys bring away little information about the communities that produce their linguistic data, correlations of linguistic variants with survey categories have been interpreted on the basis of general knowledge of the social dynamics associated with those categories. The success of this approach has depended on the quality of this general knowledge. The examination of variation and socioeconomic class has benefited from sociolinguists' attention to a vast literature on class and to critical analyses of the indices by which class membership is commonly determined. The study of gender and variation, on the other hand, has suffered from the fact that the amount of scientific attention given to gender over the years cannot begin to be compared with that given to class. Many current beliefs about the role of gender in variation, therefore, are a result of substituting popular (and unpopular) belief for social theory in the interpretation of patterns of sex correlations with variation.

Sociolinguists are acutely aware of the complex relation between the categories used in the socioeconomic classification of speakers and the social practice that underlies these categories. Thus, we do not focus on the objectivized indices used to measure class (such as salary, occupation, and education) in analyzing correlations between linguistic and class differences, even when class identification is based on these indices. Rather, we focus more and more on the relation of language use to the everyday practice that constitutes speakers' class-based social participation and identity in the community. Thus, explanations take into consideration interacting dynamics such as social group and network membership (Labov, 1972b; Milroy, 1980), symbolic capital and the linguistic marketplace (Bourdieu & Boltanski, 1975; Sankoff & Laberge, 1978; Thibault, 1983), and local identity (Labov, 1972c, 1980). The same can be said to some extent of work on ethnicity and variation, where researchers have interpreted data on ethnic differences in variation in terms of complex interactions between ethnicity, group history, and social identity (Horvath & Sankoff, 1987; Labov, 1972b; Laferriere, 1979). The study of the sociolinguistic construction of the biological categories of age and sex, on the other hand, has so far received less sophisticated attention (Eckert, Edwards, & Robins, 1985). The age continuum is commonly divided into equal chunks with no particular attention to the relation between these chunks and the life stages that make age socially significant. Rather, when the full age span is considered in community studies, the age continuum is generally interpreted as representing continuous apparent time. At some point, the individual's progress through normative life stages (e.g., school, work, marriage, childrearing, retirement) might be considered rather than, or in addition to, chronological age. Some work has explored the notion of life stage. The very apparent lead of preadolescents and adolescents in sound change has led some researchers to separate those groups in community studies (Macaulay, 1977; Wolfram, 1969), and some attention has been focused on the significance of these life stages in variation (Eckert, 1988; Labov, 1972b). There has also been some speculation about changes of speakers' relation to the linguistic marketplace in aging (Eckert, 1984; Labov, 1972a; Thibault, 1983). Most interestingly, there have been examinations of the relation of age groups to historical periods of social change in the community (Clermont & Cedergren, 1978; Laferriere, 1979). But taken together, these studies are bare beginnings and do not constitute a reasoned and coherent approach to the sociolinguistic significance of biological age.

Like age, sex is a biological category that serves as a fundamental basis for the differentiation of roles, norms, and expectations in all societies. It is these roles, norms, and expectations that constitute gender, the social construction of sex. Although differences in patterns of variation between men and women are a function of gender and only indirectly a function of sex (and, indeed, such gender-based variation occurs within, as well as between, sex groups), we have been examining the interaction between gender and variation by correlating variables with sex rather than gender differences. This has been done because although an individual's gender-related place in society is a multidimensional complex that can only be characterized through careful analysis, his or her sex is generally a readily observable binary variable, and inasmuch as sex can be said to be a rough statistical indication of gender, it has been reasonable to substitute the biological category for the social in sampling. However, because information about the individual's sex is easily accessible, data can be gathered without any inquiry into the construction of gender in that community. As a result, since researchers have not had to struggle to find the categories in question, they tend to fall back on unanalyzed notions about gender to interpret whatever sex correlations emerge in the data and not to consider gender where there are no sex correlations.

Gender differences are exceedingly complex, particularly in a society and era where women have been moving self-consciously into the marketplace and calling traditional gender roles into question. Gender roles and ideologies create different ways for men and women to experience life, culture, and society. Taking this as a basic approach to the data on sex differences in variation, there are a few assumptions one might start with. First, and perhaps most important, there is no apparent reason to believe that there is a simple, constant relation between gender and variation. Despite increasingly complex data on sex differences in variation, there remains a tendency to seek a single social construction of sex that will explain all of its correlations with variation. This is reflected in the use of a single coefficient for sex effects in variable rule or regression analyses of variation. This perspective limits the kind of results that can be obtained, since it is restricted to confirming the implicit hypothesis of a single type of sex effect or, worse, to indicating that there is no effect at all. Second, we must carefully separate our interpretation of sex differences in variation from artifacts of survey categories. I would argue that sociolinguists tend to think of age and class as continua and gender as an opposition, primarily because of the ways in which they are determined in survey research. But just as the class effect on variation may be thought of in terms of the binary bourgeois-working class opposition (Rickford, 1986), and just as there is reason to believe that the age continuum is interrupted by discontinuities in the effects of different life stages on people's relation to society and, hence, on language, variation based on gender may not always be adequately accounted for in terms of a binary opposition.

Interpretations of Sex Differences in Variation

There is a general misconception among writers who do not deal directly with variation that women's speech is more conservative than men's. Indeed, women do tend to be more conservative than men in their use of those vernacular forms that represent stable social variables. On the other hand, the very earliest evidence on variation (Gauchat, 1905) showed women leading in sound change, a finding that has been repeated in Labov's work in New York City (1966) and Philadelphia (1984), in Cedergren's work in Panama (1973), and in my own work in the Detroit suburbs. If these trends were universal, the coefficient of the sex variable (1 = female, 0 = male) in a variable rule or regression analysis of variation would always have positive sign for changes in progress and negative sign for stable variables.

But the picture is not quite as simple as this generalization suggests. First of all, men do lead in some sound changes. Trudgill found men leading in most changes in Norwich (1972a), and Labov (1972c) found men leading in some changes in Martha's Vineyard (1972) and Philadelphia (1984). Thus, there is every reason to assume that sex differences may vary from one variable to another. As Labov argued (1984), one might expect different sex correlations with old or new changes, for instance. This could still all be represented by a single sex effect in a statistical analysis, but the sign of the effect would depend on the particular variable. Second, sex does not have the same effect on language use everywhere in the population. Women's overall lead in the population could hide a variety of complex patterns among other social parameters, the simplest of which would be a sexual crossover along the socioeconomic hierarchy. Labov found just such a pattern in Philadelphia, for several vowels, with women leading at the lower end of the socioeconomic hierarchy and lagging at the upper end. Statistical analyses in these contexts require more than a single sex effect; either an interaction should be included or separate analyses done for women and men. Not only is it a mistake to claim that women are more or less innovative than men, but at this point in our research it is a mistake to claim any kind of constant constraint associated with gender. It is, above all, this mistake that characterizes much current work on sex differences in variation. It is commonplace for sociolinguists to allow the gender categories that they use to classify speakers (i.e., male vs. female) to guide their thinking about the effects of gender in variation. In particular, men and women are perceived as categorically different, indeed opposite and opposed, in their use of linguistic variables.

Hierarchy

Labov's (1966) original findings in New York City clearly lined up socioeconomic class, style, sound change, prestige, and evaluation on a single axis. The hierarchical socioeconomic continuum is also a continuum of linguistic change, wherein extent of historical change correlates inversely with socioeconomic status. At any place along this continuum, speech style reproduces this continuum, with each speaker's stylistic continuum from more casual to more careful speech reflecting a segment of the socioeconomic continuum. A causal connection between the two is based on the assumption that speakers look upward in the socioeconomic hierarchy for standards of correctness and feel constrained in their formal interactions to "accommodate" upward. Thus, there is a folk connection between old and new, formal and informal, better and worse, correct and incorrect. The notion of conservatism in language, then, takes on a simultaneously historical and social meaning. Finally, responses to matched guise tests confirm that members of the community associate the use of linguistic variables with individuals' worth in the marketplace. With this overwhelming stratificational emphasis in the study of variation, sex differences in behavior placed along this continuum are seen in relation to it; hence, when men and women differ in their use of sound change, this tends to be explained in terms of their different orientation to class.

Labov and Trudgill have both emphasized a greater orientation to community prestige norms as the main driving force in women's, as opposed to men's, linguistic behavior. Trudgill's findings in Norwich led him to see women as overwhelmingly conservative, as they showed men leading in most change. Furthermore, women in his sample tended to overreport their use of prestige forms and men tended to underreport theirs. He therefore argued that women and men respond to opposed sets of norms: women to overt, standard-language prestige norms and men to covert, vernacular prestige norms. Overt prestige attaches to refined qualities, as associated with the cosmopolitan marketplace and its standard language, whereas covert prestige attaches to masculine, "rough and tough" qualities. Trudgill (1972b:182–183) speculated that women's overt prestige orientation was a result of their powerless position in society. He argued that inasmuch as society does not allow women to advance their power or status through action in the marketplace, they are thrown upon their symbolic resources, including language, to enhance their social position. This is certainly a reasonable hypothesis, particularly since it was arrived at to explain data in which women's speech was overwhelmingly conservative. However, what it assumes more specifically is that women respond to their powerlessness by developing linguistic strategies for upward mobility, that is, that the socioeconomic hierarchy is the focus of social strategies. There are alternative views of exactly what social strategies are reflected in women's conservatism. An analysis that emphasizes the power relations implicit in the stratificational model was put forth by Deuchar (1988), who argued that women's conservative linguistic behavior is a function of basic power relations in society. Equating standard speech with politeness, she built on Brown's (1980) and Brown and Levinson's (1987) analyses of politeness as a face-saving strategy, arguing that the use of standard language is a mechanism for maintaining face in interactions in which the woman is powerless.

I would argue that elements of these hypotheses are correct but that they are limited by the fact that they are designed to account for one aspect of women's linguistic behavior only: those circumstances under which women's language is more conservative than men's. Based on the multiple patterns of sex, class, and age difference that he found in Philadelphia sound changes in progress, Labov (1984) sought to explain why women are more conservative in their use of stable variables but less conservative in their use of changes in progress and why women lead men in some changes and not in others. Although his data do not show women being particularly conservative, he based his analysis on the assumption that women's linguistic choices are driven by prestige. What he sought to explain, therefore, are cases where women's behavior is not conservative. Based on his Philadelphia data, Labov argued that women lag in the use of variants that are stigmatized within the larger community, that is, stable sociolinguistic variables and changes in progress that are sufficiently old and visible as to be stigmatized within the larger community. Women's behavior in these cases, then, is driven by global prestige norms. At the same time, women lead in changes that are still sufficiently limited to the neighborhood and local community to carry local prestige without having attracted a stigma in the larger Philadelphia community. In this case, Labov argued, women's behavior is driven by local prestige norms. If this explanation accounts for the Philadelphia data, it does not cover the New York City cases of (aeh) and (oh) (Labov, 1966), where women led in sound changes that had grown old and stigmatized. But more important, I can see no independent reason to seek explanations for women's behavior in prestige.

It is important to note at this point that three kinds of prestige have been put forth so far: (a) global prestige, based on norms imposed in the standard language marketplace; (b) covert prestige, based on opposition to those norms; and (c) local prestige, based on membership in the local community. Although the notion of covert prestige has come under attack, and conflated by some with local prestige, I have argued that all three of these forces play a role in variation (Eckert, 1989b). Later in this article, I suggest that not prestige but power is the most appropriate underlying sociological concept for the analysis of gender-based linguistic variation.

Sex Differences as Opposition

If the focus on class as a continuum has led to the interpretation of sex differences in speech as differences in orientation to the class hierarchy, the focus on sex as a two-way opposition has led also to interpreting sex differences as sex markers. Brown and Levinson (1979) argued against the treatment of sociolinguistic variables as markers, pointing out that the correlations may well be masking intervening variables. Although much work on phonological variation does not explicitly refer to variables as markers, the view of variables as markers is implicit when linguists attribute individuals' use or nonuse of a variable to a desire to stress or deny membership in the category with which it is being correlated at the moment. Related to the view of sex differences as markers is the oppositional view of gender differences in variation—a reification of a particular view of gender deriving from the ease of identifying individuals' sex category membership and reflecting the common expression "the opposite sex." Two instances can serve as examples in relation to gender.

Hindle (1979) examined one female speaker's use of variables in three situations: at work, at the dinner table with her husband and a friend (Arvilla Payne, the fieldworker), and in a weekly all-women's card game. Based on an assumption that speakers will implement vernacular sound changes more in egalitarian situations than in hierarchical ones, Hindle's initial hypothesis was that the speaker would show more extreme (vernacular) forms at the dinner table with her husband and a friend, because he believed social relations in that setting to be less hierarchical than in the other settings. As it turned out, she showed more advanced change in the card game. One might argue that this does not disprove Hindle's underlying assumption, that speakers show more vernacular variants in more egalitarian situations, since there is reason to believe that relations among a group of women playing cards on a weekly basis are less hierarchical than those between a husband and wife—perhaps particularly in the presence of a third person. However, he chose to attribute the use of extreme variants in a change, in which women lead community-wide, to accommodation to the group of women.

The theory of accommodation depends on the notion of marker, and this explanation essentially asserts that the speaker's use of the change among women was an attempt to mark herself as a fellow woman. One might consider, however, that her enhanced use of this phonological change at the card game is related to an affirmation of—indeed, perhaps a competition among equals for—some aspect of social identity that has nothing at all to do with gender. In other words, that these women are together in a particular set of social relationships that happen among women encourages them to emphasize some aspect of their social identities.

Whereas Hindle has attributed this woman's extreme use of a sound change to accommodation to women, others have attributed similar behavior to differentiation from men. Tony Kroch has argued that the curvilinear pattern frequently found in the socioeconomic stratification of linguistic variables is due to male speech only. Specifically, he speculated that if the sexes are examined separately, women's speech will show a linear pattern, reflecting the regular spread of sound change upward from the lowest socioeconomic group. The curvilinear pattern, then, is the result of a sudden drop in the use of extreme variables by men in the lowest socioeconomic group in relation to the adjacent higher group. This drop, according to Kroch, is the result of an avoidance on the part of men in this socioeconomic group of what they perceive as a female speech pattern. Labov (1984) found the pattern that Kroch predicted for the raising of the nucleus in Philadelphia (aw) (Figure 7.1), and Guy, Horvath, Vonwiller, Daisley, and Rogers (1986) found it for the Australian Question Intonation (Figure 7.2).

If one were prepared to accept this argument, Guy et al.'s data are more convincing than Labov's. However, in both cases, one could argue that it is only the lower working-class men's divergence from a linear pattern that creates enough of a woman's lead for it to acquire significance. In the case of Philadelphia (aw), aside from the working-class men's sudden downturn in use, the men lead the women in change in all socioeconomic groups. In the case of Australian Question Intonation, although the women lead in the middle class, there is virtually no sex difference in the upper working class. The lower working-class men's perception of the pattern, then, would have to be based on the speech of women at a considerable social remove—a remove that itself could be as salient as the sex difference. I venture to believe that if the pattern had been the other way around, with the lower working-class women showing the downturn, the typical explanation would have attributed their conservatism to prestige factors and upward mobility. I seriously doubt that these men's motivation for conservatism is upward mobility, just as I doubt upward mobility as an explanation for women's conservatism. But above all, it is problematic to seek the explanation of their behavior in simple differentiation from the "opposite" sex group.

I do not mean to argue that speakers never associate specific variables with gender, nor would I argue that there are no cases in which men or women avoid variables that they perceive as inappropriately gender marked. I would not even argue against the claim that men are more likely to avoid such variables than women, since there are greater constraints on men to be gender-appropriate in certain symbolic realms. However, I believe that variables that function as something like

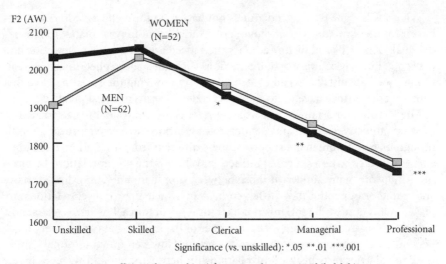

Figure 7.1 Occupation coefficients for F2 of (aw) for men and women in Philadelphia neighborhoods (from Labov, 1984).

gender markers must have some iconic value. The Arabic palatalization discussed by Haeri (1989) is a candidate for such a variable, although that case also points to intervening variables (Haeri, personal communication). But, as Brown and Levinson (1979) pointed out, a correlation with a particular social category may mask some other attribute that is also associated with that category. One that comes easily to mind in relation to gender is power. This could clearly apply in the case of Australian Question Intonation. Guy et al. (1986) described this intonation pattern as a confirmation-seeking strategy, which one can assume is associated with subordination regardless of sex (Baroni & d'Urso, 1984).

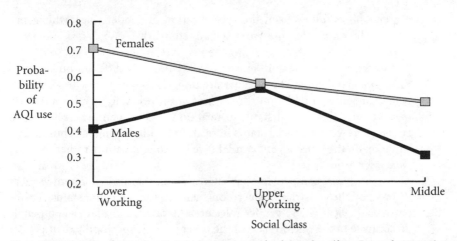

Figure 7.2 Probability of Australian Question Intonation use by class and sex (from Guy et al., 1986:37).

What I will argue is that gender does not have a uniform effect on linguistic behavior for the community as a whole, across variables, or for that matter for any individual. Gender, like ethnicity and class and indeed age, is a social construction and
may enter into any of a variety of interactions with other social phenomena. And although sociolinguists have had some success in perceiving the social practice that
constitutes class, they have yet to think of gender in terms of social practice.

There is one important way in which gender is not equivalent to categories like
class or ethnicity. Gender and gender roles are normatively reciprocal, and although men and women are supposed to be different from each other, this difference is expected to be a source of attraction. Whereas the power relations between
men and women are similar to those between dominant and subordinate classes
and ethnic groups, the day-to-day context in which these power relations are
played out is quite different. It is not a cultural norm for each working-class individual to be paired up for life with a member of the middle class or for every black
person to be so paired up with a white person. However, our traditional gender
ideology dictates just this kind of relationship between men and women. If one
were to think of variables as social markers, then, one might expect gender markers to behave quite differently from markers of class or ethnicity. Whereas the aggressive use of ethnic markers (i.e., frequent use of the most extreme variants) is
generally seen as maintaining boundaries—as preventing closeness—between
ethnic groups, the aggressive use of gender markers is not. By the same token, the
aggressive use of gender markers is not generally seen as a device for creating or
maintaining solidarity within the category. To the extent that masculine or femi-
nine behavior marks gender, its use by males and females respectively is more a
device for competing with others in the same category and creating solidarity with
those in the other category, and aggressive cross-sex behavior is seen as designed
to compete with members of the other sex for the attention of members of the
same sex.

Two other things follow from the specialization of gender roles, which may
apply also to other kinds of differences such as ethnicity.

1. To the extent that male and female roles are not only different but reciprocal, members of either sex category are unlikely to compete with (i.e., evaluate their status in relation to) members of the other. Rather, by and large,
   men perceive their social status in relation to other men, whereas women
   largely perceive their social status in relation to other women.[1] Thus, differentiation on the basis of gender might well be sought within, rather than between, sex groups.
2. Men and women compete to establish their social status in different ways, as
   dictated by the constraints placed on their sex for achieving status. This is
   particularly clear where gender roles are separate, and in fact when people
   do compete in the role domain of the other sex, it is specifically their gender
   identity that gets called into question.

Power, Status, and Other Things

All of the currently leading hypotheses about the effects of gender on variation recognize, however implicitly, that linguistic differences are a result of men's and women's place in society at a particular time and place. What differs in these hypotheses is the specificity and the depth of the causes in society and, hence, their changeability over time and from community to community.

Milroy (1980) traced sex differences in the use of vernacular variables to differences in the nature of men's and women's social networks—differences that are themselves a result of material factors. Based on the understanding that dense, multiplex, locally based social networks enforce the use of vernacular variables, Milroy argued that where economic circumstances allow women to form such networks, their speech takes on the characteristics of men's speech under the same conditions. In this case, then, the explanation for sex differences in variation does not lie in differences between men's and women's fundamental relations or orientation to society per se, but in the differences in the circumstances in which they normally find themselves. Closely related to the dynamics invoked by Milroy, particularly to the importance of work patterns on the nature of social networks and to social forces behind the use of vernacular or standard language, is the notion of marketplace. Nichols (1983) showed that differences between women as well as between women and men can be a function of their access to jobs that determine their participation in the standard language marketplace (Sankoff & Laberge, 1978). Both Milroy's and Nichols' examples suggest that it is the configuration of contact and interaction created by economic conditions that ultimately determines individuals' linguistic patterns, and in both cases the linguistic patterns may be as changeable as the economic conditions that underlie them.

The purpose of these analyses is to show that gender differences in variation are attributable to social forces that attach to women by virtue of their place in the economy. And whereas common sense supports this view, it is also evident that although employment conditions may change, the underlying relations of power and status between men and women can remain quite unchanging. So whereas economic explanations focus on the marketplace, they attribute gender differences in language to social forces that could presumably continue to operate on the individual speaker regardless of his or her personal relation to the economy. Since actual power relations between men and women can be expected to lag behind (indeed perhaps be orthogonal to) changes in relative positions in the marketplace, one can expect such a dynamic in language to outlive any number of economic changes. One might argue that the socioeconomic hierarchy, in this case, is the least of women's problems, since their powerless position is brought home to them, in a very real sense, in every interaction. Women's inequality is built into the family, and it continues in the workplace, where women are constantly confronted with a double bind, since neither stereotypic female nor stereotypic male behavior is acceptable. Thus, one might expect that some gender differences in language are more resistant to small-scale economic differences. In particular, the common claim that women are more expressive with language (Sattel, 1983) resides in deeper differences than the vagaries of the local economy.

The domestication of female labor—according to Marx, one of the earliest manifestations of the division of labor—involves a strict division of roles, with men engaged in the public marketplace and women's activities restricted to the private, domestic sphere (Elshtain, 1981; Sacks, 1974). The man competes for goods and power in the marketplace in the name of the family and controls these within the family. Thus, although the woman is solely responsible for maintaining the domestic unit, she has no direct control over that unit's capital. Although a man's personal worth is based on the accumulation of goods, status, and power in the marketplace, a woman's worth is based on her ability to maintain order in, and control over, her domestic realm. Deprived of power, women can only gain compliance through the indirect use of a man's power or through the development of personal influence.

Since to have personal influence without power requires moral authority, women's influence depends primarily on the painstaking creation and elaboration of an image of the whole self as worthy of authority. Thus, women are thrown into the accumulation of symbolic capital. This is not to say that men are not also dependent on the accumulation of symbolic capital, but that symbolic capital is the *only* kind that women can accumulate with impunity. And, indeed, it becomes part of their men's symbolic capital and hence part of the household's economic capital. Whereas men can justify and define their status on the basis of their accomplishments, possessions, or institutional status, women must justify and define theirs on the basis of their overall character. This is why, in peasant communities as in working-class neighborhoods, the women who are considered local leaders typically project a strong personality and a strong, frequently humorous, image of knowing what is right and having things under control.

When social scientists say that women are more status conscious than men, and when sociolinguists pick this up in explaining sex differences in speech, they are stumbling on the fact that, deprived of power, women must satisfy themselves with status. It would be more appropriate to say that women are more status-*bound* than men. This emphasis on status consciousness suggests that women only construe status as being hierarchical (be it global or local hierarchy) and that they assert status only to gain upward mobility. But status is not only defined hierarchically; an individual's status is his or her place, however defined, in the group or society. It is this broader status that women must assert by symbolic means, and this assertion will be of hierarchical status when a hierarchy happens to be salient. An important part of the explanation for women's innovative and conservative patterns lies, therefore, in their need to assert their membership in all of the communities in which they participate, since it is their authority, rather than their power in that community, that assures their membership. Prestige, then, is far too limited a concept to use for the dynamics at work in this context.

Above all, gender relations are about power and access to property and services, and whatever symbolic means a society develops to elaborate gender differences (such as romance and femininity) serve as obfuscation rather than explanation. Whenever one sees sex differences in language, there is nothing to suggest that it is not power that is at issue rather than gender per se. The claim that working-class men's speech diverges from working-class women's speech in an effort to avoid sounding like women reflects this ambiguity, for it raises the issue of the interaction between gender and power. Gender differentiation is greatest in those segments of society where power is the scarcest—at the lower end of the socioeconomic hierarchy, where women's access to power is the greatest threat to men. There is every reason to believe that the lower working-class men's sudden downturn in the use of Australian Question Intonation shown in Guy et al. (1986) is an avoidance of the linguistic expression of subordination by men in the socioeconomic group that can least afford to sound subordinate.

For similar reasons of power, it is common to confuse femininity and masculinity with gender, and perhaps nowhere is the link between gender and power clearer. Femininity is a culturally defined form of mitigation or denial of power, whereas masculinity is the affirmation of power. In Western society, this is perhaps most clearly illustrated in the greater emphasis on femininity in the south, where regional economic history has domesticized women and denied them economic power to a greater degree than it has in the industrial north (Fox-Genovese, 1988). The commonest forms of femininity and masculinity are related to actual physical power. Femininity is associated with small size, clothing and adornment that inhibit and/or do not stand up to rough activity, delicacy of movement, quiet and high pitched voice, friendly demeanor, politeness. The relation between politeness and powerlessness has already been emphasized (Brown, 1980) and surfaces in a good deal of the literature on gender differences in language. Although all of these kinds of behavior are eschewed by men at the lower end of the socioeconomic hierarchy, they appear increasingly in male style as one moves up the socioeconomic hierarchy until, in the upper class, what is called effeminacy may be seen as the conscientious rejection of physical power by those who exercise real global power (Veblen, 1931) by appropriating the physical power of others.

The methodological consequences of these considerations is that we should expect to see larger differences in indications of social category membership among women than among men. If women are more constrained to display their personal and social qualities and memberships, we would expect these expressions to show up in their use of phonological variables. This necessitates either a careful analysis of statistical interaction, or separate analysis of the data from each gender group, before any comparison.

Gender and Adolescent Social Categories

In this section, I discuss some evidence from adolescent phonological variation to illustrate the complexity of gender in the social scheme of things. Adolescents are quite aware of the gender differences I have discussed, particularly since they are at a life stage in which the issue of gender roles becomes crucial. By the time they arrive in high school, adolescent girls (particularly those who have been tomboys) are getting over the early shock of realizing that they do not have equal access to power. One girl told me of the satisfaction it still gives her to think back to the time in elementary school when she and her best friend beat up the biggest male bully in their class and of the difficult adjustment it had been to finding less direct means of controlling boys. In fact, she was very attractive and was aware but not particularly pleased that her power in adolescence to snub troublesome males was as great as her past power to beat them up.

Whether or not they wielded any direct power in their childhoods, adolescent girls know full well that their only hope is through personal authority. In secondary school, this authority is closely tied up with popularity (Eckert, 1989a, 1990), and as a result, girls worry about and seek popularity more than boys. And although boys are far from unconcerned about popularity, they need it less to exert influence. For a boy can indeed gain power and status through direct action, particularly through physical prowess. Thus, when they reach high school, most girls and boys have already accepted to some extent that they will have different routes to social status. In many important ways, boys can acquire power and status through the simple performance of tasks or display of skills. A star varsity athlete, for instance, regardless of his character or appearance, can enjoy considerable status. There is virtually nothing, however, that a girl lacking in social or physical gifts can do that will accord her social status. In other words, whereas it is enough for a boy to have accomplishments of the right sort, a girl must be a certain sort of person. And just as the boy must show off his accomplishments, the girl must display her persona. One result of this is that girls in high school are more socially constrained than boys. Not only do they monitor their own behavior and that of others more closely, but they maintain more rigid social boundaries, since the threat of being associated with the wrong kind of person is far greater to the individual whose status depends on who she appears to be rather than what she does. This difference plays itself out linguistically in the context of class-based social categories.

Two hegemonous social categories dominate adolescent social life in American public high schools (Eckert, 1989a). These categories represent opposed class cultures and arise through a conflict of norms and aspirations within the institution of the school. Those who participate in school activities and embrace the school as the locus of their social activities and identities constitute, in the high school, a middle-class culture. In the Detroit area, where the research I report on was done, members of this category are called "Jocks" whether or not they are athletes, and they identify themselves largely in opposition to the "Burnouts." Burnouts, a working-class culture oriented to the blue collar marketplace, do not accept the school as the locus of their operations; rather, they rebel to some extent against school activities and the authority they represent and orient themselves to the local, and the neighboring urban, area. The Burnouts' hangouts are local parks, neighborhoods, bowling alleys, and strips. They value adult experience and prerogatives and pursue a direct relation with the adult community that surrounds them. The school mediates this relation for the Jocks, on the other hand, who center their social networks and activities in the school. The Jocks and the Burnouts have very different means of acquiring and defining the autonomy that is so central to adolescents. Whereas the Jocks seek autonomy in adult-like roles in the corporate context provided by the school institution, the Burnouts seek it in direct relations with the adult resources of the local area.

Within each category, girls and boys follow very different routes to achieve power and status. The notion of resorting to the manipulation of status when power is unavailable is in fact consciously expressed in the adolescent community. Girls complain that boys can do real things, whereas boys complain that girls talk and scheme rather than doing real things. By "real" things, they mean those things that reflect skills other than the purely social and that reflect personal, and specifically physical, prowess. Boys are freer in general. For example, Burnout boys can go to Detroit alone, whereas girls must go under their protection; this seriously curtails a Burnout girl's ability to demonstrate urban autonomy. The Jock boys can also assert their personal autonomy through physical prowess. Although it is not "cool" for a Jock boy to fight frequently, the public recognition that he could is an essential part of his Jock image. In addition, Jock boys can gain public recognition through varsity sports on a level that girls cannot. Thus, the girls in each social category must devote a good deal of their activity to developing and projecting a "whole person" image designed to gain them influence within their own social category. The female Jocks must aggressively develop a Jock image, which is essentially friendly, outgoing, active, clean-cut, all-American. The female Burnouts must aggressively develop a Burnout image, which is essentially tough, urban, "experienced." As a result, the symbolic differences between Jocks and Burnouts are clearly more important for girls than for boys. In fact, there is less contact between the two categories among girls, and there is far greater attention to maintaining symbolic differences on all levels-in clothing and other adornment, in demeanor, in publicly acknowledged substance use and sexual activity. There is, therefore, every reason to predict that girls also show greater differences than boys in their use of any linguistic variable that is associated with social category membership or its attributes.

I have shown elsewhere that the most extreme users of phonological variables in my adolescent data are those who have to do the greatest amount of symbolic work to affirm their membership in groups or communities (Eckert, 1989b). Those whose status is clearly based on "objective" criteria can afford to eschew symbolization. It does not require much of a leap of reasoning to see that women's and men's ways of establishing their status would lead to differences in the use of symbols. The constant competition over externals, as discussed in Maltz and Borker (1982), would free males from the use of symbols. Women, on the other hand, are constrained to exhibit constantly who they are rather than what they can do, and who they are is defined with respect primarily to other women.

Phonological Variation

The following data on phonological variation among Detroit suburban adolescents provide some support for the discussion of the complexity of gender constraints in variation. The data were gathered in individual sociolinguistic interviews during 2 years of participant observation in one high school in a suburb of Detroit. During this time, I followed one graduating class through its last 2 years of high school, tracing social networks and examining the nature of social identity in this adolescent community. The school serves a community that is almost entirely white, and although the population includes a variety of eastern and western European groups, ethnicity is downplayed in the Community and in the school and does not determine social groups. The community covers a socioeconomic span from lower working class through upper middle class, with the greatest representation in the lower middle class.

The speakers in the Detroit area are involved in the Northern Cities Chain Shift (Labov, Yaeger, & Steiner, 1972), a pattern of vowel shifting involving the fronting of low vowels and the backing and lowering of mid vowels (Figure 7.3). The older changes in this shift are the fronting of (ae) and (a), and the lowering and fronting of (oh). The newer ones are the backing of (e) and (uh).

The following analysis is based on impressionistic phonetic transcription of the vocalic variables from taped free-flowing interviews.[2] A number of variants were distinguished for each vowel in the shift. Both (e) and (uh) have raised, backed, and lowered variants. Backing is the main direction of movement of both (e) and (uh). In each case, two degrees of backing were distinguished:

$$[e] > [\varepsilon^{\flat}] > [\Lambda]$$
$$[\Lambda] > [\Lambda^{\flat}] > [\mathfrak{I}]$$

Both variables also show lowering: [æ] for (e) and [a] for (uh). There are also some raised variants [ɛ'] and [I] for (e) (the latter occurs particularly in *get*) and [ə] and [U] for (uh). The lowest value for (ae) is [æ']. The movement of the nucleus of (ae) has clearly been toward peripherality (Labov, Yaeger, & Steiner, 1972), as the higher variants show fronting:

$$[æ'] > [\varepsilon'] > [e] > [\varepsilon'] > [e]$$

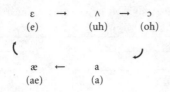

ε   →   ʌ   →   ɔ
(e)   (uh)   (oh)

æ   ←   a
(ae)   (a)

Figure 7.3   The Northern Cities Chain Shift

Two degrees of fronting were distinguished for (a):

[a] > [a] > [æ˘]

(a) also showed some raising to [aˆ] and [ʌ]. Finally, three degrees of fronting were distinguished for (oh):

[ɔ] > [ɔˇ] > [a] > [a]

(oh) also fronted occasionally to [ʌ]. Extreme variants in the main direction of change were chosen for each of the variables to represent rule application. These extreme variants are:

   (ae) nucleus = [e] or [ɛ˘], with or without offglide
   (a)   [æ] or [aˇ]
   (oh) [aˇ] or [a]
   (uh) [a] or [ɔ]
   (e)   [ʌ] or [U]

The two common social correlations for phonological variables in these data are with social category membership and sex. Sex and category affiliation are not simply additive but manifest themselves in a variety of ways among these changes. They interact in ways that are particularly revealing when seen in the context of the overall pattern of linguistic change. Table 7.1 contains a cross-tabulation by social category and sex of the percentage of advanced tokens for each vowel. Differences in the percentages shown in Table 7.1 between boys and girls and between Jocks and Burnouts for each of the changes are displayed in Figure 7.4: one line shows the lead of the girls over boys, whereas the other shows the lead of the Burnouts over the Jocks, for each of the changes in the Northern Cities Shift. As Figure 7.4 shows, the girls have the clearest lead in the oldest changes in the Northern Cities Chain Shift whereas social category differences take over in the later changes. Note that each line dips into negative figures once—at each end of the shift. The boys have a slight lead in the backing of (e) and the Jocks have a slight lead in the raising of (ae). The statistical significance of each of the differ-

TABLE 7.1 Percentage of advanced tokens of the five vowels for each combination of social category and sex (numbers of tokens in parentheses)

	Boys		Girls	
	Jocks	Burnouts	Jocks	Burnouts
(ae)	39.7 $\left(\frac{211}{531}\right)$	35.3 $\left(\frac{101}{286}\right)$	62.2 $\left(\frac{244}{392}\right)$	62.0 $\left(\frac{178}{287}\right)$
(a)	21.4 $\left(\frac{117}{548}\right)$	22.0 $\left(\frac{77}{350}\right)$	33.8 $\left(\frac{152}{450}\right)$	38.2 $\left(\frac{134}{350}\right)$
(oh)	7.4 $\left(\frac{44}{598}\right)$	10.2 $\left(\frac{34}{333}\right)$	29.8 $\left(\frac{134}{450}\right)$	38.7 $\left(\frac{131}{338}\right)$
(e)	26.2 $\left(\frac{146}{557}\right)$	33.2 $\left(\frac{113}{340}\right)$	23.8 $\left(\frac{103}{433}\right)$	30.9 $\left(\frac{103}{333}\right)$
(uh)	24.6 $\left(\frac{122}{496}\right)$	35.3 $\left(\frac{65}{184}\right)$	25.8 $\left(\frac{94}{364}\right)$	43.0 $\left(\frac{107}{249}\right)$

ences is given in Table 7.2. A treatment of variation that views variables as markers would call the fronting of (ae) and (a) "sex markers," the backing of (uh) and (e) "social category markers," and the fronting of (oh) both.

In an earlier article, I expressed some puzzlement about the lack of sex differences in the backing of (uh), having expected a simple relation between sex and any sound change (Eckert, 1988). More careful examination of the backing of (uh), however, shows that a simplistic view of the relation between gender and sound change prevented me from exploring other ways in which gender might be manifested in variation. In fact, gender plays a role in four out of the five changes in the Northern Cities Chain Shift, although it correlates only with three out of five of the changes, and the role it plays is not the same for all changes.

As can be seen in Table 7.2 and Figure 7.4, the oldest change in the Northern Cities Chain Shift, the raising of (ae), shows no significant association with category membership in the sample as a whole. The same is true within each sex group taken separately (girls: $p < .96$; boys: $p < .22$). However, the girls lead by far in this change. The second change in the Northern Cities Shift, the fronting of (a), also shows only a sex difference, once again with the girls leading. The lack of category effect holds true within each sex group considered separately (girls: $p < .19$; boys: $p < .76$).

TABLE 7.2 Significance (yes or no) of social constraints on the vowel changes that constitute the Northern Cities Chain Shift (pl-values of log-likelihood test calculated for each constraint separately using variable rule program on data of Table 7.1)

	Sex		Social Category	
(ae)	yes	$(p < .001)$	no	$(p < .77)$
(a)	yes	$(p < .001)$	no	$(p < .16)$
(oh)[a]	yes	$(p < .0001)$	yes	$(p < .001)$
(uh)	no[b]	$(p < .04)$	yes	$(p < .001)$
(e)	no	$(p < .38)$	yes	$(p < .004)$

[a] Both constraints remain significant for (oh) when the effects of the other are taken into account.
[b] The sex effect loses significance ($p < .19$) for (uh) when social category is taken into account.

The lowering and fronting of (oh) shows a significant difference by both sex and social category, and these effects appear to operate additively in a variable rule analysis:

Overall tendency: 0.182
boys: 0.300   girls: 0.700
Jocks: 0.452   Burnouts: 0.548

When the sexes are separated, however, it turns out that the category difference is only significant among the girls ($p < .009$) and not the boys ($p < .14$).

In the backing of (uh), category membership correlates significantly with backing for the population as a whole, with Burnouts leading, but sex does not. When each sex is considered separately, however, it is clear that the category difference is much greater among the girls. The backing of (e) shows a significant category difference, with the Burnouts leading, but no significant sex difference. In this case, when the two sexes are considered separately, the category difference is the same among the girls and among the boys.

Figure 7.5 compares the differences in the percentages in Table 7.1 between the Jocks and Burnouts, within the girls' and boys' samples separately. None of these differences is significant for (a) and for (ae). For (e) they are significant and identical for the two sexes. For (oh) and (uh), however, there is a clear tendency for there to be greater social category differentiation among the girls than among the boys.

These results throw into question general statements that women lead in sound change or that sex differences are indicative of sound change. In fact, in my data, the greatest sex differences occur with the older—and probably less vital—changes, involving (ae), (a), and (oh). I would venture the following hypotheses about the relation of gender to the older and the newer changes in these data. It appears that in both sets of changes, the girls are using variation more than the

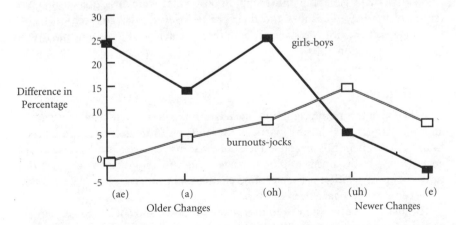

Figure 7.4 Contrast between girls and boys and between Burnouts and Jocks as differences in percentages when calculated for the combined data in Table 7.1.

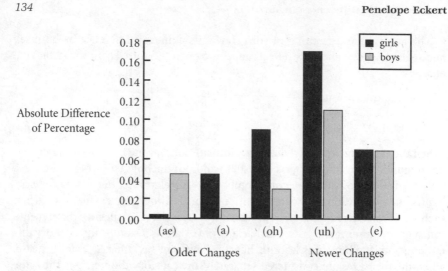

Figure 7.5 Absolute differences of percentages for Burnouts and Jocks, calculated separately for girls and boys (note that for (ae), Burnouts actually trail Jocks).

boys. In the case of the newer ones, the girls' patterns of variation show a greater difference between Jocks and Burnouts than do the boys'. In the case of the older ones, all girls are making far greater use than the boys of variables that are not associated with social category affiliation. I have speculated elsewhere that the newer changes, which are more advanced closer to the urban center, are ripe for association with counteradult norms (Eckert, 1987). The older changes, on the other hand, which have been around for some time and are quite advanced in the adult community, are probably not very effective as carriers of counteradult adolescent meaning, but they have a more generalized function associated with expressiveness and perhaps general membership. In both cases—the girls' greater differentiation of the newer changes and their greater use of older changes—the girls' phonological behavior is consonant with their greater need to use social symbols for self-presentation.

Conclusions

I would not, at this point, claim that the relation shown in these data between new and old changes is necessary, particularly in view of the fact that Labov (1984) found that women in Philadelphia led in new sound changes, whereas sex differences tended to disappear in older changes. It is apparent, then, that generalizations about the relation between sound change and gender are best deferred until more communities have been examined.

   The first clear conclusion from these data is that sex and social category are not necessarily independent variables but that they can interact in a very significant way. It is the nature of that interaction, which occurs here with (oh) and (uh), that is of interest in this article. It is not the case with these phonological variables that there are large sex differences in one category and not in the other. In other words, sex is rarely more "salient" in one category than the other. One certainly cannot say that the boys and/or girls are asserting their gender identities through language more in one category than in the other. Rather, there are greater category differences in one sex group than the other. In other words, category membership is more salient to members of one sex than the other; girls are asserting their category identities through language more than are the boys. This is consonant with the fact that girls are more concerned with category membership than boys, as well as with the fact that girls must rely more on symbolic manifestations of social membership than boys. And this is, in turn, the adolescent manifestation of the broader generalization that women, deprived of access to real power, must claim status through the use of symbols of social membership.

These data make it clear that the search for explanations of sex differences in phonological variation should be redirected. All of the demographic categories that we correlate with phonological variation are more complex than their labels would indicate. Indeed, they are more complex than many sociolinguistic analyses give them credit for. Some analyses of sex differences have suffered from lack of information about women. But it is more important to consider that where most analyses have fallen short has been in the confusion of social meaning with the analyst's demographic abstractions.

Notes

This work was supported by the Spencer Foundation and the National Science Foundation (BNS 8023291). I owe a great debt of thanks to David Sankoff for his very generous and important help with this article. The value of his suggestions for strengthening both the conception and the presentation of these arguments is immeasurable.

1. This is an oversimplification. Gender inequality imposes a canonical comparison, whereby higher and lower status accrue automatically to men and women, respectively. It is this inequality itself that leads to the tendency for intrasex comparisons and for the different terms on which men and women engage in these comparisons. Men tend to compare themselves with other men because women don't count, whereas women tend to compare themselves with other women with an eye to how that affects their relation to male-defined status. (My thanks to Jean Lave for helping me work out this tangle.)

2. The transcription of these data was done by Alison Edwards, Rebecca Knack, and Larry Diemer.

References

Baroni, Maria Rosa, & d'Urso, Valentina. (1984). Some experimental findings about the question of politeness and women's speech. *Language in Society* 13:67–72.
Bourdieu, Pierre, & Boltanski, Luc. (1975). Le fétichisme de la langue. *Actes de la recherche en sciences sociales* 4:2–32.

Brown, Penelope. (1980). How and why women are more polite: Some evidence from a Mayan community. In Sally McConnell-Ginet, Ruth A. Borker, & Nelly Furman (eds.), *Women and language in literature and society*. New York: Praeger. 111–136.

Brown, Penelope, & Levinson, Steven. (1979). Social structure, groups and interaction. In Klaus R. Scherer & Howard Giles (eds.), *Social markers in speech*. Cambridge: Cambridge University Press. 291–341.

———. (1987). *Politeness*. Cambridge: Cambridge University Press.

Cedergren, Henrietta. (1973). *The interplay of social and linguistic factors in Panama*. Ph.D. dissertation, Cornell University.

Clermont, Jean, & Cedergren, Henrietta. (1978). Les "R" de ma mère sont perdus dans l'air. In Pierrette Thibault (ed.), *Le français parlé: études sociolinguistiques*. Edmonton, Alberta: Linguistic Research. 13–28.

Deuchar, Margaret. (1988). A pragmatic account of women's use of standard speech. In Jennifer Coates & Deborah Cameron (eds.), *Women in their speech communities*. London: Longman. 27–32.

Eckert, Penelope. (1984). Age and linguistic change. In Jennie Keith & David I. Kertzer (eds.), *Age and anthropological theory*. Ithaca: Cornell University Press. 219–233.

———. (1987). The relative values of variables. In Keith Denning, Sharon Inkelas, Faye McNair-Knox, & John Rickford (eds.), *Variation in language: NWAV-XV*. Stanford, Department of Linguistics. 101–110.

———. (1988). Adolescent social structure and the spread of linguistic change. *Language in Society* 17:183–207.

———. (1989a) *Jocks and burnouts*. New York: Teachers College Press.

———. (1989b). *Social membership and linguistic variation*. Paper presented at NWAVE, Duke University.

———. (1990). Cooperative competition in adolescent "girl talk." *Discourse Processes* 13:91–122.

Eckert, Penelope, Edwards, Alison, & Robins, Lynne. (1985). *Social and biological categories in the study of linguistic variation*. Paper presented at NWAVE IV, Washington, DC.

Elshtain, Jean Bethke. (1981). *Public man, private woman*. Princeton: Princeton University Press.

Fox-Genovese, Elizabeth. (1988). *Within the plantation household*. Chapel Hill: University of North Carolina Press.

Gauchat, L. (1905). L'unité phonétique dans le patois d'une commune. In *Festshrift Heinrich Morf*. Halle: Max Niemeyer. 175–232.

Guy, G., Horvath, B., Vonwiller, J., Daisley, E., & Rogers, I. (1986). An intonational change in progress in Australian English. *Language in Society* 15:23–52.

Haeri, Niloofar. (1989). *Synchronic variation in Cairene Arabic: The case of palatalization*. Paper presented at Linguistic Society of America Annual Meeting, Washington, DC.

Hindle, Donald. (1979). *The social and situational conditioning of phonetic variation*. Ph.D. dissertation, University of Pennsylvania.

Horvath, Barbara, & Sankoff, David. (1987). Delimiting the Sydney speech community. *Language in Society* 16:179–204.

Labov, William. (1966). *The social stratification of English in New York City*. Washington, DC: Center for Applied Linguistics.

———. (1972a). Hypercorrection by the lower middle class as a factor in linguistic change. In William Labov (ed.), *Sociolinguistic patterns*. Philadelphia: University of Pennsylvania Press. 122–142.

———. (1972b). The linguistic consequences of being a lame. In William Labov (ed.), *Sociolinguistic patterns*. Philadelphia: University of Pennsylvania Press. 255–292.

———. (1972c). The social motivation of a sound change. In William Labov (ed.), *Sociolinguistic patterns*. Philadelphia: University of Pennsylvania Press. 1–42.

———. (1980). The social origins of sound change. In William Labov (ed.), *Locating language in time and space*. New York: Academic. 251–265.

———. (1984). *The intersection of sex and social factors in the course of language change*. Paper presented at NWAVE, Philadelphia.

Labov, W., Yaeger, M., & Steiner, R. (1972). *A quantitative study of sound change in progress*. Report on NSF project No. 65-3287.

Laferriere, Martha. (1979). Ethnicity in phonological variation and change. *Language* 55:603–617.

Macaulay, R. K. S. (1977). *Language, social class, and education*. Edinburgh: Edinburgh University Press.

Maltz, Daniel, & Borker, Ruth. (1982). A cultural approach to male-female miscommunication. In John J. Gumperz (ed.), *Language and social identity*. Cambridge: Cambridge University Press. 195–216.

Milroy, Lesley. (1980). *Language and social networks*. Oxford: Basil Blackwell.

Nichols, Patricia C. (1983). Linguistic options and choices for black women in the rural south. In Barrie Thorne, Cheris Kramarae, and Nancy Henley (eds.), *Language, gender and society*. Rowley, MA: Newbury House. 54–68.

Rickford, John. (1986). The need for new approaches to class analysis in sociolinguistics. *Language and communication* 6:215–221.

Sacks, Karen. (1974). Engels revisited. In M. Rosaldo & L. Lamphere (eds.), *Women, culture and society*. Stanford: Stanford University Press. 207–222.

Sankoff, David, & Laberge, Suzanne. (1978). The linguistic market and the statistical explanation of variability. In David Sankoff (ed.), *Linguistic variation: Models and methods*. New York: Academic. 239–250.

Sattel, Jack W. (1983). Men, inexpressiveness, and power. In Barrie Thorne, Cheris Kramarae, & Nancy Henley (eds.), *Language, gender and society*. Rowley, MA: Newbury House. 119–124.

Thibault, Pierrette. (1983). *Equivalence et grammaticalisation*. Ph.D. dissertation, Université de Montréal.

Trudgill, Peter. (1972a). Sex, covert prestige, and linguistic change in the urban British English of Norwich. *Language in Society* 1:179–195.

———. (1972b). *The social differentiation of English in Norwich*. Cambridge: Cambridge University Press.

Veblen, Thorstein. (1931). *The theory of the leisure class*. New York: Viking.

Wolfram, W. A. (1969). *A sociolinguistic description of Detroit Negro speech*. Washington, DC: Center for Applied Linguistics.

Part Three
Genre, Style, Performance

Metternich pointed out that one of the commonest uses of language was for the concealment of thought.

—*J.R. Firth*

Only VERY rarely does the spoken word mean what it professes to mean.
—*Paul Valery*

Most linguists and philosophers have difficulty with "non-serious" uses of language, whether these are irony, sarcasm, metaphors, lying, joking, or fantasizing. This is clearly illustrated in the exchange a few years ago between Jacques Derrida and John Searle over J. L. Austin's (1975:22) decision to exclude from his analysis of performatives, language "used not seriously but in many ways parasitic upon its normal use." Derrida teased Searle for his "confidence in the possibility of distinguishing 'standard' from 'non-standard,' 'serious' from 'non-serious,' 'normal' from 'abnormal,' 'citation' from 'non-citation,' 'void' from 'non-void,' 'literal' from 'metaphoric,' 'parasitical' from 'non-parasitical,' etc." Derrida's teasing, in part, consisted of making jokes (often relevant to the points he wishes to make) and then at the end asking whether he had taken Searle's arguments 'seriously.' Armchair linguists and philosophers can distinguish very easily and simply between 'serious' and 'non-serious' or 'literal' and 'metaphoric' because they deal with examples they (or their colleagues) have invented ('fictive discourse' in Smith's 1978 terms) and know *exactly* how these examples are to be interpreted.

Those who deal with language in use find the correspondence between form and function much less simple or direct. José Limón illustrates this by examining some examples of language that are both 'non-serious' (in the sense that they are intended to amuse) and 'very serious' (in the sense that the joking plays an important role in the society). From a few simple exchanges, Limón develops a "narrative of resistance" although the participants themselves provide an alternative interpretation.

A. L. Becker, in his "rhetorically based linguistics," aims to get away from "the world of delicate parsing" and the kind of relations "that grammarians talk about, often very intimidatingly." For many theoretical linguists language is a system *où tout se tient*, where everything hangs together. If you believe this, then you can hope to program a computer to deal with language. This is possible only if you deal with language abstracted from its context, since, as Becker observes, "language interaction is not a closed system (i.e., rule-governed)." Becker illustrates the complexity of understanding language by taking a short Burmese proverb as a text and showing how the apparently simple message may be more complex than a simple matching of syntactic form and lexical meaning might imply.

Richard Bauman shows how among coon hunters in Texas "stretching the truth" and even "[outright] lying" are not only accepted forms of behavior but even taken for granted. Contrary to the Gricean Cooperative Principle (Grice 1975), in which the assumption is that the participants are telling the truth, Bauman pointed out that "it is not at all surprising that parties on both sides of a dog trade should enter the transaction anticipating that the opposite party might lie about a dog and expect to be lied to in return." Grice's principle and its maxims have served as a fruitful stimulation for much work in philosophy and theoretical linguistics, but they are based on an idealization from actual speech behavior.

As part of his teasing, Derrida quoted Searle's justification for idealization in studying speech acts:

> In short, I am going to deal only with a simple and idealized case. This method, one of constructing idealized models, is analogous to the sort of theory construction that goes on in most sciences, e.g. the construction of economic models, or accounts of the solar system which treats planets as points. Without abstraction and idealization there is no systematization. (1969:56)

The success of an approach that requires considerable idealization away from actual language use is obvious in departments of theoretical linguistics, but their systems have only limited relevance for actual as opposed to idealized language. To understand how people use language it is necessary to look at the world with a broader view than the perspective of the scholar's study. The Chapters in Part Three give a few examples of observing interesting situations.

Suggestions for Further Reading

The starting point for all study of language in relation to culture is the volume edited by D. G. Mandelbaum, *Selected Writings of Edward Sapir: Language, Culture and Personality*. Sapir's writings are full of insights and acute observations that still provide guidance for how to look at language in use. Dell Hymes's collection, *Language in Culture and Society*, includes many provocative studies on this topic, as do R. Bauman and J. Sherzer's *Explorations in the Ethnography of Speaking* and J. Gumperz and D. Hymes's *Directions in Sociolinguistics*. A fine example of how to carry out such work is K. M. Basso's *Western Apache Language and Culture*. A different approach is shown in R. D. Abrahams, *The Man-of-Words in the West Indies*. R. Bauman deals with varieties of verbal art in *Verbal Art as Performance*. Several approaches to humor can be found in the volume edited by M. L. Apte, *Language and Humor*. The social significance of narratives is shown in B. Johnstone, *Stories, Community, Place*. Some of the liveliest work in this area has been by contextually sensitive folklorists. Two edited volumes, *Toward New Perspectives in Folklore* (A. Paredes and R. Bauman, eds.) and *Theorizing Folklore* (C. Briggs and A. Shuman, eds.), represent a wide and stimulating range of such studies. The relevance of Bakhtin's work for linguistic anthropology is clearly brought out in an article by J. Hill, "The refiguration of the anthropology of language."

References

Abrahams, Roger D. 1983. *The Man-of-Words in the West Indies: Performance and the Emergence of Creole Culture.* Baltimore: The Johns Hopkins University Press.

Apte, Mahadev L., ed. 1987. "Language and humor." *International Journal of the Sociology of Language,* vol. 65.

Austin, J. L. 1975. *How to Do Things with Words,* 2d ed. Cambridge: Cambridge University Press.

Basso, Keith H. 1990. *Western Apache Language and Culture: Essays in Linguistic Anthropology.* Tucson, AZ: University of Arizona Press.

Bauman, Richard. 1977. *Verbal Art and Performance.* Rowley, MA: Newbury House.

Bauman, Richard, and Joel Sherzer, eds. 1974. *Explorations in the Ethnography of Speaking.* New York: Cambridge University Press.

Briggs, Charles, and Amy Shuman, eds. 1993. *Theorizing Folklore: Toward New Perspectives on the Politics of Culture.* Special issue of *Western Folklore* 52 (2, 3, 4).

Derrida, Jacques. "Limited Inc a b c." *Glyph* 2:162–254.

Grice, H. P. 1975. "Logic and conversation." In Peter Cole and Jerrold Morgan, eds. *Speech Acts.* New York: Academic Press: 41–58.

Gumperz, John J., and Dell Hymes, eds. 1972. *Directions in Sociolinguistics: The Ethnography of Communication.* New York: Holt, Rinehart, Winston.

Hill, Jane H. 1986. "The refiguration of the anthropology of language." *Cultural Anthropology* 1:89–102.

Hymes, Dell, ed. 1964. *Language in Culture and Society: A Reader in Linguistics and Anthropology.* New York: Harper and Row.

Johnstone, Barbara. 1990. *Stories, Community, and Place: Narratives from Middle America.* Bloomington: Indiana University Press.

Paredes, Américo, and Richard Bauman, eds. 1972. *Toward New Perspectives in Folklore.* Austin: University of Texas Press.

Sapir, Edward. 1949. *Selected Writings in Language, Culture and Personality,* David G. Mandelbaum, ed. Berkeley: University of California Press.

Searle, John R. 1969. *Speech Acts.* Cambridge: Cambridge University Press.

Smith, Barbara Herrnstein. 1978. *On the Margins of Discourse.* Chicago: University of Chicago Press.

8

Biography of a Sentence: A Burmese Proverb

A. L. BECKER

There are three kinds of mistakes: those resulting from lack of memory, from lack of planning ahead, or from misguided beliefs.

—Burmese proverb

I call this essay "Biography of a Sentence" in order to evoke Wittgenstein's way of thinking about language as a form of life, a mode of being in the world, and so to depart from an atomistic picture of language and meaning and to move toward a contextual one. In using language one shapes old words into new contexts—*jarwa dhosok,* the Javanese call it, pushing old language into the present. All language use is, in this sense, translation to some degree; and translation from one language to another is only the extreme case. I argue here that translation for the philologist—one who would guide us across the terra incognita between distant languages—is not the final goal but only a first step, a necessary first step, in understanding a distant text; necessary because it opens up for us the exuberancies and deficiencies of our own interpretations and so helps us see what kinds of self-correction must be made. And so the goal of this essay is to begin with a Burmese proverb, a simple sentence, a minimal text, and to move step by step from a translation (provided by a bilingual Burmese) closer to the original. Each step is a correction of an exuberance or a deficiency of meaning as presented to us in the English translation.

In moving from an atomistic mode of interpretation to a more contextual one, new kinds of questions appear just as old ones lose their force. One asks not how some phenomenon is built up in a rule-governed way out of minimal bits but rather in what ways context constrains particular language—real text (i.e., remembered or preserved language). There are many ways to answer that question, depending on how one defines context. One way to see context is as sources of constraints on text. Linguists and language philosophers could agree on five or six sources of constraints, although they would group and name them differently, I suspect. Let me for present purposes identify these six kinds of contextual relations, none of which seems to me to be reducible to another:

1. *structural relations*, relations of parts to wholes;
2. *generic relations*, relations of text to prior text;
3. *medial relations*, relations of text to medium;
4. *interpersonal relations*, relations of text to participants in a text-act;
5. *referential relations*, relations of a text to Nature, the world one believes to lie beyond language;
6. *silential relations*, relations of a text to the unsaid and the unsayable.

There is nothing particularly original about these six, and there has been a great deal of work on each, except perhaps the last one. Together they define context. A text is the interaction of the constraints they provide.

The terms have one great weakness: they are all too categorial—too "nouny," too liberally neutral. As Kenneth Burke might say, their "improvisational" quality is weak. The life of a text is in the weighting and balancing and counterbalancing of the terms and figures and in the conceptual dramas they evoke. To transcend these neutral terms, one can make them active—as a text strategy—and say that a text has meaning because it is structuring and remembering and sounding and interacting and referring and not doing something else . . . all at once. The interaction of these *acts* is the basic drama of every sentence.

The sentence—simple or complex—is, in any language, the minimal unit in which all these actions are happening, in which the drama is fully staged. Only with sentences—and larger units—are there speakers and hearers and times and worlds; that is, particular speakers, particular hearers, particular times, and particular worlds. Paul Ricoeur (1981) calls sentences the "minimal units of discourse," the "minimal units of exchange." Jan Mukařovský (1977:15) wrote of the sentence as "the component mediating between the language and the theme, the lowest dynamic (realized in time) semantic unit, a miniature model of the entire semantic structuring of the discourse."

Words and phrases are *staged* only as sentences. Much of our language about sentences overlaps with our language about drama, an iconicity we share with many other languages. That is, in both there are actors or agents, goals, undergoers, instruments, accompaniments, times, and settings—all bound into an act or state, or just plain *being*, and all shaped to a context in subtle ways. To see the drama of a sentence requires only a bit of contemplation: stepping back (as a friend puts it) to take a closer look. To hide that drama with neutral terms—what Burke (1964) calls "bureaucratizing" knowledge—is to lose the essential liveliness and excitement of that contemplation. And it is to miss the considerable aesthetic pleasure one gets in contemplating a text and seeing the drama of terms and figures unfold, a good deal of it at the level of sentences.

Not all sentences are whole texts in themselves. Most are parts of larger texts. Yet there are sentences free enough of lingual context to be treated as texts. Proverbs, perhaps, which are not really self-sufficient texts but rather small texts used to evaluate (give value to) new situations. They are recurrent evaluatory statements, part of whose job is to sound like proverbs, language in the public do-main. Proverbs are a mode of sounding, referring, interacting, remembering, and shaping which are small enough to be discussable in an essay (a ratio of 1 sentence of text to 320 sentences of commentary, in this case). In larger texts, one is forced to sample.

Contemplating single sentences or very small texts brings one into the world of the grammarian, the world of delicate parsing. It thus brings one up against a very large, wildly ill-defined grammatical terminology: all the names for the categories, processes, and relations that grammarians talk about, often very intimidatingly. One can get the feeling that from grammar school to graduate school the prime use of grammar has been some variety of intimidation.

However, the *pleasures of the text* (one of the phrases Roland Barthes left us) are too important not to encourage people to enter as amateurs and to experience the whole of the journey to a distant text. There is a skill in parsing which a good lin-guist can be led to display on small persuasion, but it should be only inspiring to the amateur, not intimidating—like Billie Holiday's singing.

There are two basic ways to think about grammar (as a prelude to the contem-plation of a small text). One view leads us to think of the field of study as a sys-tem of rules that somehow map abstract and a priori semantic categories and re-lations onto phonic substance—or in different terms, map a logical deep structure onto a surface structure. Language in this structural sense is "rule governed," and the task of the grammarian is to find the most economical, least "subjective" for-mulation of the rules. Theory is exclusively formal. In this view the computer is a natural metaphor for the language-processing mind. Grammars—or tiny frag-ments of unfinished grammars—tend to be written as rules accompanied by ex-amples, illustrating problems of theory shaping (Geertz 1983:19).

There is another kind of grammar, based on a different perspective on language, one involving time and memory; or, in terms of contextual relations, a set of prior texts that one accumulates throughout one's lifetime, from simple social exchanges to long, semimemorized recitations. One learns these texts in action, by repetitions and corrections, starting with the simplest utterances of a baby. One learns to re-shape these texts to new context, by imitation and by trial and error. One learns to interact with more and more people, in a greater and greater variety of environ-ments. The different ways one shapes a prior text to a new environment make up the grammar of a language. Grammar is context-shaping (Bateson 1979:17) and context shaping is a skill we acquire over a lifetime. We learn it essentially by con-tinual internal and external corrections, in response to change and lack of change in the environment. From the first point of view, constraints common to all lan-guages tend to be structural (or logical); from the second, pragmatic (or rhetori-cal). What I call philology might also be called a rhetorically based linguistics.

The ways one shapes a text to new contexts include such operations as substi-tution of words or other larger or smaller lingual units, rearrangements, repeti-tion, expansion, inflexion, and embedding. These are all things one can do with a word or a sentence or a larger text, all general strategies, which one learns to do more and more skillfully and which become (potentially) more and more complex. The problem with stating them all as rules is that the constraints on shaping are not entirely structural; and they are not a closed system but open to context. We are not so much compositors of sentences from bits as reshapers of prior texts (the self-evident a prioris of language). The modes of reshaping are in large part conventional, but also in some unpredictable part innovative and unpredictable— except for the most formulaic of utterances. Language interaction is not a closed system (i.e., rule-governed).

Even very formulaic utterances have interesting histories. The strange imperative greeting that has blossomed (along with the three-piece smiling face) in the currency of noetic exchange over the past few years in American English has been, "Have a nice day." The reader is invited to notice how many different shapings of that formula he or she encounters over the next few days. This morning, in good New Jersey accent, I got, "Have one, y'hear," from an exuberant gas station attendant. "I will," I answered, not knowing what I was saying. In all language, there are prior norms and present deviations going on constantly.

Proverbs tend to be slower changing than nonproverbs, since they are public language and not private language and depend on recognition as proverbs in order to work. But there are a whole range of things we recognize as proverbs— not just wise, comfortable ones, but also banal clichés and even original evaluations not yet fully in the public domain. Here are a few:

He who hesitates is lost.
Well, it takes all kinds. . . .
Sometimes a man just has to stand up for his rights.
We're all in it for the money.
He leaped before he looked.

Here are some not yet in the public domain, perhaps never to be:

Progress: that long steep path which leads to me.
   Jean-Paul Sartre

Contextual shaping is only another term for grammar.
   Gregory Bateson

Art and the equipment to grasp it are made in the same shop.
   Clifford Geertz

Do not be overwhelmed by all that there is to know. It is a myth of the oppressor.
   Kenneth Koch

Public evaluatory sentences are of many sorts. One need only look through the *Oxford Dictionary of Proverbs* to see the great variety in even so small a sample. But the goal here is not to provide a classification scheme for proverbs (as Burke 1964:108 writes in his short essay on proverbs, "The range of possible academic classifications is endless"—a good and useful candidate for the public domain). They are sometimes "generic" sentences, in two senses: they are often marked by indefinite subjects and indefinite tense and thus meant to refer to a large class of phenomena; but they are also generic in the sense that they are quite overtly drawn from the past and help to identify a present text as belonging to a *genre,* a set of prior texts. They are meant to stand apart. Their power comes from one's recognition of them as shared public opinion, and one is not supposed to argue with them in situations that call for politeness. They are part of the credit of society on which one lives.

As prevailing opinions, public opinions are uttered differently than private opinions are. They need no support, since they do not depend on the adherence of individuals, and are not presented as hypotheses to be proved. They are there, to be reckoned with, as authoritative as law. We sometimes think of public opinion as a collection of private opinions (polls operate on this fallacy), rather than as a collection of evaluatory statements, there in the language—like proverbs—on which we are free to draw (Ortega y Gasset 1957:266). This collection is not identical for each of us and like much of language is broader in recognition than in use. The closer we are to people, in a communal sense, the more we share evaluations—and the less we seem willing to tolerate evaluatory differences.

There is a continuum of evaluatory utterances from those, like proverbs, which we share exactly (i.e., with identical wording) to those which we recognize as having some family resemblance with our own evaluatory stock sufficient to be accepted as equivalent or nearly so. For example, "He who hesitates is lost" is always said in just those words—even when referring to women. Here, context shaping is minimal, a matter only of one's voice, its qualities, pitches, and rhythms. By contrast, the cynical observation, "We're all in it for the money" is less frozen and more likely to be reshaped—softened or strengthened—each time it is used.

These small texts—proverbs, semiproverbs, and clichés—are a form of speaking the past. But uttering them—even with all the controls over rhythm, pitch, and voice quality that music can provide—is also to some extent speaking the present. They evoke a norm and to some degree, however small, deviate from it.

Utterances with a family resemblance to, for instance, the cliché "We're all in it for the money" include those utterances that can be seen to have a connection with it via substitution, rearrangement, repetition, expansion, inflexion, and/or embedding. As a figure, the cliché sets up points of substitution:

We are all in it for the money.
They were partly in it for the money.
He was in it because of his interest.

The sentence is a frame for the substitution of words, affixes, phrases, and whole clauses—all the levels of lingual units.

Besides substitution, context shaping can involve rearrangement and the consequent readjustments, which contribute much of the complexity to syntax (Givón 1979:235ff.):

It's the money that we're all in it for.
Money is what we're all in it for.

Or expansion:

We're all—you me and everyone—in it right now for the money we can get out of it.

Or repetition:

We're all in it for the money . . . for the money.

Or inflexion:

He's in it for the money.

Or the whole can be embedded:

I don't believe that we're all in it for the money.
Our all being in it for the money disturbs me.

(One can reduce these modes of context shaping by considering inflexion a structural type of substitution and by considering repetition and some embedding as types of expansion.) Mostly one uses combinations of these strategies to shape prior text into new contexts—and to recognize someone else's shaping.

The important thing here is not whether one can describe all the shapings that are possible, singly and in combination, and all the remedial strategies that they entail, in some formalism, but rather where family resemblance fades in the reshaping that keeps lingual strategies alive. Most people—our cousins and aunts— are not often aware of the extent to which one constantly reshapes old language into new contexts. The process is rapid, and only if there is a breakdown do we normally become conscious of it—when something doesn't *sound* right (under analysis, as Wittgenstein [1958] put it, language is on holiday).

The difference between looking at grammar as rules which map logical categories and relations onto a medium and looking at it as ways of reshaping old language to new contexts is, primarily, that in the first case one begins with a priori or "universal" categories as being common to all languages, while in the second case what is common are pragmatic or rhetorical situations—common features of the context—and what is a priori is prior text. To assume a universal logic seems to be to take very abstract representations of the categories and relations of Indoeuropean languages as inherent in all languages (see Benveniste 1971). One learns, of course, to confront all new experience in one's own language, including experience of another language. It is not difficult to assume that these categories and relations are "there" *in* the phenomena, a priori to language. However, it seems more conducive to cross-cultural understanding that one not assume an abstract realm of absolute categories and relations—some kind of extra-lingual logic—as a ground for all languages, but rather start in language, with actual remembered texts (however they are preserved). Recall Wittgenstein's (1958:114) caution: "One thinks that one is tracing the outline of the thing's nature over and over again, and one is merely tracing round the frame through which we look at it."

The meaning of a word, then, is not a combination of atomic categories and relations or underlying features or properties, but the past and present contexts it evokes. Then how do grammars and dictionaries of distant languages work? They work as abductions: one language in terms of another. A grammar of Burmese in English is an English version of certain aspects of Burmese—that is, those having English analogs. A Burmese grammar of English does not yet exist, except as a translation into Burmese of an English grammar of English; but if it did, it would be a Burmese interpretation of English in which, for instance, the simplicity of our numeral classifiers and verb particles might be noted. Grammars and dictionaries are as much cultural artifacts as newspapers or shadow plays.

In understanding a distant text, even for the writer of the most formal of grammars, there is an essential first step—a gloss or rough word-for-word translation. It is always present and is always meant to be invisible, like the invisible man, dressed in black, in the Japanese Noh drama, who moves props, adjusts costumes, and generally keeps things tidy on stage. The gloss, rather than the abstract representations of categories, features, and relations, is the underlying vehicle for understanding. The only mode that we have of understanding a distant text is first to jump to an interpretation, to guess (or have someone guess for us), and then to sort out the exuberancies and deficiencies of one's guess. One's own language is the initial model for another language, a metaphor of it (Pike and Pike 1977:69).

A philologist does well to be always self-conscious that his understanding of another language is initially metaphoric and not "pure" meaning. To do otherwise is to add to the exuberancy of thinking of logical categories as reified "things," the further exuberancy of assuming that they are the categories of one's own language. It is at this point that grammatical explanation becomes political: when we assume that there is one grammar for the Greek and the Barbarian—and it is Greek. To ask, for instance, what the passive is in Burmese is to assume (1) that "the passive" exists a priori to any language, and (2) that "it" has an English name or an English function in shaping context, whatever one calls it. To translate some Burmese clause as an English passive, however, is both necessary and reasonable.

A methodology for parsing should be a lightly held thing, as one confronts the distant text with it. When methodology and text conflict, it is the methodology that should give way first. In this sense, one's discipline is the text. Methodologies come and go, but the discipline of the text and its language remain. Perhaps a particular experience can illuminate this point.

On arriving in Burma in 1958, I began to learn Burmese from a very kind and patient old teacher, U San Htwe. As I had been taught to do, I would ask him words for things and then write them down. He watched me writing for a while and then said, "That's not how you write it," and he wrote the word in Burmese script. For the word evoked by English "speak," I wrote /pyɔ/ and he wrote 6ၛၒ. I insisted it made no difference. He insisted it did and told me I was hurting his language. And so I began, somewhat reluctantly, to learn to write Burmese: /p—/ was a central ၒ, and /-y-/ wrapped around the ၒ to make ၛ and the vowel /6–ɔ/ fit before and after it: 6ၛၒ.

This difference in medial representation made a great difference, on at least two levels. For one thing, I could not segment the Burmese syllable into a linear sequence, as I could /pyɔ/, as one can see clearly by studying the two representations. But segmentation into linear sequence is a prerequisite for doing linguistics as most of us have been taught it: normally, sounds string together to make morphemes and words, and words string together to make phrases, and so on. We analyze strings, with analog phenomena relegated to super- or subsegmental status. To write my kind of grammar I had to violate his writing.

At first it seemed to me a small price to pay, to phonemicize his language. But over the years—particularly 20 years later, in Java and Bali—I learned how that kind of written figure (a center and marks above, below, before, and after it; the figure of the Burmese and Javanese and Balinese syllable) was for many Southeast Asians a mnemonic frame: everything in the encyclopedic repertoire of terms was ordered that way: directions (the compass rose), diseases, gods, colors, social roles, foods—everything (see Zurbuchen 1981:75ff.). It was the natural shape of remembered knowledge, a basic icon.

As Zurbuchen (1981) has shown us, this notion of the syllable is the ground even of the gods: it is evoked at the beginning of every Balinese shadow play. Even though the shadow play is taught and performed orally, it begins with an invocation of the written symbol as a source of power.

Just as the boundaries of awareness become perceptible,
There is perfect tranquillity, undisturbed by any threat,
And even the utterances of the gods subside.
It is none other which forms the beginning of my obeisance to the Divine.
Greatly may I be forgiven for my intention to call forth a story.
And where dwells the story?

There is a god unsupported by the divine mother earth,
Unsheltered by the sky,
Unilluminated by the sun, moon, stars, or constellations.
Yes, Lord, you dwell in the void, and are situated thus:
You reside in a golden jewel,
Regaled on a golden palanquin,
Umbrellaed by a floating lotus.
There approached in audience by all the gods of the cardinal
      directions....(1981:vi)

These last lines, after locating the written symbol outside of time and space, describe metaphorically the shaping of the written symbol as a focal point for natural order. Zurbuchen's (1981:vi–vii) translation continues, describing the implements of writing:

There, there are the young palm leaves, the one lontar,
Which, when taken and split apart, carefully measured are the lengths and
widths.
It is this which is brought to life with hasta, gangga, uwira, tanu.
And what are the things so named?
Hasta *means "hand"*
Gangga *means "water"*
Uwira *means "writing instrument"*
Taru *means "ink."*
What is that which is called "ink"?
That is the name for
And none other than
The smoke of the oil lamp,
Collected on the bark of the kepuh-tree,
On a base of copper leaf.
It is these things which are gathered together
And given shape on leaf.
"Written symbol" is its name,
Of one substance and different soundings....

The translation, which I have taken the liberty of arranging in lines (mainly to slow down the reader), goes on slowly to evolve the story from the written symbol.

My point, however, is not to explore this image further, or to retell Mary Zurbuchen's fascinating stories, but to try to understand why U San Htwe had insisted on my learning Burmese this way. I think it was that the traditional learning was organized around that shape, that it was a root metaphor (see Lakoff and Johnson 1980), the stuff that holds learning together—just as our sequential writing lines up so well with our sequential tense system or our notions of causality and history. That is a great deal to ask anyone to give up—the metaphoric power of his writing system. And I had tried to argue with that wise old man that it did not matter.

One of the most subtle forces of colonialism, ancient or modern, is the undermining of not just the substance but the framework of someone's learning. As Gregory Bateson put it, in his oft-quoted letter to the other regents of the University of California, "Break the pattern which connects the items of learning and you necessarily destroy all quality." I see now that what I had been suggesting to my teacher, though neither of us could articulate it, was that we break the pattern which connects the items of his learning. When methodology and language conflict, it is the methodology which should give way first.

The proverb that serves as an epigraph to this paper comes from a small book my teacher gave to me just before I left Burma in 1961, after studying with him for three years and mostly reading Burmese classics, after I had grasped a bit of the language. I read with a great deal of what Keats called "negative capability": Keats spoke of Shakespeare as one who was "capable of being in uncertainties, mysteries, doubts, without any irritable reaching after fact and reason" (quoted in Dewey 1934:33). I read with half-understanding the children's histories, poems, plays, chronicles, and *jataka* tales he brought me, and heard with half-understanding his commentaries and corrections of me. I taught English to children in the morning—funny, uninhibited Burmese children—and studied Burmese in the late afternoon, at twilight, at U San Htwe's house. Just before I left, he gave me a small notebook, a child's copybook with a picture of a mountain on the front, in which he had copied lists of sets: the two thises, five thats, and fifteen whatevers. I had asked him how I might continue studying Burmese without him and this book was his solution and gift. I stared at it for years, and with the help of a Burmese friend, U Thein Swe, began to understand some of it, much later.

In the book, written in U San Htwe's fine hand, are all classes of things, abstract as well as concrete, in this world and out of it—a syllabus for study. It begins with sets of twos and grows, as if paralleling the growing complexity of one's experience, to larger and larger sets. The initial sets are sometimes obvious, like the two parents and the two strengths (strength of arm and strength of heart), but are sometimes more exotic pairs like the two worlds (the zero world—in which Buddhas, monks, supernatural beings, and so on, do not appear, exist, or flourish—and the nonzero world—in which the above appear, exist, and flourish). The sets in my book continue to sets of eighteen. (I learned later that other lists go on to bigger sets and that my teacher may have censored a bit.) To understand the sets, he said, is to understand the world, both inner and outer, seen and unseen. They represent, taken together, a taxonomy of the phenomenal and noumenal universe of at least some traditional Burmese.

Each set is itself a kind of plot from a universal plot book, around which to build a discourse. For example, a sermon can be built around, say, the four cardinal virtues (love, attention, happiness, detachment), or a political speech around those three kinds of mistakes mentioned in the epigraph (resulting from lack of memory, from lack of planning ahead, or from misguided beliefs). Or a play might be constructed around some other appropriate set, perhaps the four false hopes (hoping to get rich by reading treasure maps, hoping to get healthy by reading medical literature, hoping for wisdom by following a learned man, and hoping for a girlfriend by dressing up). These sets are assumed a priori to any discourse as impersonal frames to which nature, both human and nonhuman, properly and appropriately corresponds. A true sermon, a wise foreign policy, or a well-constructed drama can be rooted in one or more of them. One can contemplate these sets with continual fascination and increasing insight, as one learns to see things in new ways. Like a good poem, a new set can defamiliarize one's world.

The proverb used as the epigraph to this paper appears in my copybook as in Figure 8.1. U San Htwe copied this from a manuscript book that one of his teachers had given to him. Similar books were common in traditional Buddhist monastic education. They were learned first then gradually understood over the years, like most things in traditional Southeast Asian education. Memory preceded understanding, an order practiced by few in our culture other than classical pianists. The closer one gets to nonliteracy (and a chirographic culture is, in this sense, less literate than a print culture), the more a student seems to be expected to *perform* the past like a classical pianist. Language classes in traditional schools were not so much the acquiring of a neutral tool as a set of prior texts, serious cultural wisdom.

Neither had writing come to Burma, as it never does anywhere, as a neutral tool. It had come with content: a religion, a calendar, and a new set of cultural prior texts in Pali, the language of Buddhism. The new writing was, first of all, access to those Pali texts, the real sources of knowledge. Only gradually did the local language begin to be written in the new writing, at first only for translation. Later, this translation language—far from the language acts and strategies of everyday discourse (the vernacular)—began to be used for creating local texts and replac-

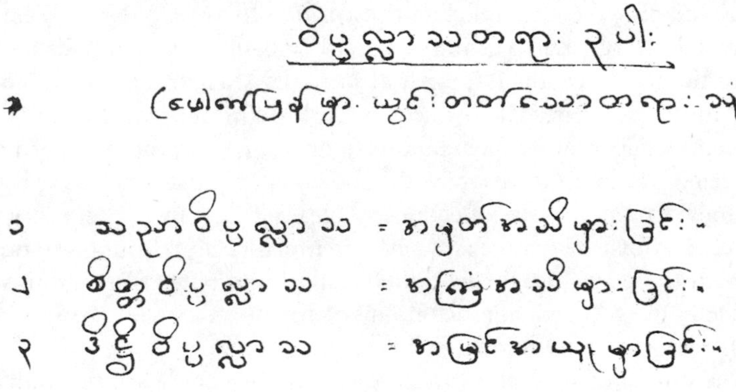

Figure 8.1

		wippallāthạ	ta ya:	thoñ:	pa:		
		error	law	3	classifier		

(hpau'	pyañ	hma:	ywiñ:	ta'	thaw	ta yạ	thoñ: pa:)
(perforate	return	error	misplace	do	connective	law	3 classifier)

1 thạ nya	wippallāthạ	=	ạ hma'	ạ thi	hma:	hkyiñ:	
perceive-mark	error		sign-mark	know-witness	error	doing	
2 sitta	wippallāthạ	=	ạ kyañ	ạ thi	hma:	hkyiñ:	
mind-thought	error		plan	know-witness	error	doing	
3 ḍiti	wippallāthạ	=	ạ myiñ	ạ yu	hma:	hkyiñ:	
opinion-doctrine	error		appear-ance	belief error	doing		

Figure 8.2

ing individual memory. Very much later, some bold innovator began to write the vernacular. In a very general way, that is what happened throughout Southeast Asia under the noetic impact of Sanskritic languages.

And so this set about mistakes is not a proverb in our sense but rather Buddhist categories indicating natural laws of human nature, stated first in Pali and then in Burmese. Phrase-by-phrase translation of this sort is also common in Southeast Asia, and no doubt elsewhere, as a way of *performing* a translation. It has had profound effect on literary styles and performance techniques, where translating is a very common speech act (Okell 1965). These traditional styles make most foreigners feel that about half the words should be crossed out: we get impatient with that extra step of glossing so many words.

In order to parse the Burmese passage, we must first transliterate it, or else learn Burmese writing. Taking the former, faster course means both addition and loss of meaning: what is lost is the powerful iconicity of the image of the Burmese syllable, the visual gesture and pace of reading it and sounding it, and the aesthetic possibilities of the shaping and combining of syllables. Using a Burmese typewriter, even, is like decorating a Christmas tree: the central symbol is struck and the carriage does not automatically jump ahead but just sits there, while one adds things above, below, before, and after the central syllable. One focuses on syllables, not phonemes.

Figure 8.2 gives an interpretation (meant to be read slowly) of the Burmese text in Roman letters, a transliteration, with rough glosses in English, taken from dictionaries and bilingual Burmese friends.

With this, let us go back to the original English translation (the epigraph of this paper) and remove from it all the exuberance we can by taking out everything that has no counterpart in the Burmese (in this passage):

three kind mistake

error memory   error plan   error belief

Everything else in the English is there because of the demands of English: existential frame ("There are. . . . "), tense, number, *of*, deictics, prepositions, connective. Nearly none of the things that give the English passage its cohesion by relating the parts to each other is left. What remains is that thin, sparse wordscape that
characterizes "literal" translation. It might be argued further that only one of the
English words comes reasonably close to the range of meaning of its Burmese
counterpart: three, (2).

The cohesion of the Burmese passage comes from grammatical phenomena
that we do not have in English or that we have but do not exploit in the way
Burmese does. One deficiency, one of the things missing from the English, is *classification*. It occurs twice, once in the top line (*pa:*) and again in the parenthetical
explanation in the second line. It is used in counting, but it also has several other
grammatical-rhetorical functions in Burmese. It evokes a universe of discourse,
that is, a particular perspective on the word classified (Becker 1975). It marks, by
its special prominence, a discourse topic, and therefore shares some of the function of the English existential sentence ("There be . . . "). The classifier *pa:* is one
of a paradigm of classifiers that mark the status of beings and some things associated with them. There are five categories, which might be conceptualized as a
center and four concentric rings radiating from that center. In the center are
Buddhas, relics, images, and the Buddhist Law. In the next ring, closest to the center are the things classified as *pa:*: deities, saints, monks, royalty, scriptures, and
Pali terms. The word *pa:* itself is felt to be related to the term for "close" by some
Burmese friends, while others are skeptical about that etymology. In the next orbit
are things associated with the head, metaphorically: people of status, teachers, and
scholars. And next are ordinary humans, followed by an outer realm of animals,
ghosts, dead bodies, depraved people, and children. A classifier is a locus on a conceptual map, not the name of a genus, all members of which have some attribute.
Animate beings are ordered according to their distance from Buddhahood: spiritual progression is a movement from animality to Buddhahood. The three mistakes as a set are Buddhist wisdom and so are closest to the center in this conceptual map.

Classifiers almost seem to add another level of reality to the world as seen
through Burmese. We are accustomed to quantifiers, like two pounds of something or three yards of something else, but we do not regularly and obligatorily
classify everyone and everything with the same unconscious thoroughness that,
by contrast, we mark relative times in our tense-aspect system. Classifiers give special salience to terms as they are introduced, marking out the topics of a discourse.
What linguists call "zero anaphora" (marking a discourse role as unchanged by *not*
mentioning it) indicates the domain of a term in a Burmese discourse. My own

Burmese was always very confusing because I kept overmentioning things, a particular form of exuberance to which English conditions us.

Most other terms a foreigner usually undermentions. These are the so-called elaborate expressions (Haas 1964:xvii-xviii; Matisoff 1973:81ff.). Although words are almost all monosyllabic in Burmese (with the exception of foreign terms like *wippallāthạ* and the other Pali terms in the text), they are used in pairs. There are examples in lines 2 through 5:

1. *hpau' pyañ*   "perforate-return" meaning to "fall-away"
                    (as from a religion)
2. *hma: ywiñ:*   "error-misplace" meaning "mistake"
3. *a hma' a thi*   "mark-know" meaning "perceiving and remembering"
                    (no English term of this scope)
4. *a kyañ a thi*   "intent-know" meaning "planning ahead," "intending"
5. *a myiñ a yu*   "appearance-belief" meaning "belief" in a broad sense.

There are no precise English equivalents for any of these pairs of terms, but via their Burkean dialectic they help us to imagine what they might mean. Like the classifiers, they tend to make phrases double-headed. Few foreigners manage this very well and so speak very *thin* Burmese, while we find them, as our name for this phenomenon suggests, elaborate.

The rhythm of good Burmese seems to demand these expressions, and rhythm is probably the most basic and powerful cohesive force in language. When two people speak comfortably to each other, they both join in the creation of a rhythm, marked by stresses, nods, grunts, gestures, and sentence rhythms. On the basis of this created rhythm they exchange words. If the conversation is not going well, the discomfort will be manifested in arhythmic responses and repairs, until they get rolling again. Speaking a language requires skill in those background rhythms, which are not the same in all languages. Our basic, elusive unease in speaking to foreigners is in large part inexplicable because it is often in large part rhythmic (Erickson and Shultz 1982; Scollon 1981). Here, the rhythmic elaborate expressions mark the parallelism of the three pairs of terms, perhaps also bringing the Burmese terms into balance with the heavier Pali terms.

Slowly, by a process of self-correction after a ventured glossing, the Burmese passage is emerging: the drama of the classifiers and the elaborate expressions. This slow emergence is the aesthetic of philology. It emerges in all the dimensions of meaning: as a structure, as a genre, as an exchange, as a sounding, and as a potential reference to (or evaluation of) an appropriate event.

If we look at the overall syntax of the text, we can clearly identify two strategies. One is the strategy of the title and its paraphrase, which might be interpreted as:

X law	three	"close" things
X taya:	*thoñ:*	*pa:*

X law three revered things
(X law three revered things)

1 *Y wippallāthạ* = *Z* error-ing
2 *Y wippallāthạ* = *Z* error-ing
3 *Y wippallāthạ* = *Z* error-ing

Figure 8.3

Here the X represents the variable term, the difference between the first and second lines. This is a particular classifier strategy, to give it a name based on its final constituent. By comparing other sets in the little book, we might make a more general formula for classifier strategies, but that would be to move away from understanding how this strategy is shaped in this context. A strategy is not an abstract pattern but an actual bit of text, used as a point of departure, either across texts or in a single text. Here, the first line is a frame for the second, in which the Pali term is paraphrased in Burmese. To give the most generalized formulation of the strategy is to move too far from the text in separating formal meaning from the four other kinds of meaning. It is possible to do so, as a long period of structural analysis has proved, yet it is also a movement away from understanding.

The second strategy is what we might call (after the distinctive sign =) an equative strategy, and it might be interpreted as: NUMBER Y *wippallāthạ* = Z erroring. This is the strategy of the final three lines. In this small text, a system has been established in which certain slots in a frame are varied, others kept unchanged (other entries in the little book almost all use variants of these strategies). These repeated strategies give structural coherence to the text and provide a ground for thematic coherence.

By looking at the relation of the three slots (X, Y, and Z), we find a further pattern. The fillers of X are modifiers of *tạya* (law). In the first line the filler is the Pali term (Burmanized) *wippallāthạ*, and this term becomes part of the *frame* of the second strategy (i.e., the term which Y modifies). In the second line, the paraphrase, the filler of X is *"hpau' pyañ hma: ywiñ: tat thaw"* (a modifying clause: "perforate-return error-misplace doing + connective term and clause particle"— a Burmese paraphrase of *wippallāthạ*, the Pali origins of which are discussed later in the paper.) Part of this Burmese paraphrase (the word *hma:* [error]) is the key framing term in the second part of the equative strategy (i.e., the term which Z modifies). The two fillers of X are Pali and Burmese, respectively, while the fillers of Y and Z are also, respectively, Pali and Burmese. Furthermore, each filler of Y is structurally parallel, as is each filler of Z. And, one might add, the number three of the first two lines constrains the number of equative figures in the list. The structural figure might be represented as in Figure 8.3.

As a structure, the text is very elegant. Each part is tightly bound into a very symmetrical overall pattern. At the lower levels of structure in this text are the varieties of relations of modifier terms to modified terms and the internal structure of the elaborate expressions:

ạ hma'	*ạ thị*	"mark know"
ạ kyañ	*ạ thị*	"plan know"
ạ myiñ	*ạ yu*	"appearance belief"

Here, the particle *ạ* marks a noun derived from a verb (Okell 1969:243). However, what phonological and semantic constraints there are on the order of these constituents is still unclear.

Probably, it takes a close parsing to make us aware how tightly structured this figure is. It is a structure used throughout the book U San Htwe gave me, and hence quite appropriately called a frame for a certain kind of language—a coherence system, a language-game, an episteme.

The kind of knowledge that these frames "contain"—to use our English metaphor for the relation of knowledge to language (Lakoff and Johnson 1980:92)—or better, that these "frames" are the formal meaning of—is for the most part originally in Pali and is being shaped into Burmese in these figures. There are two lingual interfaces here, from English back to Burmese and from Burmese back to Pali. These can be seen as two sets of prior texts, although the relations are not that simple, if we consider, for instance, the curious use of the equal sign—the source of which in Burma may well have been English—or the intrusion of Burmese into the Pali words—where a Burmese writer's possible confusion over long and short vowels in Pali led to the "misspelling" of *wippallāthạ (only* one p in Pali). Or, both these things may be U San Htwe's own deviations. One of the hardest things to know in reading a distant text is what is stereotypic and what is innovative.

The term *wippallāthạ* is a Burmese interpretation of Pali *vipallasa* from Sanskrit *viparyasa.* Edward Conze (1957, 1962a, 1962b) translates it as "perverted views." The noun *viparyasa* is from a root *as,* which means, roughly, "to throw." The whole term is used for the "overthrowing" of a wagon, or even, as a Sanskrit pundit told me, "turning a pancake." It has been translated as "inversion," "perverseness," "wrong notion," "error," "what can be upset," or "missearches"—that is, looking for permanence in the wrong places. I think it quite appropriate to call them "mistakes of interpretation" and so underscore their special relevance for philologists. "The Scriptures," writes Conze (1957:314 and 1962a:40) "identify the *viparyasas* with 'unwise attention' (*ayoniso manasikaro*)—the root of all unwholesome dharmas—and with ignorance, delusion, and false appearance." In another place, he writes, "The *viparyasa* are sometimes treated as psychological attitudes, sometimes as logical propositions, and sometimes even as an ontological condition" (1962b:39). When considered as features of the world they distort, the *viparyasas* are four in number; but when considered as *locations* in the mind they are three:

samjna	(Pali-Burmese *thanya*)	=	"perception"
citta	(Pali-Burmese *sitta*)	=	"thought"
dṛṣti	(Pali-Burmese *diṭi*)	=	"theoretical opinions"

158   A. L. Becker

All of these mistakes of interpretation lead us to habitually act as if things were different from what they are. Perception (blending in Burmese with what we might call memory) is perverted when we forget that what we perceive is impermanent, ultimately unpleasant, and not us (not to be seen ego-fully). And so we meditate on the rise and fall of the thing, breaking it down into dharmas. Thought (blending in Burmese with planning) is perverted by our wishes and fears. Both fear and hope make us overstress the permanence of things, make us close our eyes to suffering and exaggerate the importance of our own existence. Belief is perverted when we formulate a theory that the world contains permanent objects, with permanent properties, or that good outweighs suffering, or that there is a self.

These are all empirical mistakes, summarized in the formula that these views lead one to seek "the Permanent in the impermanent, Ease in suffering, the Self in what is not the self." As Conze (1962a:41) writes,

> All this we can see quite clearly in our more lucid moments—though they be rather rare and infrequent. The techniques of Buddhist meditation aims at increasing their frequency, and innumerable devices have been designed with the one purpose of impressing the actual state of affairs on our all too reluctant minds.

Even yet there remains what Ricoeur has called a "surplus of meaning"—an open-endedness about what I first saw as a proverb (translated for me by a non-Buddhist Burmese) but later came to see as a translated bit of Buddhist philosophy. We have sampled each of the contextual sources of meaning—the interpersonal uses of public language, the metaphoric power of the medium, the kinds of references the proverb might be appropriate with, the tight symmetry of its structure, and the prior (and posterior) Buddhist texts it evokes. We have moved back from translation toward the original text, and beyond. The text was our discipline and the unfinished process has been one of self-correction: removing exuberancies of interpretation, filling in deficiencies. The Burmese text eventually overtakes us, as a Buddhist injunction to philologists.

There are three kinds of perversions of interpretation, three kinds of mistakes of philology:

1. Perversions of perception, including memory = perversions of the past, of prior texts
2. Perversions of thought . . . fore-thought, planning, hopes and fears = perversions of the future
3. Perversions of appearances and beliefs = perversions of theory.

Notes

Acknowledgments. The author is grateful to Madhav Deshpande and Luis Gómez for help with the Pali terms; to Michael Aung Thwin and U Thein Swe for help with the Burmese; and to Clifford Geertz and others at the Institute for Advanced Study, Princeton, for many valuable suggestions when a version of this essay was presented there in March 1982. This paper is dedicated to Saya San Htwe, my teacher in Taunggyi, Burma, 1958–61.

References

Bateson, Gregory. 1979. Mind and Nature. New York: E. P. Dutton

Becker, A. L. 1975. A Linguistic Image of Nature: The Burmese Numerative Classifier System. International Journal of the Sociology of Language 5:109–121.

Benveniste, Emile. 1971. Categories of Thought and Language. In Problems in General Linguistics. pp. 55–64. Coral Gables: University of Miami Press.

Burke, Kenneth. 1964. Literature as Equipment for Living. In Perspectives by Incongruity. pp. 100–109. Bloomington: Indiana University Press.

Conze, Edward. 1957. On "Perverted Views." East and West 7(4):313–318.

———. 1962a. The Three Marks and the Perverted Views. In Buddhist Thought in India. pp. 34–46. London: George Allen & Unwin.

———. 1962b. The Maháyána Treatment of the Viparyāsas. Orientemus Jk. 1:34–46.

Dewey, John. 1934. Art as Experience. New York: G. P. Putnam's Sons.

Erickson, Frederick, and Jeffrey Shultz. 1982. The Counselor as Gatekeeper: Social Action in Interviews. New York: Academic Press.

Geertz, Clifford. 1983. Blurred Genres: The Refiguration of Social Thought. In Local Knowledge: Further Essays in Interpretive Anthropology. pp. 19–35. New York: Basic Books.

Givón, Talmy. 1979. On Understanding Grammar. New York: Academic Press.

Haas, Mary R. 1964. Thai-English Student's Dictionary. Palo Alto: Stanford University Press.

Lakoff, George, and Mark Johnson. 1980. Metaphors We Live By. Chicago: University of Chicago Press.

Matisoff, James A. 1973. The Grammar of Lahu. Berkeley: University of California Press.

Mukařovský, Jan. 1977. The Word and Verbal Art. John Burbank and Peter Steiner, eds. New Haven: Yale University Press.

Okell, John. 1965. Nissaya Burmese. In Indo-Pacific Linguistic Studies. G. B. Milner and Eugenie J. A. Henderson, eds. pp. 186–227. Amsterdam: North-Holland Publishing Company.

———. 1969. A Reference Grammar of Colloquial Burmese. London: Oxford University Press.

Ortega y Gasset, José. 1957. Man and People. New York: W. W. Norton & Company.

Pike, Kenneth L., and Evelyn G. Pike. 1977. Grammatical Analysis. Arlington: Summer Institute of Linguistics and University of Texas.

Ricoeur, Paul. 1981. The Model of the Text: Meaningful Action Considered as a Text. In Hermeneutics and the Human Sciences. John B. Thompson, ed. and transl. pp. 197–221. Cambridge: Cambridge University Press.

Scollon, Ronald. 1981. The Rhythmic Integration of Ordinary Talk. In Georgetown University Round Table on Language and Linguistics, 1981. pp. 335–349. Washington, DC: Georgetown University Press.

Wittgenstein, Ludwig. 1958. Philosophical Investigations. New York: Macmillan.

Zurbuchen, Mary S. 1981. The Shadow Theater of Bali: Explorations in Language and Text. Ph.D. dissertation. University of Michigan, Ann Arbor.

9

"Any Man Who Keeps More'n One Hound'll Lie to You": A Contextual Study of Expressive Lying

RICHARD BAUMAN

"There are two kinds of tales, one true and the other false," Socrates proposes to Adeimantos in the course of exploring the proper place of literature in *The Republic* (376e), and the truth value of narrative—one dimension of the relationship of stories to the events they recount—has been a basic typological criterion in the classification of narrative ever since. Folklorists, for their part, have relied rather heavily on the truth factor in classifying oral narrative forms. For some, the basic distinction rests on "the extent to which a narrative is or is not based upon objectively determinable facts" (Littleton 1965:21), whereas others are more pragmatic and relativistic, relying on local distinctions made by members of the societies in which the tales are told between "narratives regarded as fiction" and "narratives . . . regarded as true by the narrator and his audience" (Bascom 1965:4).

Recently, however, there have been increasing expressions of unease about the empirical basis and reliability of such truth-value criteria. Herbert Halpert, for example, reports frequent baffled disagreement between himself and his students in the application of the truth–fiction distinction to the sorting out of jests and anecdotes, local legends, tall tales, and personal narratives (1971:51). Robert Georges, in turn, sees the truth–fiction question as so empirically clouded in actual cases that "the only *meaningful* answer would have to be an ambivalent one" (1971:17, emphasis in the original). Arguing from a most revealing transcript of a storytelling event, Linda Dégh and Andrew Vázsonyi take a preliminary step toward formulating an empirical basis for investigating the problematics of the truth value and believability factors, at least with regard to legends. "Objective truth and the presence, quality, and quantity of subjective belief are irrelevant," they maintain (1976:119). What is important is that legend "takes a stand and calls for the expression of opinion on the question of truth and belief" (1976:119). As observed by José Limón, "In some instances 'belief' may be quite secondary to performance itself" (1983:207). That is, if one may extend the point, considerations of truth and belief will vary and be subject to negotiation within communities and storytelling situations. This would suggest that if we are interested in the place of narrative in social life, it is the dynamics of variability and negotiation that we should investigate; the issue should be transformed from a typological comparative one to an ethnographic one. Abstract, a priori, and universalistic truth-value criteria or classificatory systems for oral narrative based on them have revealed themselves to be no more empirically productive than such a priori etic schemes have proved to be in other cultural spheres. Still, evidence indicates that truth and lying may well be of social and cultural concern to members of communities with regard to stories. What is needed are closely focused ethnographic investigations of how truth and lying operate as locally salient storytelling criteria within specific institutional and situational contexts in particular societies (e.g., Heath 1983:149–89; Rickford 1986). That is what I have attempted here, in an exploration of storytelling and dog trading in Canton, Texas.

Canton is a small town of approximately 3,000 people, located about sixty miles east and a little south of Dallas. Its principal claim to fame is that on the Sunday preceding the first Monday of every month Canton becomes the scene of a large and very popular trading fair. The average attendance is about 20,000—perhaps double that on Labor Day. The fair draws traders and dealers from as far away as New York, California, Oregon, and Minnesota.

First Monday at Canton—for so it is still called, although the action has shifted to Sunday in accommodation to the modern workweek—fits into a long tradition of American trade days. These seem to have originated in this country before the middle of the seventeenth century, in conjunction with the sitting of the county courts (Craven 1949:167). These courts met as often as once a month in some convenient spot, corresponding to the shire town of England or New England. Court day was a holiday, an occasion on which county residents came into town not only in connection with court functions, but to transact all kinds of business: to discuss public affairs, hold auctions, trade, and visit on the courthouse green (Carson 1965:195–6; Fiske 1904:62–6; Verhoeff 1911:7n). County courts usually met on the first Monday of the month—hence the term "First Monday." Although the sitting of the court was the nucleus around which the court days first developed, the occasion became a social institution in its own right; Sydnor (1948:34) calls it one of the most important in the antebellum South. As political organization changed, however, and county courts developed other schedules, trade days often disengaged from court sessions to become autonomous occasions; they continued to be economically and socially important to the people of the regions in which they were held.

From the beginning, an important commodity in the trading that went on during First Mondays was horses and mules. Professional horse and mule traders were called "jockies"; thus "Jockey Day" and "Hoss Monday" are other names for the occasion, and "jockey ground" or "jockey yard" designate the area in which the trading was conducted (Sartain 1932:253). Numerous local histories and personal documents testify to the high degree of interest and excitement generated by the action on the jockey ground during the height of the trade days in the nineteenth and early twentieth centuries. But, as horses and mules declined in importance with the mechanization of Southern agriculture, First Monday trade days declined as well, to the point that very few now remain. Still, some trade days have been in continuous existence since they began, whereas others have been revived, reincarnated as flea markets.

First Monday in Canton, like most others, began in conjunction with a county court day; Canton is the county seat of Van Zandt County. The event developed in the years following the Civil War, probably during the early 1870s (Mills 1950:191–2). Like most others, too, this trade day became as much or more an occasion for coming to Canton as for attending to court business. Until 1965, the trading took place in the courthouse square, but by the mid-sixties the crowds simply got too big, and separate grounds were set aside. More than 1,000 lots are available on the trading ground, and more are being added all the time. The entire event is now sponsored by the Canton Chamber of Commerce.

Although an occasional mule or two is still hauled to Canton for trade and a considerable amount of domestic poultry is sold there as well, where animals are concerned, coon dogs are the real focus of interest during First Monday. This dog trading was an early feature of Canton First Monday. No one seems to know precisely when it began, but my oldest sources, who are past eighty years of age, remember it from their earliest visits to Canton. In 1960, a few years before the general trading left the courthouse square for separate grounds, the dog trading was moved to its own site across the highway from the main area, down on the river bottom. The dog grounds and dog trading are not part of the Chamber of Commerce operation. The grounds are privately owned, and the dog trading generally has a very different tone from the flea-market atmosphere across the road.

First, whereas many of the flea-market dealers and public are women, the people on the dog grounds are almost exclusively men. Again, the flea market attracts many urban types as well as townspeople from surrounding towns. On the dog grounds one sees mostly rural people—farmers, hunters, more blacks, and more people of lower socioeconomic status generally. The activity on the dog grounds begins in earnest on Friday night, when people begin to gather, set up tents and campers, stake out their dogs, drink, play cards, shoot dice, talk dogs, go off into the surrounding countryside to hunt, and generally have a good time.

At the peak of the trading, there are hundreds of hunting dogs of all kinds on the dog grounds, although coonhounds are clearly predominant. Some coon-dog men are as serious as other dog fanciers about breeding, standards, registration, papers, and the other trappings of "improving the breed." Most dealing in dogs at this level involves fancy stud fees, careful records, big money—into the thousands of dollars for a top dog. Many hound-dog men, however, are far more pragmatic. They just want good, working hunting dogs, and cannot afford to pay a great deal of money for them. These men tend to be less careful about the niceties of breeding, record keeping, and so on; they are satisfied with whichever dogs get together behind the shed, breeding "old Handy to old Ready." This is the group of dog traders that comes to Canton, and as a group they tend not to be highly regarded by the serious coon-dog breeders or by the townspeople in general. One citizen of Canton described dog traders to me as people for whom "making a living gets in the way." Some are professional dog jockies; most are amateurs. Their motivations for coming to Canton are various and often mixed. Some come to get "using dogs," whereas others just like to "move their dogs around" or "change faces." The professionals come to make some money, but many traders just want the activity to pay for itself—that is, to pay for the trip and for the dogs' feed.

The dominant reasons for coming to Canton, though, are to get together with other hound-dog men to talk about dogs and hunting, and to trade for its own sake, as recreation. For most traders at Canton, the economic motive is far from the top of the list; dog trading for them is a form of play, a contest of wits and words. Some men actually keep one or two dogs around at any given time just to trade and, not surprisingly, these are usually rather "sorry" dogs, "old trashy dogs that ain't worth a quarter for nothin'." One trader put it this way:

> My experience is, I'll be in Canton in the morning, be there Sunday all day, I've got a dog trade always. Reason I want to go because a man's gonna meet me there and demonstrate his dog and I'm gonna take mine. Course the one I'm gonna take ain't much of a dog. . . . Now and then I get a good dog, then I get one that ain't worth bringin' home, but still it's trade that I like to do. (Recorded by Thomas A. Green, Blooming Grove, Texas, May 31, 1968)

In other words, Canton is "where the action is" (see Goffman 1967). Of course, no dog trader is averse to making some money, and one of the stated goals of any swap is to "draw boot"—that is, to get a dog and some cash for your dog. One man told me that his fellow traders would "trade with you for ten when ten's all they got in their dog, then they'll make five on your dog." These are small sums, though. In most cases, cash profit stands as a token of having played the game well; it is a sweetener that enhances the encounter. It is also true that many of the transactions at Canton are straight cash sales, but the dynamic of these transactions is the same in all essentials as trading, and they are considered to be and labeled trades.

When I asked what brought him to Canton, one old trader, who has been coming to First Monday for more than seventy years, replied, "Well, I enjoy trading and enjoy seeing my old friends." For him, as for most others on the dog grounds, the essence of First Monday is trading and sociability. I propose in the remainder of this chapter to explore some of the interrelationships between the two activities.

As a point of departure, let us consider the following two excerpts from dog-trading encounters at Canton. The first involves two participants: John Moore, a black man in his early forties, and Mr. Byers, a white man in his early fifties. John Moore has the dogs, and Byers has just walked up to look them over.

Byers: He strike his own fox? [That is, can he pick up the fox's trail by himself?]
Moore: He strike his own fox. Strike his own fox. Clean as a pin, strike his own fox. [Pause] And he'll stand to be hunted, he'll stand to be hunted [Byers interrupts—unintelligible]. What is that?
Byers: He run with a pack good?
Moore: Oh yes, oh yes. And he'll stand . . . he'll stand three nights out a week. He has did that and took off—ain't seen him waitin' behind that. [Unintelligible.] He'll stand three nights out a week. I've known that to happen to him. [Pause]

I try to be fair with a man 'bout a dog. Tell the truth about a dog. Tell you what he'll do. If there's any fault to him, I wanna tell the man. If I get a dog from a man, if there's any fault to him, I want him to tell me.

I bought . . . we bought some puppies from a man, we asked him, said, "they been vaccinated?" Said, "now we gonna buy the puppies," say, "now if they been vaccinated, we wanta know if they ain't." Say, "now, what we's gettin' at, if they ain't been vaccinated distemper's all around." We wanted 'a vaccinate 'em.

And he swore they was vaccinated and after we bought 'em they died, took distemper and died. Then he told a friend o' ours, he say he hate that he didn't tell us that the dogs, the puppies, wasn't vaccinated.

See, and I begged him, "I tell you somethin' man, we gonna buy the puppies, gonna give you a price for 'em," I said, "but there's one thing we just wanta know if they been vaccinated." And then turned right around . . . then turned right around and told the man that they hadn't been vaccinated. And here I begged him, "I'm beggin' you, gonna buy the dogs, puppies, at your price."

Byers: I traded two good coon dogs for two Walker dogs [a breed of hounds]—
Moore: //Mmm hmm.
Byers: //—supposed to be good fox dogs.
Moore: Mmm hmm.
Byers: Sumbitches wouldn't run a *rabbit*.
Moore: You see that?
Byers: Boy, I mean they wouldn't run nothin'.
Moore: I tell you for . . . what is your name?
Byers: Byers.
Moore: Mr. Byers, this here is John Moore, everybody know me here. I can take you to some people in here any day—I'm talkin' about some rich, up-to-date people—I have sold dogs to, and they'll tell you. . . . I'm talkin' 'bout for hunnerd dollars, some hunnerd dollar dogs, seventy-five dol-

lar dogs, fifty dollar. . . . I haven't got a dog over there for fifty dollars. You can't raise one for that, 'cause a sack o' feed down there where we live cost you four fifty for fifty pounds, what we feed the hounds on, we feed the hounds on, and then we get scraps from that slaughter pen to put in. And if I tell you somep'n 'bout a dog I'm not gon' misrepresent him. Not gonna misrepresent him.

You see that little ol' ugly gyp [bitch] there? She'll git in the thicket. . . . We was runnin' the Fourth o' July, I think it was, runnin' a big gray fox. Across the road runnin' right down 'side this culvert, oh, 'bout like that. [Unintelligible.] You've seen it where, that's what, briar, you know, you know briar up under there, you know, know what I'm talkin' 'bout—these ol' . . . where . . . got them stickers on, 'bout like that [holds up his finger], 'bout that size, got that runner, big runner to 'em. And just had the place solid.

And we had a fox under there, and got him under there 'bout three o'clock, and he stayed there till it got daylight, he stayed under there to daylight. The road on east side o' that place.

And daylight come and them ol' feet comin' out from under round there drove her all buggy. He just walked in them briars. Place he could get in, you'd just see him every while just walkin'. You could hear that gyp now smell that fox. He got him hot, he just walk in them briars.

That little gyp come up in now, and she come up, man, there, like this fox, far like to the middle o' this pickup, quite that far—come out, shot out from under there, wasn't long before she come out just sprawled on her belly.

There she is, right there. There she is right there. [To dog] Yeah, come over here. (Recorded Canton, Texas, July 31, 1971)

In the second encounter there are three participants, only two of whom are heard in this excerpt: Homer Townsend and Herman Smith. Townsend's son is interested in Smith's dogs, but his father does the talking.

Townsend: Will them ol' dogs you got catch a rabbit?
Smith: Yeah.
Townsend: Really get up there and catch one?
Smith: Yes sir. I'd buy another one that'll outrun 'em.
Townsend: Well, a man told me a while ago they wouldn't hardly *run* a rabbit.
Smith: I tell you what I'll do. I'll take the man out here and *show* him. That's all I can do. . . . that's the *best* way, is to take him out and show him. I'll buy another 'un that can run with 'em . . . uh, keep 'em or sell or buy another 'un that could run with 'em, see. . . .
Townsend: [Interrupts] He's interested in some dogs, some greyhounds, and, uh, that man says they wouldn't hardly run a rabbit.

Smith: [Angrily] I'll *show* you! That's all I can do. You know me, I don't *lie*
about these dogs. I tried 'em out, see, I tried them dogs out before I
ever bought 'em, see. And I do the *coon* dogs thataway. I wouldn't
give a dime for nary a dog I didn't know on this ground until I
hunted him.

    I sold one last . . . uh . . . summer and the man asked me what I'd
take. I said, "I won't even price him till you go huntin.'" I said, "I sell
mine in the *woods!*" And when we went huntin', he treed three
coons. Come out, and he said, "Whatcha want for that dog?" I said
two-fifty. And he went countin' out them twenty-dollar bills.

    I got a little ol' gyp out there I've had three years. And she's three
years old—she's been treein' coons ever since she was a year old!
And she's still in my pen! And I got one o' her puppies mated to that
'un yonder . . . that's the one over there. Took him out the other day,
just started trainin' him, you know.

    That's the reason I got them greyhounds, 'cause I can see 'em, see? I
can't hear a thing outta this ear. I gotta go with somebody and they
got a bunch of trash and. . . . No, somebody got one to run with 'em,
I'll buy 'em this morning.

Townsend: [Leaving] Well, we'll talk to you a little bit . . . after a while.

Smith: [Loudly] I'll take 'em out here and *show* you! That's the way I am. I
don't lie about these dogs. I ain't . . . I don't believe in it.

    I bought a dog here 'bout three or four months ago down here
from an ol' man and ended high nigh walkin' him! And he was
tellin' me about that dog, trainin' young dogs and this 'n' that, and I
give him thirty dollars for it, and I *give* him to that little boy down
there. That hound don't tree. I *give* him to him. I wouldn't lie to
him, I *give* it to him! I don't lie about it. I'll buy 'em on the tree or
sell 'em on the tree, I don't care about the money. I don't lie about
these dogs. You hear anything very long and you'll say it's all right,
you know what I mean? (Recorded by Donna West, Canton, Texas,
November 1, 1970)

    For our purposes, two features stand out from these excerpts. First, the partic-
ipants clearly devote a considerable amount of interactional attention to the issue
of truthfulness and lying; and, second, one of the devices they resort to in ad-
dressing this issue is telling stories. Anyone who is at all familiar with hound-dog
men, coon hunters, or otherwise, will feel no surprise at hearing they have some
involvement in lying and storytelling. Georg Simmel suggests that "sociological
structures differ profoundly according to the measure of lying which operates in
them" (1950:312), and coon hunting certainly ranks fairly high on this scale.

    To an audience familiar with coon hunters, the association between lying and
coon hunting is so well established that it constitutes an expressive resource for

performance. The humorous monologue of the featured speaker at a Fourth of July celebration in Pekin, Indiana—an area near the Indiana-Kentucky border that is full of coon hunters—included the following introduction to a series of hunting stories:

> You know, now, somebody's accused me of lying, and I told somebody one time how bad it hurt me to lie, and they said, "you must be in awful pain, then, buddy." But I have had to lie some just to get by, you understand? I didn't want to lie, I was pushed into it. I done a lot of coon hunting, and when you go out with a bunch of coon hunters you got to lie just to stay with 'em.
>
> I can see by looking that there's no coon hunters in this audience today. I'm glad I did, I didn't want to insult anybody. But when you get out there in the field with a bunch of coon hunters, and get you a chew of tobacco in your mouth, and the dogs start running, you better start telling some lies, or you won't be out there long. (Byron Crawford, recorded Pekin, Indiana, July 4, 1978)

Or, as summed up for me with artful succinctness by a Texas coon hunter, "any man who keeps more'n one hound'll lie to you."

One type of lying associated with coon hunting, and of long-standing interest to folklorists, is the tall tale, the traditional tale of lying and exaggeration. Hunting has always been a privileged domain for tall tales: *The Types of the Folktale* (Thompson 1961) established the hunting tale as a special subgroup of tales of lying (types 1890–1909), and the standard American tall-tale collections are full of hunting windies (see Baughman 1966: types 1890–1909 and motifs X1100–1199, and references therein).

Traditional tall tales are told at Canton, but not often. Since the regulars have heard them over and over again, they tend largely to save them for newcomers not yet fully integrated into the coon-hunting fraternity (cf. Toelken 1979:112). The following tale, widely recorded, was addressed by a veteran hunter to a nineteen-year-old novice in the group:

> This ol' boy, he had him a coon dog. He had him a little coon [hide-] stretcher, looked like a piece of wire, V-shaped. He'd bring it out of the house, he had that coon dog, and it'd go out in the woods, kill him a coon, bring it back to the house, and all that boy had to do was just skin that coon out, put on that stretcher and skin. He was doing that for about two or three years, and was plum proud of his dog, and everything, and was telling everybody in town how good that dog was.
>
> One day his mama told him to take the ironing board outside to fix it; there was something wrong with it. That dog seen that ironing board and that dog hadn't showed up yet.[1] (Recorded Canton, Texas, June 2, 1973)

Tall tales such as this one play upon the generic expectations of another type of story which is ubiquitous among hound-dog men: narratives of personal experience about the special qualities and hunting prowess of particular dogs. The story of the dog and the ironing board/hide-stretcher followed closely on the heels of this one:

A: I run a coon down the creek back down home at Fred's a couple weeks
    ago. . . .
B: Yeah?
A: And I couldn't get him out, couldn't get in there to him, so Speck and I got
    . . . I caught Speck to lead him off now, "let's go, Speck."
    Went on down there, struck another coon and treed it. He jumped it out, and old Speck just whirled and left there, and I didn't know where in hell that sumbitch went.
    First time I heard him opened up back down on the tree. He went back there and checked the hole, that coon had come out and he treed that sumbitch down there [laughing].
C: Yeah.
D: Sure did. Dog's smart.
A: That durn coon came outa that hole. He went and treed that coon.
C: Yeah. That's what me and Bud done one night. Treed one down there. . . .
A: [Interrupting] He was thinkin' about that coon, wasn't he? (Recorded Canton, Texas, August 1, 1971)

Stories like this one dominate the sociable encounters of coon hunters wherever they come together, including the dog-trading grounds at Canton. These accounts stick close to the actual world of coon hunting and to the range of the possible—though not, in the best of them, to the ordinary. The extraordinary, the "reportable" in Labov's terms, is necessary if a personal narrative is to hold the listener's attention (Labov and Fanshel 1977:105). A dog like old Speck that can remind itself of a piece of unfinished business and go back to finish it off after treeing another coon is special, though believable. Why not, then, a dog that will catch a coon on order, to fit his master's hide-stretcher? The more common story of personal experience, told straightforwardly as truth, contextualizes the tall tale; it contributes to the latter's humorous effect by establishing a set of generic expectations that the tall tale can bend exaggeratedly out of shape. The effect is reciprocal, of course: The obvious exaggeration of the tall tale creates an aura of lying that colors the "true" stories as well.

When we juxtapose the personal narrative and the tall tale, actually two dimensions of "lying" become apparent. First, the unusual but not impossible events of the former are transformed into the exaggeratedly implausible events of the latter. Thus tall tales are lies, insofar as what they report as having happened either did not happen or could not have happened.

There is more, though. The tall tale presented above is told in the third person, which distances it somewhat from the narrator, and contrasts with the characteristic use of the first-person voice in the personal narrative. A common feature of tall-tale style, however, is also the use of the first person (Brunvand 1978:136–7), either directly ("I had an old coon dog that would go out in the woods. . . .") or as a link between the narrator and the third-person protagonist ("I knew an old boy, he had a coon dog . . . "). This device occurs in the second traditional tale we will consider below. When the first-person voice is employed, a second dimension of "lying" comes into play. The use of the first person brings the tall tale closer to personal narrative; it allows the story to masquerade for a while as a "true" personal narrative, until the realization that what is being reported is impossible shatters the illusion. In other words, these first-person tall tales are what Goffman calls "fabrications," "the intentional effort of one or more individuals to manage activity so that a party of one or more others will be induced to have a false belief about what it is that is going on" (1974:83). What appears to be going on is an account of actual events; what is really going on is a lie masquerading as such an account—a double lie. The man who tells such a tale in the third person is a liar; the man who tells it in the first person is a tricky liar, a con man. Thus two potential dimensions of "lying" enter into the expressive ambience of coon hunters: outright lies and fabrications.

As I have noted, though, traditional tall tales are not very common at Canton. But even without them, the aura of lying persists around the personal dog stories because, although recounted as true, they are susceptible to creative exaggeration, another dimension of "lying," for at least two major reasons. First, like all natural sociable interaction, the encounters of coon hunters are at base about the construction and negotiation of personal identity. In them, sociable narratives are a vehicle for the encoding and presentation of information about oneself in order to construct a personal and social image (Bauman 1972). In Watson and Potter's apt formulation, "social interaction gives form to the image of self and the image of the other; it gives validity and continuity to the identifications which are the source of an individual's self-esteem" (1962:246). The way to establish that you are a good coon hunter is to show that you have good hounds and are thus knowledgeable about quality dogs—even more so if you have trained them yourself. Thus, because hunting stories are instruments for identity building, for self-aggrandizement (Labov and Waletzky 1967:34), there is a built-in impulse to exaggerate the prowess of one's dogs with hyperbole ("When he trees, hell, if you ain't give out, you're plum gonna get him of starvation before he comes away from there"), or by selection (omitting mention of the faults of a dog you're bragging on) as a means of enhancing one's own image (cf. Gilsenan 1976:191). This tendency toward "stretching the truth," as it is often called, has been widely reported in men's sociable encounters (see, e.g., Bauman 1972; Bethke 1976: Biebuyck-Goetz 1977; Cothran 1974; Tallman 1975). It is one more factor that gives hound-dog men the reputation of being liars.

The other factor that promotes the expressive elaboration of the hound and hunting story is that, whatever its referential and rhetorical functions, it constitutes a form of verbal art. That is, it is characteristically *performed*, subject to eval-

Figure 9.1

uation, both as truth and as art for the skill and effectiveness with which it is told
(Bauman 1977:11). The aesthetic considerations of artistic performance may demand the embellishment or manipulation—if not the sacrifice—of the literal
truth in the interests of greater dynamic tension, formal elegance, surprise value,
contrast, or other elements that contribute to excellence in performance in this
subculture. "Stretching the truth," which chiefly exaggerates and selects, is not exactly the same as the outright lying of the tall tale. Nevertheless, although the two
activities can be terminologically distinguished to point up the contrast between
them, they are usually merged, and the term "lying," in an unmarked sense, is used
to label both (see Figure 9.1). Fabrication, our third analytically distinguished
type of lying, has no folk label.

For these reasons, then, some expectation of lying attends the telling of these stories about special dogs and memorable hunts. Realizing this, the tellers frequently
resort to various means of validating their accounts (cf. Ben-Amos 1976:30–2).
These range from verbal formulas like "I guarantee," to the testimony of witnesses
(as in the above story), to offers to demonstrate the dog in action. One man concluded a lengthy story about the hunting prowess of his hound as follows:

> You don't believe it, take and let your dogs run a coon loose, and I'll lead her, anybody
> tonight, anybody got their damn good cold-nose dogs, and if she don't run that coon
> and tree that coon, it's gonna be somethin' that ain't never happened. She'll run that
> sumbitch till by god, she'll tree that sumbitch. (Recorded Canton, Texas, August 1, 1971)

But even such emphatic attempts at validation often contain elements that subtly undermine the intended effect. In the statement just quoted, the owner backs
up his previous claim about his dog's ability to follow a cold trail to the tree by
stating that it has *never* failed to do so. Whereas the dog in question did in fact
have a far higher success rate than most others, both the owner and several of the
onlookers knew of times when it had failed, as any dog must once in a while. So,
despite these attempts at validation, the expectation persists that hound-dog men
will lie when talking about their dogs.

Occasionally, among intimates, someone may make a playful thrust at discred-
iting a story. To cite one example from Canton, a man, spotting an old friend who
was giving an account of a recent hunt to a circle of fellow hunters, called out as
he approached, "What you doin', lyin' to these people?" This is joking, however.
The interesting and noteworthy thing about the sociable storytelling of hound-
dog men is that, although it is strongly recognized as susceptible to lying, the lying
is overwhelmingly licensed as part of the fundamental ethos of sociability. That is,

by not challenging the truthfulness of another's stories, one may reasonably expect to be accorded the same license in presenting one's own image-building narratives and crafting one's own artful performances. Then too, it is only susceptibility we are talking about; not every personal narrative about dogs and hunting involves lying, nor is it always clear or consciously recognized as to which do and which do not. There is merely a persistent sense that every story might. To call another man a liar in this context, then, is to threaten his "face," with some risk and no possible advantage to oneself; whereas to give apparent acceptance to his accounts is to store up interactional credit toward the unchallenged acceptance of one's own tales.

Hunting tall tales and ordinary dog stories do not exhaust the repertoire of storytelling at Canton. The special character of First Monday for the hunters who attend is that it is an occasion for dog trading; not surprisingly, then, trading itself constitutes an important conversational resource for those who gather there. Like the hunting tall tales, some of the trading stories are traditional fictions, part of the national—even international—treasury of lore about shrewd trades, deceptive bargains, gullibility, and guile. To underscore his observations about a smart fellow trader, a dog jockey from Oklahoma who almost never misses a First Monday at Canton told the following story:

> And they're smart, too. I know an ol' boy, by god, he fell on a damn scheme to make some money, you know? Got hisself a bunch o' damn dog pills. 'Stead o' them damn . . . he called 'em "smart pills," you know, and by god, he'd sell them damn things, and an ol' boy'd come along, and he'd sell 'em a little to 'em, and tell 'em how smart they'd make 'em, you know, an' he'd get a dollar a piece for 'em.
>
> An ol' boy come along, and he sold him one.
>
> He said, "hell, I don't feel any smarter than I did."
>
> He said, "I found sometimes when you're pretty dumb it takes several of 'em, by god, to get you smartened up."
>
> He bought another one, took it, stood around there a few minutes, and said, "now, I ain't no smarter than I was."
>
> "Boy," he says, "you're something', you're just pretty dumb. You . . . you've got to take four or five for you."
>
> Well, he bought another one, took it, so he stood around, and the said, "man, them things ain't helping me a damn bit."
>
> He said, "I told you, you was pretty dumb." He said, "by god, you're gonna have to take another one."
>
> So he bought another one, by god, and he took that son of a bitch and rolled it around in his damn hand, and he reached up to taste it, and he said, "that tastes just like dog shit."
>
> He said, "boy, now you smartenin' up."[2] (Recorded Canton, Texas, June 5, 1977)

Let us examine this story in the light of our discussion thus far. Linked to the conversation that precedes it, and opened in the first person ("I know an ol' boy . . . "), the story appears at first to be a conventional personal narrative of the kind that is told as true. Ultimately, it is revealed as a humorous fiction. Like the traditional tall tale told in the first person, then, this story is both a lie and a fabrication. Its content, however, endows it with an additional dimension of deception. The trader here has clearly swindled the dupe by playing on his expectation that the "smart pills" would make him wiser by virtue of their medicinal powers. That, after all, is how pills work. The trader, of course, has made no such explicit claim. He has merely advertised his wares as "smart pills," and they do in fact make the dupe smarter—he wises up to the fact that he has been paying a dollar each for pellets of dog dung.

This story is one of a type of traditional tale in which the shrewd trader, although not actually telling an untruth—and thus not lying in a limited, literal sense—lies in effect nevertheless, at least in the sense set forth by Charles Morris (1946:261): "lying is the deliberate use of signs to misinform someone, that is, to produce in someone the belief that certain signs are true which the producer himself believes to be false." In the story above, the trader's ploy is actually a kind of fabrication, insofar as he induces the dupe to believe that he is taking pills that will affect him medicinally, whereas in fact such effect as they have is the result of his realization that this belief is false. The tale thus underscores in expressive form the semiparadoxical fact that traders can lie by telling the truth. The "smart pills" deception is at least arguably a "benign fabrication," in Goffman's terms (1974:87), leading as it does to the enlightenment of the dupe. However, "exploitive fabrications" (ibid.:103) also abound in this body of folklore and, as we shall see, in actual trading as well.

My impression, unverified by conclusive data, is that traditional tales about trading, like the one I have just presented, are less generally familiar to the population of the dog grounds at Canton than are the traditional tall tales about dogs and hunting. The latter are appropriate, in a general sense, whenever coon hunters come together sociably, whereas the former are more likely to be familiar to those with a regular involvement in trading, a much smaller group. In the setting of a First Monday, though, trading tales are highly appropriate, and I have heard more traditional stories about trading than traditional tall tales about hunting on the dog grounds.

Still more common are personal narratives about trades in which the teller himself was involved. Some of these, interestingly, are about being taken. Dog trading is, after all, a contest, and even the canny trader can be bested occasionally, as in the following account:

A: That's that little Trigg [a breed of hound] I's tellin' you about.
B: I bought one o' them one time, Cal, was the funniest thing I got in.
        When I swapped for her, and give some money, in Texarkana, old boy
        said, "I guarantee her." Said, "she's one of the finest coon dogs I've ever
        had in the woods in my life."
           I carried that dog home, I pitched her out, first thing she hit was a
        deer. I think a day or two later, I finally found her. And I mean she
        wouldn't run *one* thing on earth but a deer, not anything.

So I carried her back to Texarkana and just give her away. Yes sir. And *five* minutes after the boy drove off with that dog, a guy drove up and said, "do you know where I can find a deer dog anywhere for sale?"

C & D: [Laugh]

B: I'll bet he hadn't got two mile outa town, when . . .

D: [Interrupting] Outa town dog and all?

B: Yeah. Ain't no tellin' what he'd give for the dog, and she was perfect. I mean she was a straight deer dog. Wouldn't run nothin' else. But that's my luck. (Recorded Canton, Texas, August 1, 1971)

In this story, the teller loses out not once, but twice. He is victimized by being lied to outright by another trader—note the inevitable preoccupation with lying—and then compounds the problem by giving away the deer dog, worthless to a coon hunter, moments before he is presented with a golden opportunity to sell it at a handsome profit. Still, he is philosophical about it; he introduces the story as the *funniest* experience he has had with Trigg hounds and chalks up the whole experience to luck.

Whereas admitting that one has been taken in a trade might seem to expose one to some risk of losing face, the risk is apparently offset by the reportability and performance value of a good story. And, after all, it did take an outright lie on the trader's part to accomplish the deception. Moreover, any trader worth his salt has plenty of stories about how he bested someone else in a trade by the exercise of wit, cleverness, or deception. The same man who lost out twice on the deer dog told the following story, recounting a classic example of the short con, a fabrication par excellence.

Last time I went over to Canton, I had a dog I called Blackjack. He was just about as sorry a dog as I ever had owned. He wouldn't do nothin' but eat. Take him huntin' and he lay out under the pickup.

So I decided I'd take him over to Canton, and I did, and I met a friend of mine over there, named Ted Haskell, out o' Corsicana. I told Ted, I said, "now, you go up that alley up yonder and meet me 'bout half-way where they's tradin' dogs yonder, and then we'll introduce ourselves. You . . . we'll . . . sell this dog, and I'll give you half what I get outa it."

I met ol' Ted, and he says, "well, ol' Blackjack," he says, "I haven't had a coon race since I sold him," he says, "where'd you get him?"

"I got him over to Palestine."

"Well, I declare, I wisht I had him back," he says, "what are you askin' for' him?"

I said, "I'll take thirty dollars."

Well, they began to gather 'round and listen and listen. We kept talkin' 'bout him. He'd brag on Blackjack. And finally, an ol' boy eased up and called me off and says, "I'll give twenty dollars for him."

And I said, "Well, pay me." Well, he paid me.

Course I told Mr. Haskell mighty glad I'd met him, and he turned and went one way, and I went the other way, and we met at the pickup and divided the money. I come home, and he come back to Corsicana.

So I'm sure that man felt about like I did when I bought him, 'cause he wasn't worth carryin' a-huntin'. (Recorded by Thomas A. Green, Blooming Grove, Texas, May 31, 1968)

Stories like this one manifest a significant ambivalence about lying and other swindles, especially about lying—whether outright lying, stretching the truth, or fabrication—in conducting the trading itself. As I have noted, dog trading is viewed by the confirmed traders as a game of strategy in which, like many other games of strategy, deception occupies a central and accepted place. There is a long tradition in American folklore and popular literature of admiration for the shrewd trader, from the Yankee peddler to the Southern horse trader, who makes his way through the world by wit and words, part of "the traditional sympathy which storytellers have for rascals and crooks" (Benjamin 1969:106; cf. Dorson 1959:47–8; Ferris 1977; Green 1968, 1972). The numerous entries in Baughman's *Type and Motif-Index of the Folktales of England and North America* (1966) under K134, Deceptive horse sale (or trade), as well as such literary pieces as the horse trader in Longstreet's *Georgia Scenes* or the recent popular collections of horse-trading tales by Ben Green (1968, 1972; see also Welsch 1981), suggest that Americans enjoy hearing about shrewd traders and therefore, at some level at least, accept their crooked dealings (cf. Boatright 1973:146). The interplay between the trader's verbal skill in trading and his verbal skill as a storyteller is probably significant here; the two are complementary aspects of his overall image as quick-witted and shrewd, one who manipulates men and situations—whether trading encounters or social gatherings—to his own advantage (cf. Benjamin 1969:101). Good traders are not reluctant self-publicists; one Canton regular told me with obvious pride: "I'll tell you what you can do. You can put me right out there on that road, barefooted, if it wasn't too hot, and before I get home, I'll have a pair of shoes, I want to tell you."

Nevertheless, whereas chess, for example, is unequivocally and only a game, in which such strategic deception as may occur is completely contained within the play frame, dog trading is not so unambiguous. Whereas trading is certainly engaged in as play by many of the participants at Canton, the play frame is almost never overtly acknowledged. The only instances I observed that were openly marked as play were framed by such obviously inappropriate offers as five dollars plus a toothless old dog for a proven hound in prime condition. Otherwise, the public construction placed upon the trading encounter depicts it as a serious business transaction, and it is *always* susceptible to being understood as such by one or both participants.

Here is the crux of the matter. The traditional American ideal demands, if not absolute honesty in business transactions, at least the maintenance of the public fiction that the participants are telling the truth (cf. Simmel 1950:314). Thus lying does not accord with the public construction of a dog-trading transaction, nor is it consistent with the actual understanding of those who consider a dog trade straight business, not a game. The trader who lies about a dog during the conduct of a trade may see himself and be seen by some other traders as a master player, gulling the marks as they deserve, but he may also be despised as a swindler who cheats honest people. No harm is done by telling stories about shrewd or crooked trades—indeed, such accounts may be relished for their performance value—but actually hoodwinking someone is a different matter. It makes the difference between Goffman's benign and exploitative fabrications (1974:87, 103).

At the same time, therefore, that a trader is telling a well-formed and entertaining story in which he beats someone by a classic confidence trick, he may also be at pains to disavow any dishonesty. The veteran trader who unloaded Blackjack by trickery and obviously relished telling about it had just a few minutes before beginning his story made a gesture at resolving the moral dilemma by framing his trading swindles as the excesses of youth: "Most men my age won't lie about a dog; but just before you get to my age, they'll lie and tell you any kinda tale just to get to sell you a dog."

Having explored the relationship between lying and storytelling among the dog traders at Canton to this point, we can now return to the excerpts from the trading encounters with which we began our exploration. The strong preoccupation with lying and storytelling that characterizes both encounters should be relatively more comprehensible in light of the preceding discussion.

The rich expressive tradition of storytelling associated with hound-dog men and dog traders—the tales of hunting and trading and the personal narratives about both activities—as well as the conception of dog trading as a game of strategy in which the goal is often to get rid of a worthless dog at a profit help endow dog trading at Canton with a considerable aura of lying and deception. These expressive forms both reflect and sustain the sense that misrepresentation of one sort or another permeates the institution, and many participants can confirm from first-hand experience that lying is indeed a factor to be reckoned with. It is not at all surprising that parties on both sides of a dog trade should enter the transaction anticipating that the opposite party might lie about a dog and expect to be lied to in return. At the same time, either man (both parties if a trade is involved, only the seller if it is to be a cash sale) might in fact be ready and willing to lie to unload a dog. Yet even if one is ready to lie, to acknowledge as much is impossible; it would violate the public construction that dog trading is an honest business transaction and would very likely undermine the interactional foundation of the trading relationship itself.

The strategy that emerges from the expectations and conventions of dog trading is that one should take pains during an actual transaction to *dispel* the aura of lying that surrounds it. The most direct means of doing so is by explicit insistence on one's truthfulness and by disavowal of lying (cf. Bakhtin 1968:162). In the encounters under examination, both John Moore and Herman Smith employ this means of establishing their trustworthiness. John Moore volunteers early in the encounter: "I try to be fair with a man 'bout a dog. Tell the truth about a dog, tell you what he'll do. If there's any fault to him, I wanna tell the man." And then, employing the powerful rhetorical device of identification (Burke 1969:20–3), Moore puts himself in Byers's position: "If I get a dog from a man, if there's any fault to him, I want him to tell me." A little later, to validate the information he is providing about his dogs, he insists: "If I tell you somep'n 'bout a dog, I'm not gon' misrepresent him. Not gonna misrepresent him." In the second encounter, Herman Smith is rather seriously challenged by Homer Townsend; he reiterates with some vehemence throughout the encounter, "I don't lie about these dogs!" These are all disclaimers of outright lying or of stretching the truth by selection or distortion. I have not recorded or observed any instances in which a participant disavowed pulling off a fabrication, although it is conceivable that such disavowals might occur.

Another means of establishing one's veracity in a trading encounter is to offer to let the dogs prove the claims made for them, just as the tellers of dog stories do in sociable encounters. This is Herman Smith's main trust; he offers repeatedly to "take 'em out here and show you." He also resorts to the identificational strategy of putting himself in the place of the buyer. When he is buying dogs, he tries them out: "I wouldn't give a dime for nary a dog I didn't know on this ground until I hunted him." By trying out the dogs he is offering before having bought them, Smith has, in effect, already acted on Townsend's behalf, and Townsend is safe in buying them now.

For our purposes, perhaps the most interesting means by which the dog traders seek to establish and substantiate their identities as honest men is in telling stories. If we examine these stories, we see that they are closely related to the sociable narratives discussed at length earlier in this chapter—specifically, to personal narratives about the performance of particular dogs and to personal narratives about trading experiences.

Three narratives appear in the excerpt from the first trading encounter—two told by John Moore and one very minimal one told by Mr. Byers. Moore clearly tells his first story, about being victimized in a trade by buying some puppies that the seller falsely assures him had had their shots, as a rhetorical strategy to convey his negative attitudes toward a trader who would tell an outright lie about a dog. By implication, he emphasizes his own trustworthiness in a context wherein trickery and deceit are widespread. Moore's central rhetorical purpose is to distance himself from dog traders who lie, and his story is obviously and strongly adapted to that purpose. Much of his narrative is given over to establishing this polarization (Labov 1979) between the dishonest trader and Moore himself, as customer. The trader's lie is doubly destructive because it was both unnecessary, since Moore was going to buy the dogs whether or not they had had their shots, and cruel, since it resulted in the death of the dogs. The evaluative dimension of the narrative is heavily elaborated, both through repetition (both the query to the trader about whether the puppies were vaccinated and the narrative report of those queries are repeated) and lexical intensifiers (emotion-laden words like "swore," "hate," "begged") (Labov and Waletzky 1967:37–8). The point is that Moore gave the trader ample and repeated opportunity to tell the truth, but he remained firm in his lie; and everyone suffered as a result, even the liar himself, since the death of the puppies brought him remorse ("he hate that he didn't tell us . . . ").

Byers too has been taken in a trade. He comes back with his account of having traded once for two dogs that were supposed to be good fox dogs and then discovering that the "sumbitches wouldn't run a *rabbit.*" This story establishes that he has already been victimized at least once in a trade and, by implication, that he does not intend to let it happen again. As he is not the one whose honesty is on the line, however, having no dog to trade, his story is rather minimal—just long enough to make his point, without attempting to be strongly persuasive. Still, there is not a clause in his narrative that lacks a clearly evaluative element.

Moore goes on to reaffirm his bona fides by mentioning his satisfied customers, including "some rich, up-to-date people." Then, picking up on Byers's apparent interest in fox dogs, Moore points out a fox dog among his own string, and proceeds to tell an extended story about her prowess in a recent hunt in order to build up her credentials—a sales pitch in narrative form. Stories of this kind are especially motivated during trading transactions because one cannot tell from merely looking at a dog what its hunting abilities are. Straightforward enumeration of the dog's qualities could also get the information across, but corroborating narratives, convincingly told, may add verisimilitude to the seller's claims. Skill in storytelling may thus enhance the overall rhetorical power of the sales pitch. One must maintain a delicate balance, however, because stories are also considered vehicles for creative or duplicitous misrepresentation. Hence the usefulness of combining such narratives with additional claims to honesty, as Moore does both directly and by telling his story about a dishonest dog trader in order to distance himself from such practices. As the one offering the dogs, Moore has to tell stories that are persuasive enough to establish both his honesty, as in the first story, and the dog's quality, persistence, toughness, and so on, as in the second. In sociable interaction, there is no immediate negative consequence if your audience does not accept the truth of your story; in trading encounters, others must accept your story sufficiently to be persuaded to *act* on it (it is hoped by trading for or buying your dog).

The second excerpt contains two stories, both told by Herman Smith, the man with the dogs. Townsend has rather seriously challenged him with offering dogs that won't perform. Smith accordingly counters with a story to demonstrate that, far from being willing to risk a customer's dissatisfaction or skepticism, he would actually *refuse* to conclude a sale until the dog has proven itself in the woods. This is not just honesty, it's superhonesty. Smith's second story is in the same vein: Having been taken in by an unscrupulous trader who lied about the treeing ability of a dog, Smith would not himself stoop to selling the worthless hound, but gave it away to a little boy. Any man who gives dogs to little boys can't be all bad. Here is another instance of extreme polarization between the dishonest trader and the honest man: The unscrupulous trader places profit over honesty, whereas Smith values honesty over profit ("I don't care about the money. I don't lie about

these dogs"). Just so there is no question about his own honorable values, he repeats the relevant points again and again.

Honesty . . .	Over Profit
I wouldn't lie to him.	I *gave* him to that little boy down there.
I don't lie about it.	I *give* him to him!
I don't lie about these dogs.	I *give* it to him!

Interestingly, this story compromises one of Smith's earlier claims to
Townsend—that he himself tries out all the dogs he acquires before buying them.
If he had done so in this case, he would not have had a worthless dog fobbed off
on him. But it is more important to tell an emphatic story for its rhetorical effect
than to worry about a minor inconsistency like this. Should Townsend pick up on
it, this inconsistency could undermine Smith's claims to scrupulous honesty.

This second story of Smith's so closely parallels the story of the deer dog, discussed earlier, that a brief comparison can highlight certain significant differences
generated by the differing contexts in which they occur and their respective functions within these contexts. In both stories the narrator acquires a dog from someone who lies to get rid of it and then, discovering that the dog does not perform
as expected, gives it away. The story of the deer dog, told for entertainment in sociable interaction, is connected to the discourse that precedes it solely by the fact
that the dog in question was a Trigg hound, and the previous speaker had pointed
out a Trigg in his own string of dogs. No more is needed for the story to be appropriate in this sociable context. The extra twist at the end of the story, in which
a customer appears for the dog immediately after it has been given away, makes
the tale unusual and endows it with entertainment value. There is credit to be
gained, as a performer, in telling it. The event sequence consists of six principal
episodes, most of which have subepisodes:

1. Trading for the dog in the expectation that it was a coon dog
2. Taking it home
3. Taking it on a disastrous trial hunt, in which it turns out to be a deer dog
4. Having to search for the now apparently worthless dog
5. Returning to Texarkana to give it away
6. Being approached by someone looking for a deer hound exactly like the one
   just given away

The evaluative dimension of the story serves to highlight the reportability of the
experience, the humor and irony of the situation.

Herman Smith's story, however, is more strongly motivated and rooted in its
conversational context. Smith's prospective customers are leaving, apparently because they don't believe his dogs are any good, and he is very concerned to establish his trustworthiness as a dog trader. The narrative line of the story is minimal:

1. Trading for the dog

2. Discovering that it won't perform as promised
3. Giving it away

More important by far is the rhetorical impact. The rhetorical power of the story resides in the fact that, unlike the unscrupulous trader, Smith spurned the opportunity to swindle someone else with a worthless dog; instead, he gave it away to the little boy. This is the point that he emphasizes most strongly in his story. Most of the work of the narrative, the thrust of its heavy evaluative dimension, aims at a polarization between the dishonest trader and the honorable narrator. Note, however, that this story, like those of John Moore and Mr. Byers, does also involve a trader who is not as honest as Smith presents himself to be, one who lies outright about a dog. Thus we come full circle: The very story that is told in the course of a trading encounter to dispel any suspicion of the trader's dishonesty reinforces the aura of lying that surrounds trading in general. Any man who keeps more'n one hound'll lie to you.

Dog trading at Canton First Monday brings together and merges two important figures in American tradition, the hunter and the trader. Both are strongly associated with storytelling as subjects and performers, and both are major exponents of the widely noted (though not exclusively) American predilection for expressive lying. Since at least the time when a distinctive body of American folk humor first emerged during the early years of the American republic, the hunter and the trader have occupied a privileged place in American folklore. Dog trading at Canton is a thriving contemporary incarnation of this American folk tradition. The tall tales and personal narratives of its participants place them in unbroken continuity with the generations of hunters, traders, and storytellers that have given American folklore some of its most distinctive characteristics. At the same time, First Monday dog trading offers a richly textured arena for the ethnographic investigation of the nuances of expressive lying, the negotiation of truthfulness and lying as action and evaluation in the conduct of social life.

The narratives that are the instruments of these negotiations do not fall into clear-cut categories of factual and fictional, truthful and lying, believable and incredible, but rather interweave in a complex contextual web that leaves these issues constantly in doubt, ever susceptible to strategic manipulation whenever a trade is joined.[3]

Notes

1. Baughman (1966), motif X1215.8 (aa): Master shows dog a skin-stretching board; the dog brings in a raccoon just the size of the board. Master's mother puts ironing board outside one day. The dog never returns.

2. Thompson (1955–8), motif K114.3.1: *Virtue of oracular pill proved.* The dupe takes it. "It is dog's dung," he says, spitting it out. The trickster says that he is telling the truth and demands pay.

3. An earlier version of this chapter appeared in Bauman (1981).

References

Bakhtin, Mikhail M. 1968. *Rabelais and His World,* Hélène Iswolsky, trans. Cambridge, MA: MIT Press.

Bascom, William. 1965. "The forms of folklore: Prose narratives." *Journal of American Folklore* 78:3–20.

Baughman, Ernest W. 1966. *Type and Motif-Index of the Folktales of England and North America.* The Hague: Mouton.

Bauman, Richard. 1972. "The LaHave Island General Store: Sociability and verbal art in a Nova Scotia community." *Journal of American Folklore* 85:330–343.

———. 1977. Verbal Art as Performance, repr. ed. 1984. Prospect Heights, IL: Waveland Press.

———. 1981. "'Any man who keeps more'n one hound'll lie to you:' dog trading and storytelling at Canton, Texas." In Richard Bauman and Roger D. Abrahams, eds. *"And Other Neighborly Names": Social Process and Cultural Images in Texas Folklore.* Austin: University of Texas Press, 79–103.

Ben-Amos, Dan. 1976. "Talmudic tall tales." In Linda Dégh, Henry Glassie, and Felix J. Oinas, eds. *Folklore Today.* Bloomington: Indiana University Press, 25–43.

Benjamin, Walter. 1969. *Illuminations.* New York: Schocken.

Bethke, Robert D. 1976. "Storytelling at an Adirondack inn." Western Folklore 35:123–139.

Biebuyck-Goetz, Brunhilde. 1977. " 'This is the dyin' truth': mechanisms of lying." *Journal of the Folklore Institute* 14:73–95.

Boatright, Mody C. 1973 [1961]. "The oil promoter as trickster." In Ernest Speck, ed. *Mody Boatwright, Folklorist.* Austin: University of Texas Press, 145–162.

Brunvand, Jan. 1978. *The Study of American Folklore,* 2nd ed. New York: Norton.

Burke, Kenneth. 1969 [1950]. *A Rhetoric of Motives.* Berkeley: University of California Press.

Carson, Jane. 1965. *Colonial Virginians at Play.* Williamsburg, VA: Colonial Williamsburg.

Cothran, Kay L. 1974. "Talking trash on the Okefenokee Swamp rim." *Journal of American Folklore* 87:340–356.

Craven, Wesley Frank. 1949. *The Southern Colonies in the Seventeenth Century, 1607–1689.* Baton Rouge, LA: Louisiana State University Press.

Dégh, Linda, and Andrew Vázsonyi. 1976. "Legend and belief." In Dan Ben-Amos, ed., *Folklore Genres.* Austin, TX: University of Texas Press, 93–123.

Dorson, Richard M. 1959. *American Folklore.* Chicago: University of Chicago Press.

Ferris, Bill. 1977. *Ray Lum: Mule Trader, an Essay.* Memphis, TN: Center for Southern Folklore.

Fiske, John. 1904. *Civil Government in the United States.* Boston: Houghton-Mifflin.

Georges, Robert. 1971. "The general concept of legend: some assumptions to be reexamined and reassessed." In Wayland D. Hand, ed., *American Folk Legend: A Symposium.* Berkeley: University of California Press, 1–19.

Gilsenan, Michael. 1976. "Honor, lying and contradiction." In Bruce Kapferer, ed., *Transaction and Meaning: Directions in the Anthropology of Exchange and Symbolic Behavior.* Philadelphia: Institute for the Study of Human Issues, 191–219.

Goffman, Erving. 1967. "Where the Action Is." In E. Goffman, ed., *Interaction Ritual.* New York: Doubleday Archor,

———. 1974. *Relations in Public.* New York: Harper and Row.

Green, Ben K. 1968. *Horse Tradin'.* New York: Knopf.

————. 1972. *Some More Horse Tradin'*. New York: Knopf.

Halpert, Herbert. 1971. "Definition and Variation in Folk Legend." In Wayland D. Hand, ed., *American Folk Legend: A Symposium*. Berkeley: University of California Press.

Heath, Shirley Brice. 1983. *Ways with Words*. Cambridge: Cambridge University Press.

Labov, William. 1979. "*A Grammar of Narrative*." Lecture presented at the University of Texas at Austin, October 10, 1979.

Labov, William, and David Fanshel. 1977. *Therapeutic Discourse*. New York: Academic Press.

Labov, William, and Joshua Waletzky. 1967. "Narrative analysis: oral versions of personal experience." In June Helm, ed., *Essays in the Verbal and Visual Arts*. Seattle: University of Washington Press, 12–44.

Limón, José E. 1983. "Legendry, metafolklore and performance." *Western Folklore* 42:21–27.

Littleton, C. Scott. 1965. "A two-dimensional scheme for the classification of narratives." *Journal of American Folklore* 78:21–27.

Mills, W. S. 1950. *History of Van Zandt County*. Canton, TX.

Morris, Charles. 1946. *Signs, Language and Behavior*. New York: Braziller.

Rickford, John R. 1986. "Riddling and lying: participation and performance." In Joshua A. Fishman, ed., *A Festschrift for Charles A. Ferguson*. The Hague: Mouton.

Sartain, James Alfred. 1932. *History of Walker County, Georgia*, vol. 1. Dalton, GA: A. J. Showalter.

Simmel, Georg. 1950. *The Sociology of Georg Simmel*. Kurt Wolff, ed. and trans. Glencoe, IL: Free Press.

Sydnor, Charles S. 1948. *The Development of Southern Sectionalism, 1819–1848*. Baton Rouge, LA: Louisiana State University Press.

Tallman, Richard. 1975. "Where stories are told: a Nova Scotia storyteller's milieu." *American Review of Canadian Studies* 5:17–41.

Thompson, Stith. 1955–1958. *Motif-Index of Folk Literature*. 6 vols. Bloomington, IN: Indiana University Press.

————. 1961. *The Types of the Folktale*, 2nd rev. ed. Helsinki: Folklore Fellows Communication no. 184.

Toelken, Barre. 1979. *The Dynamics of Folklore*. Boston: Houghton-Mifflin.

Verhoeff, Mary. 1911. *The Kentucky Mountains*, vol. 1. Louisville, KY: John P. Morton.

Watson, Jeanne, and Robert J. Potter. 1962. "An analytic unit for the study of interaction." *Human Relations* 12:245–263.

Welsch, Roger, ed. 1981. *Mister, You Got Yourself a Horse*. Lincoln, NE: University of Nebraska Press.

10

Carne, Carnales, and the Carnivalesque: Bakhtinian *Batos,* Disorder, and Narrative Discourses

JOSÉ E. LIMÓN

And when he came to the place where the wild things are
they roared their terrible roars and gnashed their terrible teeth
and rolled their terrible eyes and showed their terrible claws
till Max said, "Be still!"
and tamed them with the magic trick
of staring into all their yellow eyes without blinking once
and they were frightened and called him the most wild thing of all
and made him king of all wild things
"And now," cried Max, "let the wild rumpus start!"

> —*From the children's book by Maurice Sendak,* Where
> the Wild Things Are, *in which a mischievous little boy,*
> *Max, visits the Wild Things.*

At two in the afternoon a periodically unemployed working-class man in Mexican-American south Texas puts hot chunks of juicy barbecued meat with his fingers on an equally hot tortilla. The meat or *carne* has marinated overnight in beer and lemon juice before being grilled. Antoñio, or Toñio, passes the meat-laden tortilla to one of the other eight mostly working-class men surrounding a rusty barbecue grill, but as he does so, the hand holding the food brushes against his own genital area, and he loudly tells the other, "*¡Apaña este taco carnal, 'ta a toda madre mi carne!*" (Grab this taco, brother, my meat is a mother!).[1] With raucous laughter all around, I accept the full, dripping taco, add some hot sauce and reach for an ice-downed beer from an also rusty washtub.

Some 50 years ago the Mexican thinker, Samuel Ramos, published his well known and still culturally authoritative *Profile of Man and Culture in Mexico*

(1962), an interpretive general narrative history of its subject since its indigenous beginnings. Ramos was trying to explain what he saw as the reduced sense of Mexican cultural life and its contradictions in his time. As part of his contemporary account, a kind of climax to his narrative, Ramos turns into an anthropological, if distanced, observer of everyday Mexican life, particularly male life. For example, the Mexican *pelado* or lower-class man

> belongs to a most vile category of social fauna; . . . a form of human rubbish. . . . Life from every quarter has been hostile to him and his reaction has been black resentment. He is an explosive being with whom relationship is dangerous, for the slightest friction causes him to blow up (1962:59).

According to Ramos, the Mexican lower-class man's

> explosions are verbal and reiterate his theme of self affirmation in crude and suggestive language. He has created a dialect of his own, a diction which abounds in ordinary words, but he gives these words a new meaning. He is an animal whose ferocious pantomimes are designed to terrify others, making them believe that he is stronger than they and more determined. Such reactions are illusory retaliations against his real position in life which is a nullity (1962:60).

For Ramos, these verbal pantomimes, these explosive linguistic reactions are of a particular kind. This lower-class man's "terminology abounds in sexual allusions which reveal his phallic obsession; the sexual organ becomes symbolic of masculine force." The reproductive organs are a symbolic source of "not only one kind of potency, the sexual, but every kind of human power" as this man "tries to fill his void with the only suggestive force accessible to him: that of the male animal" and, continues Ramos, "so it is that his perception becomes abnormal; he imagines that the next man he encounters will be his enemy; he mistrusts all who approach him" (1962:59–61).

In this paper I discuss what Foucault calls discourses of power as these concern Mexican-American south Texas where I was raised, my current fieldwork site and still a place characterized by sharp class and ethnic divisions as it has been since Zachary Taylor's army first conquered the area in the 1840s during the United States-Mexico War (Foley 1978; de Leon 1982, 1983; Montejano 1987). You have already heard two examples of such discourse: one, the expressive, all male humor of a group of *batos* (guys, dudes) articulated in and through the ritualistic consumption of barbecued meat in southern Texas, an event called a *carne asada*; and, two, Samuel Ramos' narratively embedded commentary on the language and culture of the Mexican male lower class, a discourse tradition continued by Octavio Paz in the 1950s and applied directly to the Mexican-Americans of south Texas in the 1960s by anthropologist Joseph Spielberg (1974).

Mindful of Marcus' recent call upon Marxist ethnographers to also provide analyses of the culture of the dominant as well as the dominated (1986), I have, in another paper tried to show how this second set of discourses, this interpretive tradition begun by Samuel Ramos, functions as a discourse of power in a larger international scope (Limón 1987). At critical moments in Mexican and Mexican-American history, this interpretive tradition unintentionally helps to ratify dominance through its negative psychologistic interpretation of the Mexican male lower class and their language. As Ramos' commentary clearly illustrates, this discourse casts these classes in the idiom of human rubbish, animality, aggressiveness, and abnormality, a view, I might add, considerably shared by those—both Anglo and Mexican-American—who hold class power in southern Texas.

My chief purpose here, however, is to begin to develop an alternative understanding of this lower-class male culture; to develop a third narrative discourse, if you will, one which I would like to think Foucault might have called an archaeology of subjugated knowledges and practices, this in an effort to demonstrate the power of such knowledges and practices as a discourse of the dominated, discourses often in narrative form. My analysis will draw from recent Marxist perspectives on language, on the anthropology of natural symbols but centrally on Bakhtin's sense of the carnivalesque.

However, even as I go about this central purpose, I want to call attention to the purpose itself. That is, I want to keep before the reader my own effort to narrativize these subjugated narratives. To be sure, this effort is in a different political direction from Ramos and Paz but is nonetheless itself an authoritative narrative, which, as Foucault would remind us, is never wholly free from the influence of dominating power. This latter issue will become more evident in my conclusion.

In the construction of our own ethnographic narratives, we are inevitably faced with the problem of rhetorically managing what we are pleased to call "the data." How much is enough so as to persuade and not bore or overwhelm? And, where do we place it in the structural development of our own text? What is the proper relationship between the data and our interpretive analysis, recognizing full well that the selection and organization of the data have already taken us a long way toward our understanding of it? With these issues in mind, I continue with my strategy of juxtaposing narrative discourses from the dominant and dominated, reminding you once again of my own emerging ethnographic narrative.

Later that afternoon on a hot August Saturday in 1981, another man, an auto parts salesman, in a ten-year-old pickup drives up to our barbecue session in the outskirts of McBurg.[2] He brings with him a couple of pounds of tripe that will eventually be added to the other internal organs and to the *fajita*, or skirt steak, now turning golden brown and sizzling in its fat on the barbecue grill. His *tripitas*—for all the meat parts are expressed in the diminutive—are turned over to Poncho, house painter, and the latest cook at the grill. Jaime, this new arrival (otherwise known as "el Midnight" because he is quite dark), begins to shake everyone's hand in greeting saying, "*¿Como estas?*" (How are you doing?) and so on. Expecting my turn, I put down my beer and dry my hand on my jeans, but Jaime never makes it past the second man he greets, Simón.

Simón, otherwise known as "el Mickey Mouse" because of his large ears, has been a construction laborer most of his adult life, except for the three years he spent at the state prison when he got caught on the highway to Austin transporting marijuana for the consumption of the students at the university. "*¡Que pendejada!*" "*¡Tiré un beer can y me paró el jurado!*" (What stupidity! I threw out a beer can and the cop stopped me!)

Simón takes Jaime's hand as if to shake it but instead yanks it down and holds it firmly over his own genital area even as he responds to Jaime's "*¿Como estas?*" with a loud "*¡Pos, chínga ahora me siento a toda madre, gracias!*" (Well, fuck, now I feel just great, thank you!) There is more laughter which only intensifies when "Midnight" in turn actually grabs and begins to squeeze "el Mickey's" genitals. With his one free hand, for the other is holding a taco, el Mickey tries to pull on Jaime's arm unsuccessfully. Finally in an effort to slip out of Jaime's grip, he collapses to the ground cursing and trying to laugh at the same time and loses his taco in the process. Jaime, however, has gone down on his knees and manages to maintain his grip even as he keeps saying over and over, "*!Dime que me quieres, cabrón, dime que me quieres!*" (Tell me you love me, godammit, tell me you love me!) El Mickey finally says "*Te quiero, te quiero*" but as soon as he is released, he continues, "*Te quiero dar en la madre!*" (I want to beat the hell out of you) playing on the double meaning of quiero as "want" and "love." He takes a few semi-mock punches at Jaime's torso and receives a few in return, both carefully avoiding the face. Everyone is still laughing as el Mickey and Midnight, still on their knees, hug each other to a stop. As they help each other up, Jaime tells Mickey, "*Dejando de chingaderas, anda a traer otro taco y traile uno a tu papa*" (All screwing around aside, go get another taco and bring one for your father), referring, of course, to himself. Doing or saying *chingaderas* (fuck ups) is how these men label and gloss this activity, also sometimes *pendejadas* and *vaciladas* (stupidities, play routines). See Spielberg (1974).

In the 1950s another distinguished Mexican intellectual had this story to tell about the Mexican lower-class male personality and his language. "It is significant," says Octavio Paz, "that masculine homosexuality is regarded with a certain indulgence insofar as the active agent is concerned." The passive agent is an abject, degraded being. "This ambiguous conception," he continues, "is made very clear in the word games or battles—full of obscene allusions and double meanings— that are so popular in Mexico City" (1961:39).

> Each of the speakers tries to humiliate his adversary with verbal traps and ingenious linguistic combinations, and the loser is the person who cannot think of a comeback, who has to swallow his opponent's jibes. These jibes are full of aggressive sexual allusions; the loser is possessed, is violated, by the winner, and the spectators laugh and sneer at him (1961:39–40).

Octavio Paz continues this commentary translated into English in 1961. "The Mexican macho," he says, is a humorist who commits *chingaderas*, that is, unforeseen acts that produce confusion, horror, and destruction. He opens the world; in doing so, he rips and tears it, and this violence provokes a great sinister laugh . . . the humor of the *macho* is an act of revenge (1961:81).

"Whatever may be the origins of these attitudes," Paz tells us, "the fact is that the essential attribute of the *macho*-power almost always reveals itself as a capacity for wounding, humiliating, annihilating" (1961:82).

It is almost six o'clock in this evening outside of McBurg at what our host Chema likes to call his *rancho*, which amounts to less than one-quarter acre of dry, wholly undeveloped land with only a few mesquites to provide some shade from the hot south Texas sun. Chema bought the land, called "ranchettes" by local real estate agents, when he came into a little money from a worker's compensation settlement. He fell from a truck while doing farm labor for extra money. Massaging his lower back for the still lingering pain, he says "*El pínche abogado se quedó con la mitad*" (The fucking lawyer [Mexican-American] kept half). Chema's only real notion for improving the property is to build an inevitable brick barbecue pit, but until he can afford it, he will have to haul the portable rusty one on the back of his pickup out to the *rancho*.

A few more men have come with more meat and beer and a few have left, playfully taunted by the others "*Tiene que ir a reportar a la vieja*" (He has to go report to his old lady), knowing that eventually they'll have to go report to their "old ladies." The eating, drinking, and the talk are still thick, and *conjunto* polka music is playing from a portable radio, although later this will be replaced by guitar playing and singing of, on the one hand, *corridos* or Mexican ballads with accompanying *gritos* (cries) and, on the other, American tunes from the 'fifties such as "In the Still of the Night" by the Five Satins to which everyone will sing a cacophony of appropriate *sho do be do be doos*.

One of the men keeps insisting that he has to go; with equal insistence he is told to have another beer and to make a taco out of the very last of the cherished delicacy, *mollejitas* (glandular organs), but he is particularly insistent because his kids need to be picked up at the movies where, we discover, they have been watching Steven Spielberg's *E.T.—The Extra Terrestrial*. Octavio is almost ready to leave when Chema, our host and ranch owner asks him: "*Aye, 'Tavo. Sabes como se dice 'E.T.' en espanol?*" (Hey 'Tavo, do you know how to say E.T. in Spanish?) Before Octavio can even try to reply, a grinning Chema answers his own question correctly by saying, "*Eh Te*" but he is also holding his hand over his genitals and gesturing twice with it as he pronounces the two syllables. *Eh Te* does of course mean E.T. in Spanish, but it is also the way a toddler might pronounce *este* (this one), dropping a consonant "s" but meaning *this or this one* as in *este papel* (this paper). In saying *Eh Te* and with his double gesture, Chema is calling attention, particularly Octavio's attention, to his penis—this one. But things get better . . . or worse, as the case may be. Chema continues his interrogation of Octavio: "*Y, como se llaman los dos hermanitos de E.T.?*" (and, what are the names of E.T.'s two little brothers?).

Chema demonstrates the answer with another genital double gesture, this time answering his own question with the Spanish *Eh Tos,* again exploiting the baby play language pronunciation of *estos* meaning *these,* referring, of course, to *these two* meaning his own testicles. Everyone, including Octavio, is laughing and all of us cannot help but look as Chema does his gestures and baby talk, and he isn't through yet. "And what," he asks, "is the name of E.T.'s mother?" This time, however, Octavio who has obviously been conducting his own ethnography of this speech act, beats Chema to the answer with his hand at his crotch, loudly and triumphantly proclaims the answer, "*¡Mama Eh Te!*"; this time, Octavio has exploited the original *este* (this one) and he has also exploited the charged ambiguity of *mama* in Spanish, which, depending on accent and syntax can mean "mother" or "suck." Laughing with the others, Octavio finally makes his way to the movie *E.T. or Eh Te* to pick up the kids; Chema is shaking his head and laughing and complaining about all of the meat juice he has managed to rub all over his crotch.

By seven or eight, more people start dispersing, a few latecomers arrive, a fire has been started, and one of the guitarists sings the "Corrido of Jacinto Trevino" about a brave south Texas Mexican who shot it out with the Texas Rangers in 1906 in the town of Brownsville just down the river from McBurg (Paredes 1976). Finally, thinks your ethnographer, I get some real folklore of resistance and not all of these *chingaderas.*

For at that moment, some years ago, I am troubled, at least intellectually, by what I have reexperienced, having gone through such events several times in my life in south Texas but also in a few cantinas in Monterey, in Los Angeles, in Mexico City. Are Ramos and Paz right when they speak of sexual anxiety, of wounding, and humiliation? Are the *chingaderas* "unforeseen acts that produce confusion, horror and destruction" amid a "great sinister laugh?" And, at that time it did not help to have reread a recent anthropological study of such south Texas male humor specifically in this area near McBurg in which Joseph Spielberg, also a native south Texan, concludes that this humor "can be characterized as verbal aggression aimed at another when he is most vulnerable" by his "own lack of discretion in bodily functions, social circumstances or by revealing his sentiments." In the tradition of Ramos and Paz, Spielberg also believes that "the principal theme of this humor" is "humiliation" (1974:46).

These discourses troubled me then for they did not speak well of these, my people, and perhaps, they do not speak well of me, for, frankly, although with some ambivalent distance, I had a good time that Saturday afternoon and have had a good time since.

I had indeed gone to racially and structurally dominated southern Texas in 1981 looking for a folklore of resistance, carrying in my head the examples furnished by Genovese, by Gutman, by E. P. Thompson and George Rudé and ultimately by Gramsci. I found instead a powerful sexual and scatological discourse—part of a greater Mexican working-class folk tradition, but a tradition I saw as delegitimatized by the powerful authoritative intellectual discourses of Ramos and Paz and in a more circumscribed but still effective way, by Spielberg. And I found difficult, and perhaps still do, its relegitimization because this is at least the implicit burden of those who approach such materials from a Marxist cultural perspective. Certainly one alternative is simply to deny the burden and accept Ramos and Paz or perhaps some species of functionalist argument where these behaviors are seen as adaptive steam valves. From this perspective as everyone leaves Chema's ranch, they feel well adjusted to the labors they will face on Monday.

How can one rethink these materials as a narrative of resistance provided by Marxist social historians, especially when the materials do not nicely lend themselves to such a reading as do black spirituals and the crafts of English artisans? And how can one do this if one has to contend with an extant authoritative interpretive discourse, especially one developed by members of the same general cultural group, such as Spielberg?

In the intervening years I have read new sources, reread old ones, and have been developing an analysis of such discourses so as to address this question. The task is made more interestingly difficult by George Marcus, who, in the essay cited earlier, takes Paul Willis to task, and by implication other Marxist ethnographers, for privileging working-class culture as a seamless discourse of anti-capitalist resistance (1986). As I think of Chema, Midnight, Mickey Mouse, Octavio, and others, I ask, how does one develop a different story about these men without lapsing into an uncritical romanticism of resistance everywhere; how does one do this without abandoning the concept of the social whole and one's native and political sympathy with the dominated? And, finally, how does one produce a narrative construction, one's ethnography, that does not wholly objectify and violate the "feel" of such events?

Writing with a Difference

We may begin this alternative reformulation by examining the central sexual symbolization that lies at the heart of the speech play and gesture that I have noted. Tonio's, Jaime's, Samuel's, Octavio's, and Chema's obvious and expressive manipulations of body and speech would certainly seem consistent with Samuel Ramos' observation that the Mexican lower-class man's

> terminology abounds in sexual allusions which reveal his phallic obsession; the sexual organ becomes symbolic of masculine force. In verbal combat he attributes to his adversary an imaginary femininity, reserving for himself the masculine role. By this stratagem he pretends to assert his superiority over his opponents (Ramos 1962:59–60).

For these commentators, aggression and its generative conditions—inadequacy and inferiority—are directly expressed in this humor through anal references and the theme of male sexual violation. I would not deny the existence of these values and meanings, given my earlier argument for the historical production of aggression, nor that these performances may in part be expressing them. I would, however, argue that these might be multivocal symbols possessing several meanings and not reducible to a single one that fits a preconceived psychoanalytical scheme. It is too easy to rely on a wild psychoanalysis when dealing with such physical references.

Mary Douglas has warned us of the dangers and shortcomings of such simple psychologistic readings when they concern rituals dealing with the human body (1978). Some psychologists are fond of treating such rituals not as social acts, but as the expression of private and personal infantile concerns. "There is," she believes, "no possible justification for this shift of interpretation just because the rituals work upon human flesh . . . " (1978:115). Those who make this interpretive reduction

> proceed from unchallenged assumptions, which arise from the strong similarity between certain ritual forms and the behavior of psychopathic individuals. The assumption is that in some sense primitive cultures correspond to infantile stages in the development of the human psyche. Consequently such rites are interpreted as if they express the same preoccupations which fill the mind of psychopaths or infants (1978:115).

Douglas argues for an alternative analytical model for the understanding of the human body in relation to society—one that is "prepared to see in the body a symbol of society, and to see the powers and dangers credited to social structure reproduced in small on the human body" (1978:115). A society's definition and treatment of the body and bodily pollution is, in her estimation, a critical symbolic key for grasping its perceptions of its own structure and of its external relationships. Such pollution—all forms of matter issuing from the body's orifices as well as entering through them—may acquire symbolic proportions as do necessarily the orifices themselves. The Coorgs of India, for example, are an isolated mountain community sharing with other castes a fear of what is "outside and below" their group. In their ritual behavior they "treat the body as if it were a beleaguered town, every ingress and exit guarded for spies and traitors" (1978:123).

I would submit that the *mexicano* on both sides of the border also has something to fear. This fear may not be simply an infantile concern with one's *palomilla* (gang) and simple sexual dominance. Rather, the themes of anality, pollution, and bodily penetration may also be symbolic expressions of an essentially political and economic concern with social domination, not from below, as with the Coorg, but from above—from the upper levels of the structure of power in both countries. The marginalized working and unemployed classes where these expressions abound constitute a body politic symbolically conscious of its socially penetrable status. What Douglas claims for the Coorgs may be at least partially applicable for Octavio, Samuel, Chema, and my other friends:

> For them the model of the exits and entrances of the human body is a doubly apt symbolic focus of fears for their minority standing in the larger society. Here I am suggesting that when rituals express anxiety about the body's orifices the sociological counterpart of this anxiety is a care to protect the political and cultural unity of a minority group (1978:124).

There is certainly some evidence for this view in the often noted tendency of the Mexican male, particularly the lower-class male, to turn to the expression *chingar*—meaning sexual violation—to also express social violation, as my friends often do when speaking particularly of their political/economic relationships: "*Me chingaron en el jale*" (I got screwed at work) or during one of the regular political discussions at the *carne asada*, "*Pos gano Reagan, y ahora si nos van a chingar*" (Well, Reagan won, now we're really going to get screwed) and, finally, "*la vida es una chinga*" (life is being constantly screwed), which represents a quite reasonable perception of social conditions for these men in this part of the world.

Others, the dominant Mexican-American and Anglo upper classes—*los chingones* (the big screwers)—as these men commonly refer to them, always have the ability to *chingar*, and it is entirely to the point that these are also men, and it is here, I suspect, that we can find a possible reason for the conversion of this potential male social violation into the symbolic idiom of homosexuality. The routines, I will remind you, are called "*chingaderas.*" When Antonio seemingly threatens me with the meat that has passed by his genitals; when Octavio triumphantly says "*¡Mama Eh Te!*", they may indeed, as all Western men do, be expressing their latent anxiety about homosexuality. However, I am suggesting, partially following Mary Douglas' lead, that we need not just stop here.[3] These men may also be reenacting, in the idiom of homosexuality, their sense that the world beyond Chema's *rancho* is also full of constant violation by other men—*los chingones*—and one must learn to play that too-serious game as well![4]

But as I write of play and games, I want to introduce another critical alternative perspective that speaks to a central flaw in Ramos, Paz, and Spielberg's understanding—or lack of it—of this speech play. It is important to recognize that even as my friends introduce the seemingly aggressive idiom of sexual and social violation, they do so in a way that reframes that aggressive speech and gesture into play. Ramos, Paz, and Spielberg extract the sexual symbols in this play and give them their shallow reductive interpretations. They are not appreciative of these scenes as dynamic forums that interactionally produce meaning. Their focus always is on those discrete "aggressive" verbal symbols. As such they are like those anthropologists who, according to Peacock,

> tend to pay too little heed to the dynamics of (cultural) performances, to report from the performances only those tidbits of content which lend support to his portrait of the values and organization of the society in which the performances are found. . . . This kind of analysis which fails to grasp the essence of symbolic performances can yield no full appreciation of social dynamics (1968:256).

This difference in interpretive emphasis is crucial, for their "tidbits of content" analysis leads these analysts to ignore the way in which the aggressive meaning of the literal language, such as it is, is transformed into its exact opposite through the intercession of interactional speech play and art.

To begin with, *mexicanos* frame such scenes as ludic moments through native markers such as *relajando* and *llevandosale* (carrying on, bantering, playing), as in "*nomas estabamos relajando*" (we were just playing). We have a clear recognition of a play world in which open aggression can appear *only by mistake*. Such a mistake can occur when a novice or an unacculturated person fails to "recognize" the scene, or when he is less than competent in the requisite artistic skills. This latter consideration is crucial, for whatever latent aggression exists is not only rendered socially harmless but is turned into a basis for solidarity. The participants do this by interactionally creating an artistically textured discourse through skillful manipulations of allusion, metaphor, narration, and prosody.

Through interactionally produced play, the aggression of the world is transformed into mock aggression, mock fighting through artistic creativity which does not deny the existence of aggression but inverts its negativity. Ultimately this transformation is of greater social significance. What Bateson notes for nonhuman animals is also fundamentally true for these human artistic performers. These men mean something other than what is denoted by their aggressive language. Such language becomes like the "playful nips" which "denote the bite but it does not denote what would be denoted by the bite" (Bateson 1972:180). Art and play ultimately create paradox and fiction.

> Paradox is doubly present in the signals which are exchanged within the context of the play, fantasy, threat, etc. Not only does the playful nip not denote what would be denoted by the bite for which it stands but the bite itself is fictional. Not only do the playing animals not quite mean what they are saying but, also, they are communicating about something which does not exist (1972:182).

Aggression is what would be denoted by an actual bite—it is that something that is the hidden textual model for the playful nip, but is itself not denoted and therefore is negated at the moment of interaction. The playful nips of skillful artistic language produce a paradoxical effect, namely the interactional production of solidarity, or as Latin Americans everywhere would say, *confianza*. Anthony Lauria notes that in Puerto Rico, "to indulge in *relajos* of any sort in the presence of anyone is to engage in a relation of *confianza*—of trust and familiarity with that person" (1964:62). As Lauria also notes, the ultimate paradoxical social result of the expressive scene is not aggression, humiliation, and alienation, but rather *respeto*. This is the significance of ending a verbal exchange in mock punches, a hug, and a laugh. In one of Bateson's metalogues his persona and that of his daughter engage in conversation.

Daughter: Why do animals fight?
Father: Oh, for many reasons, territory, sex, food . . .
Daughter: Daddy, you're talking like instinct theory. I thought we agreed not to do that.

Father: All right. But what sort of an answer do you want to the question, why animals fight?
Daughter: Well, do they deal in opposites?
Father: Oh. Yes. A lot of fighting ends up in some sort of peace-making. And certainly playful fighting is partly a way of affirming friendship. Or discovering or re-discovering friendship.
Daughter: I thought so . . . (1972:18).

The artistic disclosure of friendship and respect in the *palomilla's* interaction is not, in and of itself, ideological. That is, in a social vacuum, one could only construe it as play, friendship, and solidarity pure and simple. But, of course, these expressive scenes do not emerge in such a vacuum; they appear and are embedded in a political economy and a hegemonic culture that produces marginalization and alienation such as prevails among this class of *batos* in south Texas.[5]

In these particular socioeconomic circumstances play and its concomitant friendship become eminently ideological. As an emergent cultural performance, they represent an oppositional break in the alienating hegemony of the dominant culture and society.

In a provocative article, Hearn correctly notes that both mainstream and orthodox Marxist social science construe play as an ontologically secondary activity to the instrumental "real" world of politics and economics (1976–77). There is in such a construal a reproduction of capitalist categories of experience, a particularly unfortunate situation for Marxists. Hearn offers a corrective formulation of play that draws upon the work of two nonorthodox Marxist theoreticians, Habermas and Marcuse. He notes the former's idea of language as symbolic interaction that "has a transcendental self-reflexive capacity which permits it to give expression to contradictions between appearance and reality, potentiality and actuality." Because it is not totally and automatically bound to reproduce the social order, "language has the potential for emancipating people from a dependence on reified cultural controls." As such, people have in their language "the capacity for reflexivity and transcendence which enables the creation of evaluative standards, allows the expression of contradictions, and supplies a conception of potentiality, of 'what can be' " (Hearn 1976–77:147). These critical possibilities are greater for that least commodified and instrumentalized language—the emergent verbal art of marginalized peoples.

Hearn finds similar properties in Marcuse's concept of play. For Marcuse human play is the autonomous production of a dramatized, albeit temporal vision of an alternative social order. In authentic, that is noncommodified play, there is an emergent promise of "freedom from compulsion, hierarchy, inequality, and injustice" (1976–77:150). In its very ontology, play is neither secondary to instrumentalism nor is it its total denial. Rather it emerges as a critique, a constraint, and a transcendence of all instrumental activity. Ultimately, play—the free-flowing artistic exchanges of the men at Chema's *rancho*—has a subversive quality.

> In play while the limitations of the existing reality are exposed, a more satisfying—more equitable and just—order is celebrated. . . . To the extent that play affirms the possibility of a "better world" it retains the potential for highlighting the negativity of and contributing to the subversion of the prevailing arrangements (Hearn 1976–77:150–151).

Mexicans and their verbal art draw upon the domains of language and play explored by Habermas and Marcuse to produce a single phenomenon—human speech play. Through such speech play the participants continually produce a world of human value—of *confianza* and *respeto.* Created in collective equality, such momentary productions negate the alienating constraints of the historically given social order that exists for *mexicanos* and affirm the possibilities of a different social order. They momentarily overturn the alienating effects even while they remind these men of the real aggression in the world, that of *los chingones.*

Because the dominant discourse of power—that of Ramos, Paz, and Spielberg—has focused exclusively on the language of such scenes, I too have felt obligated to pay special attention to language even while recognizing that language is only part of a cultural contextual scene. Indeed, as I have suggested, it is the failure to recognize this total context of play that flaws this dominant discourse. But in the world of Chema's *rancho,* it is necessary to recognize other symbolic elements that also constitute this play world as a temporary forum of non-alienation.

For example, this play scene is itself framed in another form of play—a kind of visible joke—namely, the very existence of Chema's *rancho,* that undeveloped little piece of land surrounded on all sides by huge ranches with oil drills; just a few miles away, for example, lie the beginnings of the King Ranch, parts of which, according to Mexican legend, were bought and paid for in Mexican blood. Chema's *rancho* is itself a source of constant humor, especially when, after a few beers, Chema begins to tell the other guys of his big plans for this little place. Inevitably someone will ask him, where are you going to put the cow? And, how is the bull going to screw her when you can't get them both on the place at the same time? The ultimate joke, of course, is the existence of this "ranch" dedicated not to capitalist mass agriculture but to friendship and play. While not a necessary condition, the very existence of this visible joke—this humorous incongruity—is productive of more jokes and play. As Mary Douglas says, "if there is no joke in the social structure, no other joke can appear" (1968:366).

Finally, there is my title—*carne, carnales,* and the carnivalesque. As the name of this event—*carne asada*—clearly indicates, and, as I have suggested throughout, *carne* (meat) and its preparation and consumption are of central concern here. If, as Mary Douglas says, food is a code, then where in society lies the precoded message and how does this message speak of hierarchy, inclusions, and exclusions (1971:61)? What kind of meat is this socially and what, if anything, is its message?

These men are preparing and consuming those parts of a steer—the internal organs and the *faja,* or skirt steak, that are clearly undervalued, low prestige meats in the larger social economy, and, given their economic resources, that is not unexpected. As an old Anglo rancher in the area told me, "We used to call that stuff 'Mexican leavings.' " What interests me is the way in which such meat parts, symbolically linked to capitalist cattle ranching, are culturally mediated to convert them from low-prestige, rather tough and stringy protein into tasty, valued, social food. The use of the affectionate diminutive to name and linguistically "soften" this food—*fajita, mollejita, tripita*—is a case in point here and parallels the physical softening of the protein in much-valued, secret marinades. (Indeed, it is rumored with awe and disgust that the marinade for Chema's meat—which is considered the best—has a touch of urine in it, some say from his wife. When I hesitantly asked Chema about this, he said it was absolutely not true; he would never ask his wife to do such a thing. After a few seconds, he added, with a grin, "only a man's piss will do!") In this cultural mediation we get food that is an ever-present reminder of their class status but which in its preparation symbolically negates that status; food material that begins with low status and exclusion results in food prepared in pride, good taste, and social inclusion.

The preparation and consumption of this meat also speaks to class difference in another way. The food is simply prepared, with the only utensils present being a sharp knife to cut the meat and the chilis, tomatoes, and onions for the sauce, and a fork to turn the meat. The sauce is prepared in the bottom parts of beer cans cut in half, and spoons are fashioned from the metal of the upper half. This preparation becomes a way for these guys to distinguish themselves from the dominant Others—*los chingones*—who use plates, knives, forks, cups, and napkins. They also eat awful things like potato salad and lettuce with their meat, which is bought and barbecued for them by their Mexican servants from across the border, who cross the bridge to work in their large, fashionable homes.

Finally, I am most interested in the way the consumption of food is a kind of interactional parallel to the charged language that paradoxically generates friendship. Everyone brings their low-prestige meat—a symbol of societal aggression—and contributes it to a central collective pile; everyone, at some point or another, takes a turn at shooing flies away, broiling and cutting the meat; and making the sauce.

The tacos are made by everyone in random fashion and, since there are no plates, they are passed along by hand, sometimes going through two or three sets of hands. These men at Chema's *rancho* and many others throughout south Texas and, I might add, in the Texan outposts of central California, prepare and consume their once low-prestige food collectively and nonhierarchically even as they playfully assault each other with the charged language of friendship. The felt result is another discourse of power, a power that does not dominate but liberates them, if only for brief moments, from the contexts of alienation beyond Chema's *rancho* where race and structure still prevail. In this world, Chema's *carne* is closely linked to *carnales,* a kinship term used among brothers or close male friends.

In the 1960s Chicano college students spoke in too self-conscious and slightly forced ways of *carnalismo.* These men never use this term; although, when they hear it, they can sense what it means. Rather, they freely use the term *carnal*—a folk term for brother or buddy, which seems to me to be an appropriate native gloss for their cultural practice. In one too conscious and too keenly ideological moment, Chinito ("little Chinese man"), a young man with "Asian" features and the most educated among them (one year of college) holds up a piece of raw fajita and says *"esta carne es pa' mis carnales, esto es el carnalismo"* (this meat is for my brothers, this is brotherhood). Another man, pained slightly by this apparent intrusion of linear ideology, immediately replies, *"Mira cabron,"* and going for his own genitals, says, *"esta es la carne que te voy a dar"* (Look, goddammit, this is the meat I'm going to give you). And it is only at this moment, when the others laugh hesitantly, that we see the possibility and the tones of real aggression. The world of too-conscious ideology has intruded and must be rejected. One does not speak ideologically of friendship and community, one practices it in the symbolic action of meat, body, and language.

To unify these various revisionary perspectives, I want to think of these scenes as a present-day example of what Bakhtin calls the unofficial culture of the Middle Ages, the folk culture of Grotesque Realism, of the carnivalesque. The playful, sexual, and scatological language, the concern with minimalist consumption of meat taken from the internal, stomach-centered parts of the animal, the concern with the body—all of these involve what Bakhtin called degradation, a principal aspect of the carnivalesque. But this is not degradation as the imprisoning bourgeois discourse of Ramos and Paz would have it.

> Degradation here means coming down to earth, the contact with earth as an element that swallows up and gives birth at the same time. To degrade is to bury, to sow, and to kill simultaneously, in order to bring forth something more and better. To degrade also means to concern oneself with the lower stratum of the body, the life of the belly and the reproductive organs; it therefore relates to acts of defecation and copulation, conception, pregnancy, and birth. Degradation digs a bodily grave for a new birth; it has not only a destructive, negative aspect, but also a regenerating one. To degrade an object does not imply merely hurling it into the void of nonexistence, into absolute destruction, but to hurl it down to the reproductive lower stratum, the zone in which conception and a new birth take place. Grotesque realism knows no other lower level; it is the fruitful earth and the womb. It is always conceiving (Bakhtin 1984:21).

However, in adopting this Bakhtinian perspective on unofficial culture, heteroglossia, and the carnivalesque, one also has to note its political limitations and its uneasy relationship to Marxism. In a recent critical review of this issue, Young seriously and persuasively questions the Marxist status of Bakhtin's thought on the carnivalesque in culture (Young 1985–86). Taken without critical revision, Young argues, Bakhtinian "carnival offers a liberal rather than a Marxist politics" (1985–86:92). That is, Bakhtin has offered a semi-idealist sense of an essentialist-humanistic oppositional Other expressed in the carnivalesque as a transcendence of an unspecified general Foucauldian-like domination. Only by specifying the historical moment and social location of the carnivalesque, as Fredric Jameson would have us do, only by specifically accounting for its class (and race) antagonistic character in a specific context, can the carnivalesque be read as an expression of class contestative discourse in the manner that I have tried to do (Jameson 1981:83–87). For it is specifically against the ruling bourgeois official culture of contemporary south Texas, including that of both Anglos *and* Mexican-Americans, that one must understand my friends. Their discourses of sexuality, the body, and low-prestige food exactly counterpoint the repression and affectation of these ruling sectors throughout the region, a dominating culture whose most visible expression, for example, is the upper-class celebration of George Washington's Birthday in Laredo, Texas, not far from Chema's *rancho*.

However, a Marxist perspective on the carnivalesque also obliges us to note that its ideological and material character is not one of undiluted seamless "opposition." Two points may be made here. First, the critical carnivalesque of these men is to some considerable degree predicated on a model of their own dominating patriarchy and exclusion of women from these scenes. Second, in the long term, their feasting on beef and beer on an almost daily basis is likely contributing to serious health problems among the working-class male population of this area (Lyndon B. Johnson School of Public Affairs 1979).

> "Now stop!" Max said and sent the wild things off to bed
> without their supper.
> And Max the king of all wild things was lonely and wanted to
> be where someone loved him best of all.
> Then all around from far away across the world he smelled
> good things to eat
> so he gave up being king of where the wild things are.
> But the wild things cried, "Oh please don't go—
> we'll eat you up—we love you so!"
> And Max said, "No!"
> The wild things roared their terrible roars and gnashed
> their terrible teeth and rolled their terrible eyes and
> showed their terrible claws
> but Max stepped into his private boat and waved goodbye (Sendak 1963).

Epilogue: The Centipede Who Played Free Safety

So there you have my narrative, which, though now fleshed out with new theoretical references, had already begun to take this form even as I concluded the period of fieldwork that had generated it. Successful, I thought, was I in producing an ethnographic account that could stand as a critical counternarrative to that of the great Mexican bourgeois thinkers and its localized application by Spielberg. Successful was I, I thought, in giving narrative critical voice to the dominated against those who in their discourses of power would reproduce and enhance the domination in their everyday lives. And, as such, this essay could have ended a paragraph ago were it not for the centipede—the centipede who played free safety.

As I prepared to leave McBurg, *los batos* decided to have a *despedida* (a farewell party) in my honor, naturally a *carne asada*. This time, however, rather than Chema's *rancho,* we decided to gather at a local bar—Tenorio's—where in addition to partying, it was also decided that I would make a "speech" (their term) about what I had "learned," the whole thing in an idiom and ethos of play consistent with the event. We all gathered outside in a kind of patio behind the bar and with fajita tacos and beer for fuel, I meandered my way through a kind of "folk" version of my present story. A variety of commentary followed ranging from *"Bien de aquellas"* (real good) to *"puro pedo"* (pure shit) to loud "Hmmm's" to quiet long pulls on beers. Most of them at least agreed that my rendering was better than those of Ramos and Paz, which they unambivalently thought of as *"puro pedo."*

And then the centipede, unexpectedly, made his appearance. Chinito, the local college dropout who knew something about the esoterica and secret rituals of our sacred discipline had, from the beginning, been unhappy with my fieldwork enterprise. But, he had not actually said so or specified his objections until a little too much beer plus my leave-taking provided the necessary disinhibition to his repressed critique. Like one of the young antagonistic villagers that James Fernandez encountered in the Fang village of Gabon, this fellow, with even greater antagonism, wanted to know "what reason did I have for wanting to know such things?" (Fernandez 1986:173). As with most antagonistic and therefore rhetorical questions, my questioner came equipped with his own answer, to wit: "You want to tell *them* about us!" with a heavy emphasis on "tell" and "them"—which, of course, was quite true, although I wouldn't have put it quite that way. Rather, I would have said, or tonally implied, that, yes, I did want to tell *them* about Mexican-American critical ideological responses to *their* domination. We debated the question, there next to the barbecue pit, and generated just about as much heat with raised voices, which eventually led to a bit of body posturing—he, forward, me, backward—my most vivid recollection of that instant being, "Oh, shit, did the summer grant cover health insurance?"

This emerging disorder of a different kind—this intrusion into the somewhat spontaneous communitas of the *carne asada* that afternoon—could not be permitted by the rest of the guys, who had a stake not only in the maintenance of the communitas but in making sure that I, friend/guest/ "professor," wasn't mistreated. Yet, to varying degrees, they too had probably wondered "what reason did I have for wanting to know such things?" which, after my best explanations and in the final analysis, I may not have fully answered to their total satisfaction, a probably impossible thing. It was at that point, after several of my friends persuaded my interrogator to calm down, that one of them, *"la tuerca"* (the screw nut), a car mechanic, offered the following. He opened with a local introductory marker for joking narratives:

¡Watcha, Limón. Pesca este pedo y píntalo verde! [Lookit, Limón. Catch this "fart" and paint it green.] These two *antropolocos* [anthropologists] got a grant, you know. To go to

Africa to study the natives. But when they got there, all the *batos* [dudes] had split for the mountains. Left a sign in the village. "Gone to the mountains, *bros,* see you next winter!" "So now what are we going to do, Bruce?" said one of them.

"Well, gee, I don't know, Horace." So they sat around getting bored. Once in awhile one of them would find some native shit, and they'd get all excited thinking they were still around. But no, it was old shit. One day, one of them said, "You know, we're not doing anything. Why don't we organize all of the jungle animals into football teams and have a game?" So they did. They chose up. A tiger for me. A tiger for you. A hippo for me. A hippo for you. We each get a gazelle for running backs.

And then they started the game. The giraffe kicked off for one team, and the other team had its cheetah back to receive. And the game went on. But since both teams had pretty much the same animals, they were tied by the end of the first quarter. But then the elephant who was playing linebacker on one team got hurt when somebody stepped on its trunk. So the other team with its hippo fullback and nobody to stop him up the middle started getting ahead. *¡En chinga carnal!* [Fucking them over, *bro!*]

They went into the third quarter, and the hippo started right up again, but all of a sudden, he went down with a crash at the line of scrimmage and he had both knees injured. So both coaches and the teams gathered around, one coach worried about his player and the other one wanted to know who brought the hippo down. "Was it you, turtle?" "No, coach, I couldn't react fast enough!" "How about you, chimp?" "No, coach, I was up on the goal posts!"

Then they heard a little voice coming from under the hippo, "I got the bastard, I got the bastard!" They turned the hippo over and there was a little centipede holding tightly to the hippo's leg. So after they got him off, the coach asked him, "How did you do it, centipede?" And, the centipede said, "Well, coach, I was playing free safety and when I saw that the hippo had the ball, I just ran up and met him at the line of scrimmage!"

"But why didn't you do that in the first half?" asked the coach.

"I wasn't playing the first half, coach."

"Well, where the hell were you?"

"Say man," said the centipede, "don't fuck with me, I was in the locker room putting on my goddamn tennis shoes!"

(Much laughter; Chinito and I look sheepish, I think.)

What is *this* about I asked and continue to ask myself? Two anthropologists, marked as elite *and* effeminate by the use and intonation of the personal names, *Bruce* and *Horace,* fail to find their "natives" when they arrive in Africa armed with their inevitable grant. Given an active presence by the narrator, the natives have "split" and by virtue of the sign they leave behind, they are also given voice. The often deactivated subject of anthropology is restored in the same way that it (they) were restored when I was questioned. So far, perhaps, so good. But why—and this was the largest piece of the puzzle for me—do our anthropologist/protagonists then turn immediately to the organization of jungle animals into football teams and a game? Are the latter so many surrogate "natives"; and is this a satirical comment on the obsessive anthropological quest for order, any order, at all costs? After all, we can't very well just sit around. Is it this that makes us "antropo-locos" (crazy anthropologists)?

But why football? Why not? Isn't it the Balinese cockfight of American culture where our capacity for highly organized systemic violence is displayed most evidently in the frame of "game" and at a profit? But juxtaposed to anthropology as its close semantic cousin? Was this what I had been doing, organizing their play this way? Is this what we all do? Order up what Fernandez calls "the play of tropes in culture" into ethnographies that organize the polyphony into narrative forms that are metaphorically related to violence and profit?

Having organized my "natives" for the sake of my own orderly narrative game, I was ready to take leave of them when the game started breaking down. For I suspect that, perhaps, in the role of one coach, I had gotten ahead of them, run up the score by having gained much with relatively little in return, save for a book that would tell "their" story for the benefit of others. Did I, in fact, as I prepared to leave, require some marked opposition to stop my tough running game?

Which brings us to the centipede. Here the animal symbolism becomes even shiftier and more multivocalic. Is this the antagonist who brought me down, reframed in narrative play and thereby given symbolic license? Why a centipede? Well, it makes for the punch line, but why a centipede who acts this way, sitting out the first half, laboriously putting on fifty pairs of tennis shoes so that he can get in the game? And why does he play free safety?

Let me momentarily avoid my own problem and digress to suggest that the centipede is a pretty good symbolic rendition not only of my personal antagonist who disordered my ethnographic narrative game, but of these guys as a group and probably of Mexican-Americans as they see themselves relative to the sociopolitical game of which anthropology is part.

To fully exploit this particular reading, you have to know your football, including the knowledge that the free safety, as his name implies, is a defensive back not bound to the standard zone defense where a defender protects a particular portion of the backfield. Rather, he is set deep in the backfield and free to roam it, protecting against deep and short passes but also free to come up and stop a running play, as our centipede did. You may, perhaps, also need to know that in the folklore of the National Football League, free safeties, along with split ends, are thought to be marginal, temperamental, moody guys who love to hit. To this knowledge, shared by my barbecue friends who are avid watchers of the sport, we can add the following concerning the centipede, which is found plentifully in south Texas. It is small and nasty, frequents dark places, and will painfully sting by clinging ferociously and venomously. Nonetheless, they are lesser creatures certainly in comparison to tigers, lions, and so on.

And that may be how Mexican-Americans see themselves and are, in fact, seen in American popular, political, *and* anthropological discourse. There at the margins, not fully dangerous or exotic; socially and politically lesser but not enough to make them a real problem or a real attraction for the imagination. To be sure, every so often they come up fast and make a hit—Cesar Chavez, Henry Cisneros—but most of the time there they are at the margins. (Like the coach,

Anglo liberals sometimes ask me the political equivalent of "where were you in the first half?" which is, "why didn't Mexican-Americans turn out to vote in the last election?" usually for an Anglo liberal candidate. To which, like the centipede, I sometimes feel like saying, "Say, man, come on. Maybe they're in the locker room slowly and laboriously putting on the necessarily social, educational, and cultural equipment to come out and play for themselves.")

But you see, here I am digressing in my own interest, once again, returning to my safe and politically hip narrative role of explaining how Mexican-Americans express their cultural opposition to *Them* including the dominant discourses of intellectual power. I am neatly avoiding the fragmenting problem for my own work, namely, what does the centipede have to do with me, with my ethnographic narration?

The centipede, I propose, is the critical carnivalesque turned in my direction. Even as I was rewriting their mostly oppositional voices into my own narrative, thereby rendering it oppositional to those of Ramos and Paz, my friends offered me pointed instruction on the limits of my rewriting. In their disordering deconstruction of the ethnographic project, they remind me (us) that however "liberating" a narrative discourse we propose to write, it is one always intimate with power, and many of our "informants," "subjects," "consultants," "teachers," "friends" know it. That these particular friends permit me to rewrite them is itself testimony to their understanding that there are better and worse discourses—that some are, indeed, *"puro pedo"*—that there are sites of struggle far from Chema's *rancho* where such discourses contest for hegemony in other cultural spheres and where my pale rewriting may be to some purpose.

But it is important to note that their critical reminder itself comes in the form of the carnivalesque, as if to say that anthropology itself is not and should not be immune to its disorderly character. Indeed, I want to go a step further and take this lesson at full formal value for the production of my ethnographic narrative. Used with imagination, this empowering gift of the carnivalesque can lend not only ideological content but also an ideology of critical form, as Jameson (1981) might say, to our ethnographic practice. Along with other critical resources we can incorporate the carnivalesque into our ethnographic practice, creatively disordering it so that it also stands as a formal counterhegemonic practice countering the "normal" and often dominating practice of ethnography.[6] I believe this is what Fischer is recommending when he argues for an ethnography based formally on the postmodern practices of ethnic autobiography, practices such as inter-reference, critical juxtaposition, ironic humor, parody, the return of the repressed, alternative selves, and bifocality which, in my estimation, are synonymous with the carnivalesque (1986). To some degree at least, I have been experimenting with this formal appropriation of the critical carnivalesque here even as I also write manifestly against the *ideas* of domination. Finally, at the heart of this gift of the carnivalesque is a reflexive critical self-awareness of our status as ethno-graphers: writers of people. For, as my friends and the centipede reminded me, this postmodernity of the carnivalesque must also include the keen sense of critical reflexivity that goes with such discourse, the sense that we must always decenter our own narrative self-assurance lest it be saturated with dominating power. Ultimately, as Stephen Tyler reminds us, when ethnography is truly critical, such a function

> derives from the fact that it makes its own contextual grounding part of the question and not from hawking pictures of alternative ways of life as instruments of utopian reform (1986:139).

Notes

Acknowledgments. Portions of this paper were presented as lectures at Stanford University (1986) and at the annual meetings of the American Ethnological Society in St. Louis (1988). My special thanks to Renato Rosaldo for the former invitation and to Charles Briggs for the latter. The research was conducted under the partial auspices of a grant from the National Research Council and the Ford Foundation sponsored by the Language Behavior Research Laboratory at the University of California, Berkeley.

1. All formal names and nicknames are fictitious.

2. McBurg is also my general fictional name for the towns—very close to each other—in South Texas were these men live. It is a composite of two large Anglo-dominated towns—McAllen and Edinburg. These were established as "American" towns at the turn of the century as part of the Anglo-American agricultural capitalization and social dominance of the area. It is in this general area where Madsen (1964) and Rubel (1966) conducted their fieldwork. For a fine critical account of these two projects and their insensitivity to language and humor, see Paredes (1978).

3. I say "partially" for I appropriate only Douglas' fine descriptive insights, not her Durkheimian interpretive framework. Clearly I am moving in a different left direction.

4. In a footnote, anthropologist Patricia Zavella notes a closely related male-centered verbal performance among California Mexican-Americans *who are nonetheless from South Texas*. I have never heard the expression *chingar mentis* in South Texas, so it is possibly a California label for this same kind of verbal performance. I quote Zavella:

> In an analysis of *chingar mentis* behavior (which means to fuck over minds), I concluded that it is a male form of verbal art similar to "playing the dozens" by young black males. I observed young Chicano males from South Texas spreading false stories or spontaneously duping someone through group verbal performance. According to the performers the point of these hilarious deceptions was just to *chingar mentis,* but I argue they develop male solidarity and prestige among the participants (Zavella 1987:25).

5. In a recent article announcing the Vice-Presidential nomination of Senator Lloyd Bentsen, who is from this area, David Rosenbaum of the *New York Times* has succinctly captured this world better than any set of social statistics:

> the 67-year-old Senator has deep roots in Texas. He comes from one of the richest and most prominent families in the Rio Grande Valley of south Texas, where the great wealth of a few families contrasts with the poverty of the overwhelmingly Mexican-American citizenry (Rosenbaum 1988).

6. In a perceptive insight Young, after Benjamin, notes the way Bakhtin's *Rabelais and His World* could be read as itself a carnivalesque text in formal counterhegemonic response to Stalinist domination (Young 1985–86:78).

References

Bakhtin, Mikhail. 1984. Rabelais and His World. Bloomington: Indiana University Press.
Bateson, Gregory. 1972. A Theory of Play and Fantasy. *In* Steps to an Ecology of Mind. pp. 177–193. New York: Random House.
de Leon, Arnoldo. 1982. The Tejano Community, 1836–1900. Albuquerque: University of New Mexico Press.
————. 1983. They Called Them Greasers: Anglo Attitudes Toward Mexicans in Texas, 1821–1900. Austin: University of Texas Press.
Douglas, Mary. 1968. The Social Control of Cognition: Some Factors in Joke Perception. Man: The Journal of the Royal Anthropological Institute 3:361–376.
————. 1971. Deciphering a Meal. *In* Myth, Symbol, and Culture. Clifford Geertz, ed. pp. 61–81. New York: W. W. Norton.
————. 1978[1966]. Purity and Danger: An Analysis of the Concepts of Pollution and Taboo. London: Routledge & Kegan Paul.
Fernandez, James. 1986. Persuasions and Performances: The Play of Tropes in Culture. Bloomington: Indiana University Press.
Fischer, Michael M. J. 1986. Ethnicity and the Post-Modern Arts of Memory. *In* Writing Culture: The Poetics and Politics of Ethnography. James Clifford and George E. Marcus, eds., pp. 194–233. Berkeley: University of California Press.
Foley, Douglas. 1978. From Peones to Politicos: Ethnic Relations in a South Texas Town. Austin: University of Texas, Center for Mexican American Studies.
Hearn, Francis. 1976–77. Toward a Critical Theory of Play. Telos 30:145–160.
Jameson, Fredric. 1981. The Political Unconscious: Narrative as a Socially Symbolic Act. Ithaca: Cornell University Press.
Lauria, Anthony, Jr. 1964. Respeto, Relajo, and Interpersonal Relations in Puerto Rico. Anthropological Quarterly 3:53–67.
Limón, José E. 1987. Mexican Speech Play: History and the Psychological Discourses of Power. Texas Papers on Latin America. No. 87–06. Austin: University of Texas Institute of Latin American Studies.
Lyndon B. Johnson School of Public Affairs. 1979. The Health of Mexican Americans in South Texas. Policy Research Project No. 32. University of Texas at Austin.
Madsen, William. 1964. The Mexican-Americans of South Texas. New York: Holt, Rinehart, and Winston.
Marcus, George E. 1986. Contemporary Problems of Ethnography in the Modern World System. In Writing Culture: The Poetics and Politics of Ethnography. James Clifford and George E. Marcus, eds. pp. 165–193. Berkeley: University of California Press.
Montejano, David. 1987. Anglos and Mexicans in the Making of Texas. Austin: University of Texas Press.
Paredes, Américo. 1976. A Texas-Mexican Cancionero. Urbana: University of Illinois Press.
————. 1978. On Ethnographic Fieldwork among Minority Groups: A Folklorist's Perspective. *In* New Directions in Chicano Scholarship. Recardo Romo and Raymund Paredes, eds. pp. 1–32. La Jolla: Chicano Studies Center, University of California at San Diego.

Paz, Octavio. 1961[1951]. The Labyrinth of Solitude: Life and Thought in Mexico. New York: Grove Press.

Peacock, James. 1968. Rites of Modernization: Symbolic and Social Aspects of Indonesian Proletarian Drama. Chicago: University of Chicago Press.

Ramos, Samuel. 1962[1934]. Profile of Man and Culture in Mexico. Austin: University of Texas Press.

Rosenbaum, David E. 1988. A Candidate Who is More Like Bush: Lloyd Millard Bentsen, Jr. New York Times, July 13, p. 1.

Rubel, Arthur. 1966. Across the Tracks: Mexican Americans in a South Texas Town. Austin: University of Texas Press.

Sendak, Maurice. 1963. Where the Wild Things Are. New York: Harper and Row.

Spielberg, Joseph. 1974. Humor in a Mexican-American Palomilla: Some Historical, Social, and Psychological Implications. Revista Chicano-Requeña 2:41–50.

Tyler, Stephen A. 1986. Post-Modern Ethnography: From Document of the Occult to Occult Document. *In* Writing Culture: The Poetics and Politics of Ethnography. James Clifford and George E. Marcus, eds. pp. 122–140. Berkeley: University of California Press.

Young, Robert. 1985–86. Back to Bakhtin. Cultural Critique 1:71–92.

Zavella, Patricia. 1987. Women's Work and Chicano Families: Cannery Workers of the Santa Clara Valley. Ithaca: Cornell University Press.

Part Four
Language as Social Practice

Language lets us choose.

—Norbert Dittmar 1988:xi

What the norms do, then, is to give all speakers a grammar of consequences. Speakers are free to make any choices, but how their choices will be interpreted is not free.

—Carol Myers Scotton 1988:155

Daniel Jones, in his book on the phoneme, defined a language as "the speech of one individual pronouncing in a definite and consistent style" (1962:9). Such a rigorous definition is admirably honest in making clear the basis on which his study is founded. It is, however, not a very helpful definition for those who are interested in how language is used in a particular community. With the exception of Chomsky's "ideal speech-community," variation in language is endemic everywhere. The existence of alternatives implies choice, and choice is generally meaningful. Whether the choice is between two distinct languages or within a single language, the choice between two alternatives can be significant. The chapters in Part Four illustrate the kinds of social and political consequences that may result from such choices.

Donald Brenneis's study of Fiji Indian gossip focuses on interactions among the content of gossip, the events within which it is conducted, and the stylistic features that make the intense coperformance characteristic of this genre possible. Understanding the "politics" of gossip in Bhatgaon requires a multidimensional approach: It furthers overt political ends through its scurrilous commentary about absent others, but it also implicitly weaves together and strengthens social relationships among the participants themselves. Brenneis's study also draws upon a relatively detailed transcript of particular gossip sessions; such features as overlap between speakers and the rhythmic pacing of individual turns are critical in how gossip works in Bhatgaon.

Fred Myers describes a situation among the Pintupi in Australia's Northern territory, where the use of language is influenced by the need to maintain the "relatedness" that gives the group its cohesion. The Pintupi are reluctant to use language confrontationally in situations that are potentially divisive. This makes it difficult to arrive at decisions in meetings where there are opposing interests: "Maintaining respect . . . dictates the removal of individual assertiveness from public speech." The function of the meeting is more to reaffirm membership in the group than to achieve a result. Myers is "concerned with the way forms of speaking come to acquire meaning for participants."

Michael Silverstein shows how in the United States, Standard English is a commodity that has become "the object of a brisk commerce in goods-and-services" in which experts and advertisers encourage speakers to acquire it "for a price." The notion of a standard language has been frequently discussed (e.g., Bartsch 1987, Joseph 1987, Macaulay 1973, Milroy and Milroy 1985), but Silverstein emphasizes the role of Standard English as "a cultural emblem" rather than as a medium of communication. He also links the symbolic value of Standard English to the "English only" movement as conforming to the ideology that the standard language is "the essential medium of corporate survival and personal success."

Judith Irvine deals even more explicitly with the notion of value, looking at the "communicative economy" (Hymes 1974) of a Wolof community in Senegal, West Africa. Irvine describes two speech styles, "noble speech," associated with higher castes, and "griot speech," used by low-ranking groups. These are not separate languages (although French and Arabic are also used in the community) but each style has an appropriate function. In the case of praise-songs offered by griots to patrons, the rewards are openly material. In this sense, the use of language is, as Irvine suggests, "part of a political economy, not just a vehicle for thinking about one."

Jane Hill shows how in the Malinche Volcano region of central Mexico the Mexicano language (Nahuatl), despite its limited value in the mainstream Spanish-speaking community, is "the language of intimacy, solidarity, mutual respect, and identity as a campesino." However, the higher status of Spanish is recognized by the frequent use of Spanish loan words when speaking in a "power code" register of Mexicano. At the same time, even those who assert their identity by using Mexicano do not control the language in its traditional form. The symbolic value of Mexicano does not guarantee its survival as a full-functioning language.

Each of these Chapters deals with the role that language plays in a particular society. These are the topics that traditionally crop up in courses on language and culture. But the purpose of studying these cases carefully is not simply to see them as alien ways of behavior. As G. K. Chesterton observed: "The whole object of travel is not to set foot on foreign land; it is at last to set foot on one's own country as a foreign land." By looking at the significance of language in other cultures we may come closer to understanding our own.

Suggestions for Further Reading

Other examples of politically significant uses of language can be found in the collections of D. L. Brenneis and F. R. Myers, eds., *Dangerous Words: Language and Politics in the Pacific; Disentangling: Conflict Discourse in Pacific Societies,* edited by K. A. Watson-Gegeo and G.

M. White; and *Responsibility and Evidence in Oral Discourse,* edited by J. H. Hill and J. T. Irvine. Different forms of face-saving are examined in P. Brown and S. Levinson, *Politeness: Some Universals in Language Usage.* The classic works on interaction are those by E. Goffman: *The Presentation of Self in Everyday Life, Frame Analysis,* and *Forms of Talk.* Ethnographic studies of particular language situations are provided by K. H. Basso, *Western Apache Language and Culture;* W. F. Hanks, *Referential Practice: Language and Lived Space Among the Maya;* G. Urban, *A Discourse-Centered Approach to Culture: Native South American Myths and Rituals;* and J. Siegel, *Language Contact in a Plantation Environment: A Sociolinguistic History of Fiji.* M. Moerman provides a rare example of combining an ethnographic and conversation analytic approach in *Talking Culture: Ethnography and Conversation Analysis.* W. Chafe and J. Nicholls, eds., *Evidentiality: The Linguistic Coding of Epistemology* gives examples of different ways of expressing stance in a variety of languages. The debate over "English only" is set out clearly in the collection of materials edited by J. Crawford, *Language Loyalties,* and discussed by him in *Hold Your Tongue.*

References

Bartsch, Renate. 1987. *Norms of Language: Theoretical and Practical Aspects.* London: Longman.

Basso, Keith H. 1990. *Western Apache Language and Culture.* Tucson, AZ: University of Arizona Press.

Brenneis, Donald L., and Fred R. Myers, eds. 1984. *Dangerous Words: Language and Politics in the Pacific.* New York: New York University Press.

Brown, Penelope, and Stephen Levinson. 1987. *Politeness: Some Universals in Language Usage.* Cambridge: Cambridge University Press.

Chafe, Wallace, and Johanna Nichols, eds. 1986. *Evidentiality: The Linguistic Coding of Epistemology.* Norwood, NJ: Ablex.

Crawford, James. 1992. *Hold Your Tongue: Bilingualism and the Politics of "English Only".* Reading, MA: Addison-Wesley.

Crawford, James, ed. 1992. *Language Loyalties.* Chicago: University of Chicago Press.

Dittmar, Norbert. 1988. "Foreword to the series 'Sociolinguistics and language contact.'" In Norbert Dittmar and Peter Schlobinski, eds. *The Sociolinguistics of Urban Vernaculars: Case Studies and Their Evaluation.* Berlin: de Gruyter: ix–xii.

Goffman, Erving. 1959. *The Presentation of Self in Everyday Life.* Garden City, NY: Doubleday.

———. 1974. *Frame Analysis.* New York: Harper.

———. 1981. *Forms of Talk.* Philadelphia: University of Pennsylvania Press.

Hanks, William F. 1990. *Referential Practice: Language and Lived Space Among the Maya.* Chicago: University of Chicago Press.

Hill, Jane H., and Judith T. Irvine, eds. 1993. *Responsibility and Evidence in Oral Discourse.* Cambridge: Cambridge University Press.

Hymes, Dell. 1974. *Foundations in Sociolinguistics: An Ethnographic Approach.* Philadelphia: University of Pennsylvania Press.

Jones, Daniel. 1962. *The Phoneme: Its Nature and Use* (2nd edition). Cambridge, MA: Heffer.

Joseph, John Earl. 1987. *Eloquence and Power: The Rise of Language Standards and Standard Languages.* London: Frances Pinter.

Macaulay, Ronald. 1973. "Double Standards." *American Anthropologist* 75:1324–1337.

Milroy, James, and Lesley Milroy. 1985. *Authority in Language: Investigating Language Prescription and Standardisation.* London: Routledge & Kegan Paul.

Moerman, Michael. 1988. *Talking Culture: Ethnography and Conversation Analysis.* Philadelphia: University of Pennsylvania Press.

Scotton, Carol Myers. 1988. "Code switching as indexical of social negotiations." In Monica Heller, ed., *Codeswitching: Anthropological and Sociolinguistic Perspectives.* Berlin: Mouton de Gruyter: 151–186.

Siegel, Jeff. 1987. *Language Contact in a Plantation Environment: A Sociolinguistic History of Fiji.* Cambridge: Cambridge University Press.

Urban, Greg. 1991. A *Discourse-Centered Approach to Culture: Native South American Myths and Rituals.* Austin: University of Texas Press.

Watson-Gegeo, Karen A., and Geoffrey M. White, eds. 1990. *Disentangling: Conflict Discourse in Pacific Societies.* Stanford: Stanford University Press.

11

Grog and Gossip in Bhatgaon: Style and Substance in Fiji Indian Conversation

DONALD BRENNEIS

The central question in the anthropological study of gossip has long been, What is gossip about? Gluckman (1963:308), for example, suggests that gossip and scandal "maintain the unity, morals and values of social groups. . . . they enable these groups to control the competing cliques and aspiring individuals of which all groups are composed." For Gluckman the content of gossip—the message it conveys—is primarily concerned with the implicit, sometimes negative articulation of group values. Paine (1967:282), by contrast, argues that "gossip, whatever else it may be in a functional sense, is also a cultural device used by an individual to further his own interests"; gossip contains information about others, shaped strategically to suit the speaker's ends (see also Cox 1970; Szwed 1966). From both perspectives the proper objects of study are the texts and topics of gossip; disagreement lies in how these materials and their implications are to be evaluated.

In this paper I argue that as important as the question of what gossip is *about* may be, our anthropological preoccupation with it has prevented us from looking at gossip itself in any great detail. To some extent this reflects a broader cultural notion that language is primarily a descriptive tool, a way of making propositional statements about the world (see Myers and Brenneis 1984 for a more detailed discussion). Our interpretations have concentrated on what gossip says about people and values and have largely ignored how it is said. In so doing we have neglected the nonreferential features and implications of gossip as an activity. A few anthropologists, notably Edmonson (1966), Gossen (1974), and Abrahams (1970), have drawn attention to the stylistic character of gossip itself, analyzing it in terms of community ideas of verbal art, license, and decorum; others such as M. Goodwin (1980, 1982) focus on its interactional character and ways by which language use generates social relationships. When Edmonson, Gossen, and Abrahams consider the content of gossip, it is essentially as a way of getting at style; the rhetorical effects of what gossip is about are neglected. Goodwin, by contrast, considers prosodic, syntactic, and interactional features in some detail; her analysis centers on relationships between particular syntactic forms; especially embedding (Goodwin 1980:689), and the presentation of information. In this she uses stylistic features as a way of understanding the organization of content and the establishment of a recurring interactional frame ("he-said-she-said") that ramifies throughout social relationships. I seek to broaden still further our understandings of gossip by reference to larger sociopolitical features of community life in which gossip clearly plays an important role.

This paper examines a variety of verbal interaction, herein glossed as "gossip," in a Fiji Indian rural village. This type of talk, labeled in village Hindi by the Fijian loan word *talanoa*,[1] is one way of speaking within the larger domain of *batcit* ("conversation" or "discussion"). *Talanoa* is not a clearly demarcated genre in itself. Certain stylistic, semantic, and contextual features are associated with it, but they are evident to some extent in other kinds of conversation as well; villagers speak of *talanoa* in degrees. *Talanoa* is not the only way in which information about absent others is conveyed in Bhatgaon, but that it is talk about absent others is central to its definition. As the private, essentially illicit discussion and evaluation of others, *talanoa* is regarded by many villagers as *fakutiya bat* ("worthless doings")[2] This negative evaluation extends to the language of *talanoa* as well, as it draws on the forms and vocabulary of local, rustic Fiji Hindi rather than on those of the Standard Fiji Hindi used for public occasions. Despite these negative features, villagers clearly delight in *talanoa* and relish both the scandals themselves and the highly stylized ways in which they are discussed.

Approaching *Talanoa*

In my consideration of *talanoa* I am guided by four premises. First, *talanoa* cannot be treated in isolation but must be seen as part of the expressive and communicative repertoire of a community; its character and implications are tied to those of other ways of speaking. Second, gossip is both about something and something in itself. It works in both referential and nonreferential ways at the same time (see Silverstein 1976), and a consideration of gossip should not be limited to one or the other. Third, gossip necessarily involves two kinds of social relationships—those between the gossipers and their subject and those between the gossipers themselves. The functions of gossip in the two relationships are quite different, as are the ways in which those functions are accomplished. Finally, the stylistic features of *talanoa* in Bhatgaon are both striking and substantial. They not only mark *talanoa* but have a great deal to do with its effectiveness. The formal features of *talanoa* operate in different and quite specific ways vis-à-vis both the kinds of relationships mentioned above and the larger social context.

Bhatgaon: A Fiji Indian Community

Bhatgaon is a rural village of 690 Hindi-speaking Fiji Indians located on the northern side of Vanua Levu, the second largest island in the Dominion of Fiji.

The villagers are the descendants of north Indians who came to Fiji between 1879 and 1919 as indentured plantation workers. Bhatgaon was established in the early 1900s and now (July 1980) includes 91 households. There has been little migration to or from the village for the past 20 years, and there is a wide age-span among the villagers. Most families lease rice land from the Government of Fiji; although they may work as seasonal cane cutters or in other outside jobs, most men consider themselves rice farmers. Rice and dry-season vegetables are raised primarily for family use, although surplus produce may be sold to middlemen. Leaseholds are generally small, and rice farming does not offer Bhatgaon villagers the same opportunities for wealth available in sugarcane-raising areas. Since 1974 a number of village men have been able to spend four months in New Zealand doing agricultural work under Fiji government auspices.

Both men and women are politically active in the community, but they take part in very different ways and in different settings. Men are the performers in such public political events as religious speechmaking and insult singing (Brenneis 1978; Brenneis and Padarath 1975). Women may speak in mediation sessions as witnesses, but these important political events are organized and run by men. Political participation by women generally occurs in less public settings, as does much male politicking through *talanoa*.

Among males an overt egalitarian ideology prevails. Although ancestral caste appears to influence marriage choice to some extent (Brenneis 1974:25), it has few daily consequences in Bhatgaon. As one villager said, *Gaon me sab barabba hei* ("In the village all are equal"). This public ideology is manifest in such practices as sitting together on the floor during religious events and equal opportunity to speak. The roots of this egalitarian outlook lie in the conditions of immigration and indenture, central among them the difficulty of maintaining subcaste identity and purity and the disappearance of the hierarchical division of labor which helped sustain the caste system in north India (Mayer 1972; Brown 1981; Brenneis 1979). Egalitarian values are reinforced by the relative similarity in wealth throughout Bhatgaon. Such egalitarianism, however, is problematic in several important respects. First, not every villager is a potential equal. Sex is a crucial dimension; men do not consider women their equals. Age is also consequential. Adolescent boys (*naujawan*) are accorded less respect than older, married men (*admi*). As there are no formal criteria or ceremonies to mark the transition from *naujawan* to *admi*— to social adulthood—disagreements about how one should be treated are common and often lead to serious conflict between males of different ages.

A second problematic aspect of Bhatgaon egalitarianism is the delicate balance between people who should be equals. One of the hallmarks of such an egalitarian community is that individual autonomy is highly prized. Equals are those who mutually respect each other's freedom of action. Attempting too overtly to influence the opinions or actions of another is a violation of this equality. Further, individual reputation is central to one's actual social position. A man's reputation is subject to constant renegotiation through his own words and deeds and through those of others. Villagers are quite sensitive to perceived attempts by others to lower their reputations; the fear of reprisal by the subject of a gossip session has an important constraining effect upon the form of those sessions. Reputation management is a constant concern in disputes, for conflict often arises from apparent insult, and the remedy lies in the public rebalancing of one's reputation with that of one's opponent.

A number of men are recognized as *bada admi* ("Big Men") because of their past participation in village affairs, religious leadership, education, or other personal accomplishment. They also gain respect through the successful management of the disputes of others. Their status is always under stress, however, as obtrusive attempts to assert authority or to intervene in the problems of others abuse the autonomy of other men. Successful Big Men do not exercise their informal power ostentatiously. Continued effectiveness as a respected advisor depends on an overt reluctance to assume leadership. Even when requested to intervene in a dispute, Big Men are often unwilling; they fear both being identified with one party's interests and being considered overeager to display power. The willing exercise of authority leads to its decline.

Although there is a police station 5 km away, there are no formal social control agencies in Bhatgaon itself. The village has a representative on the district advisory council, but he is not empowered to regulate affairs within Bhatgaon. With the decline of caste as an organizational feature of Fiji Indian life, such bodies as caste councils are no longer available for conflict management. Conflict in Bhatgaon remains largely dyadic, the concern of the contending parties alone; yet, as long as the disputes are dyadic, the chances of a settlement are slim. The face-to-face negotiation of a serious dispute is usually impossible, as open accusation or criticism of another is taken as a grievous insult. The offended party might well express his displeasure through nonverbal, nonconfrontational violence—for example, cutting down his opponent's banana trees. While such vandalism would not be praised, other villagers would interpret it as the natural result of direct confrontation or insult and would not intervene. Only a *kara admi* ("hard man") would risk such revenge through direct discussion; most villagers resort to more indirect strategies.

It is difficult to enlist third parties in the management of a conflict, but such triadic participation is crucial. The recruitment of others, not as partisans but as intermediaries and mediators, is a central goal of disputants. Compelling the interest and involvement of disinterested parties is therefore a major end in dispute discourse. Not surprisingly. avoidance remains the most common means of managing conflict.

Central to an understanding of discourse in Bhatgaon is a consideration of the sociology of knowledge in the community. As in any society, both what people talk about and how they talk about it are to some extent informed by what they know, what they expect others to know, and what they and others should know. However, just as local organization and social values were transformed during immigration, indenture, and postplantation life, expectations concerning the social distribution of knowledge were also dramatically altered from those characteristic of north Indian villages.

The radical leveling of Indian immigrant society in Fiji had obvious implications for the allocation of knowledge in Bhatgaon. While in north India the differential distribution of knowledge had both reflected and sustained a system of ranked but interdependent caste groups, in Fiji the groups were at best ill defined; the division of labor in part responsible for the division of knowledge no longer existed. Secular knowledge became, in effect, open to all.

In Bhatgaon, at least, there was a corresponding democratization of sacred knowledge as well. The reformist *arya samaj* sect has as a central tenet the notion of *sikca* ("instruction"). Members are expected to educate both themselves and others in religious practice and understanding. The stated purpose of most types of public communication, from hymns to religious speeches, is mental and spiritual improvement (Brenneis 1978, 1983). Although reform Hindus are a minority in Bhatgaon, their stress on instruction has had a considerable effect on orthodox villagers.

The generally egalitarian nature of social life in Bhatgaon has a counterpart in the relatively equal opportunity of all villagers to pursue knowledge, both sacred and secular. The sacred has become shared knowledge, no longer, in most cases, the property of a particular group. It is important to note, however, that where egalitarian ideals are stressed, continuing symbols of one's membership in a community of peers are necessary. One must not only feel membership but be able to display it publicly. Apparent exclusion from the community is taken very seriously, and knowledge continues to define one's social identity.

A crucial way of demonstrating one's membership is through sharing in what is "common knowledge" in the community—what "everyone" knows. Sacred and technical knowledge can be included in this, but it is relatively unchanging. The real action lies in the dynamics of everyday life; familiarity with local events and personalities is necessary. No one, however, knows everything, and some villagers are considerably better acquainted with particular incidents than are others. This differential participation in common knowledge lies at the root of *talanoa* in Bhatgaon.

The general features of male speaking in Bhatgaon derive in large part from the community's character as an acephalous, egalitarian one in which individuals are concerned both with their own reputations and freedom of action and with maintaining those of others, particularly of men with whom they are on good terms. One's enemies present a more complex situation. Their reputations are tempting targets, but too overt or successful an attack might lead to immediate revenge or preclude future reconciliation, as the insult would be too grievous to remedy.

These broad features of life in Bhatgaon underlie a speech economy the salient feature of which is indirection.[3] One rarely says exactly what one means. Instead, in a variety of public and private performance genres, speakers must resort to metaphor, irony, double entendre, and other subtle devices to signal that they mean more than they have said. Such indirection is clearly a strategy for critical junctures, for situations in which overt criticism or comment would be improvident or improper. Public occasions recurrently pose the same dilemma: one must both act politically and avoid the appearance of such action. The perils of direct confrontation and of direct leadership in the village have fostered oblique, metaphoric, and highly allusive speech. Understanding political discourse in Bhatgaon therefore requires both the interpretation of texts in themselves and the unraveling of well-veiled intentions.

In such genres as *parbacan* ("religious speeches") oblique reference is particularly marked. *Parbacan* are oratorical performances with ostensibly sacred content given at weekly religious services. Their contents are not ambiguous in themselves; it is easy for the Hindi-speaking outsider familiar with Hinduism to follow an analysis of, for example, the fidelity of Sita, the wife of the epic hero Ram. The relationship between such a text and its intended function, however, remains quite opaque. The audience knows that some speakers have no hidden agenda while others are using *parbacan* for political ends.[4] Such indirection both precludes revenge and pricks the curiosity of others, who feel they should understand what is really going on. A successful *parbacan* compels the interest and involvement of potential third parties.

Even in those events where relatively direct reference is necessary, such as *panchayats* ("mediation sessions"), procedural rules severely limit what can be discussed. *Panchayat* testimony focuses on specific incidents rather than ranging freely over the history of disputants' past relations (cf. Gibbs 1967; Nader 1969; Cohn 1967); further, it is elicited through quite direct and topically restricted questions. No decisions are reached in such mediation sessions. A coherent public account of disputed events is produced through testimony; participants and audience are left to draw their own conclusions about the implications of the account. Again, the effects of a concern for individual reputation and autonomy are evident (Brenneis 1980).

A second important feature of men's talk in Bhatgaon is that the culturally ascribed purpose of most genres of public, generally accessible performance is *sikca* ("instruction"). Whatever intentions individual speakers might have, their texts must focus on such topics as moral and spiritual improvement; their apparent motives must be didactic. Such genres as *parbacan* work politically by joining sacred teaching with covert secular interests. The political implications of mediation sessions are more overt. They provide authoritative and licit public explanations—though not evaluations—of particular incidents; villagers can refer to these authoritative accounts in later discussions without fear of revenge. Mediation sessions "teach" not so much through their content as through the manner in which they are conducted—that is, in a neutral spirit and with proper respect for individual sensibilities.

Private conversation (*batcit*), whether *talanoa* or not, is not limited by this concern for instruction. Its topics may range from national politics to the weather, the selection of a topic depending on the participants and their shared interests, not on generic requirements. Most *batcit* is neutrally evaluated: conversation does not offer the same scope for instruction as speechmaking, but it is rarely inherently bad. One of the important features of *talanoa* is that it is clearly considered *fakutiya* ("worthless"). That *talanoa* is seen as worthless or wasteful reflects the villagers' evaluation of its content: nothing of value can be gained from such conversations. One can, nonetheless, learn a great deal from such talk, especially given its potential dangers.

Talk is evaluated not solely in terms of topic. Artfulness, fluency, and wit are highly prized along dimensions specific to each genre. Speechmakers, for example, should display a good knowledge of standard Fiji Hindi, a large Sanskritic vocabulary, and a knack for apposite parables. While *talanoa* is considered worthless in itself, men who excel in it are much appreciated. In distinction to other kinds of *batcit*, *talanoa* is clearly a variety of verbal performance—it "involves on the part of the performer an assumption of responsibility to an audience for the way in which communication is carried out, above and beyond its referential content" (Bauman 1977:11; see also Hymes 1975). As shall be evident below, it is a somewhat singular kind of performance—focusing on stigmatized subjects, using a low-prestige variety of Hindi. Nonetheless, it is an important type of verbal art in the village.

Genres of verbal activity in Bhatgaon are linked together not only in terms of the expressive repertoire of the village but in an inferential web as well. Given the indirect character of public communication, a crucial question is how one learns the background information in terms of which these oblique references can be interpreted. My own initial sense was that *parbacan* made sense because of what the audience had learned or would learn through gossip, that *talanoa* would carry the real communicative burden behind the scenes. However, a more detailed consideration of *talanoa* has shown the process to be considerably more complex. How one learns what is going on in the village remains very problematic.

Talanoa as Text

Most *talanoa* sessions take place in the early evening when the day's work is completed and village men sit with a few friends or kinsmen and drink *yaqona*, a beverage made from the roots of the *Piper methysticum* tree and frequently referred to as "grog." *Yaqona* drinking has long been a ceremonial focus in Fijian life; Fiji Indian grog drinking is considerably less ritualized. The drink has relatively few physiological effects and does not so much intoxicate as provide a focus for relaxed and amiable conviviality. Grog is most frequently drunk inside the *belo*, a thatched sitting house found on most village homesteads. Drinking may go on for several hours, after which the men eat dinner and retire for the night.

While women from the household might sit in the *belo* doorway and occasionally join in conversation, grog drinking and *talanoa* are chiefly male activities. This
is not to say that women do not gossip, but their gossip occurs in different settings
and is not labeled *talanoa*. Only fairly close friends who may be kin as well participate in *talanoa* sessions. The men drop by to drink and chat; rarely is a formal
invitation extended. Occasionally, someone comes with a particular purpose in
mind, but more frequently sociability is the goal. The gossiping group is in most
cases small, rarely exceeding four men; should an additional man join the group,
especially one who is not an intimate, the topic will most likely change. At a grog
party most of the talk is *batcit* ("general conversation"). From time to time speakers will move to topics and styles associated with *talanoa* and then return to less-
marked discussion.

The linguistic code used in *talanoa* is frequently referred to as *jangli bat* ("jungle talk"), a local variety of Fiji Hindi. *Jangli bat* is usually contrasted with *shudh
Hindi* ("sweet Hindi"), a dialect considerably closer to Hindi as spoken in India:
Shudh Hindi is the language of religious oratory and public events; it is the "vernacular" used for early instruction in elementary school. *Jangli bat* is associated
with home, farm, and informal conversation. The two varieties are not clearcut alternatives, however, but represent two ends of a continuum. The language of *talanoa* is considered to be the most *jangli* variety available, at the same time a
source of shame and of rural pride.

The generic boundaries of *talanoa* are somewhat fuzzy and include both topical and stylistic elements. *Talanoa* must be about the less-than-worthy doings of
absent others. In addition, a complex of stylistic features are linked with *talanoa*,
though they need not all be present for a conversation to be so classified. The texts
in the appendix of this paper represent a moderately marked piece of *talanoa* and
a considerably more striking one. Villagers use such terms as "light" or "deep" to
describe how extreme a particular conversation is; the second transcript is of a
very heavy conversation.

"*Talanoa* at Dharm Dutt's", while only a moderate example of *talanoa*, displays
many of the characteristics of *talanoa*—differences between it and "*Talanoa* at
Sham Narayan's" are primarily a matter of degree. The two speakers in the first
transcript are an elderly man (R) and his deceased younger brother's son (DD), a
close neighbor and a good friend. DD also participates in the conversation at
Sham Narayan's house. The others involved are HN and SN, brothers, sons of
DD's mother's sister, and very close friends of DD. I was also present at both sessions, making the tape recordings which the transcripts in part represent.

The incident discussed at Dharm Dutt's house was a dispute about the amount
of money that villagers recently returned from seasonal work in New Zealand
should pay to the village road fund. Before leaving for New Zealand the men had
signed a promissory letter agreeing to give the village F$150 each for sponsorship
in the labor program. They did not make as much money as expected in New
Zealand, and most were reluctant to pay the full amount. Lal Dutt, the village rep-

resentative on the district advisory council and the instigator of the promissory letter, refused to accept less than the promised amount. By the time DD and R were discussing the issue, a number of attempts at resolving the disagreement had been made, several catalyzed by Praya Ram, an older village man who is often considered to be a *bada admi* ("Big Man"). The first part of the transcript is a narrative of several stages in the dispute, while the latter portion includes more evaluatory comments and suggestions for how the disagreement should be handled.

In the second transcript, HN, DD, and SN are discussing the remarkable events of the night before at Praya Ram's house, where he lives with his wife and his married son Vajra Deo and his wife and their children. The entire family had been threshing and bagging rice for storage on the previous day, in the course of which they got Praya Ram's blanket dirty. That evening a number of family members drank locally produced rice whiskey, getting quite drunk in the process; Praya Ram was not home and did not drink with them. Upon his return, however, he found the house full of intoxicated people and his sleeping blanket still dirty from the threshing. A series of altercations followed, during which Vajra Deo fled the house with a rope, seriously threatening to hang himself. Praya Ram chased him and some of the quickly gathered spectators with a knife. By the time a number of neighbors had reached the house, everything was again quiet. The next day Praya Ram called the police to come and interview his family. They came to the village, talked with a few people, and left. Almost all of the second transcript consists of a narrative of these events.

The most striking feature of these transcripts is how difficult it would be to reconstruct the underlying events on the basis of the *talanoa* texts themselves. To some extent contextual cues help in making sense of what is said, but generally participants in *talanoa* sessions must come to them with some understanding of what is being discussed. *Talanoa* is in part referential—it is about something—but it is a very opaque kind of referentiality.

One major feature contributing to this opacity is the lack of any orientation in *talanoa* narratives (Labov and Waletzky 1967; Kernan and Sabsay 1982). One is never told why a story is being told, and the links between the account and preceding discourse are never made clear. Instead, the *talanoa* performer leaps right in *medias res*, frequently identifying his character obliquely, if at all. This feature contrasts markedly with most accounts of gossip in other communities, where the identification of those being talked about is considered an essential, initial part of any gossiped story (see, e.g., Haviland 1977:51; M. Goodwin 1982). While the usual absence of orientation and identification suggests that *talanoa* does not meet the generic standards for well-formed narratives generally found in the literature, it is clear that these features are not necessary from the villagers' point of view.[5]

A particularly marked feature of *talanoa* discourse is the remarkable frequency with which the word *bole* (literally, the third-person singular present form of the verb "to speak") appears.[6] Further, *bole* rarely appears with a subject, a generally unacceptable occurrence in even *jangli* Hindi. *Bole ki* ("says that") frequently oc-

curs with a subject as a quotative frame in Awadhi, the Indian variety of Hindi
from which Fiji Hindi is most directly descended (R. Miranda 1982:personal communication), but the particular form and frequency of *bole* in *talanoa* appears to
be a peculiarly Fiji Indian phenomenon. The confusions possible in this use of *bole*
are further compounded by the fact that it sometimes is used to mean something
much like the English "I hear" or "They say," and at other times is used to quote
unidentified speakers. In either situation the use of *bole* has the effect of distancing
the speaker from the subject about which he is speaking; it is not one's own account
but something which has been heard (see also M. Goodwin 1980; Vološinov 1971).

In the first transcript *bole* almost always occurs in contexts where reported
speech might be occurring. For example, DD says (1.8): *tab Praya Ram bole hamlog dusre aidia lagai bole dusre skim lagai aise nahi thik hei.* The second *bole* has
Praya Ram as subject; its text (*Dusre skim . . . nahi thik hei*) works both syntactically and semantically as a quote. In the second transcript, the deeper *talanoa*, a
solely quotative interpretation of *bole* is difficult to sustain. In HN's speech (2.9),
for example, there is no obvious subject. Further, while any single "quoted" phrase
following *bole* might reasonably be taken as reported speech, it is highly unlikely
that the entire string of phrases is intended as quotation.

Bole is not the only verb to lack a subject. Especially in the second transcript actions frequently appear without apparent actors. Subject deletion is not a feature
of ordinary *jangli bat*, and such passages as HN's first long turn (2.7) are syntactically quite confusing. The confusion is heightened by a fairly free variation in
verb form between the simple past tense (in *jangli* Hindi the third-person singular form ends in *-is*, as in *kaderis*, or "chased") and what strictly is the impolite imperative form (*-ao* or *-io* endings, as in *lagao*, or "fasten"), which is characteristic
of the plantation-pidginized Hindi spoken between laborers and European su-
pervisors. From their linguistic context it is clear that verbs with the latter endings
should be understood as past tense.

Although it is not evident in the transcripts, rapid and rhythmic delivery is
characteristic of *talanoa*. *Bole* plays an important role in this, as it divides the discourse into syntactic and rhythmic chunks. It frequently is stressed and length-
ened vis-à-vis the rest of the text, and these stress patterns give a pulsing feel to
the *talanoa* as a whole. *Talanoa* displays a number of other prosodic features as
well. Assonance and alliteration are quite marked, and exaggerated intonation
contours and volume variation frequently occur. The repetition or near repetition
of words and phrases are common, as are plays with word order. Reduplication
(*garmi-garmi*, "hot" or "angry"; 1.20) and partial reduplication (*polis-ulis*, "police"; 2.3) are common in *jangli* Hindi but particularly marked in *talanoa*.

All of these features have a great deal to do with a larger structural feature of *talanoa*. *Talanoa* rarely has a single performer. While one man may do most of the
talking, usually at least one other will participate in the performance. One's auditors are not limited to grunts of encouragement but are expected to contribute to
the construction of a narrative. Overlaps between speakers are fairly frequent in

talanoa in contrast to ordinary village discourse. Such overlaps lead not to conversational repair but to continuity between two speakers; they contribute to the coproduction of *talanoa* narratives.[7]

The stylistic features described above are instrumental in the coordination of the speakers' performances. *Bole*'s rhythmic and segmenting effects are particularly important as they mark potential entry points for the other speaker. An example of this is in the second transcript, where HN joins in (*Ha. Bole . . .*) while DD says "*Kahe bole . . .*" (2.16, 2.15). Such junctures allow for a continuing flow of talk from speaker to speaker.

Most transitions between *talanoa* speakers do not involve overlap but are linked through some stylistic feature. Direct repetition of the preceding speaker's words is fairly common, as are word order plays between speakers (see, e.g., 2.4—2.7). Speakers also frequently maintain the tempo and meter set by their predecessors. Although there may be two or more performers. *talanoa* is one performance, united in subject and style.

The degree to which there is such coperformance appears to be one of the dimensions along which heavy and light *talanoa* are distinguished. The first transcript is close to a one-man show; R's participation is, with a few exceptions, limited to supportive murmurs and questions intended to further D's account. All of the stylistic features of *talanoa* are present but to a moderate extent. In the second transcript HN initiates the *talanoa* in the midst of a more general conversation, but DD quickly joins in as a coauthor. Features present in the first example are exaggerated in the second.

There are no other genres of adult male discourse which display the stylistic and organizational features of *talanoa*, nor are there any in which joint performance occurs. *Talanoa*, however, is remarkably similar to children's arguments in the village (Lein and Brenneis 1978). Children's arguments are characterized by exaggerated prosodic features, self- and other-repetition of both texts and stylistic strategies, the use of shared rhythmic framework, and considerable coordinated overlap between speakers. The texts of arguments are considerably more direct than those of *talanoa*, and the *bole* construction is not used. Apart from particular similarities, *talanoa* and such arguments share a remarkable sense of verbal playfulness. The manipulation of forms and the simultaneously competitive and cooperative construction of a joint performance provide pleasure for participants and audience alike. Adults do not argue like children do; in rare moments of direct confrontation between disputants playfulness is never evident. What I suggest here is that communicative styles learned in one type of context in childhood become part of one's repertoire; in later life these styles can be adapted to new settings and uses.[8]

Talanoa as Activity

Gossip necessarily involves the gossipers in two simultaneous social relationships: with each other and with the subjects of their talk. In this concluding section I ex-

plore the relationships between the formal features of *talanoa* and these two social dimensions. In so doing I also suggest the very important nonreferential functions which *talanoa* appears to serve.

Perhaps the central concern of gossipers about their subjects is that their comments do not lead to irreparable damage; one gossips as frequently about friends
as enemies. One way of trying to prevent such difficulties is to limit gossiping to
trustworthy auditors. Even with care, however, information leaks are possible. The
relative opacity of *talanoa* texts and the systems of indirect reference sustained
through the *bole* construction help to make speakers less than fully culpable for
their commentary. It is not fortuitous that the use of *bole* developed in the relatively amorphous social world of Fiji Indian villages: it provides an effective way
of distancing speakers from their speech, of allowing them denial as defense. Such
responsibility as speakers have is shared with their co-authors; joint performance
helps to shield gossipers from anger and possible revenge.

If the effects of *talanoa* style in relations with subjects are largely preventive, the
same stylistic features have a quite different role in regard to the gossipers themselves. First, the same indirection that helps to prevent revenge from others also
leaves open the options of one's listeners. The possibility of multiple interpretation helps to maintain the autonomy of participants: they are not forced to accept
a straightforward and unambiguous account. Second, the stylistic and organizational features of *talanoa* allow—indeed, almost compel—a kind of conversational duet. Rhythm, repetition, syntactic play, and the *bole*-defined chunking of
discourse not only invite coparticipation but enable a remarkable degree of stylistic convergence on the part of the speakers. As Gumperz (1982) has recently argued, divergences in conversational style can lead to the definition and maintenance of social differentiation. Convergence can have the opposite effect,
emphasizing the shared qualities and social identities of the speakers.

It is clear that *talanoa* is *about* something; it concerns village events, people, and
standards for evaluation. Information is transmitted, even if individuals must
know a great deal already to make sense of what they hear. Gossiping is also an
event in itself, one in which relationships of solidarity and artful complicity are
each time reproduced anew.

Appendix

The following *talanoa* transcripts are intended for general readers rather than Indianists;
diacritical markings have been omitted. Numbers in parentheses indicate the length of
pauses in seconds; brackets indicate overlaps.

Transcript 1: *Talanoa* at Dharm Dutt's, 7 July 1980

1.1   R: HOYGAYA FAISALA?
               Completed decision?
               Has a decision been reached?

1.2   *DD*:   NAHI NAHI KUCH NAHI.
                      No no at all no.
                      Not in the least.
                      (1)

1.3   *R*:   KAL RAHA KI KAHIA RAHA?
                      Yesterday was or when was?
                      Was it yesterday or some other time?
                      (1)

1.4   *DD*:   KAL TO PRAYA RAM SENICER TO BATAYA RAHA NE? HAMLOG
                      Yesterday so Praya Ram Saturday so said had no? We
                      Praya Ram said Saturday yesterday, didn't he? Our . . .

                      KE..(1) .. TUMHE BATAYA RAHA BATAYA RAHA MORDAYA ME.
                      of..(1).. You said had said had cemetery in.
                      You said he said it would be in the cemetery.

1.5   *R*:   HA, HA, HA.
                      Yes, yes, yes.

1.6   *DD*:   HARDGAYA BOLE.
                      Changed says.
                      Says it was changed.
                      (4)

1.7   *R*:   HARDGAYA?
                      Changed?

1.8   *DD*:   TA BOLE HARDGAYA. . . .
                      So says changed. . . .
                      So says it was changed. . . .

                      TAB PRAYA RAM BOLE HAMLOG DUSRE AIDIA LAGAI BOLE DUSRE
                      So Praya Ram says we another idea propose says another
                      So Praya Ram says we'll propose another idea, says we'll propose

                      SKIM LAGAI AISE NAHI THIK HEI.
                      scheme propose this not good is.
                      another scheme; this one is no good.

1.9   *R*:   HA.
                      Yes.

1.10   *DD*:   BOLE BATAI DENA TUMHE NAHI AI NAHI HAMLOG HARDAI DEGA.
                      Says tell give you not come not we change will give.
                      Says to tell you not to come, that we will make a change.

1.11   *R*:   OO.
                      Oh.

1.12   *DD*:   TAB KAL HAM JANNO MALTAI- . . . U STIRING KAMITI
                      Then yesterday I think Multi- . . . that steering committee
                      Then, I think it was yesterday, the Multi-racial, no, the

                      MITING RAHA U RAJ KUBER KE GHAR PAR RAT ME.
                      meeting was that Raj Kuber of house at night in.
                      steering committee meeting was that night at Raj Kuber's.

1.13   *R*:   OO.
               Oh.

1.14   *DD*:   BOLE PATA NAHI KIYA NISCAY KARO. KOI BOLE
               Says knowledge not which decision make. Someone says
               Says he has no idea which decision was made. Someone said

               BYAS DEDIS.
               Byas gave.

1.15   *R*:   UM HUNH. KITNA?
               Um hunh. How much?

1.16   *DD*:   EK SAU PACAS.
               One hundred and fifty.

1.17   *R*:   PURA?
               All?

1.18   *DD*:   HA.
               Yes.

1.19   *R*:   KAMTI DETE TABO THIK RAHA.
               Less give then fine was.
               If he'd given less, it would have been fine.

1.20   *DD*:   HA. TAB PHIR RAJ DHAN KE LADKA AI RAHA HAM JANNO KAPHI
               Yes. Then again Raj Dhan of son come had I know plenty
               Yes. Then again I've heard that Raj Dhan's son came and gave

               GARMI-GARMI KARIS USE.
               hot-hot did to him.
               him a hot time about it.

1.21   *R*:   HA.
               Yes.

1.22   *DD*:   BOLE TUM KAHI DEDIU?
               Says you why given?
               Says why had you given?

1.23   *R*:   HA.
               Yes.

1.24   *DD*:   KAHI DEDIU BOLE HAM BATAYA RAHA NAHI DENE .. . .
               EK DEDIS TO DEKH
               Why given says I said had not give .. . . One gave so look
               Why did you give? I said not to give . . . One has given, now

               PARI SAB KE LAGBAG . . . (4) .. TO HARI PRATAP KALAYA
               RAHA TO BOLE
               must all similar..(4) .. So Hari Pratap gone had so says
               all must do so .. (4) .. So Hari Pratap went over there and says

               RAJ DHAN WALLA TO NAHI DE MANGE.
               Rai Dhan folks so not give want.
               that Raj Dhan's family did not want to give.

1.25 *R:* HA.
      Yes.

1.26 *DD:* BOLE KAMTI DIEGA. HAM BOLA KI JO GAYA RAHIN INKE
      Says less will give. I said that who gone had he
      Says I'll give less. I said that whoever had gone must.

      CHAHIYE MITING BATORKE JANTA SE BATAU KI HAMLOGIN
      must meeting called people from tell that we
      having called a meeting, tell people that we

      GAYA RAHA JARUR LEKIN PAISE UTNE NAHI MILA.
      gone had certainly but money that much not available.
      certainly went, but we did not make as much money as we hoped.

      HAMLOG NAHI SAKIT HEI ETNA DIU EK SAU DE
      We not able are that much give one hundred give
      We cannot give that much. Some can give one

      SAKIT HAI YA PACASSI DE SAKIT HOI NA? . . . DUI CAR ADMI
      able are or eighty-five give able are no? . . . Two four men
      hundred, some eighty-five, okay? A few men

      PAGALA HEI SAB PURA NAHI PAGALE HEI. HAM JANNO KOI TO
      crazy are all totally not mad are. I know some so
      are crazy but not everyone's that way. I know several who

      BATAYA TO THIK HEI.
      said so fine is.
      said it would be fine.

1.27 *R:* NAHI KAMTI ME TO RAJI HOI JATE.
      Not less in so agreement be goes.
      If it's not less, people will be in agreement.

1.28 *DD:* HA.
      Yes.

1.29 *R:* PACASSI DOLAR NE BHAIYE?
      Eighty-five dollars no brother?
      Eighty-five dollars would be all right, brother?

1.30 *DD:* HA. KUCH DE DETE NAHI?
      Yes. Whoever bit give gives no?
      Yes. Whoever gives a bit is giving, no?

1.31 *R:* SACHE BAT.
      True words.

1.32 *DD:* PATA NAHI KAISE MAMALA HEI. ABHI KUCH PATA NAHI
      Knowledge not what sort fight is. Now some idea not
      I don't know what the trouble's all about. Now I don't know

      LAGA KA FAISALA BAYE KAL. NOTIS TO MILA HEI
      take if decision was yesterday. Notice so available is
      if a decision was made yesterday. There's been notice, so

INKE JALDI PAISE BHAR DIU JALDI SE JALDI.
to them quick money pay give quick from quick.
they should pay the money quite quickly.

1.33   *R:*   SACHE BAT ..(2).. LEKIN APAS ME BATWAI KE AUR KAMTI HOI
True words .. (2) .. But own on tell of other less is
True enough ..(2).. But one told the other less than he was

SAKATA RAHA. KAMTI KAREK TO BOLET RAHA.
able was. Less having done so said had.
able. He did less than he said he had.

1.34   *DD:*   HA. ULOG DUNO PAGALE HEIN. LAL DUTT TO GAON KE PAGALA
Yes. They two crazy are. Lal Dutt so village of crazy
Yes. Those two are madmen. Lal Dutt is the craziest one

HAI YE HEI USKE KOI TANG NAHI HEI KAISE KAREK CHAHIYE.
is is his at all idea not is how done must.
in the village and has no idea at all how things should be done.

AUR U JON HEI ULOG PAGALE HEI. LAL DUTT ULTA BAT
And he who is they crazy are. Lal Dutt backwards talk
And those other folks are mad! Lal Dutt has been talking

BATAWE TO ULOGIN KE CHAHIYE MITING BALAU. YA KOI KAMITI
spoke so they of must meeting call. Some committee
nonsense, so they must call a meeting. Some committee.

SANATAN DHARM KAMITI YA STIRING KAMITI UNKA BOLAI LIYE.
Sanatan Dharm committee or steering committee them call take.
whether the Sanatani or steering committee, call them.

TA KOI KAMITI BATAI DE KI AISE AISE BAT
Then some committee tell give that this way this way affair
Then they can tell some committee what the nature of the

HEI. YA RASTE KAMITI RUPAN PRADHAN HEI UNKE BALAU
is. Or road committee Rupan chair is him call
problem is. Or call the road committee—Rupan is the chair—

KI HAMLOG DE MANGE HEI JARUR AISE AISE
that we give want are certainly this way this way.
say we certainly want to give, that Lal Dutt made us

LAL DUTT SAIN KARAI RAHA AUR BATAYA RAHA KI TUMLOGIN
Lal Dutt sign cause had and said had that you
sign things this way, that he made us sign saying

SAIN KAR DIU JITNA DE DENA. TO SAKIT RAHA KUCH
sign make give how much give give. So can was somewhat
how much we would give. So it could be somewhat

SUDHAR HO NAHI. LEKIN ULOGIN KUCH NAHI KARE. IDHARSE
simple is not. But they at all not did. From here
simple, no? But they did nothing at all. Just running

UDHAR DORE HE JUTE-PHUTE. KOI ACHA TANG SE KAM NE
there run is lying, at all good idea from work not
around wildly, lying, doing nothing profitable.

KARE NAHI. TAB E TO ETNA GARBARI .. (1) .. RUPAN NE BATATE
did not. Then e so so much trouble .. (1) .. Rupan ne said
thoughtless. And from that so much grief. . . . Rupan could say.

KI DEKHO AISE AISE BAT HEI HAMLOG MANGIT HEI
that look this way this way issue is we want are
look, this is how things are—we want to give

PAISE DEGA LEKIN PAISA MANGE PURA BADA RASTA ME
money will give but money want all big road on
money but want to make sure it is all used for the main

LAGE SAB.
placed all.
village road.

1.35   R: HA.
              Yes.

1.36   DD: YA NAHI DETE WE ME DETE BOLTE SAB KI HAMLOG PACAS PACAS.
              Or not give it in give said all that we fifty fifty
              Or if not giving as much as they agreed, at least to say

              DEGA.
              will give.
              they'd give fifty dollars.

1.37   R: UM-HMH.
              Um-hmh.

1.38   DD: TODA ADMI KE KAM ME AWA AUR HAMLOG JADA UNNATI
              Few men of work in come and we great improvement
              Help has come from only a few men's work; we haven't made

              NAHI KAR PAWA. UTNA PAISA KAMAI NAHI PAWA
              not make able. That much money raise not able
              a great improvement. We haven't raised much money.

              KALI CHE SAT AT SAU. LAWA OMAN SE DUI SAU
              only six seven eight hundred. Take it from two hundred
              only six to eight hundred. Take two hundred dollars from

              DOLAR RASTAM DEDE TO HAMAR BHAKI KA. TAB KOI
              dollar road give so our remaining of. Then some
              that, give it to the road; we'll keep the rest. Then there'd

              FAISALA HOI LEKIN ILOGIN PATA NAHI KAISE ULTA-PHULTA
              decision is but they idea not how upside-down
              be some decision, but they don't know what they're doing.

              GARBARIYANI HEI IDHARSE UDHAR KARE HEI.
              mixed-up is from here there do are.
              just getting everything mixed-up.

1.39   *R:*   UM-HUNH ..(3).. KHUSI ULOGINKE .. (1) .. TANG SE BAT
              Um-hunh .. (3) .. pleasure theirs .. (1) .. sense from issue
              Um-hunh .. (3) .. It's their choice .. (1) .. It would be nice

              KARTE TO THIK RAHE.
              make so fine would be.
              to make some sense out of all of this.

1.40   *DD:* ETNA MAMALA NAHI HOTI. . . .
              This much trouble not have been. . . .
              There need not have been all this trouble. . . .

Transcript 2: *Talanoa* at Sham Narayan's, 3 July 1980

2.1   *HN:* TA U BAT ..(3).. EE VAJRA DEO KAL CHATAK
              So that issue ..(3).. Ee Vajra Deo yesterday occasion
              What about that? . . . Ee Vajra Deo really made a great

              KARDIYA RAHA.
              created had.
              stir yesterday.

2.2   *DD:* HAM SUNA UPAR SABERE WAHA TAK   ⌈ GAYA RAHA.
              I heard there in the morning there to   *went had.*
              I heard this morning they had gone as far   as that place.

2.3   *HN:*   AJ POLIS-ULIS
                                                       Today police
                                                    ⌊ Today the police

              AIN. . . . FASI LAGAI RAHA. BOLE DUNU PIET RAHIN.
              came. . . . Noose fastened had. Says both drinking were.
              came. . . . He'd tied a noose. Says both were drinking.

              BOLE PIET RAHIN ISE TODA JADA RAT HOGAYA RAHI.
              Says drinking were so a bit late night become had.
              Says they were drinking. and so it became late at night.

2.4   *DD:* NAU BAJE LAGBAG   ⌈ HOI NA?
              Nine o clock approximately   *is no?*
              About nine o'clock.   wasn't it?

2.5   *HN:*   NAU BAJE LAGBAG.
                                                       Nine o'clock approximately.
                                                    ⌊ About nine o'clock.

2.6   *DD:* DUNU KAT PIN.
              Both totally drunk.

2.7   *HN:* BOLE DUNU PIN KAT BOLE BAS DONO LARAIN BOLE
              Says both drunk fully says enough both fought says
              Says both were quite drunk; says they fought with each other;

              PRAYA RAM BOLE BHAG JAO KADERIS BOLE GAYE RASI LEKE
              Praya Ram says away go chased says went rope taking
              says Praya Ram says scram and chased them; they went taking

CHADKE JAMUN PED PE FASI LAGAO CHOTU BOLE SAB GHARAWE
went jamun tree on noose fastened. Chotu says all house in
a rope and tied a noose on the jamun tree. Chotu says all were

CHOTKANA JAI BOLE BAPA LOTIO JAB CHOTKANA
little fellow go says father returned when little fellow
at home, and the little guy says father is back; the little

GAI BOLE LEKE CHURI RAPETIS CHOTKANA TO BHAGA GHAR
went says taking knife chased little fellow so fled house
guy left; says he took a knife and chased the little guy so

E. CHOTKANA RAPETIS TO BHAGA CHAR E.
from. Little fellow chased so fled house from.
he fled the house. He chased the little guy so he fled.

U DARWAWAT RAHA. BAS SAB RONA PITNA BOLE EK
He terrified was. Enough all crying drinking says one
He was terrified. So everyone was crying, drinking. Says

TARAF SE CHILAI ROWAI KALI YAHA BIKARI GHAR LE ROYE
side from shout cry only there Bikari house at crying
from that side there was nothing but crying and shouting;

SUNAI.
was heard.
they heard it as far away as Bikari's.

2.8   *DD*:   LONDE BOLE TIS JANNE HAMLOG GAWA.
Children says thirty people we went.
The children said more than thirty people went there.

2.9   *HN*:   HA BAHUT BOLE TIS JANNE KOI GAYE TIS RAHA BOLE
Yes many says thirty people who went thirty were says
Yes, many people, says, says thirty, says thirty or

TIS BATIS JANNE KE BOLAT RAHA GAYE BOLE.
thirty thirty-two people of said had went says.
thirty-two people. he said, went there. says.

2.10   *SN*:   BOLE GAYE HUAN KUCH PONC GAYEN KUCH DEVIDINLOG
Says gone had some arrived went some Devidin's folks
Says some had arrived as far as Devidin's house.

KE GHAR LE. KUCH NARA TALAK GAYE BIKARI KE GHAR KE
of house to. Some ditch to went Bikari of house of
Some got as far as the ditch, some only as

KOI DUI LADKE GAYE RAHA TALAK KALI. KUCH FIR LOTAIN.
some two boys gone had to only. Some again returned.
far as Bikari's house. Some went back home.

2.11   *DD*:   BOLE HUWA JATJAT BATI KALAS BHUT GAYE. BOLE SAB
Says there going lanterns finished off went. Says all
Says that as they were going there the lights went out.

SOYGAYA KALAS. PONCAT PONCAT.
gone to sleep finished. Arriving arriving.
Says all had gone to sleep. Just as they were arriving.

2.12   *HN*:   HA. BOLE EKDUM GHAR ME SAKIT BOLE
Yes. Says immediately house at arrived says
Yes. Says that just as soon as they got to the house, says

VAJRA DEO NIKALGAYA. | BOLE PRAYA RAM POLIS ME GAYA RAHA
Vajra Deo came out. | *Says Praya Ram police to gone had*
Vajra Deo came out. | Says Praya Ram had gone to the police

2.13   *DD*:   BOLE POLIS. . . . | HA, TO. . . .
says police. . . . | Yes, then. . . .

2.14   *HN*:   AYA RAHIN DIN ME BOLE ADMILOG SOCIN BOLE PRAYA RAM
Come had day in says men thought says Praya Ram
The police came today. Says people thought, says Praya Ram

NAHI RAHIT TO AUR JANNELOG SOCE RAHIN BOLE KI KAHE
not was so and people thought had says that told
wasn't there, and people thought, says, that he'd

ETNA GAON KE NI ETNA DOR KE GAYE RAHIN JANTA.
such village of in such run of gone had know.
never heard of such running around in a village.

2.15   *DD*:   KON KON MAMALA RAHA? | KAHE BOLE. . . .
What what trouble was? | *Told says. . . .*
What was it all about? | I've heard. . . .

2.16   *HN*: | HA. BOLE ILOG KE BOLE U KAR
                             | *Yes. Says they of says he done*
                             | Yes. Says of them, says he did

DIN ILOG DOR KI GAYIN TO DEKHIN PRAYA RAM APNE GAYA.
had they run of went so saw Praya Ram self went.
something. They fled running so he saw Praya Ram himself go.

2.17   *DD*:   PRAYA RAM BATIS. . . . | BOLE. . . .
Praya Ram said. . . . | says. . . .

2.18   *HN*: | BIKARI BOLET RAHA.
                             | *Bikari said had.*
                             | Bikari had said.

2.19   *DD*:   BOLE BAHUT GUSSAN BOLAT RAHA TUMLOG CELLE JAO BOLE.
Says very angry said had you(pl) leave go says.
Says he said, very angrily, for them to leave at once.

BOLE FIR ROHIT RAHA PRAYA RAM BOLE KA KARI. . . . U
says again cried had Praya Ram says what doing. . . . He
Says they cried again; Praya Ram says what are you doing?

BATAWAT RAHA BESWA GAYA RAHA BOLE LATCHMI UDHAR SE AWE
said had Beswa gone had says Latchmi there from came
He said Beswa had gone; says Latchmi had not come from

NAHI.
not.
over there.

2.20   *HN:*   HA.
               Yes.

2.21   *DD:*   BOLE CELLE JAO NAHI TO CHURI-URI MAR DI BOLE EKDUM
               Says leave go not then knife hit give says totally
               Says leave at once or I'll hit you with my knife. Says

               PAGALEN HEI NAHI?
               crazy are not?
               they're totally mad, aren't they?

2.22   *HN:*   HA.
               Yes.

2.23   *DD:*   BOLE HAMLOG NAHI MANA AUR AGHE GAWA TO PRAYA RAM
               Says we not believe and forward went so Praya Ram
               Says we didn't believe him and went on. So Praya Ram

               NIKALA BOLE KAMAR KE PICE JAGARA BAYE. KAMARWALA
               came out says blanket of after fight was. Blanket about
               emerged, says the fight was about a blanket. The whole

               BAT RAHA.
               issue was.
               thing was over a blanket.

2.24   *HN:*   HAMLOG KE VISCAY KUCH NAHI MALUM. KALI I BAT BOLE
               We of topic at all no idea. Only this issue says
               We had no idea about that topic. All we knew was that

               KI   DHARU PIN ETNA. . . .
               that   *whiskey drunk this much.* . . .
               they   had drunk so much whiskey. . . .

2.25   *DD:*   EE U DHAN RAKHAIN NAHI?
                                      Ee they rice put away not?
                                        Ee, they were storing threshed rice, right?

2.26   *HN:*   HA.
               Yes.

2.27   *DD:*   KAMAR MAILAI GAYA RAHA HAM JANNO
               Blanket dirtied gone had I know.
               They got the blanket dirty in the process. I know.

2.28   *HN:*   HA.
               Yes.

2.29   *DD:*   VAJRA DEO BATAYA RAHA DHOHI DENA KUN CIS KAR DENA
               Vajra Deo said had wash give some thing do give
               Vajra Deo had told them to wash it or do something with

               PATEL KE RAHA. TO DHOHE NAHI TO ADHEK TAIM BAYE TO
               Patel of was. So washed not so covering-up time was so
               it. It was the boss's. So it wasn't washed and when it was

HAM JANNO BAS. . . . BOLE KAHI NAHI DHOHIN TO CELLA
I know enough. . . . Says why not washed so proceeded
time to go to bed that was all. . . . Says why didn't you wash

BAT.
issue.
it, and things got started.

2.30   *HN*:   HAI, HAI, KOI VISCAY WAHI TO. . . .
               Yes, yes, some topic that so. . . .
               Yes, yes, something like that. . . .

2.31   *DD*:   EKDUM SARA BAT. LAD PADE BOLE DHARU PIS.
               Totally shameful issue. To carry on says whiskey drunk.
               What a shameful affair! To carry on like that while drunk!

Notes

Acknowledgments. Research in Bhatgaon was sponsored by Harvard University, N.I.M.H., the Haynes Foundation, N.E.H., and Pitzer College. I would like to thank Wynne Furth, Fred Myers, Bette Clark, Ronald Macaulay, Elinor Ochs, Sandro Duranti, and Emanuel Schegloff for their comments and suggestions concerning the transcripts discussed in the paper. Earlier versions of this paper were presented to the Department of Anthropology, University of California, Berkeley, and in the session on "Ethnographic Approaches to Verbal Interaction Across Social and Cultural Contexts" at the 81st Annual Meeting of the American Anthropological Association. I would like to thank participants in these events for their guidance. Michael Silverstein, Judith Irvine, Andrew Arno, Roger Abrahams, Dell Hymes, Norman E. Whitten, Jr., and the anonymous reviewers for *American Ethnologist* also provided very helpful criticism and encouragement.

1. *Talanoa* is one of the relatively few loan words taken into Fiji Hindi from Fijian. In Fijian it means general conversation rather than gossip per se. Its use in Fiji Hindi carries some connotation of idle chatter, sustaining the Fiji Indian stereotype of Fijians as given to pointless socializing. That it is a loan word suggests, as I explore in detail later, that this form of discourse is a development in Fiji rather than an importation from India.
2. *Fakutiya* is a particularly rich term in Fiji Hindi; it implies silliness, worthlessness, sloth, immorality, and eristic behavior generally.
3. Bhatgaon villagers themselves make a clear distinction between *kara* ("hard") or *sita* ("straight") talk and *shudh* ("sweet") talk which is parallel to my distinction between direct and indirect discourse; only on certain infrequent occasions would the usual village man speak "straight."

"Indirection" as communicative style has yet to be defined in such a way that the controlled crosscultural study of it can be carried out. Various strategies of indirection, however, are strikingly associated with egalitarian social relations (see, e.g., Atkinson 1984; Rosaldo 1973; Strathern 1975; McKellin 1984; Myers and Brenneis 1984). Specific motives for indirection remain quite variable. In the Pacific communities discussed in the articles cited above, for example, indirection serves to preclude further conflict, while in the well-known Black American speech strategy called "signifying" the intent may be "bringing about future confrontation through indirection" (M. Goodwin 1982:800; see also Mitchell-Kernan 1972).

4. Speakers with political motives frequently cue their listeners to the possibility of second meanings through the use of a range of keying devices, notable among them the "coy reference," the use of relative clauses with indefinite antecedents (discussed in detail in Brenneis 1978).

5. Other genres in the village, for example *katha* ("sacred narratives") and *dristant* (religious exempla), come much closer to meeting the Labov and Waletzky (1967) criteria. *Talanoa* differs not only from scholarly definitions of narrative but from other folk genres within the village as well.

6. I am indebted to Ronald Macaulay for suggesting that given this salient characteristic, *talanoa* be referred to as "shooting the *bole*."

7. Conversational analysts such as Schegloff (1982) and C. Goodwin (1981) argue convincingly that ordinary talk is a shared achievement, one in which participants attend constantly to a range of formal ordering and cueing devices. Their argument arises from a programmatic position that conversation is a coordinated exchange between individual speakers; from that point of view conversation is best seen as joint accomplishment. While *talanoa* can be characterized in terms of such conversational organization, any focus on the individual speaker would obscure one of its central features, that it is an instance of coperformance, rather than a merely cooperative one. *Talanoa* is an emergent performance, not a formulaic one. Burns (1980) and Watson-Gegeo and Boggs (1977) discuss somewhat similar examples of the coperformance of narratives.

8. This observation draws in part on Ochs's (1979) suggestion that linguistic forms characteristic of speech during childhood remain in the repertoire of adults and are used in certain situations. Ochs is concerned primarily with morphosyntactic forms, while I focus on discourse structure.

References

Abrahams, Roger D. 1970. A Performance-centered Approach to Gossip. Man (NS) 5:290–391.

Atkinson, Jane Monnig. 1984. Wrapped Words: Poetry and Politics among the Wana of Central Sulawesi, Indonesia. *In* Dangerous Words: Language and Politics in the Pacific. Donald Brenneis and Fred Myers, eds. pp. 33–68. New York: New York University Press.

Bauman, Richard. 1977. Verbal Art as Performance. *In* Verbal Art as Performance. Richard Bauman, ed. pp. 3–58. Rowley: Newbury House.

Brenneis, Donald. 1974. Conflict and Communication in a Fiji Indian Community. Ph.D. dissertation. Department of Social Relations, Harvard University.

————. 1978. The Matter of Talk: Political Performances in Bhatgaon. Language in Society 7:159–170.

————. 1979. Conflict in Bhatgaon: The Search for a Third Party. *In* The Indo-Fijian Experience. Subramani, ed. pp. 41–56. St. Lucia: University of Queensland Press.

————. 1980. Straight Talk and Sweet Talk: Political Discourse in a Community of Equals. Working Papers in Sociolinguistics No. 71. Austin, TX: Southwestern Educational Development Laboratory.

————. 1983. The Emerging Soloist: *Kavvali* in Bhatgaon. Asian Folklore Studies 42:67–80.

Brenneis, Donald, and Ram Padarath. 1975. About Those Scoundrels I'll Let Everyone Know: Challenge Singing in a Fiji Indian Community. Journal of American Folklore 88:283–291.

Brown, Carolyn Henning. 1981. Demographic Constraints on Caste: A Fiji Indian Example. American Ethnologist 8:312–328.

Burns, Allan F. 1980. Interactive Features in Yucatec Mayan Narrative. Language in Society 9:307–319.

Cohn, Bernard S. 1967. Some Notes on Law and Change in North India. In Law and Warfare. Paul Bohannan, ed. pp. 139–159. Austin: University of Texas Press.

Cox, Bruce. 1970. What Is Hopi Gossip About? Information Management and Hopi Factions. Man (NS) 5:88–98.

Edmonson, Munro. 1966. Play: Games, Gossip and Humor. In Handbook of Middle American Indians. Manning Nash, ed. pp. 191–206. Austin: University of Texas Press.

Gibbs, James. 1967. The Kpelle Moot. In Law and Warfare. Paul Bohannan. ed. pp. 277–289. Austin: University of Texas Press.

Gluckman. Max. 1963. Gossip and Scandal. Current Anthropology 4:307–316.

Goodwin, Charles. 1981. Conversational Organization: Interaction Between Speakers and Hearers. New York: Academic Press.

Goodwin, Marjorie Harness. 1980. "He-Said-She-Said": Formal Cultural Procedures for the Construction of a Gossip Dispute Activity. American Ethnologist 7:674–695.

———. 1982. Instigating: Storytelling as Social Process. American Ethnologist 9:799–819.

Gossen, Gary. 1974. Chamulas in the World of the Sun: Time and Space in a Mayan Oral Tradition. Cambridge: Harvard University Press.

Gumperz, John. 1982. Discourse Strategies. New York: Cambridge University Press.

Haviland, John B. 1977. Gossip, Reputation and Knowledge in Zinacantan. Chicago: University of Chicago Press.

Hymes, Dell. 1975. Breakthrough into Performance. In Folklore: Performance and Communication. Dan Ben-Amos and Kenneth Goldstein, eds. pp. 11–74. The Hague: Mouton.

Kernan. Keith T., and Sharon Sabsay. 1982. Semantic Deficiencies in the Narratives of Mildly Retarded Speakers. Semiotics 42:169–193.

Labov, William, and Joshua Waletzky. 1967. Narrative Analysis: Oral Versions of Personal Experience. In Essays in the Verbal and Visual Arts. June Helm, ed. pp. 12–44. Seattle: University of Washington Press.

Lein, Laura. and Donald Brenneis. 1978. Children's Disputes in Three Speech Communities. Language in Society 7:299–323.

Mayer, Adrian. 1972. Peasants in the Pacific: A Study of Fiji Indian Rural Society. Berkeley: University of California Press.

McKellin, William. 1984. Putting Down Roots: Information the Language of Managalase Exchange. In Dangerous Words: Language and Politics in the Pacific. Donald Brenneis and Fred Myers, eds. pp. 108–127. New York: New York University Press.

Mitchell-Kernan, Claudia. 1972. Signifying. Loud-talking, and Marking. In Rappin' and Stylin' Out: Communication in Urban Black America. Thomas Kochman, ed. pp. 315–335. Urbana: University of Illinois Press.

Myers, Fred, and Donald Brenneis. 1984. Introduction: Language and Politics in the Pacific. In Dangerous Words: Language and Politics in the Pacific. Donald Brenneis and Fred Myers. eds. pp. 1–29. New York: New York University Press.

Nader, Laura. 1969. Styles of Court Procedure: To Make the Balance. In Law in Culture and Society. Laura Nader, ed. pp. 69–91. Chicago: Aldine.

Ochs, Elinor. 1979. Planned and Unplanned Discourse. *In* Discourse and Syntax. Talmy Givón, ed. pp. 51–79. New York: Academic Press.

Paine, Robert. 1967. What Is Gossip About? An Alternative Hypothesis. Man (NS) 2:278–285.

Rosaldo, Michelle Z. 1973. I Have Nothing to Hide: The Language of Ilongot Oratory. Language in Society 2:193–223.

Schegloff. E. A. 1982. Discourse as an Interactional Achievement: Some Uses of "Uh Huh" and Other Things that Come Between Sentences. *In* Analyzing Discourse: Text and Talk. Deborah Tannen. ed. pp. 71–93. Washington, DC: Georgetown University Press.

Silverstein, Michael. 1976. Shifters, Linguistic Categories and Cultural Description. *In* Meaning in Anthropology. Keith Basso and Henry Selby. eds. pp. 11–56. Albuquerque: University of New Mexico Press.

Strathern, Andrew. 1975. Veiled Speech in Mount Hagen. *In* Political Language and Oratory in Traditional Societies. M. Bloch, ed. pp. 185–203. New York: Academic Press.

Szwed, John. 1966. Gossip, Drinking and Social Control: Consensus and Communication in a Newfoundland Parish. Ethnology 5:434–441.

Vološinov, V. N. 1971. Reported Speech. *In* Readings in Russian Poetics: Formalist and Structuralist Views. Ladislav Matejka and Krystyna Pomorska, transls. pp. 149–175. Cambridge, MA: MIT Press.

Watson-Gegeo, Karen, and Stephen Boggs. 1977. From Verbal Play to Talk Story: The Role of Routines in Speech Events among Hawaiian Children. *In* Child Discourse. Susan Ervin-Tripp and Claudia Mitchell-Kernan, eds. pp. 67–90. New York: Academic Press.

12

Reflections on a Meeting: Structure, Language, and the Polity in a Small-Scale Society

FRED R. MYERS

Observation shows us, first, that every polis (or state) is a species of association, and, secondly, that all associations are instituted for the purpose of attaining some good—for all men do all their acts with a view to achieving something which is, in their view, a good. We may therefore hold that all associations aim at some good; and we may also hold that the particular association which is the most sovereign of all, and includes all the rest, will pursue this aim most, and thus be directed to the most sovereign of all goods. This most sovereign and inclusive association is the polis, as it is called, or the political association

—(Aristotle 1967:1252a)

In May 1981, a critical meeting took place at Papunya, an Aboriginal community in Australia's Northern Territory. The participants included members of the Aboriginal Village Council of Papunya and Pintupi Aborigines from the surrounding outstation communities. These groups had disputed the use of a truck that had been granted by the government to the outstations but funded legally through the administrative mechanism of the Papunya Council (incorporated as Lyappa Congress). Miffed by Papunya control of resources vital to their autonomy, the Pintupi, among themselves, had discussed intensively their desire to have their funding separated from Papunya administration.

As the meeting to voice their problems began, with the requested attendance of senior representatives of the Department of Aboriginal Affairs in Alice Springs, a Papunya councillor asserted that there was no problem: "We're all one country, one Council—eh?" This was precisely the disputed issue, of course, since the Pintupi were at that moment attempting to establish themselves as a separate, autonomous body. Yet, as if bound by the unspoken code of face-to-face encounter, one of the previously outspoken Pintupi rose and enthusiastically seconded this assertion. "Yes, one country, really."

After watching a month's preparation for this meeting and conscious of the message the DAA would conveniently take about Pintupi wishes to establish their own communities further west, for a moment I actually considered speaking up myself. But I held my breath when another Pintupi assented, "One council." My heart pounded and I looked around; it appeared the meeting would end without any open airing of their grievances, although only an hour had passed since the Pintupi had explained their wish for autonomy to these same DAA representatives. With relief I heard, finally, one unusually persistent man assert undiplomatically, "No. We want separate money, separate banking."

After years of association with the Pintupi, I recognized that he had violated common meeting practice. And I understood how, ironically, the Pintupi ability to sustain their political autonomy and identity depends on adopting forms of sociality somewhat alien to them.

Ethnocentric Europeans once characterized tribal societies as "group-oriented," but a later generation of researchers has been rather impressed with the value placed on autonomy (cf. Briggs 1970; Lee 1979; Myers 1979; Rosaldo 1980). To be sure, this is never a simple matter. For the Pintupi, personal autonomy lies in the capacity to choose which social relations to sustain. Such relations are, it would seem, fragile—the cost of freedom. On the other hand, personal autonomy depends paradoxically on sustaining relations—shared identity—with others. Herein lies the problem of the polity, and the internal contradiction of many societies.[1] The subjective dimension of this political problem was acutely grasped by Róheim (1945) in his interpretation of central Australian Aboriginal cultures. What he discusses in Freudian terms as the loss of a loved object and the desire to complete oneself through incorporating it reflects the dilemma my Pintupi informants faced in gaining autonomy through relations to others.

This paper is a consideration of the significance of this dilemma, using as illustration the speech events (Hymes 1972) known as "meetings" among Pintupi-speaking Aborigines of Australia's Western Desert. While the lives of these formerly foraging people have changed dramatically in the past 30 years of contact with Euro-Australian society, a particular Pintupi conception of the polity continues to inform the organizational work of speech at meetings. Attending to the form and significance of this linguistic activity in Pintupi life illuminates some vital features of their political culture. Viewing speech as a form of action not only reveals the polity as a problematic achievement, but as a construction of quite specific form. At the same time, we are able to comprehend how language as a social artifact can be vital to sustaining political structure in this small-scale society.

In analyzing the relationship between speech and sociopolitical context, then, my emphasis is on the structural necessity of sustaining that context. I will show that (1) meetings constitute the Pintupi polity as an organized framework within which certain principles (rules or precedents) are held applicable and binding, and that (2) the principle or value (Aristotle's "most sovereign of all goods") that defines this jurisdiction is "relatedness"—a concept I define in reference to their notion of "kin" (*walytja*). In other words, the Pintupi polity has an emergent character, marked by enormous flexibility yet apparent to the observer and participants as it is constituted through activities of speaking. In such actions, the relationship of Pintupi political culture to subjective feeling and a sense of shared identity is manifest.

This relationship between feeling and polity is not accidental. Such a temporary polity as the Pintupi maintain, as with many small-scale societies, is constituted by "feeling" in the sense that people residing together consider themselves to share identity. Where individuals can easily opt out of particular collectivities, a flexibility permitted by traditional Pintupi band organization (Myers 1982), acceptance of membership represents a participant's sentimental orientation.

That social and cultural analysis of linguistic acts might illuminate the active if not obvious concerns of participants in political relations should not be surprising. Not only do our informants consider speech to be important, but recent ethnographic studies indicate that speaking has structural significance in many small-scale societies (Bloch 1975; Irvine 1979; Myers and Brenneis 1984; Paine 1981; Rosaldo 1973, 1980; Sansom 1980). In maintaining that certain forms of speaking should be seen as definite forms of social action, I do not claim a single universal significance for language or for any feature, as Bloch (1975) did for "formality." Rather, I hope to suggest how the significance[2] of different formal features of speech is defined by their relationship to the larger system of social relations in which they take place.

The Polity

The question of how we might understand the political organization of small-scale societies when, as is commonly the case, there are no obvious institutional forms (kingships, chiefdoms, village councils, and so on), is well known to anthropologists. Nearly 50 years ago (Evans-Pritchard 1940; Evans-Pritchard and Fortes 1940) the problem of acephaly was met by pointing to the way other institutions (kin groups, feuding, and so on) carry out "political function." Yet such studies have rarely considered how the maintenance of a political arena itself—of a polity, so to speak—might be the substance of political activity.

In Aboriginal Australia especially, the substance or value of the polity has been obscured too often by an emphasis on geographically based local groups (cf. Strehlow 1970:128–129). What I might characterize as the "building block view"—no centralization of authority for a tribe but smaller geographical groups centralized around a leader—ignores the concrete relations among those who are temporarily coresiding, on which the daily enactment of the polity rests. In Pintupi society, at least, the polity is not a permanent, concrete grouping organizationally, nor is it the reflex of authority.

My attention to the relationship between speech and this sort of temporary polity is based in part on observations of the limitation on the authority of collective decision making in Pintupi meetings. Despite urging by white authorities to do so, talk at Pintupi meetings does not press on toward a topic, relentlessly to solve a problem. At first this puzzled me as much as it frustrated well-intentioned advisors interested in Pintupi self-determination. Gradually, I came to understand the nature of talk at meetings differently. For Pintupi, the meeting must first sustain the very occasion of its performance. This is so because there is no preexisting, assured organizational framework of political action within which people live, yet they are in need of each other. Thus, the force of their speaking is concerned mainly to sustain relations among the participants under a rubric of being related to each other—but always maintaining the identity as autonomous equals that is so marked a feature in Pintupi life more generally. My argument is that speech at meetings mediates between two dialectically related values that are central to any political identity for Pintupi: relatedness and autonomy. The social form of language—minimally including speaker, hearer, messages, and the capacity to be coordinated and shared—facilitates the process of mediation through which the polity is continually renegotiated.

While the meetings are partly an artifact of the postcontact situation, I believe that they nonetheless make clear a more general condition. As in many small-scale societies, the Pintupi polity is a difficult and precarious achievement, not simply to be taken for granted. For them, the nature of this sort of polity imposes constraints on meetings as speech events. The organizational work of speaking as a form of social action, I will argue, is rooted in the precontact system of local organization that placed little emphasis on maintaining any residential community through time.

Ethnographic Context

In asking what is accomplished in Pintupi meetings, my analysis concerns the relationship between a form of speaking and the larger social context. The Pintupi discussed here are Western Desert Aboriginal people, hunter-gatherers who came to live in the area of Papunya, a settlement of some 600 Aboriginal people situated 150 miles west of Alice Springs, Northern Territory.[3] Many Pintupi reside in small satellite communities called "outstations," which surround Papunya at distances of anywhere from 3 to 100 miles and depend on the larger settlement for most of their goods and services. The residents of the area represent groups of differing cultural, linguistic, and historical backgrounds, but government administrative convenience and economy in the early contact period led to their settlement in a single community. For many, contact began in the 1920s and 1930s, and from that time the autonomous foraging way of life in small mobile bands became increasingly abbreviated as people moved to missions and settlements. The Pintupi continued an independent way of life in their western homelands until the late 1950s and early 1960s, when they joined the others in sedentary life in the large, permanent settlement of Papunya. Here, much to the chagrin of those who administered to Aboriginal welfare and envisioned the long-term goal of assimilation, the Pintupi maintained a certain distinctiveness. But the frequent, regular pattern of movement—aggregation and dispersion—in relation to the seasonal and local distribution of resources ended.

Life in contemporary Pintupi communities depends largely on regular social service payments to the unemployed, widows, and pensioners and some limited employment by the administration of the communities. While as much as 40 percent of the meat consumed in outstation communities may be procured by hunting and foraging, cash is necessary for staple supplies of flour, tea, sugar, and tobacco, as well as for clothing and the gasoline needed for the vehicles now used in foraging and visiting expeditions, and other desired items. As in the traditional subsistence economy where sharing resources among coresidents of a band was morally obligatory, those without direct access to cash are provided with food, clothing, and the like through kinship ties to fellow residents.

In all contemporary communities in this desert area, the basic facilities of water bores and tanks, most of the transport vehicles that assure basic supplies, housing, health care, and other community facilities are provided and maintained through a variety of government grants. Given that few Pintupi desire to return to a complete foraging lifestyle, the existence of particular remote outstation communities is largely determined by governmental agreement to provide services. These are applied for, granted to, and administered by an institution that had no precedent in precontact Pintupi life: the Village Council.

Initially administered by government representatives, after 1973 control of Papunya passed into the hands of an elected Aboriginal Village Council that was itself created by earlier government policies in the 1960s. In addition to representing local Aboriginal communities to the branches of the Australian government, Village Councils were envisioned—by white Australians in any case—as the authoritative and legislative representative of those communities. Such bodies were expected to help preserve order and regulate community life, to decide on how to deploy community resources, and to decide on employment.

The organizational situation in which Pintupi find themselves is not entirely strange to them. Shared identity—through kinship ties, affinality, and ceremony—continues to represent the basis of their access to valued and necessary resources. Thus, they have adapted to settlement conditions in ways familiar to them, only lacking the geographical flexibility that underlies an individual's freedom to move away from difficult circumstances. In meetings, settlement people work to sustain and reproduce the shared identity that culturally underwrites their continued association.

Contemporary Pintupi political life must be defined at least partly by their inclusion in the Australian welfare state and the fact of European political hegemony. As a result, the Pintupi live now in larger and more permanent aggregations than anything they had known before. The frequency (at least weekly) and size (10 to 20 participants) of gatherings as well as the relative social distance among participants would not have been matched in foraging conditions, when residential groups rarely exceeded 30–50 persons. Additionally, the meeting is to some extent the creation of Australian government policies that sought to establish responsible, self-governing Aboriginal community structures with which they could deal. Encouraged by government support of self-determination, however, the limited autonomy of the movement to remote outstations has allowed the reemergence of local Aboriginal conceptions of political order. The fragile polities are the forms of sociopolitical organization that are reasserting themselves in the contemporary situation. Regardless of external form, meetings are a clear expression of Pintupi values and understandings of the polity, which are often at odds with those being imposed from outside.

The few occasions of meetings that occurred around the preparation of ceremonial events—the very antithesis of European matters—were similar to patterns I describe below. While the English term "meeting" is the marked form, it is not insignificant that Pintupi currently refer to *all* collective gatherings using both the loan word and the Pintupi unmarked form, *wangkinpa*, which means generally "speaking." Indeed, the Pintupi sense of the difference between "Aboriginal" and "whitefellow" styles of speaking allows me to suggest that public speech events have always borne a significant relationship to the negotiation and renegotiation of the polity in Pintupi terms. Thus, the lack of political force of meetings in contemporary contexts does not only reflect the futility of collective Aboriginal political action in the face of Euro-Australian control of critical resources. While this may be the case, such a view dismisses the critical weight that Pintupi place on balancing autonomy and relatedness in all forms of collective identification.

The Phenomenology of Relatedness

In the Pintupi view, the category of "meeting" includes any significant group discussion with an agenda or a common concern. Gatherings to discuss plans for initiation or other ritual matters, inquests relating to death, and the like are all described as meetings. Many of the meetings I observed took place in the context of the Village Councils. That meetings of this sort are largely male activities may have resulted in an impression of male dominance, but such a view reflects the very difficulty at hand: it simply assumes that the deliberations of such bodies have authority over women (cf. Bell and Ditton 1980). That they have authority at all is problematic. Indeed, little attention has actually been given to what these meetings accomplish or to the substance of "politics."[4]

To understand the significance of meetings—the work they do—we must begin to place them within the social relations of their use. The tension between "relatedness" and "differentiation" (as expressed in conflict and violence) defines the central dilemma for Pintupi life and is the field in which meetings are to be understood. This dialectic is not mystifying. The terms are my own labels for a structural opposition rooted in Pintupi concepts. Elsewhere, I have explicated the importance of what I here call "relatedness" (Myers 1979, 1986) in terms of the way Pintupi ideas of shared identity, compassion for others, grief, and so on, are formulated around the concept *walytja*. That this term can be translated in some contexts as "kin" or "relative" and in others as the possessive "one's own" or the reflexive "oneself" shows its general application to the problems of relational identity. What is clear is that sustaining the impression of relatedness to coresidents constitutes a real and basic quality of Pintupi social life. So great is the emphasis on open sociality that it comes to dominate the ability of any group to define itself as a bounded entity.[5]

However, "differentiation"—its opposite—is also a fact of life, in the form of conflict and violence (*pika*, fight or argument), as well as the willingness to stand up against threat. Pintupi descriptions of the past as "like army all the time" and their fear of attack by revenge parties under cover of night are indications of this potential. Conflict and intimidation are regular occurrences in Pintupi communities as individuals try to influence each other. Despite the value on shared identity, fighting prowess is highly valued and both men and women are proud of their abilities. But these are not warrior people. Fighting is not so much an attempt at dominance as an assertion of autonomy. In this sense, conflict and relatedness define each other structurally as values: it is the possibility of conflict or differentiation that gives relatedness its special value. Ultimately, they are two different trajectories of autonomy. Thus, fighting and threat are commonly understood as responses to the rejection of relatedness.

The Pintupi meeting is one transformation of this dialectic between relatedness and differentiation. It is necessary to understand, however, that in Pintupi social life relatedness is the ontologically primary value, and that differentiation is experienced as a breach. Much Pintupi public speaking is constitutive of this fundamental image of society. For example, Pintupi avoid the appearance of egotism, self-assertion, or private willfulness (all considered shameful) and accept identity with others as part of the self.[6] This identity is represented subjectively by the cultural formulation of emotions such as "shame" (*kunta*), "compassion" (*ngaltu*), and "homesickness" (*watjilpa*) that tie the self to others (Myers 1979). The Pintupi emphasis on relatedness itself, as opposed to *kinds* of relationships, is foregrounded by the unimportance of distinctions in the kinship system. For the Pintupi, the fact of being a "relative" (*walytja*) is more important than what particular kin status one has. Since all relatives must "help" (a loan word from English) each other, there is no simple way to establish priorities.

Furthermore, a wide extension of relatedness is an important component of Pintupi life, illustrated in an extended classificatory kinship system, subsections and in numerous named, ceremonially constituted relationships. A tendency to assimilate categorically distant but well-known kin to categories reflecting close (that is, "one countryman") relations also exhibits Pintupi willingness to extend the substance of relatedness. As a person grows older, the field of relatives increases in breadth and complexity. From them come the valuables of Pintupi life, including food, spouses, rights in ceremony, protection, and so one. One's relatives are likely to be found in all geographical directions and, though each is related to ego, they may not be related to each other. This quality of the social field is a source of strain. One cannot ignore ties with some neighbors to concentrate on just a few relations, because those neglected may prove necessary in the long term. Yet, choosing among them to allocate one's attention is, at times, difficult to avoid.

Being a relative requires regularly demonstrating the relationship. Creating and maintaining relatedness necessitates interaction, reciprocity, and exchange, yet this is not always possible. A man who kills a kangaroo must decide which people will receive a share. Frequent neglect is regarded as a rejection of relatedness—of kinship—and leads those who fail to get a share to complain about "not being loved."[7] Those who give nothing are "hard" (*purli*, stone), that is, without feeling. The problem of managing relatedness is apparent in the lives of older men who talk about how to delay ceremonial obligations to one set of people while satisfying another. While men of prominence are skillful in managing complex relations over time, one cannot ever satisfy all expectations. Conflict, division, or differentiation are inevitable, although people work to reduce the instability, to suppress distinctiveness, by making choices less insulting (or less obvious) to others. This often occurs in discussions of landownership when speakers typically include those present with them at the time as "co-owners."

Finally, the traditional system of local organization did not offer much structural basis to sustain divisions in any enduring fashion. The larger regional system—by which I mean the relationships that exist between different localities of the total area—was and is still built out of egocentric or dyadic links among individuals. Pintupi local organization was characterized by a flexibility of movement, maximizing access to resources in the desert through a system of multiple claims by individuals to association with several different landholding groups (Myers 1982, 1986). Local groups—both landowning groups and residential ones—are crystallized out of dyadic categories of relatedness that have been established among a territorially broad range of people. The system of openness and flexibility continues to operate, although in changed circumstances, in modern settlements where Pintupi still draw on wide-ranging ties to sustain residential alternatives. Aggregations, or collective formations, are outcomes of ongoing social processes. Conditions of life in the Western Desert, then and now, give value to shared identity as a means for obtaining other people's labor, support, and temporary resources. People need each other's help, and the most extraordinary fact is how the rubric of relatedness is usually restored after conflict. It is important to realize that this Western Desert focus on extensive dyadic relatedness among individuals in a region differs from forms of territorial organization found elsewhere in Aboriginal Australia that identify individuals first with a discrete group and integrate *these* into a larger system. For the Pintupi, an individual's social identity is not subsumed by any particular aggregation.

It is well known that rituals such as male initiation prescriptively bring together people of geographically separated social areas. One of the principal consequences of such events has been the reproduction of relatedness as a component of the regional system, but this is not just any sort of relationship. That these ceremonies—clearly the most important in Western Desert life—are organized on the principle of alternate generation moieties is critical in my view. These generational categories transcend local group affiliation, giving such segments no place in the regional structure. Thus, participation on the basis of a social identity formulated through generational moieties emphasizes what might be called *overall relatedness*. In emphasizing this principle as basic, Pintupi social structure differs from that of other regional organizations in Australia, a point to which I will return below.[8]

The Problem of Meetings

The ceremonial forms discussed broadly above address the perennial dilemmas of differentiation posed for many foraging people by life in dispersed, localized groups. Meetings, however, tend to deal more with idiosyncratic threats to relatedness among those whose lives impinge on each other; such threats have become especially frequent in postcontact life.

The subjective, moral dimensions of relatedness are a notable element of speech in meetings. Initially, this appears to administrators and anthropologists only as a problem, a limitation on the legislative effectiveness of meetings. As reported for other small-scale societies as well (Bell and Ditton 1980; Brenneis 1984; Frake 1963; Lederman 1984; Meggitt 1962; Rosaldo 1973; Weiner 1976), Pintupi meetings rarely resulted in decisions or plans for concerted action.[9] However, the outcome ceases to be a "problem" when these events are placed in broader perspective. Rather, three issues seem fundamental regarding the relationship of these events to the rest of Pintupi social life. First, to whom are its actions relevant? Second, in what way are they relevant? Third, do its actions (decisions, deliberations) have a status hierarchically superior to other forms of social action (that is, as rule to application)?

The establishment of Aboriginal councils by government policy envisaged a model of authority that related this assembly to a community in terms of representation, in Euro-Australian terms. These assemblies were expected to act for the community in representing Aboriginal opinion to whites and in making policy and regulations binding on members. Pintupi perceptions differed. No matter how much respect members of the Council might enjoy as individuals, their decisions were usually seen as without authority when they attempted to impose new regulations on community residents. One man's objection to the creation of a no-liquor rule by the Council particularly illuminates the issue: "It's only their idea," he insisted; "They [the Councillors] are just men like me." Viewed as encroachments on the autonomy of others, such attempts are treated as egoistic, coercive, and self-willed by Pintupi; one should be ashamed. When the Council did seek to impose sanctions, claims on their sympathy on grounds of relatedness inevitably caused them to relent. Thus, a decision to banish two irresponsible youths from a settlement in 1974 was rescinded when the young men asked to be trusted, to be given another chance, and drew attention to their status as relatives.

The frequency with which such events occurred raised questions for me about the social construction of "law" itself, of rules to which action must conform. Where egalitarian relations prevail, how is legitimacy—authoritative social consensus—to be established for new rules?

The Dreaming and the Meeting

In fabricating authority, the problem the Pintupi face more generally is how to remove the constructions of men from their identification with subjectivity, personal will, interest, and responsibility (Munn 1970; Myers 1979, 1980a, 1980b). For example, the normative foundation of Pintupi life has been traditionally guaranteed through a mythological construction known as The Dreaming: those critical events external to human action—retold in myth, song, and ritual—that created the present-day world of landscape, natural species, and social institutions. This cosmogony presented certain social practices and principles as ontologically basic to cosmic order (cf. Stanner 1956). They were not human creations and therefore represented no encroachment by an equal other on one's autonomy. Further, they were incumbent on everyone.

By rendering the concept, alternatively, as "The Law," Pintupi direct attention to the moral imperative bound in these structures: as things were done in The Dreaming, so they should be done in the present. To objectify contemporary human decisions into guiding principles requires representing them as religious revelation, not just consensus among a group of men. While this kind of objectification may constitute authority, there are limitations to what such a polity can do (cf. Meggitt 1962:253). However, the point is that the Pintupi polity is concerned as much with preserving autonomy (with reference to authority outside the self) as it is with legislating.

It is revealing, therefore, that the process embodied by the Pintupi strategy in meetings so clearly resembles the moral movement of The Dreaming. A speaker presents his own position as representing that of an external, authoritative source. Hence, a man who was reluctant about a proposed move to a new settlement referred to the opposition that had been expressed by officers of the Department of Aboriginal Affairs, and thus did not deny relatedness by committing *himself* against the sense of a gathering. Similarly, it was common for Pintupi Council members to present their decisions as ideas coming from the white Australian(s) employed as Community Advisor(s) and thus to abjure responsibility for them. Though Advisors served at the Council's behest and were without authority, Council members used them as convenient representatives for an authority that stood outside the Pintupi social world.[10] These forms of political maneuvering take place in a contemporary context. However, the use of an authority external to the self in order to deny subjectivity, personal will, and responsibility is an indigenous practice applied to new circumstances. While meetings are obviously a different domain from The Dreaming, as cultural constructions they accomplish similar goals.

Speech Style

The political strategy of Pintupi meetings is demonstrated and informed by a close analysis of the salient style of speech. Several features are particularly noticeable in speeches at meetings: (1) opening with oratorical self-deprecations, such as "I'm going to tell you a little story, nothing really"; (2) depersonalization of an account, as in presenting one's own position as coming from outside; (3) indirectness in discussing the substance of conflict; and (4) noncontradiction of others. These are more than idiomatic because to violate these canons is thought to "set up" fights.

Participation in these speech events is marked by a concern with "shame" and with those sentiments constitutive of relatedness. Commonly, "shame" (*kunta*) is understood as a consequence of being exposed in a failure to recognize one's relatedness and thus malleability to others; such action lacks the "compassion" (*ngaltu*) expected of relatives who share identity. Not only are direct refusal and open contradiction of another shameful, but so also are other forms of self-importance, willfulness, and lack of control. Maintaining respect (that is, avoiding *kunta*), on the other hand, dictates the stylistic removal of individual assertiveness from public speech. The same effacement is often developed further by a depersonalizing obliqueness and indirectness of discourse, so that the substance of conflict is disguised.[11] Even when two successive speeches in a meeting are directly opposing, therefore, the speakers usually do not refer to each other.

Although speech in meetings follows more explicit turn-taking rules than in ordinary conversation, interruption is still frequent, as it is in most forms of Pintupi talk (Liberman 1981:114). Liberman describes the turn-taking procedures, of serial turns instead of "you-me" pairs addressed to each other, as contributing to the "anonymization" of the product. Understood as joint production rather than assertive interruption, such procedures lead to an outcome that is not associated with anyone in particular. Pintupi men contrasted their usual meeting practice with the special organization of a meeting that they described as "whitefellow way." The latter style implies a single speaker at a time and "listening without talking."[12]

The characteristic Pintupi orientation of presenting the events of this world as conforming to an already objectivized, external authority or "law" (as with The Dreaming) is reflected here in meeting speech. The organization of discourse has the effect of creating a sense of a meeting as a set of discrete bits from which speakers' egotism, will, and responsibility are detached. It is as if the outcome—the consensus no one opposes—is "found" rather than created, and the group reflexively derives from it. No one's autonomy is diminished. An awareness of this reflexive property of meetings and of "consensus" in constituting a polity as much as in formulating a policy is very much part of Pintupi culture.[13]

Within these constraints, meetings are delicate achievements, consisting of movements between "centralization" and "peripheralization." Meetings tend to move back and forth between a predominance of unfocused side conversations and the achievement of a central focus (Irvine 1979). A meeting *attempts* to construct a central focus—one of topic and/or personnel. When it breaks down, the event is characterized by a lot of side-talking. It becomes conversation. Certain talented speakers are successful and gain prestige from bringing meetings to fruition, sustaining a focus within a framework of "anonymization."

The substance of Pintupi strategies is clarified in the way meetings, typically, appeared to end in assent. A speaker catches the drift of the main sentiments and phrases them for the whole group present. Strangely, however, while this "phrasing" of the sentiment seems to be a climax or turning point in the event, nothing may come of it. What, then, does it accomplish?

Meetings and the Problem of Relatedness

Examples of this kind of performance—in addition to that in the introduction—clarify the question of what is accomplished. Together, they suggest that the meeting does not *stand for* but *is* the polity for Western Desert Aborigines. Therefore, meetings designed for the airing of conflict are, by definition, unlikely to achieve that end, since they conflict with the Pintupi notion of polity as relatedness.

The encounters between the Pintupi and the Papunya Council are instructive. The Pintupi lived mostly on outstations around Papunya, but still on land that belonged to the traditional Aboriginal residents of Papunya, who controlled the Council. Although the outstations were granted their own money by the government, it was administered through the Papunya Council, and they had disagreed with the latter about who could be hired by the outstations. The Pintupi spoke among themselves of their desire to separate from Papunya. When joint discussions took place between the Pintupi and people from Papunya—even under the rubric of disagreement—Papunya spokesmen emphasized how they help their relatives in the outstations. This sort of help or exchange, in the Pintupi view, makes people "one countrymen" (*ngurra kutjungurrara*) or "from one camp"—the primary category of relatedness. Thus, Papunya people implied, they should be all one Council.

An emphasis on the unity of Papunya and the outstations was characteristic of joint meetings. Usually, as such a meeting progressed, Pintupi men who had once spoken privately for separation and autonomy stood and assented to the view that they were all "from one country, one Council," and therefore did not desire a split (as my introductory example illustrates). To do otherwise would be to deny the shared identity and mutuality of being related, and these are the only bases on which coresidence and continued association (or meeting) could take place. In other words, a significant constraint on any meeting that takes place is the assertion of relatedness or identity that underlies social interaction. The recognition of this frame is what makes meetings "collaborations for the production of congeniality" (as Liberman [1981] called them). The emphasis is on producing or sustaining a sense of shared identity, or of having "one word" (Sansom 1980). When consensus in actuality cannot be reached, it is not disagreement that is publicly announced. Those who are capable of bridging dissension in difficult situations, usually men of real oratorical skills, are highly valued and sought out.

As the central domain in which consensus can occur, the very process of the meeting *is* the polity and defines it, however momentarily. Because it exists only as long as people view themselves as related, the polity is not a structure, an outside referent that is simply to be taken for granted and not an enduring accomplishment. Severe opposition and debate would deny the very basis on which resolution could take place at all. Recognizing this, the Pintupi would rather not have a meeting until some of the opposition has diminished. To do otherwise is an invitation to violence, what they call "setting up" a fight.

Having a meeting is itself a social achievement. It is a recognition of some common level of sociality, and because that fact dominates it, the appearance of disagreement is uncomfortable, a contradiction. In this sort of egalitarian structure, the actors must work to sustain the context of "relatedness" that underlies the possibility of continued interaction. Debate and confrontations that threaten the context are suppressed.

This is not simply my reading of it, but that of participants as well. For example, amid a controversy during an initiation in Papunya, a white Australian who worked for the outstations had attempted to set up a separate meeting for outstation people to decide about using their truck independently from Papunya influence. Unable, in that context as guests, to enact distinctiveness, the outstation people had ignored him. When members of the Papunya Council spoke against him, he was upset that no one openly defended him. Afterwards, however, several Pintupi explained that there was nothing to worry about because the Papunya people could not fire him: it was "only talk." Pintupi silence was not assent to criticism or willingness to dismiss him; rather, their silence sustained the continued association with Papunya that was still necessary and desirable. Agreement recognizes one's relatedness to those present but does not compromise autonomy outside the context.

The following example illustrates how important the appearance of agreement is to participants. In addition to showing how a speaker's position varies with the context in which he acts, it demonstrates the way in which individual speakers focus the event. (This case followed on the strain in relations between the Pintupi and other Aboriginal groups in Papunya and was, despite appearances, a step toward moving back west to their own country in the Kintore Range.) Upon deciding they were going to move to a new, autonomous outstation, the Pintupi requested help from the Department of Aboriginal Affairs. At the resulting meeting to discuss their plans, the DAA representatives told the Pintupi men not to hope for much financial support from the government and stressed the difficulties of a · move. Most of the men had already been talking of moving, yet as the meeting progressed, one of those previously most vocal about the need for a move stood to tell the meeting that they did not want to move west. "We have to stay here." His remarks were clearly addressed to the source of power at the meeting, the white "bosses," and he was phrasing what he took to be the inevitable conclusion of the meeting. Just five minutes later, he spoke to me in a fashion that indicated he still planned to move. Nonetheless, he had undoubtedly enjoyed his moment in the limelight.

For the Pintupi, relatedness is not constituted by the meetings alone. In this sense they may differ from some other "egalitarian societies." Among the Ilongot (Rosaldo 1973, 1980), for example, speaking is all that sustains the overarching rubric of a polity that might be described as the context of interaction (Myers and Brenneis 1984). For the Pintupi not everything is negotiable. Not only does The Dreaming as moral imperative provide an objectified, inescapable context for some actions, but also on the basis of the classificatory kinship system, we should regard relatedness as ontologically preexisting; threats to its continuation are overcome through meetings. As indicated by the substance and increasing frequency of meetings, it appears that their significance may be intensified with the problems brought in by contact with Euro-Australian society.

Participation and Its Consequences

The meetings do not seem to result in a plan of action that is binding on those who are not present. Rather, the events play a significant role in sustaining relatedness as the context in which a limited polity can exist. If the force of speaking often seems more concerned with sustaining the occasion itself, then taking part in this production is of some consequence.

Who can perform is a vital element in the significance of these events. Demonstrating the right to be heard seems very close to what participants in meetings perceive as important. They often seem less concerned with a particular outcome than they are with taking part in its production. Such demonstrations are the real protection of their status. Common features of speech at meetings— the repetition of what has already been said and the concern to be the one who phrases shared sentiments—make sense in this light. Not surprisingly for a society with egalitarian tendencies, there is little power to coerce others. People are more concerned with the recognition of their autonomy as the right to be consulted and the expectation of being heard. As with drama, understanding what meetings do depends as much on recognizing who is on stage and who is off as it does on following the lines themselves.

Almost all the meetings that occurred within sight of the main camp were dominated by men.[14] Not only women, but also young men rarely spoke in public and little attention was paid to those who tried. Fearing "shame," they were reluctant to put themselves forward. Indeed, their performance was inhibited not only because the young were much less adept at the stylistic flourish characteristic of the best speaking done by their elders,[15] but also because they were less certain that they knew enough about the ritual life to speak about matters that might impinge there. Obviously, the systems of age and gender differentiation work together here.

One important result of the restriction on who can speak is in symbolic action: it produces, in every event, a tangible representation of the social order as consisting of those who speak and those who listen. This image identifies initiated older men with knowledge and sociality.

While men do not make decisions binding on women, participation in meetings does affect sexual politics because of the value meetings have for everyone. The management of relations among men has consequences for Pintupi social life that derive from men's critical position in the tension between relatedness and differentiation. In the Western Desert, male-centered initiatory ritual is the idiom of most of the regional activity through which the broadest relatedness is constituted.[16] Generally, adult men have a greater number of relationships established through ceremony with other individuals from afar than women have.[17] They are also more concerned in daily life with the sustaining of "distant" relations. The problem of how to allocate "value" (in terms of sacred objects and ceremony) is especially significant for older men and precariously managed. That the serious violence and threats that follow on differentiation (or mismanaged choice) are ultimately men's business is clear when danger is afoot. When a group is under threat of violence—or when a woman feels threatened—people congregate and travel with male kin for protection.[18]

This is the context that gives value to the activity of meetings. In these meetings, adult men produce determinations sensitive to the parties present, sustaining a rubric of relatedness that maintains they are members of a single group, or (as they say) "from one camp." Because of what these relations entail for *everyone*, social value accrues to those who perform in this context, according prominence to those who may speak without giving them a power to coerce. The meeting is political not as a form of coercion as much as for the part it plays in reproducing the structures that make domination possible—the differentiation of older and younger men and the existence of men as a corporate body.

Negotiation and the Polity

The limitation of the jurisdiction of a meeting and the precariousness of its achievement in terms of decision and regulation are obvious. At best, consensus is the account of those present; it must be sensitive and responsive to the entrance of new persons into the social field. However, the widespread quality of relatedness and the mutuality of rights make it difficult within any aggregation to consult all those who have an interest and a claim in a formulation. How is it possible to establish a determination that does not unalterably differentiate some people?

Indeed, their emphasis on sustaining the sense of relatedness has consequences for all Pintupi social activity. A sense of looseness, negotiatedness, or temporariness was what was prominent in Pintupi social action.[19] Rules and norms—so amply and prominently present not only in Meggitt's (1962) description of the neighboring Warlpiri but also in my own brief visits among them—were rarely stated by Pintupi. Although norms obviously exist for Pintupi, the problem is precisely in *what* sense they do. In the mundane course of fieldwork, I quite frequently had the opportunity to experience the characteristic Pintupi consultation with those whose interests or rights might be affected by a decision. Once, for example, my "father," N., planned to sing some songs for me to tape and analyze. He assured me emphatically that it was all right to do so. "Women can hear them," he said. Then he turned to an older man and asked him, "Is it okay?"

The issue of recording the songs depended on whether they were secret and who owned them, but these matters do not seem to have an accepted interpretation even among the Pintupi themselves (although, because of my involvement, this case is not unambiguous on that score). N., a man of ritual standing who knows the Law, was not merely asking for permission or information from an elder. Rather, in making public his intention and displaying awareness of another man's rights, he recognized that what is appropriate or acceptable to people may change (cf. Williams 1985).

The need to consult those whose interests are at stake is a major constraint on Pintupi action and explains why many forms of activity follow such an extreme path of negotiation. One could never be certain who might extend a claim to be included. Pintupi typically avoid the unnecessary differentiation of others as unrelated or, as they say, "nothing to do" (*mungutja*). The recognition that one's rights are rarely exclusive of those of other people makes consultation an essential part of life. This is especially true when one needs, equally, the recognition of others to sustain claims of one's own. Further, the threat of violence by one whose claim might otherwise be regarded as weak—as with a marriage bestowal—could lead to acceptance.

The concerns of relatedness and consultation place a substantial limitation on the Pintupi polity. This is particularly true in regard to achieving an authoritative consensus, as one can grasp in discussions concerning land and ritual. If decisions are taken without those who have a right to be consulted, violence or sorcery are possible. The issue of relatedness informs the strategy of participants in recent meetings to establish legal ownership of Aboriginal land or to plan distribution of royalties from its use. Men may absent themselves from discussions about land in order to avoid the pressure for consensus and to show who really is "boss." Others hesitate to talk without them. Conversely, some use the value on congeniality by coming to meetings drunk and, without shame, pushing their own position while sober parties are reluctant to contradict (J. Stead, personal communication).

The maintenance of relatedness over such a broad field has its effect on the Pintupi polity. As compared with the clan-organized Yulngu (the "Murngin") of northeast Arnhem Land who have well-organized moots (Williams 1973), the Pintupi polity has no clearly defined social center in which authority resides. It is never quite certain who should be included in considering a problem, who believes he or she has a right to be consulted. An important Western Desert custom reported by informants may illustrate the problem of jurisdiction: when a person is accused of serious sacrilege, a "firestick" (*tjangi*) is sent from group to group to inform men of the region about the "trouble" and to gain legitimacy from the relevant polity for the sanctions appropriate as Law. What is significant is the diffuseness of the authoritative body, the breadth of those considered to have a right to be consulted.

Even for the Pintupi, though, everything is not always and forever up for grabs in that there are some objectified norms around which negotiation occurs. Much of Pintupi social life—in ritual transmission to the young—is directed toward the social reproduction of these hierarchical orderings that counteract negotiability. Punishment of one who transgresses a major Dreaming law is not open to consideration; claims of relatedness with the victim and compassion are countervailed by an external authority that commands greater moral claim. It is more common, perhaps, for the stable center of unquestioned principles to be sustained indirectly, entailed by negotiation. Because the achievement of consensus in meetings is, I have argued, a search for objectified forms, the consensus *reproduces* these previously objectified forms as effective and viable (cf. Giddens 1979:71).

For Pintupi, relatedness is egocentric and unsubordinated to group membership; its network quality makes it essentially dyadic in form. The polity, a temporary jurisdiction among those who regard themselves as related and subordinated to a binding set of principles, is not predicated on membership in groups, has no offices and no enduring structure. That it is based on the creation and maintenance of dyadic relations gives a special quality of intimacy, fragility, and subjective responsibility to interaction among autonomous equals. For the Pintupi, especially, the polity is one of "feeling," in that the jurisdiction of relatedness—of shared identity—must constantly be renegotiated among those who participate. Hence, the principle held sovereign within this jurisdiction is relatedness. That any action must conform to this value reproduces it but limits, at the same time, its enduring accomplishments.

The Cultural Subject and the Polity: The General Case

Far from being distinctively Pintupi, the value on relatedness is reported in many descriptions of Aboriginal social life (and elsewhere in the world). What differs is the field to which this value may apply and the way in which it can be employed by participants, that is, the way this value is situated in a larger structure. In the Western Desert there is an enormous value placed on relatedness in terms of a whole region, not structured as the integration of lower level units. Indeed, so important is *overall relatedness* that the local units at the lower levels of the system are not clearly bounded. Whereas other Aboriginal groups have more definitively formed and bounded social units, Pintupi stress the relation of all to all: they "are all family." Without a basis on which one can legitimately refuse or exclude another, the questions of who are and who are not "relatives" *(walytja)* are always problematic and never taken for granted. Thus, avoidance of overt differentiations and an attempt to sustain the rubric of overall relatedness are essential to determinations such as meetings. These sociological conditions seem to underlie the stylistic features and the general awareness of negotiation that we have seen to characterize speech in such circumstances.

One must not lose sight of the specific qualities of the Pintupi case. That other small-scale polities are less fragile is highly revealing. It would be absurd to suggest that the problem of relatedness and autonomy is equally the political focus in all these societies. The possibility of autonomy, for instance, would seem to be limited by the relations of production in which an individual is located. But these are not only the subjective entailments of certain material forms of organization in a vulgar sense; it is the total structure of social relations that gives differing value to relatedness and autonomy. Thus, the relative flamboyance and more clearly delineated structures of leadership in Arnhem Land on the tropical north coast are the consequences of a system of social reproduction that does not emphasize the sustaining of overall relatedness as the Pintupi do. In Arnhem Land relatedness is, so to speak, structurally circumscribed. That the fragility and intimacy of a system built out of dyadic ties is not even general throughout Aboriginal Australia has important implications for ascribing subtle differences in cultural emphasis to structural variation in foraging societies.

This has further consequences. Despite anthropological platitudes about Aboriginal people "philosophizing" about kinship, I found the Pintupi relatively disinclined to reflect on their social system as an abstracted object, in contrast to the Warlpiri. Instead, Pintupi comments and reluctance emphasized the negotiated quality of social life and their sense of it as always under construction. They focus on what individuals do and the experiences to which their concepts are relevant.

However, the concern to maintain relatedness by considering the claims of others need not be as central for other Aboriginal societies as it is for the Pintupi. And where individuals are aggregated into enduring groups first and through these into a larger system, there are predictable subjective consequences. Such is manifestly the case for the polity among the well-known Yulngu of northeast Arnhem Land (see Warner 1937; Shapiro 1969; Morphy 1977; van der Leeden 1975; Williams 1973). Here the region is integrated, politically and ecologically, through alliances between structured patrilineal clans ordered into a system of *named* patrimoieties. Such groups have an objective status of a given reality beyond the choice of participants: they are objectifications. The dependence of the structures of alliance on arranged marriage leads to a concern with temporal continuity, with the reproduction of these relationships through time, as evidenced in elaborate mortuary ceremonies, clan differentiation, and inherited leadership. Thus, meetings and determinations are often held *within* the jurisdiction of the clan alone (Williams 1985). Within these meetings, the maintenance of "one word" among participants is important, but the boundaries of participation are clearly drawn (the clan) and particular individuals who represent the group appear to control the event. Who is and is not included within this jurisdiction is far less negotiable: a determination need not satisfy outsiders. One's relationship to others outside the clan is mediated by membership in it. In Arnhem Land, then, a wider, regional system exists, but *this* system of relatedness is achieved through a rather different means of reintegrating *accepted* distinctions. At one level of the polity, at least, a secure objectified base exists. Participants seek to reproduce this basis for action; the strategy is different from recreating it anew.

In contrast, the Pintupi system is predicated on the denial of repeated and defined particular political relationships, in favor of overall, diffuse regional integration. Consequently, in the Western Desert social attention to temporal continuity in terms of mortuary, clan structure, or even the reproduction of alliances, is insubstantial. The social concern with an individual's marriage, so vital to alliances in the north, is far less pronounced in Pintupi life.

What is critical, then, is the level of social organization on which a value (like relatedness) or an event (a meeting) appears. The fact that *overall relatedness* is the structure that is reproduced through time among the Pintupi, rather than the structuring of difference and alliance as it is in Arnhem Land, is responsible for very different emphases on the part human beings can play in creating, altering, or affecting the things of this world. Because relatedness is not constrained within a higher level of structure in Pintupi society, it has no limits of application. Thus, negotiation is never fully concluded and decisive choices rarely made. Only The Dreaming remains as a control, a structure beyond individuals and binding them to itself, but it is, correspondingly, felt more intensely as an imperative here than anywhere else. It is not accidental that Western Desert people are known throughout Australia for their conservatism and the strength of their adherence to the Law. In Arnhem Land, on the other hand, individuals appear more constrained by membership in a group and political alliances of the past, but are freer in the invention of song, dance, and innovation. Individuals build names for themselves, amass a wealth in bestowals, and constitute alliances that last for generations. This difference is, of course, precisely the consequence foretold in Simmel's (1950) discussion of dyadic relationships in contrast to those submerged in groups: because of their fragility, the freedom to choose the relationship decreases the freedom to act. That these variations exist and seem to be systematic argues that we must attend to kinds of structural differences in the polity of small-scale societies that we have not conceptualized well heretofore.

Conclusion

In analyzing the organizational work of speech at Pintupi meetings, I have tried to place speaking as a form of action within a larger theory of social value. This is, then, something of a structural sociolinguistics, concerned with the way forms of speaking come to acquire meaning for participants. In the Pintupi case, the meeting is dominated by the requirements of immediacy. I have argued that talk at Pintupi meetings is concerned mainly to sustain relations among the participants under a rubric of being related to each other but also as autonomous equals. Without an overarching and preexisting organizational framework of political action, such talk must continually define its own context. In a sense, it constitutes its own referent. Recognizing the value and meaning of this form of social action is simply to recognize that the structural content of any activity must be understood in terms of its relationship to the total system of relations. Thus, without placing action within a larger totality, we cannot foretell what it is that participants are treating concretely in their activity, linguistic or otherwise.

In linking event and structure, the analysis has more general theoretical implications. The conditions of the Pintupi meeting are embedded in a larger political economy that shares some features with other tribal societies, particularly the segmentary quality in which there is no genuine jurisdiction between segments. Yet the structural differences between the Pintupi regional system and others have important consequences, giving special importance to the meeting and, ironically, limiting its capacity for legislative accomplishment. In some of these societies (cf. Strehlow 1970, Williams 1973), if there is no overarching authority at the societal level, it clearly exists at a lower segmental level and has been identified with concrete groupings. What is informative about the Pintupi case is that the organization of society at the higher level (region) affects the relations of the polity existing at lower (infrastructural) levels and is mediated by speech. Here, where access to resources in a region is organized primarily through extensive dyadic ties, the very relations among those of a locality are affected, made flexible but more problematic. Without other levels of structure that can be relied upon, the Pintupi polity, more than most, is what I characterize as a polity of "feeling," and the meeting is a vehicle of communion, not so much representing a social grouping as constituting it. I would suggest that the organizational work I ascribe to Pintupi meetings has correlates among other small-scale societies, but that the level of social integration sustained by this kind of linguistic action might differ in those cases.

Finally, and perhaps most significantly, by drawing our attention to the special problem of constituting and sustaining a political arena, the analysis of these meetings provides us with a basis for comparison. This case foregrounds what other societies have achieved in creating a polity and how they have done so: the particular structures have their own dynamics and their own limitations. It is not only important that we continue to build our comparative models of political process before they "disappear," however. In seeing the persistence of indigenous forms in contact, I hope to have shown how anthropological knowledge can help ameliorate some dilemmas in the struggle for self-determination faced by the people with whom we work.

Notes

Acknowledgments. I would like to thank the following people for their useful comments and criticism of earlier drafts of this paper: Jane Atkinson, T. O. Beidelman, Don Brenneis, Bette Clark, Faye Ginsburg, Annette Weiner, and anonymous reviewers. They are not responsible for difficulties that remain in the analysis here. Finally, my most profound gratitude goes to the many Pintupi who have treated me with kindness, love, and patience. An earlier version of the paper was given as part of the symposium "Papers presented in Honor of Mervyn Meggitt: Ethnography and Theory," held at the 1982 Meetings of the American Anthropological Association. Research with the Pintupi—at Yayayi, Northern Territory (1973–75), at Yayayi and Yinyilingki (1979), and at New Bore and Papunya, Northern Territory (1980–81)—was supported by NSF Doctoral Dissertation Improvement Grant No. GS 37122, NIMH Fellowship No. 3F0IMH57275–01, and research grants from the Australian Institute of Aboriginal Studies. The ethnographic present is 1981.

1. I use the word "polity" in this paper to distinguish my object of consideration both from the *Homo politicus* of political process as formulated in Swartz, Turner, and Tuden (1967) and from the easily identifiable formal political institutions. By leaning toward this less positivist construct, I hope to avoid as well the notion that small-scale societies are prepolitical.

2. I conceive the term "significance" to include the notion of "value," thereby avoiding a division between meaning and action that would contradict the basic thrust of my analysis. Part of an act's meaning or significance is the value it acquires.

3. See Myers 1976, 1986.

4. A similar concern has developed in the work of Sansom (1980), Williams (1973, 1985), and Liberman (1981).

5. For readers unfamiliar with Aboriginal ethnography, the sort of relatedness I describe below is specific to the Western Desert and takes on different forms in other Aboriginal societies. I discuss these differences at the end of the paper.

6. This is why I have emphasized "identity" in my writing and appears to be corroborated by Liberman (1981).

7. I quote here an English usage from one dispute. There are important similarities here with the !Kung San (Lee 1979; Marshall 1961) and the Trobriand Islands (Weiner 1976).

8. That moiety organization could be analyzed as the transformation, on a higher level, of basic principles of the structure was suggested by reading Turner (1979).

9. In central Australia, Bell and Ditton argue that contemporary male councils have a "wider ranging jurisdiction than any body [traditionally] enjoys in Aboriginal society" and that a "council of male elders did not constitute the only decision-making mechanism in Aboriginal society and probably did not exist in any formal sense in the past" (1980:13). These comments suggest the limits on the jurisdiction of any such gathering.

10. Reay (1970) presents interesting parallels in the use of outsiders at Borroloola.

11. For a discussion of "indirection" in speech as a general strategy for coordination around a common goal, see Myers and Brenneis (1984:14–16).

12. Rosaldo (1973, 1980) discusses a similar contrast, in "traditional" and "Christianized" speech styles, for the Ilongot.

13. Attempting to come to terms with the process by which a group's "word" defines it as a social unit, Sansom (1980) calls its result a "determination." Williams (1985) calls it a "standing account."

14. In the past (1973–81), Pintupi women tended to regard meetings as "men's business," and rarely spoke even when they did attend. At Kintore in 1982, however, a few women were Council members and women spoke at meetings on subjects that were of concern to them (Bette Clark, personal communication). Still, men continue to run the meetings. The place of these events as part of contemporary sexual politics involves two issues. One concerns a shift in the balance of power between the sexes in contemporary life: where Councils control resources, men's meetings may intrude on women's autonomy more than they once did. The second issue concerns the differing integrative scope of men's and women's activities in the Western Desert.

15. These include in-law avoidance registers and ceremonial euphemisms.

16. This is *not* to deny power to Pintupi women or to deny their own experience of autonomy. Women's "business" is their own and it is valuable. Nor is it simply to associate women with "kinship" as against "society" or "politics." Recent accounts show that women's ritual *is* addressed to varieties of social disharmony, thereby securing the social system at certain levels of relationship (Bell 1980; Hamilton 1984). It is necessary, however, to see the activities of males and females within a total system, acting at different levels or dialectically to limit each other.

17. These are characterized by restraint in behavior, including the use of special speech registers.

18. These patterns continue to be important. Women tend to associate their activity with the "single women's camp" consisting of their close kin. Men, on the other hand, are likely to congregate in larger groups that transcend this differentiation and in which the forms of speech stress the "relatedness" of all present.

19. See Sansom (1980) for a similar description of Aboriginal fringe camps in Darwin.

References

Aristotle. 1967. The Politics. E. Barker, transl. *In* Aristotle. A. Edel, ed. New York: Dell.

Bell, Diane. 1980. Daughters of the Dreaming. Ph.D. dissertation. Australian National University.

Bell, Diane, and Pam Ditton. 1980. Law: The Old and the New. Canberra: Central Australian Aboriginal Legal Aid Service.

Bloch, Maurice. 1975. Introduction. *In* Political Language and Oratory in Traditional Society. M. Bloch, ed. New York: Academic Press.

Brenneis, Donald. 1984. Straight Talk and Sweet Talk: Political Discourse in an Occasionally Egalitarian Community. *In* Dangerous Words: Language and Politics in the Pacific. D. Brenneis and F. Myers, eds. pp. 69–84. New York: New York University Press.

Briggs, Jean. 1970. Never in Anger. Cambridge: Harvard University Press.

Evans-Pritchard, E. E. 1940. The Nuer. Oxford: Oxford University Press.

Evans-Pritchard, E., and M., Fortes, eds. 1940. African Political Systems. Oxford: Oxford University Press.

Frake, Charles. 1963. Litigation in Lipay: A Study of Subanun Law. Proceedings of the 9th Pacific Science Congress, Vol. 3.

Giddens, Anthony. 1979. Central Problems in Social Theory. Cambridge: Cambridge University Press.

Hamilton, Annette. 1984. A Complex Strategical Situation: Gender and Power in Aboriginal Australia. *In* Australian Women: Feminist Perspectives. N. Grieves, ed. pp. 69–85. Melbourne: Oxford University Press.

Hymes, Dell. 1972. Models of the Interaction of Language and Social Life. *In* Directions in Sociolinguistics. J. Gumperz and D. Hymes, eds. New York: Holt, Rinehart & Winston.

Irvine, Judith. 1979. Formality and Informality in Communicative Events. American Anthropologist 81:773–790.

Lederman, Rena. 1984. Who Speaks Here? Formality and the Politics of Gender in Mendi, Highland Papua New Guinea. *In* Dangerous Words: Language and Politics in the Pacific. D. Brenneis and F. Myers, eds. pp. 85–107. New York: New York University Press.

Lee, Richard B. 1979. The !Kung San: Men, Women, and Work in a Foraging Society. New York: Cambridge University Press.

Liberman, Kenneth. 1981. Understanding Interaction in Central Australia: An Ethnomethodological Study of Australian Aboriginal People. Ph.D. dissertation. University of California, Los Angeles.

Marshall, Lorna. 1961. Sharing, Talking, and Giving: Relief of Social Tensions Among !Kung Bushmen. Africa 31:231–249.

Meggitt, M.J. 1962. Desert People. Chicago: University of Chicago Press.

Morphy, Howard. 1977. "Too Many Meanings": An Analysis of the Artistic System of the Yolngu of Northeast Arnhem Land. Ph.D. dissertation. Australian National University.

Munn, Nancy. 1970. The Transformation of Subjects into Objects in Walbiri and Pitjantjara Myth. *In* Australian Aboriginal Anthropology. R. Berndt, ed. pp. 141–163. Nedlands: University of Western Australian Press.

Myers, Fred. 1976. To Have and To Hold: A Study of Persistence and Change in Pintupi Social Life. Ph.D. dissertation. Bryn Mawr College.

———. 1979. Emotions and the Self: A Theory of Personhood and Political Order Among Pintupi Aborigines. Ethos 7:343–370.

———. 1980a. The Cultural Basis of Pintupi Politics. Mankind 12:197–213.

———. 1980b. A Broken Code: A Pintupi Political Theory and Contemporary Social Life. Mankind 12:311–326.

———. 1982. Always Ask: Resource Use and Land Ownership Among Pintupi Aborigines. *In* Resource Managers. N. Williams and E. Hunn, eds. pp. 173–196. Boulder, CO: Westview Press.

———. 1986. Pintupi Country, Pintupi Self: Sentiment, Place, and Politics Among Western Desert Aborigines. Washington, DC: Smithsonian Institution Press.

Myers, Fred, and Donald Brenneis. 1984. Introduction: Language and Politics in the Pacific. *In* Dangerous Words: Language and Politics in the Pacific. D. Brenneis and F. Myers, eds. pp. 1–29. New York: New York University Press.

Paine, Robert, ed. 1981. Politically Speaking: Cross-Cultural Studies of Rhetoric. Philadelphia, PA: Institute for the Study of Human Issues.

Reay, Marie. 1970. A Decision as Narrative. *In* Australian Aboriginal Anthropology. R. Berndt, ed. pp. 164–173. Nedlands: University of Western Australian Press.

Róheim, Geza. 1945. The Eternal Ones of the Dream. New York: International Universities Press.

Rosaldo, Michelle. 1973. "I Have Nothing to Hide": The Language of Ilongot Oratory. Language in Society 2:193–223.

———. 1980. Knowledge and Passion: Ilongot Notions of Self and Social Life. Cambridge: Cambridge University Press.

Sansom, Basil. 1980. The Camp at Wallaby Cross. Canberra: Australian Institute of Aboriginal Studies.

Shapiro, Warren. 1969. Miwuyt Marriage. Ph.D. dissertation. Australian National University.

Simmel, Georg. 1950. The Sociology of Georg Simmel. K. Wolff, transl. and ed. New York: Free Press.

Stanner, W. E. H. 1956. The Dreaming. *In* Australian Signpost. T. A. G. Hungerford, ed. Melbourne: F. W. Cheshire.

Strehlow, T. G. H. 1970. Geography and the Totemic Landscape in Central Australia: A Functional Study. *In* Australian Aboriginal Anthropology. R. Berndt, ed. pp. 92–140. Nedlands: University of Western Australia Press.

Swartz, M., A. Tuden, and V. Turner, eds. 1967. Political Anthropology. Chicago: Aldine.

Turner, Terence. 1979. The Gê and Bororo Societies as Dialectical Systems: A General Model. *In* Dialectical Societies. D. Maybury-Lewis, ed. pp. 147–178. Cambridge: Harvard University Press.

van der Leeden, A. C. 1975. Thundering Gecko and Emu: The Mythological Structuring of Nunggubuyu Patrimoieties. *In* Australian Aboriginal Mythology. L. R. Hiatt, ed. pp. 46–103. Canberra: Australian Institute of Aboriginal Studies.

Warner, W. Lloyd. 1937. A Black Civilization. New York: Harper & Row.

Weiner, Annette. 1976. Women of Value, Men of Renown. Austin: University of Texas Press.

Williams, Nancy. 1973. Northern Territory Aborigines Under Australian Law. Ph.D. dissertation. University of California, Berkeley.

———. 1985. On Aboriginal Decision-Making. *In* Metaphors of Interpretation: Essays in Honour of W. E. H. Stanner. D. Barwick, J. Beckett, and M. Reay, eds. pp. 240–269. Canberra: Australian National University Press.

13

When Talk Isn't Cheap: Language and Political Economy

JUDITH T. IRVINE

Perhaps one of the most durable legacies of Saussure's *Course in General Linguistics* is its radical separation of the denotational sign (qua sign) from the material world. This conception of the sign has endured not just because of the effectiveness of Saussure's own formulation, but probably also because it was consonant with ideas already having a long history in the Western intellectual tradition—most particularly, the separation of mind from body.[1] It was also consonant with emerging views in American anthropology and linguistics at the time. The Boasian concern for the independence of linguistic form from race and culture (given the technological emphasis common in conceptions of culture in the early years of this century) similarly led many scholars to promote the autonomy of linguistics as a discipline and to turn their attention away from the political and economic conditions of speech. Although the Boasians and their descendants included major figures and schools who focused on relationships between language and culture, they did so largely by defining culture in terms of knowledge and ideas. The obverse side of this tradition is represented by those anthropologists and other scholars who, in studying a material and political economy, ignored or played down the study of language, and sometimes even saw themselves as aligned against the "idealists" or "culturalists" who drew on linguistic models and verbal data.

Recent years, however, have seen some uneasiness with this dichotomy, and some attempts at rapprochement. Within linguistics, the consideration of language use and context has reached out to the material and historical conditions of linguistic performance. Thus, for example, linguists like William Labov portray speech as varying according to speakers' socioeconomic class and other affiliations relating to economic and political interest. The implication is that the class connotations of variants influence the direction of change in the linguistic system. From a more sociological point of view, we see in some quarters a new or renewed concern with ideology, including its linguistic articulation, in the control of material production and distribution (for example, Rossi-Landi 1983). Still, in these views, however much the world of ideas and the world of goods may influence each other, language remains firmly locked in the former—the world of ideas. Linguistic signs stand for aspects of the marketplace; they influence it but are not of it.

Language has more roles to play in a political economy than these. And, problematic though the term "political economy" may be in some respects,[2] it may offer clues as to what those roles are. To recognize that the study of economy must include institutions, practices, and values, as well as goods—and that the values and interests governing much of its operation necessarily involve political processes and relations, not just the autonomous flow of markets—is to begin to move beyond the dichotomy that excludes linguistic phenomena from the economic realm. The allocation of resources, the coordination of production, and the distribution of goods and services, seen (as they must be) in political perspective, involve linguistic forms and verbal practices in many ways—as this paper will demonstrate.

The other side of the problem, and the one more central to my discussion, lies in our conception of language. In linguistic anthropology a fruitful approach began with the work of the anthropologically oriented sociolinguists Hymes and Gumperz, with their attention to speaking as a socially and culturally constructed activity. This school's significance for the problem of language's relationship with political economy might not be obvious from a cursory glance at some of its early texts, since the early years of the "ethnography of speaking" sometimes tended to focus on cognitive questions (for example, the concept of communicative competence) and to emphasize ideas about speaking as part of a larger, cultural system of ideas, rather more than the verbal acts themselves. But while these initial emphases were not inconsistent with the relegation of linguistics to an "idealist" camp, the shift toward a concern with speaking as a social activity opened the way to a more productive conception of relations among language, culture, and society—and, from there, the way beyond the materialist/idealist dichotomy.[3]

The present paper builds upon that base. It also draws upon recent conceptions of a semiotics inspired as much by Peirce as by Saussure (see Mertz and Parmentier 1985; Silverstein 1980, 1984), for we need to conceive of linguistic phenomena, and the functions of the linguistic sign, more broadly than in the usual structuralist readings of Saussure if we are to move beyond the materialist/idealist conundrum. As I have suggested above, we also need conceptions of economy and of value that are comprehensive enough to include linguistic resources and verbal activities. Toward that end, in this paper I consider a case where linguistic objects and performances are exchanged for cash and goods—a case where language's involvement in an economy is perhaps most direct. This is a type of economic function of linguistic phenomena that, I believe, deserves an attention it has not had. It is, however, only one type of relationship between language and economy, and to be properly understood it needs to be compared with others.

Part I of this paper, therefore, lays that groundwork: it summarizes and compares some views of the relations between linguistic phenomena and economy (best thought of as political economy). I shall lay out a range of possibilities as to what those relations can be. Part II will explore a more specific topic: a comparative economy of compliments. Ethnographic illustrations in the paper derive largely from my own fieldwork in West Africa (Senegal). As Part II emphasizes, among other things the Senegalese case presents compliments that are paid for in cash—an example of linguistic phenomena as objects of economic exchange.

A major purpose of these discussions is to show that the roles language and speech can play in a political economy are not mutually exclusive. Even though some of these "roles" correspond to views already articulated in the linguistic and sociological literature, views that are sometimes seen as competing, what they actually represent are coexisting functions of language. Rather than rival theories or separate sets of ethnographic cases, they concern different dimensions of language use. Because of language's semiotic complexity (its multiple levels of patterning, and the multifunctional nature of the linguistic sign), there are multiple possibilities for its relationship with a material world. All the types of linkage between linguistic phenomena and political economy mentioned in Part I could be found coexisting in the same community—even in the same verbal performances, as we shall see in Part II.

In outlining language's many relationships with the material world, my object is not to claim it for a "materialist" camp, or to attack the materialist/idealist dichotomy merely by inverting it. Indeed, I argue that cultural systems of ideas are crucial to an understanding of language's full range of roles in a political economy. Language is a complex social fact that can be looked at from many angles, including the economic. It is only by appreciating language's complexity that we can transcend the conundrum.

I. Types of Linkage Between Linguistic Phenomena and Political Economy

The linkages compared here can be distinguished in several ways: according to what sign-function they emphasize (denotational reference, indexicality, and so on); according to what kind of linguistic and social diversity they encompass; and according to how they connect language with the social division of labor—as its instrument, as its index, or as part of its substance. That is, does linguistic diversity impede social cooperation? Does the variety of verbal behaviors merely index social groups, divisions, or roles formed on mainly nonverbal bases, or is the variety of verbal performance a precondition for (and thus a defining characteristic of) the social division of labor itself—as the practices constituting a social role, or as the objects of economic activity?

As I suggested earlier, the notion that signs may have an economic and political dimension is hardly new. Nor are most of the extant statements on the subject inherently faulty. They are, however, incomplete. Some reduce language to only one of its functions, for example referential propositionality.[4] Some describe an indexical relationship but give little account of it. And most omit a consideration of linguistic phenomena as possible *objects of exchange*—exchanged against what we consider to be material objects, not only against other linguistic signs.

Propositionality: Signs Denote Objects and Activities in the Material World

The first kind of relation between language and economy is the most familiar one: linguistic signs denote objects, the natural world, and economic skills and activities. They label persons and groups; and they refer to, and make predications about, the forces of production and the coordination of efforts. Because signs refer to the external world, a society's productive efforts can be organized and a division of labor becomes possible.

In discussing this referential function of language and its communicative implications, however, many writers both in linguistics and in the social sciences have done more than merely elaborate on these statements. Instead, some have assumed that referential communication is the *only* function of language, and that language must be uniform in order for referential communication to work. They assume, therefore, that a social division of labor depends on linguistic homogeneity, or at least is facilitated by it. Bloomfield wrote, for example:

> In the ideal case, within a group of people who speak to each other, each person has at his disposal the strength and skill of every person in the group. The more these persons differ as to special skills, the wider a range of power does each one person control. Only one person needs to be a good climber, since he can get fruit for all the rest; only one needs to be a good fisherman, since he can supply the others with fish. *The division of labor, and, with it, the whole working of human society, is due to language* (1933:24, italics in the original).[5]

Notice that this discussion of the "ideal" case envisions a diversity of skills in the socioeconomic realm but not in the linguistic: "Obviously the value of language [for social cooperation] depends upon people's using it in the same way" (1933:29). Homogeneity in linguistic usage is assumed necessary to ensure referential communication. Utterances *refer* to economic skills, to their realization in acts and events, and to their coordination. Thus Bloomfield's conception of language's role in a social division of labor rests entirely on the referential function.

It would be unjust to Bloomfield to suggest that he never acknowledged the existence of diversity in linguistic skills or performances within a speech community. Indeed, he paid more attention to this than did many other scholars of his day and later (see Hymes 1967). But the rubrics under which he considered diversity—as material to eliminate from his science of language, or as relevant only to historical processes such as "intimate borrowing"—are inimical to any serious sociolinguistic view. For the most part he saw linguistic diversity as incidental to social and regional boundaries, or as contingent upon them. The product of "lines of weakness" in communication, diversity (for him) interferes with shared reference, and thus with economic cooperation or any other aspect of community. The "literary genius" (Bloomfield 1933:46) is the only figure he mentions whose social position is actually constituted by special linguistic skills.[6]

This picture of linguistic homogeneity as basic to communication and hence to social coordination is a familiar one—as are some of the critiques of it—and I do not want to dwell on it at length.[7] Only two further remarks are worth making here. First: although some aspects of the picture have been condemned, it has not been thrown out altogether. Sociolinguists like Hymes and Gumperz have attacked Bloomfield's (and Chomsky's) portrayal of the homogeneous speech community, and they replace it with a notion of the organization of linguistic diversity; but they do not wholly abandon the view that social coordination is facilitated if the parties to it share some common code. Instead, Gumperz and Hymes shift the emphasis to *interpretation*, as what is shared, rather than performance. In this way referential accuracy can be preserved under multilingual (or multi-varietal) conditions, although denotational reference is not the only function of language sociolinguists envisage.

Second: much investigation remains to be done on just *how* language facilitates coordination of a social division of labor. For example, within the linguistic system the study of directives (requests and commands) is especially relevant, because it concerns the verbal management of the flow of goods and services in an economy. The few studies we have of directives in social and cultural context suggest that, in conspicuously task-oriented situations, speech coordinating the tasks is often reduced and simple compared to speech of other kinds, or speech in other settings.[8] (The reduction and "simplicity" of linguistic form in pidgins and trade languages originating in labor or market settings might be relevant also.) Another, more sociological aspect of linguistic involvement in coordinating a division of labor concerns how people participate in organizational discussions. For instance, a single spokesperson may represent a group and carry out the communicative tasks necessary for its coordination with other groups.[9] In short, coordinating a material division of labor does not universally *require* a very complex system of signs held in common among all coordinated parties.

However, to the extent that a code is held in common, or at least that a semantic system is, it may also facilitate cooperation—or at least co-optation—in an indirect way: by incorporating an ideology that supports a particular socioeconomic system. The lexicon labeling social groups and economic activities, and perhaps also a system of metaphoric constructions and semantically generative principles, would presumably be the main places in the referential structure to look for this.

Indexicality: Signs Index Social Groups, Categories, and Situations Entering into the Relations of Production

I turn now to the second type of relation between signs and political economy—to a view that has become familiar to us under the rubric of sociolinguistics: a view of the speech community as an organization of linguistic diversity, having a repertoire of ways of speaking that are indexically associated with social groups, roles, or activities.[10] In other words, there is a diversity on the linguistic plane that indexes a social diversity. Studies of correlations of this sort, especially as social dialectology, have become commonplace. Less common is any attempt to explain the correlation—why a *particular* linguistic variety should mark a particular social group, except for reasons of external historical contingency, such as the demographic one of migration of ethnic groups speaking different languages. Indeed, most of these studies either state or imply that the social diversity is formed independently from its linguistic marking: for example, Labov's use of an already-existing sociological survey of the Lower East Side that provided a 10-point index of socioeconomic class, based mainly on occupation and income.

Among all these cases and their correlations, what kinds of distinctions might be useful? One possibility has been to distinguish dialects from registers—that is, to distinguish codes associated with persons and groups from codes associated with situations. This classification makes a convenient starting point, but it becomes complicated when—as is so frequently the case—a variety historically associated with one social group is adopted by another to mark a social situation. Similarly, Labov's studies of speech styles and socioeconomic class have shown how the type of linguistic variation that signals class also signals differences in style (thus, situation), in one and the same sociolinguistic process (Labov 1972).[11]

Another approach has been to characterize "types of linguistic communities," distinguished according to degrees of internal differentiation. In an early paper by this title ("Types of Linguistic Communities," 1962) Gumperz proposed that language distance among codes in a repertoire is correlated with degrees of social complexity—social differentiation internal to the community—in an evolutionary scheme ranging from bands through "larger tribal groups" to modern urban-industrial societies (1971[1962]:105). Gumperz (private communication) no longer subscribes to this scheme and its evolutionary implications. He had suggested it at a time when (as he noted, pp. 104–105) "reliable cross-cultural information on speech behavior [was] almost nonexistent." Counterexamples now abound: compare the studies of urban social dialectology in the United States and Britain, where "language distance" between social classes consists largely in phonetic detail, with cases such as the Vaupés region in the northwest Amazon, a small-scale egalitarian social system where mutually unintelligible languages are associated with descent-group-like units in a network of marriage alliances.

Although I too discard this particular evolutionary hypothesis, a valuable aspect of the 1962 paper was its attempt to draw some explanatory link between the form of the social division of labor and the nature of its linguistic indices—in contrast to correlational studies that assume the relationship is entirely arbitrary, or entirely external to the linguistic system. With this problem in view I think it is still useful to look at the topology of linguistic differentiation and social differentiation, and to pay attention to the kind of linguistic phenomena involved. For "language distance" let us substitute some other properties of codes: their *discreteness* and their *autonomy* from other codes in a communicative system. In other words, the question is how functionally independent of one another they are, regardless of their genetic relationship and structural comparability. This might allow us to compare several kinds of sociolinguistic systems: (1) systems where the socially indexing linguistic alternants form a set of discrete usages, versus systems where they are gradient (for example, multilingualism versus differences in vowel height). This contrast concerns the alternants' linguistic form.[12] (2) Systems where the socially indexing alternate varieties are limited to a narrow semantic range, or a set of topically specific items (as with some kinds of respect vocabularies), versus varieties that can apply over a wide referential range (such as dialects differing mainly in phonetics). This contrast concerns the extent to which the socially indexing variety is simultaneously involved with the referential function. (3) Systems where the relevant codes are autonomous (at least potentially), in the sense that they can be independently described or characterized, versus systems where some codes can only be defined relative to other codes (for example, by the addition of a surface-level rule, as with Pig Latin and many other play languages, and also the gender-linked codes of some American Indian languages).

Where these alternants index social groups and roles, I would suggest that their contrasts might have some connection with a cultural ideology of role relations—such as, whether the roles they mark are thought of as essentially autonomous, defined independently of one another, or as dependent and complementary; whether a role is thought to be part of a person's basic identity, thus applying to all situations and governing what other roles he/she may take on; and whether, in principle, the roles (or groups) are exclusive and sharply bounded, as opposed to allowing degrees of participation, or mobility and shifting among them (see Goodenough 1965; Nadel 1957).

A good example of the kinds of cases we might look at in this light would be "antilanguages" (Halliday 1976): argots spoken by groups (or in roles) culturally defined as opposing, or inverting, prevailing norms—such as thieves, prisoners, and revolutionaries. As Halliday points out, the linguistic phenomena characterizing these codes cannot be accounted for simply by the need for secrecy or for group boundary markers, although those needs are present. Instead, the codes' origin in *counter-societies* is reflected in many aspects of their linguistic form, for instance in their elaboration of lexicon and metaphor relevant to their special activities and their attitudes toward the normative society, and in their frequent use of formal inversions and reversals, such as metathesis. Also significant is their conspicuous avoidance and violation of forms recognized as "standard" (consider, for example, Reisman's [1974] description of "contrapuntal" speaking in Antigua as a counter to conventions of orderly turn-taking associated with the social forms of white colonial society and its heirs; see also Kochman 1972). These anti-languages are clearly not autonomous codes, then, although the normative codes on which they depend may be. The anti-language is not, and has never been, anyone's native tongue, nor are all its formal characteristics simply arbitrary. Both functionally and formally it is derived from the normative code, just as its speakers define their social role in opposition to the normative society.

The language (and culture) of gender, in different societies, might be another suitable set of cases, some perhaps even showing the characteristics of "antilanguages" (in cases where sex roles are culturally conceived of as antagonistic). The question is whether the forms of speaking associated with males and females reflect, in some way, cultural conceptions of their social identities, in relation to each other and in relation to other kinds of statuses an individual may hold.[13]

My point is that indexical correlations between realms of linguistic differentiation and social differentiation are not wholly arbitrary. They bear some relationship to a cultural system of ideas about social relationships, including ideas about the history of persons and groups. I do not mean that linguistic variation is simply a diagram of some aspect of social differentiation—as correlational studies often in effect suggest—but that there is a dialectic relationship mediated by a culture of language (and of society).

As a more detailed example, an ethnographic case from West Africa illustrates these suggestions about code discreteness and autonomy.[14] Among rural Wolof of Senegal, there is a series of ranked, endogamous occupational groups, called "castes" in the ethnographic literature on the region. As I have described (Irvine 1975, 1978b, 1982), caste differences are culturally associated with differences in speech style. A style connected with high rank (*waxu géér*,[15] "noble speech") contrasts with a style connected with low rank (*waxu gewel*, "griot speech," so named after the bardic caste which in some respects is said to epitomize low-ranking groups). Linguistically, the phenomena that most conspicuously distinguish the two speech styles are gradient in form and/or application: prosodic differences, such as pitch, loudness, and speed of talk; and the proportional use of emphatic particles and parallel and/or repetitive constructions. The prosodic phenomena in particular can only be defined relative to one another. There is no pitch frequency that absolutely marks a voice as high-ranking or low-ranking, only relatively low or high pitch. The two speech styles are *complementary*, mirror-images diverging from a neutral middle ground to the extent that a social situation defines differences in social rank as relevant.

Contrast this complementarity in Wolof speech styles, then, with the speech of another "caste" group, the Lawbé (Woodworkers). A semi-nomadic population said to have migrated into Wolof territory from a Pulaar-speaking region to the north, the Lawbé are bilingual: they speak Wolof during their temporary visits in Wolof villages (during which they are hired by villagers to cut down trees and carve wooden utensils from them), but they speak Pulaar in their encounters with Pulaar-speakers (the similarly semi-nomadic cattle-herding Peul and the sedentary Tukulor). Wolof villagers claim that the Lawbé also speak Pulaar among themselves, and that their command of that language shows they are "not Wolof."

Given the dearth of published studies of the Lawbé (and I have not closely observed them myself), it is not clear *what* they speak among themselves—whether what the Wolof claim about them is true or, if true, whether it holds for all Lawbé groups or only some of them. What does seem to be clear, however, is that Wolof villagers assign the Lawbé a different ethnic origin and a separate history, to match their control of a separate language, Pulaar. These same Wolof villagers also describe the Wolof system of caste occupations, its associated symbolism, and so on, as if it were complete without Woodworkers—that is, as if Woodworkers were simply a late, tacked-on addition to an already autonomous, self-sufficient social system. In contrast, they describe nobles and griots as complementary ranks such that neither could exist without the other. Without nobles, or without griots, there would be no Wolof caste system at all.

Now, it is probably true that the Lawbé, or at least some Lawbé, are descendants of migrants from a historically separate system to the north, and that their linguistic behavior, as compared with Wolof nobles and griots, is the result of historical facts. But this cannot be the whole story, because historical documents attest that there used also to be Wolof Woodworkers, called by a different name *(seeñ)*, and taking their place on lists of Wolof caste occupations.[16] So I would suggest that Wolof villagers' ideas about the history of Woodworkers and their place in an overall set of caste roles have at least partly shifted to match their linguistic behavior and their residential marginality, in a broader cultural scene that ideologically links language differences with historical autonomy (and with regional boundaries rather than caste boundaries).

In this case, we see two kinds of code/role relationships: the speech styles of nobles and griots, nonautonomous styles that can only be defined relative to one another, like their speakers' social roles; and the separate language, Pulaar, whose speakers are culturally assumed to have an autonomous history matching their autonomous code.[17] There is an iconic link here between the *kind* of linguistic differentiation and the *kind* of social relationship it marks, at least in the cultural ideology.

Two other languages present on the Wolof sociolinguistic scene—Arabic and French—can also be considered in the same light. These languages are of interest because they are relevant to the connections between a rural Wolof village and the national and international systems that impinge upon it, and also because we can see these connections mediated, again, by the ideology of language just described. For Wolof villagers, Arabic is the language of Islam, the dominant religion among Wolof for many centuries. Although villagers are well aware that Arabic is also the language of the modern Arab nations, including neighboring Mauritania, for the majority of the community the religious connotations predominate and a form of classical Arabic is the only variety of that language they know.[18] Indeed, many villagers, of various castes and age groups, know some Arabic;[19] in contrast, far fewer people know (or admit that they know) French, the language of colonialism, despite the long-established presence of French-speaking schools, radio, and so on.

The level of acquisition of French, especially before the 1970s, has been low compared with its availability in terms of exposure and opportunities for systematic instruction.

From the linguist's point of view, of course, Arabic and French are equally unrelated to any form of Wolof; the three are historically, and denotationally, autonomous. But some Wolof villagers have not always seen them that way. In 1970 I was told that Arabic "is really Wolof underneath, at heart. . . . Only the pronunciation is different." French, on the other hand, was said to be quite alien, even formed in a different part of the body. Thus the local ideology of language was tending to assimilate Arabic into the repertoire of "Wolof" linguistic varieties because of its functional integration into social life, while French remained (in that view) a "foreign" language belonging properly only to non-Wolof, and not readily acquirable by true Wolof ethnics, except perhaps for persons of low rank.[20]

Since local ideology linked the nature of linguistic differentiation (between Arabic, Wolof, and French) with the nature of the social relationships and activities it indexed, ideas about language were likely to shift if there were some major change in the social situation. It is not surprising, then, that the advent of Senegalese independence, by altering some aspects of the political and economic connection with France, eventually affected villagers' ideas about French, now the official language of the Senegalese state.[21] While no one has told me that French "is really Wolof," by 1984 it was apparent that many people who used to consider French unlearnable and unspeakable had changed their minds.

Note, however, that the linguistic ideology whose modifications are described here is no simple reflex of the change of government or even of a shift in economic opportunities. The attitudes toward language in general (and French and Arabic in particular) found in this rural Wolof locality differ from those in some other areas of Senegal, where (for example) French sometimes penetrated earlier, even though instructional opportunities were fewer and economic opportunities no greater. What we see here is a particular rationalization of a particular local experience, a rationalization informed by a framework of other ideas about language and about the kinds of people who speak in certain ways.

It should be clear, therefore, why this discussion of indexical values of linguistic phenomena, and the topology of linkages between codes and social relationships, does not propose a direct analogy between linguistic and social differentiation that would claim to predict the one from the other. To attempt such prediction would be to ignore the role of linguistic ideology—the cultural (or subcultural) system of ideas about social and linguistic relationships, together with their loading of moral and political interests—which is a crucial mediating factor. And I should also emphasize that the cultural system (including the linguistic ideology) is a *mediating* factor, not necessarily a causative one. In some cases it may merely rationalize a set of sociolinguistic differences, rather than shape them. The usual assumption that some historical contingency of a nonlinguistic sort, such as migration, has brought about a present-day sociolinguistic scene may often be true enough; but it is not all we need to consider. The cultural reformulation of that scene (its persons, groups, and codes) according to some rationalizing criterion is also relevant, perhaps sometimes inventing as much history as it reflects.[22]

Incorporation: Linguistic Phenomena Are Included in the Economy as Practices and as Commodities

One of the reasons correlational sociolinguistic studies fall short of revealing the full involvement of linguistic phenomena in political economy concerns the fact that forms of speaking are not always merely an index of some independently generated social differentiation but may indeed *effect* social differentiation. The division of linguistic labor is not just an analogy with the division of labor in society, or even a homology (as some have said; see Rossi-Landi 1983), but, in some ways, part and parcel of it. That is, while linguistic phenomena may denote the forces of production, and they may index the relations of production, they may also be among those forces, and they may be objects of economic activity. I turn now to that "communicative economy," to borrow a term used by Hymes (1974:4, 26) to describe the organization of a society's system of communicative (not just linguistic) institutions, vehicles, and contexts. In this view, verbal skills and performances are among the resources and activities forming a socioeconomic system; and the relevant knowledge, talents, and use-rights are not evenly, randomly, or fortuitously distributed in a community (see Bourdieu 1977, 1982; Hymes 1971, 1973). The fact of uneven distribution is itself economically relevant.

Verbal Skills as Economic Resources (and as Practices Constituting a Social Role)

One way in which linguistic goods enter the marketplace is simply as a consequence of indexical correlations like those noted above. This process is discussed at length by Bourdieu (1977, 1982), who sees it as a process of "conversion" between a "linguistic marketplace" and a material one. In a class-based society, he points out, where social classes and class-linked activities correlate with linguistic variation, the linguistic varieties acquire differential value that translates into economic value. Access to high position and prestigious social circles may require, or seem to require, the ability to speak or write in a prestigious language, variety, or style, whose acquisition becomes the focus of economic activity.[23] People who fail to acquire the high variety, such as a national standard, at their mother's knee must pay for instruction later on, whether through tutoring, how-to books (more often how-not-to), newspaper columns about "proper speaking," or state subvention through the school system.

Bourdieu's discussion focuses on the European industrial nations, especially France, and on the acquisition of standard language among other indices of membership in the bourgeoisie. Much of the argument applies elsewhere too, however, even in pre- or less-industrialized settings. Any case of diglossia, or a case where there are linguistic forms that (for at least some of the population) can only be acquired through special education, will be somewhat parallel. In all these cases code acquisition—actually, second-code acquisition—is surrounded by economic activity because of the perceived value, and distributional scarcity, of the linguistic variety to be acquired.

Now, while Bourdieu's view of the "linguistic marketplace" is clearly useful to our inquiry, it is not without complications. For example, it tends to reduce language to presuppositional indexicality and to derive language's role in political economy entirely therefrom. Little room is left for any statement made in one of the available varieties to make a difference to the political and economic situation—to be anything other than a symptom of it.[24] As Woolard (1985) points out, moreover, Bourdieu's statements on the value of class-linked varieties in the linguistic market, and his emphasis on the institutional domination of a language, are oversimplified. Questions remain as to whether the linguistic market is ever fully integrated, and whether the population that does not control a dominant variety regards its domination as legitimate (1985:740–741).

These questions about integration and legitimacy are especially relevant to Third World situations and the link between local sociolinguistic systems and the languages of national and international relations.[25] Senegal's "linguistic market," for example, is far from integrated. The political dominance of French was long acknowledged in Wolof communities without being considered legitimate, while, in contrast, members of other ethnic groups often favored French as the alternative to Wolof domination. Within the particular Wolof village described here, changes in the legitimacy of French have already been mentioned; but even though French is no longer resisted as much as before, differences in the legitimacy of French and Arabic show up in the economics of their acquisition. Economic activity surrounding acquisition of Arabic takes place at the grass-roots level, where villagers pay for their children's (and sometimes their own) instruction, while economic activity directed toward the acquisition of French—dominant but far less legitimate, in the local view—takes place at the level of the state.[26]

Despite complications, however, it is evident that linguistic skills can be economic resources, and even if some skills are merely status markers their acquisition may be the focus of economic activity. Still, as regards how linguistic phenomena can be economic resources, grammatical competence in a high-valued code is not the only aspect of language to look at. We must also consider skills in the appropriate use of language and in the management of discourse—skills that fall outside "grammatical competence" as usually defined, and that do not depend on the differentiation of a set of codes. Many social roles and statuses are at least partly defined in terms of discourse management: teacher, lawyer, or psychiatrist, for example. Even where verbal skills are not crucial to the performance of some particular social role they may be crucial to gaining access to it; see studies of gatekeeping interviews by Gumperz and his associates (Gumperz 1982; see also Erickson and Shultz 1979).

Among rural Wolof, skills in discourse management are essential to the role of the griot (bard), whose traditional profession involves special rhetorical and conversational duties such as persuasive speechmaking on a patron's behalf, making entertaining conversation, transmitting messages to the public, and performing the various genres of praise-singing. Not everyone who might be born with the appropriate raw talent can become a professional bard—for that one must be born into the griot caste. But within that category, the most talented and skillful griots earn high rewards and are sought after by would-be patrons, such as village-level political leaders (or those who seek leadership positions). High-ranking political leaders do not engage in these griot-linked forms of discourse themselves; to do so would be incompatible with their "nobility" and qualifications for office. But their ability to recruit and pay a skillful, reputable griot to speak on their behalf is essential, both to hold high position and to gain access to it in the first place.

Note that political systems in other African societies (and societies elsewhere in the world too, for that matter) commonly include spokesperson roles, such as the Ashanti "linguist" who speaks on behalf of the king. In contemporary states public relations personnel, press secretaries, and professionals in the communications industry are statuses somewhat resembling these traditional spokesperson statuses and in Senegal, at least, have often drawn their personnel from among the bardic castes.[27]

This point—that some social roles are constituted by discourse management—has been made often by Hymes and others, and I shall not belabor it, even though it is important to our understanding of political processes and access to political positions. I shall just emphasize that its implications reach beyond the cognitive (questions of communicative competence), to include how we conceive of economy. Thus, one must consider the place of verbal skills and rights in a system of transactions that includes both material and nonmaterial goods, services, and values. It is perhaps not a question of looking at a "communicative" economy, therefore, or at some sort of linkage between a sociolinguistic system and an (independently conceived) economic system, but, instead, just at an economy, from which the verbal must not be excluded.

Indeed, linguistic elements and utterances may themselves be goods and services, exchangeable against other goods and services, including material goods and cash. The next sections shift to this focus.

Authentications: Signs Accompany Commodities and Give Them Value

In a 1975 paper, "The Meaning of Meaning," Hilary Putnam presents what he calls a "division of linguistic labor." The discussion turns in several ways on the reference of terms for natural kinds, such as elm and gold. Putnam writes:

> We could hardly use such words as "elm" and "aluminum" if no one possessed a way of recognizing elm trees and aluminum metal; but not everyone to whom the [linguistic] distinction is important has to be able to make the distinction [between the things or

substances].... Gold is important for many reasons: it is a precious metal, it is a monetary metal, it has symbolic value (it is important to most people that the "gold" wedding ring they wear *really* consist of gold and not just *look* gold), etc.... Everyone to whom gold is important for any reason has to *acquire* the word "gold"; but he does not have to acquire the *method of recognizing* if something is or is not gold. He can rely on a special subclass of speakers. [These are people who have the job of] *telling whether or not something is really gold* [1975:227–228; italics in the original].

In other words, these people are experts whose knowledge (for example, knowledge of some test for telling whether a metal is really gold), while not itself linguistic, nevertheless renders their usage of the term *gold* authoritative. The economic and symbolic value of gold for the wider community depends on this. Any gold object circulating in the community must be accompanied by some convincing testimonial to its being authentically gold, if it is to command its full value. The testimonial may be oral or written (for example, when the state stamps its insignia on a gold coin).

Most often, we are probably relying not just on a single testimonial statement, but on a *chain of authentication*, a historical sequence by which the expert's attestation—and the label (expression) that conventionally goes along with it—is relayed to other people.[28] For example, I claim that the necklace I wear is made of gold because I acquired it from a trustworthy person who said it was, and who in turn acquired it from a "reliable" dealer, who in turn acquired it from a reliable source, and so on back to a point at which some expert actually did make the tests that enabled him or her to declare this metal to be gold. Thus my valued commodity (the necklace) is accompanied, not just by one special kind of statement (the authoritative testimonial), but by two: the authoritative and the derivatively authoritative (reportive—all the statements after the expert's, in the chain of authentication).

This kind of process applies not just to gold, but to any exchangeable item invested with social value, where only an "expert" can tell if it "really" is what it purports to be. Such items include not only material objects, but also verbal items like magic spells or other texts. Just *what* is invested with what sort of value, and which persons get into the position to speak authoritatively about the value, must vary from one society to another. What this process suggests, however, is that perhaps *any* system of prestations and counter-prestations—that is, an economy (in a broad sense)—will necessarily include authoritative statements as part of the exchange system. When I pay for the gold necklace, I am paying not only for the necklace itself but also for the chain of authoritative statements that accompanies it. And if I take it to be appraised, I am paying for the statement alone.

Utterances as Commodities Exchangeable for Material Goods

The above discussion of testimonials focused on statements accompanying an object of exchange, statements necessary if the object is to have its full exchange-value. I turn now to cases where a verbal statement *is* the object of exchange.

Although the appraisal of a piece of jewelry meets this criterion in a way, it only does so because it is part of a longer series of transactions whose object is the jewelry, not the statement. What we consider now are verbal "goods" and practices having value in their own right. Thus, a view of economy that can incorporate verbal practices and products will be useful for understanding systems where linguistic texts can become alienable property, and systems where some forms of speaking are institutionalized and receive financial reward.

What the verbal goods and services are, and where they enter an overall economy, will vary from one sociocultural system to another. Presumably, *any* aspect of a speech act might, separately or in combination with other aspects, be the source of its economic value in a particular system. In any given case we might ask: What aspects of the verbal performance bear the value? Who holds rights in them? Who benefits? Who pays—and in what coin?

For example, magic spells may be as much the property of a community (as with some Trobriand magic [Malinowski 1978 (1935)]) or lineage (as with some Wolof spells) as gardening land is. According to Malinowski (1978 [1935]:64), however, although the community "owns" the major form of gardening magic and has the right to benefit from its application, only one person, the *towosi*, has the right and the ability to perform community gardening spells, though he may delegate the office to a junior relative. All members of the community who expect to benefit from the performance must contribute payments for it—just as they pay for other kinds of specialist services, material or otherwise.[29]

In its capacity as community property, Trobriand gardening magic is apparently inalienable; but verbal properties may be alienable too. Silverstein (n.d. a) describes proper names in Northwest Coast societies as "investment property" and "heirloom antiques," alienable during the lifetime of a bearer. People used to try to accumulate as many names as possible and to control their bestowal (on themselves or on others). Sometimes the bearer of a name would vacate it, bestowing it on some junior relative. Acquiring a new name involved a ceremony in which an audience assembled and called the new bearer by it—receiving, in exchange, large quantities of material valuables. As Silverstein writes: "The wealth thus constitutes a back-prestation in response to the audience's having come and called the new bearer by that name, this act effectively validating the claim to it as being at a certain ranked ordinality with respect to their names (n.d.a).

Consider, too, the case of "the sick who do not speak" (Sansom 1982). Among Aboriginal Australians of Darwin fringe camps, a person who has undergone a major episode of illness may not verbally recount the story of the illness.[30] The right to tell the "sickness story" is given over, instead, to the persons who "helped him through"—in partial recompense for the debt arising from their care. The story, Sansom argues, is a bit of property exchanged against caregiving, in a community that places little store in material investments.

Although Darwin camp members treat the telling of "sickness stories" as a privilege, in other societies some kinds of talk may be treated as a burden one pays someone else to undertake. The high-ranking Wolof noble pays a griot to make a public announcement for him, because loud public speaking is something he would be "ashamed" and "unskillful" at doing.[31] On many public occasions the noble whispers briefly in the griot's ear, and it is then the griot who volubly and elaborately performs the speech for the audience. In this case, then, the act of public utterance is a service for which the griot is paid in cash.

These examples could be multiplied. It seems preferable, however, to explore one case in greater depth. Accordingly, the following section offers a more extended example of this kind of relation between language and economy. It concerns a particular type of verbal goods—statements of praise and compliment—and the verbal services of the flatterer, among village Wolof as compared with contemporary middle-class Americans. But while one of my purposes is to examine some verbal objects of exchange, the material I present also reflects other linkages between language and political economy, especially the indexical relation discussed earlier. Thus the example illustrates the fact that language is always multifunctional—and its relation to economy is, therefore, manifold.

II. The Multifunctionality of Linguistic Signs:
A Wolof Example

Recently there appeared a cartoon in the *New Yorker* magazine, entitled "Flattery getting someone somewhere" (M. Stevens, 28 July 1986). "You're looking great, Frank!" says a man in business suit and necktie to another, perhaps older, man with glasses and bow tie. "Thanks, Chuck! Here's five dollars!" Bow Tie replies, handing over the cash. The joke depends, of course, on the notion that the exchange of compliments for cash should not be done so directly and overtly. We all know that Chuck may indeed flatter Frank with a view to getting a raise, or some other eventual reward; but it is quite improper in American society to recognize the exchange formally, with an immediate payment. A compliment should be acknowledged only with a return compliment, or a minimization, or some other verbal "goods." If it is to be taken as "sincere," it is specifically excluded from the realm of material payments.

Some cultural systems do not segregate the economy of compliments from the economy of material transactions and profits, however. It is doubtful, for example, that the cartoon would seem funny to many Senegalese.[32] With a few suitable adjustments for local scene, the transfer it depicts is quite ordinary. There is, in fact, a category of persons—the griots—specializing in flattery of certain kinds, among other verbal arts. The income they gain from these activities is immediate and considerable, often amounting to full-time employment for those whose skills include the fancier genres of eulogy.

Let us return to a consideration of the social system in which these transfer, and institutionalized acts of eulogy, occur. As I mentioned earlier, the Wolof (and, indeed, most other Senegalese peoples from the Gambia River north) traditionally had a complex system of social stratification usually called a "caste" system. Though undermined by government policies and other factors the caste system retains considerable importance on the rural scene, and even on the urban scene too, according to some observers (see, for example, Silla 1966). Thus Wolof society is a hierarchical one in which hierarchy is an explicitly acknowledged value. It is also personalistic, a patronage system where person and position are closely identified. Compliments to the person are directly relevant, therefore, to the construction of high position, political and otherwise.

The lower ranks of rural Wolof society engage in various kinds of activities—agricultural labor, smithing, weaving, and so on—whose product, delivered to their patron, enhances his or her position and role as redistributor.[33] The higher ranks, as patrons, compete among themselves for political position and influence. Access to such positions is supposed to be based on genealogical rank and moral qualifications as well as on one's ability to attract and maintain a large clientship; but ideologically these criteria are almost indistinguishable from one another, for one's moral character, personality, reputation, and ancestry are all considered to be linked.

Verbal activities fit into this local system of production in several ways, most notably as one of the kinds of productive activities low-ranking persons provide for the higher-ranking. Thus verbal praise enhances the reputation and attractiveness of a would-be patron. It is comparable to physical enhancement, such as hairdressing, and requires a similar reward. (Actually, eulogizing and hairdressing are often done by the same people, or at least by members of the same social category, the griots.) Moreover, the griots' performances supposedly—that is, in the ideology of the system—contribute more directly to the system of production and distribution as well, because their liveliness and excitement arouse the addressees to carry out their own allotted role more energetically and enthusiastically. That is, praise directed to a patron stimulates him/her to (re-)distribute largesse more generously, while other kinds of performances, such as the drumming and singing directed to a work party laboring on a patron's behalf, rouse laborers to work more vigorously. Physical aspects of the performance are relevant to how this works, or so informants suggest: the forceful gush of humanly shaped, vibrating air (breath) stimulates the energy of the recipient, just as the air blown from a bellows arouses a fire.

The propositional contents of compliments and praise are of course dependent on a cultural system and the kinds of attributes locally invested with social value. Among rural Wolof, personal beauty is in some respects subordinated to "beauty of birth" (*rafet-juddu*), the subject matter of much of Wolof praise, especially of its most institutionalized form, praise-singing (as the Wolof term *woy* is often translated; praise-oratory might be a better term). I shall examine this oratorical form in more detail in what follows. But note that in doing so I am not departing so far from Chuck and Frank's conversational compliment as it might appear. Wolof conversational compliments are often formulaic praise-utterances derived from, or alluding to, the extended forms of praise-oratory. Thanks for a gift, for example, always includes praise and very frequently draws upon these formulaic expressions, or other allusions to praise-oratory. A difference between full-fledged praise-oratory and its conversational vestiges is that the former are performed only by griots, while the latter may be produced by anyone. But the griots' praise-singing is, for Wolof, a cultural model or prototype for praise-utterance in general.

Indeed, except for compliments between lovers, only this type of compliment is proper.[34] Otherwise, anything departing too far from the model is suspect, suggesting an indecent envy or exposing the addressee to the attentions of witches. "Departing too far" means a compliment focusing only on physical appearance or possessions, *and* uttered by someone of same or higher rank than the addressee. (Neither condition alone would be problematic. Lower-ranking people, like a griot speaking to a noble, may freely comment on appearance and possessions; while a high-ranking person may comment on ancestors and generous deeds.)

Returning, then, to the contents of praise: the content of a griot's praise-song normally focuses on the praiseworthy ancestry of the addressee—the ancestry that qualifies him or her for high rank and has contributed to the character and the physical being he or she is. Although the performance includes comments explicitly eulogizing particular ancestors (their generosity, strength, rectitude, beauty, great deeds) and the addressee, much of it consists in naming the ancestors and connecting them to kings or village founders or other heroic figures. Merely setting forth the names would be eulogy in itself, a display of the addressee's verbal family heirlooms, as it were. That the most elaborate displays of genealogical eulogy are performed at life-crisis events and family celebrations is only appropriate, therefore, as are outbursts of eulogistic performance at local-level political gatherings. Praise is not limited to those occasions, however, and in fact the shorter forms of eulogy and compliment need no special scheduling to occur.

Since I have described some aspects of praise-singing elsewhere (Irvine 1978a), I shall focus here on just a few relevant matters: some characteristics of praise-singing as a kind of sign. For some of these the Peircean trichotomy of icon, index, and symbol is useful, because it allows us to see praise-singing as a complex semiotic gesture uniting all three types. As icon, praise-singing formally illustrates the roles of laborer and redistributor: the singer is both verbally and physically active, declaiming the praise long and loud, and with energetic, dramatic gestures. Meanwhile the recipient (the high-ranking patron) is silent and motionless, perhaps even hidden from view behind a curtain (depending on the occasion). His/her sole appropriate movement is to hand over the cash that pays for the performance.

These iconic, formal considerations shape several aspects of the linguistic register in which praise-oratory is performed—"griot speech" *(waxu gewel)*, as opposed to "noble speech" *(waxu géér)*. As I described earlier (and see Irvine 1975), "griot speech" is loud, high-pitched, rapid, verbose, florid, and emphatic, with assorted phonological, morphological, and syntactic devices linked to those characteristics. It is the appropriate style for all expressions of praise and/or thanks, by anyone (griot or not), and for other verbal expressions of rank lower than one's addressee;[35] but, as its name implies, it is conventionally associated with griots, as the professional eulogizers who carry the style to an extreme. Thus the speech style of praise is an index of the speaker's (relatively low) rank and social identity. In a larger sense it also indexes the traditional system of ranks and sources of authority, as compared with other sources such as the French-speaking colonial regime and the national state.

Another indexical function, too, links the praise-song's eulogistic and genealogical content to its addressee, at whom the griot dramatically points. That is, the praise-song indexes the praisee (addressee) because it is pointedly directed at him/her. This addressee is also the praise-song's principal referent, however. The praisee is named, and this name, together with the genealogical statements expanding upon and providing background to it, are part of the performance's symbolic dimension. Here it is important that the griot display the patron's genealogy coherently and convincingly, mentioning only persons of good reputation, and linking the patron to famous heroes and to the ancestors of other notables, perhaps even higher-ranking. Should the griot fail to do this—that is, should he state the relationships incoherently, or reveal skeletons (family relationships) the patron would prefer to keep in the closet, or spend so much time on other lineages that he fails to display the patron's own genealogy adequately—the performance will no longer qualify as truly complimentary. Of course, griots may fail in these ways conspicuously and on purpose, if they are unsatisfied with the payment they have been offered.

This mention of payment brings me to the economic value of praise-singing, an aspect of it for which Peirce's trichotomy is no longer particularly illuminating. It is not illuminating because Peirce focuses on the relations between the sign and what it stands for—not on what it may be exchanged for.[36] But the praise-song costs, and this aspect of it is crucial. It is one of the unavoidable, large expenses a Wolof notable must incur on his way to attaining political position and maintaining any claim to rank; and, moreover, it is a sign of his ability to pay. During a performance a griot may even display the money he receives, so that all may see and admire the person being praised as a potential patron for their own services. In an important sense, then, the exchange-value of the sign is an understood part of it.

Let us consider what that value rests upon. Wolof praise-songs are a form of property, in that exclusive rights are asserted over them. The rights are of two kinds: rights over the genealogical and historical *content* of the praise-song (it is the patron's genealogy, and in principle at least the griot must obtain permission before performing it for any other addressee); and rights over the *performance* of it. (Rights to perform the long, formal versions of praise-singing accrue only to griots of particular families, although griots may transfer these rights to other griots. In no circumstances may the patron perform "his" [or "her"] own song.)

The value of the performance depends in part on the gloriousness of the content—how praiseworthy the family history really has been, and how important the family has been in political and religious hierarchies—but it depends much more on the skill and reputation of the performing griot. Though even the clumsiest griot receives something for praising a patron, knowledgeable and skillful griots are much in demand and their performances highly paid. This is especially the case when, for example, two nobles from the same lineage are competing for a lineage title and, in the process, for the services of the most famous griots who know their lineage history. And those famous performers, in turn, are careful to keep the supply of trained performers down, in order to keep the price up (as one young griot complained to me).

Thus the complexities of the overall market in which praise-song performances are situated affect their exchange-value (in cash or goods), and are the reason one may indeed, I think, speak of exchange-value here rather than just use-value. Linguistic phenomena are not all limitlessly and publicly available, like fruits on the trees of some linguistic Eden. Some of them are products of a social and sociolinguistic division of labor, and as such they may be exchanged against other products in the economy.

Under what circumstances do utterances or linguistic forms become products exchangeable against other kinds of goods? Perhaps, as material in this paper suggests, when the sign (or some aspect of it) is a scarce good, invested with value—either because knowledge of the relevant linguistic form is unequally distributed, or because performance of it cannot be universally undertaken. That is, performance might be an exclusive right, or it might require time and effort, or other costs to the producer—including, for example, as in the Wolof case, an implication of lower rank (a cost explicitly recognized as requiring remuneration, and carrying the right to receive largesse).

In these pages I have only scratched the surface of a comparative economy of compliments and praise, and how they do or do not link up with other forms of transaction in a given society. Moreover, these are certainly not the only kinds of utterances worth looking at as objects of exchange. My purpose, however, was to suggest that the project is worth undertaking—that utterances, and indeed various aspects of linguistic form and its production, *can* be viewed as prestations, and thus as part of a political economy, not just a vehicle for thinking about one.

Conclusion

I began by mentioning Saussure and suggesting—as, indeed, it has become fashionable to do—that I would take some post-Saussurean, post-structuralist position, in regard to his segregation of the sign from the material world. Actually, part of this position is not so very novel. Anthropology has a long tradition of looking at the material objects exchanged in a cultural system partly in terms of their sign value. A good example would be Evans-Pritchard's discussion of cattle among the Nuer (Evans-Pritchard 1940, 1956). In some circumstances the sign-value of the Nuer ox can be so predominant, and its material substance so irrelevant, that you can substitute a cucumber for it. What I argue for here is, in a way, a parallel treatment of the verbal sign. Ultimately, the goal—which I do not pretend to have reached, though I hope to have moved in its direction—must be a more comprehensive conception of "value," so that the various kinds of sign-values and material values can be seen in their complex integration.

Thus, linguistic forms have relevance for the social scientist not only as part of a world of ideas, but also as part of a world of objects, economic transactions, and political interests. The verbal sign, I have argued, relates to a political economy in many ways: by denoting it; by indexing parts of it; by depicting it (in Peircean terms, the iconic function, illustrated here for Wolof praise-singing); and by taking part in it as an object of exchange. These multiple functions may all co-occur, because they merely reflect the multifunctionality of language in general.

Saussure's segregation of sign-value from the world of material values is linked to his focus on only one of language's functions—its role as vehicle for referential communication. To acknowledge that language has many functions, and therefore that signs relate to the material world in many ways, including as objects of exchange, is important to understanding language's role in a political economy. An opposition between "idealists" and "materialists" that assigns the study of language only to the former is—as social theorists increasingly recognize, on other grounds—a false dichotomy.

Notes

Acknowledgments. Earlier versions of portions of this paper were presented at the annual meetings of the American Anthropological Association in 1984 and 1986, as no. 7 in the *Working Papers of the Center for Psychosocial Studies* (Chicago, IL), at the University of Massachusetts/Boston, and at Brandeis University. For helpful comments I am grateful to the audiences at these meetings; to the anonymous reviewers for *American Ethnologist;* and to Annette Weiner, Michael Silverstein, Bill Hanks, and Paul Friedrich. Financial support for fieldwork in Senegal was provided by the National Institutes of Health, the National Science Foundation, and Brandeis University; I am also grateful for institutional support from the Institut Fondamental d'Afrique Noire and the Centre de Linguistique Appliqué de Dakar, and for the help and cooperation of Senegalese officials, consultants, and hosts.

1. See discussions in, for example, Coward and Ellis 1977 and Derrida 1972.
2. Unlike political scientists, apparently, many anthropologists make a close connection between the term "political economy" and debates over a Wallerstein-derived world-system approach, on which this paper takes no particular stand. One of the issues in the debate, however, is the degree of importance to be assigned to local social relations and their "culture" (I put the word in quotation marks since some writers contest its applicability). To the extent that anthropological views of culture have been bound up with language, then,

this paper contributes to the debate by considering the way we think about relations between linguistic phenomena and the forces of production.

3. See Hymes 1961 and 1973.

4. Those that reduce language to presuppositional indexicality are equally problematic. This criticism, differently worded, has been leveled at the writings of Bourdieu (see Thompson 1984).

5. Underlying this conception of language's role in social cooperation was Bloomfield's enthusiasm for behaviorist psychology. See his 1931 obituary of the psychologist A. P. Weiss, which draws a more explicit connection between language, its speakers' nervous systems, and cooperation among members of a speech community (1970:237–238).

6. But see his discussion, in the last chapter of *Language,* of the roles of traditional grammarians, schoolteachers, and administrators as supported by the conventions of linguistic standardization.

7. For a useful historical summary, see Weinreich, Labov, and Herzog 1968.

8. As regards the form of directives, this difference in settings is sometimes confused with matters of politeness or rank, I believe. For studies of directives in social and cultural context, see for example, Ervin-Tripp 1976 and Irvine 1980.

9. See, for example, Barth 1972 on the political integration of Pathan-speaking social segments into a Baluchi system. Despite the language difference, Barth argues, Pathan segments are easily attached to the Baluchi political hierarchy because a single bilingual spokesman suffices for the communicative needs of the political relationship and its economic arrangements. There is no need for the ordinary Pathan-speaker to convey personal opinions or discuss individual contributions, as (Barth suggests) might be required in a more egalitarian political system, such as is found among other Pathans.

10. "Index" is used here in the Peircean sense of that sign-function in which the sign represents its object by contiguity (as smoke is a sign of fire), rather than by resemblance (as with a picture of a fire) or by rules and conventions (as with the word "fire").

11. Although Labov's conception of "style" differs from that of other scholars, the general point—that variation marking groups and variation marking situations appear to be closely linked wherever we have the information to investigate the relationship—still holds, I believe. See Irvine 1985.

12. A similar contrast, however, might concern categorical versus variable application of a rule.

13. For a recent discussion of the language and culture of gender see Silverstein 1985. For an extended ethnographic example see Abu-Lughod 1986.

14. Fieldwork was carried out in Senegal in 1970–71, 1975, and (briefly) in 1977 and 1984.

15. The transcription of Wolof expressions is based on the phonemic system developed by the Centre de Linguistique Appliqué de Dakar and officially adopted by the Republic of Senegal in 1971. The system is phonetically fairly transparent: /waxu géér/ = [waxu geer]; /gewel/ = [gɛwɛl]; and so on.

16. The relation between *seeñ* and *lawbé* is complex. Yoro Dyao (Rousseau 1929, from a turn-of-the-century manuscript) briefly describes both groups; see also Kobès 1875. Abdoulaye Diop (1981) considers them to have been subcastes, but argues that the *seeñ* were eventually absorbed into a different low-caste category, not into the *lawbé*.

17. That is to say, Pulaar is a language distinct from any form of Wolof, whose existence and form owe nothing to Wolof as far as we know (though the two languages are geneti-

cally related), and which has both formal and functional completeness within the main communities of its speakers, the Tukulor and Fula. For Lawbé, it is historically and denotationally autonomous, but has an indexical value within the Wolof system.

18. Note that the village from which my description is mainly drawn is far from the Mauritanian border. In Wolof villages further north, or among Wolof-speakers in Mauritania itself, native speakers of Arabic would be much more conspicuous, and the relationship with them would, no doubt, alter the ways their language is thought of by the local Wolof population.

19. Villagers' competence in Arabic is almost entirely passive. They may recite formulaic prayers, and those who know Arabic best read texts and listen to religious speeches on the radio; but they compose nothing.

20. The views of Wolof city-dwellers might well have been quite different from this, even at the time. Wolof villagers acknowledged that French was more widely used in town, but they also claimed that city-dwellers were likely to be people of dubious ethnic, caste, and moral background.

21. Senegal gained its independence from France in 1960. Ties with France remained close, however, and a sizable French population stayed on—including, locally, a community of French technical personnel. For some time after independence, therefore, many villagers apparently still thought of French in colonial frameworks—whence the statements I heard in 1970. In subsequent years the French population in Senegal dropped sharply, especially in rural areas outside the tourist zone.

22. See also Silverstein's (n.d.b) discussion of comments on British regional dialects by the Queen's English Society.

23. Silverstein (n.d.b) calls this "commoditization."

24. Again, see Thompson's (1984) critique.

25. For a Mexican example involving the autonomy of Mexicano-speaking peasant communities, see Hill 1985.

26. The acquisition of varieties of Wolof itself should not be left out of the economic picture, although this part of the linguistic "market" operates in a different way (further evidence, presumably, of the lack of integration of the Senegalese "linguistic market").

27. See Silla 1966.

28. See Putnam (1975:246) on the transmission of reference, and Kripke 1972 on the transmission of proper names, from performative nomination or "baptism" through subsequent, warranted referential usage.

29. See also Weiner 1984.

30. The former patient does, however, bear a nonverbal sign of the illness, such as a tic, a scar, or a recurrent cough (Sansom 1982:183).

31. See Irvine 1975, and Part II below. These attitudes are part of a larger sociolinguistic ideology connecting griots (and the lower ranks in general) with noisy activity and the high ranks with quiet, sometimes inert, solidity.

32. Except insofar as it might seem funny to see Americans or Europeans behaving like griots and their patrons.

33. Though I refer principally to "traditional" activities, and have not space to consider the complexities introduced by contract labor and "modern" trades, patronage and values generated through personalistic networks are important there also.

34. Actually, another proper type of compliment focuses on the addressee's religious goodness and piety. In practice, however, these compliments seem usually to merge with the praise-singing type, "goodness" being evidenced by birth and generosity.

35. This is something of an oversimplification. In some circumstances a speaker draws on only some features of the register, not others.

36. Some scholars consider that what the sign may be exchanged for, and what it stands for, are the same: hence Saussure's analogy between money and language, and the connection drawn between *valeur* and *signification*. I believe the equation is problematic, however, particularly as regards the analogy with money. Because money is a system that is maximally structured by exchange-value and minimally by use-value, it makes a tempting analogy for language if one conceives of linguistic signs as those that are maximally structured by denotational sign-value in a system and minimally by any other kind of function. But these forms of "value" may still be distinguished. Moreover, the analogy between money and language may make it difficult to conceive of any other relation between them.

References

Abu-Lughod, Lila. 1986. Veiled Sentiments: Honor and Poetry in a Bedouin Society. Berkeley: University of California Press.

Barth, Fredrik. 1972. Ethnic Processes on the Pathan-Baluch Boundary. *In* Directions in Sociolinguistics. J. Gumperz and D. Hymes, eds. pp. 454–564. New York: Holt, Rinehart, and Winston.

Bloomfield, Leonard. 1933. Language. New York: Holt, Rinehart, and Winston.

———. 1970[1931]. Obituary of A. P. Weiss. *In* Leonard Bloomfield Anthology. C. F. Hockett, ed. Bloomington: Indiana University Press.

Bourdieu, Pierre. 1977. The Economics of Linguistic Exchanges. Social Science Information 16(6):645–668.

———. 1982. Ce que parler veut dire. Paris: Fayard.

Coward, Rosalind, and John Ellis. 1977. Language and Materialism. London: Routledge and Kegan Paul.

Derrida, Jacques. 1972. Positions. Paris: Editions de Minuit.

Diop, Abdoulaye-Bara. 1981. La société Wolof: tradition et changement. Paris: Karthala.

Erickson, Frederick, and Jeffrey Shultz. 1979. The Counselor as Gatekeeper: Social Interaction in Interviews. New York: Academic Press.

Ervin-Tripp, Susan. 1976. Is Sybil There? The Structure of American English Directives. Language in Society 5:25–66.

Evans-Pritchard, E. E. 1940. The Nuer. Oxford: Oxford University Press.

———. 1956. Nuer Religion. Oxford: Oxford University Press.

Goodenough, Ward. 1965. Rethinking Status and Role. *In* The Relevance of Models for Social Anthropology. ASA Monographs no. 1. M. Banton, ed. pp. 1–24. London: Tavistock.

Gumperz, John J. 1962. Types of Linguistic Communities. Anthropological Linguistics 4:28–40. [1971, Language in Social Groups. pp. 97–113. Stanford, CA: Stanford University Press.]

———. 1968. The Speech Community. *In* International Encyclopedia of the Social Sciences, vol. 9. David L. Sills, ed. pp. 381–386 New York: Macmillan. [1971, Language in Social Groups. pp. 114–128. Stanford, CA: Stanford University Press.]

Gumperz, John J., ed. 1982. Language and Social Identity. Cambridge: Cambridge University Press.

Halliday, M. A. K. 1976. Anti-Languages. American Anthropologist 78:570–584.

Hill, Jane H. 1985. The Grammar of Consciousness and the Consciousness of Grammar. American Ethnologist 12:725–737.

Hymes, Dell H. 1961. Functions of Speech: The Evolutionary Approach. *In* Anthropology and Education. F. C. Gruber, ed. pp. 55–83. Philadelphia: University of Pennsylvania Press.

———. 1964. Introduction: Toward Ethnographies of Communication. *In* The Ethnography of Communication. Gumperz and Hymes, eds. American Anthropologist 66 (6), part 2:1–34. [1974, Foundations in Sociolinguistics. pp. 3–27. Philadelphia: University of Pennsylvania Press.]

———. 1967. Why Linguistics Needs the Sociologist. Social Research 34 (4):632–647.

———. 1971. On Communicative Competence. *In* Sociolinguistics. J. B. Pride and J. Holmes, eds. pp. 269–293. Harmondsworth: Penguin.

———. 1973. Speech and Language: On the Origins and Foundations of Inequality in Speaking. Daedalus (summer): 59–86. [also published as Language as a Human Problem. Bloomfield and Haugen, eds.]

———. 1974. Foundations in Sociolinguistics. Philadelphia: University of Pennsylvania Press.

Irvine, Judith T. 1975. Wolof Speech Styles and Social Status. Working Papers in Sociolinguistics 23. Austin: Southwest Education Laboratory.

———. 1978a. When is Genealogy History? Wolof Genealogies in Comparative Perspective. American Ethnologist 5:651–674.

———. 1978b. Wolof Noun Classification: The Social Setting of Divergent Change. Language in Society 7:37–64.

———. 1980. How Not to Ask a Favor in Wolof. Papers in Linguistics 13:3–50.

———. 1982. Language and Affect: Some Cross-Cultural Issues. *In* Contemporary Perceptions of Language: Interdisciplinary Dimensions. H. Byrnes, ed. pp. 31–47. (GURT 1982, Georgetown University Round Table in Language and Linguistics.) Washington, DC: Georgetown University Press.

———. 1985. Status and Style in Language. Annual Review of Anthropology 14:557–581.

Kobès, Mgr. A. 1875. Dictionnaire wolof-français. Saint-Joseph de Ngasobil: Mission Catholique.

Kochman, Thomas, ed. 1972. Rappin' and Stylin' Out: Communication in Urban Black America. Urbana: University of Illinois Press.

Kripke, Saul. 1972. Naming and Necessity. *In* Semantics of Natural Language, 2nd ed. D. Davidson and G. Harmon, eds. pp. 253–355. Dordrecht, Holland: D. Reidel.

Labov, William. 1972. Sociolinguistic Patterns. Philadelphia: University of Pennsylvania Press.

Malinowski, Bronislaw. 1978[1935]. Coral Gardens and Their Magic. New York: Dover.

Mertz, Elizabeth, and Richard Parmentier, eds. 1985. Semiotic Mediation. Orlando, FL: Academic Press.

Nadel, S. F. 1957. The Theory of Social Structure. London: Cohen and West.

Putnam, Hilary. 1975. The Meaning of Meaning. *In* Mind, Language and Reality: Philosophical Papers 2. H. Putnam, ed. pp. 215–271. Cambridge: Cambridge University Press.

Reisman, Karl. 1974. Contrapuntal Conversations in an Antiguan Village. *In* Explorations in the Ethnography of Speaking. R. Bauman and J. Sherzer, eds. pp. 110–124. New York: Cambridge University Press.

Rossi-Landi, Ferruccio. 1983. Language as Work and Trade: A Semiotic Homology for Linguistics and Economics. South Hadley, MA: Bergin and Garvey.

Rousseau, R. 1929. Le Sénégal d'autrefois. Etude sur le Oualo. Cahiers d'Yoro Dyao. Bulletin du Comité d'Etudes Historiques et Scientifiques de l' A. O. F. 12 (1–2):133–211.

Sansom, Basil. 1982. The Sick Who do Not Speak. *In* Semantic Anthropology. ASA Monographs no. 22. D. Parkin, ed. pp. 183–196. London: Academic Press.

Saussure, Ferdinand de. 1966. Course in General Linguistics. Ch. Bally and A. Sechehaye, eds. Wade Baskin, trans. New York: McGraw-Hill. [original publication in 1916].

Silla, Ousmane. 1966. Persistence des castes dans la société wolof contemporaine. Bulletin de l'IFAN séries B, 28(3–4):731–769.

Silverstein, Michael. 1980. The Three Faces of "Function": Preliminaries to a Psychology of Language. *In* Proceedings of a Working Conference on the Social Foundations of Language and Thought. M. Hickmann, ed. pp. 1–12. Chicago: Center for Psychosocial Studies.

———. 1984. The Functional Stratification of Language in Ontogenesis. *In* Culture, Communication, and Cognition: Vygotskian Perspectives. J. V. Wertsch, ed. New York: Cambridge University Press.

———. 1985. Language and the Culture of Gender: At the Intersection of Structure, Usage, and Ideology. *In* Semiotic Mediation. E. Mertz and R. Parmentier, eds. New York: Academic Press.

———. n.d.a. The "Value" of Objectual Language. Paper Presented at the 1984 Annual Meeting of the American Anthropological Association.

———. n.d.b. "Standardization and Metaphors of Linguistic Hegemony. Paper Presented at the 1986 Annual Meeting of the American Anthropological Association.

Thompson, John, ed. 1984. Symbolic Violence: Language and Power in the Writings of Pierre Bourdieu. *In* Studies in the Theory of Ideology. pp. 42–72. Cambridge, England: Polity Press.

Weiner, Annette. 1984. From Words to Objects to Magic: "Hard Words" and the Boundaries of Social Interaction. *In* Dangerous Words: Language and Politics in the Pacific. D. Brenneis and F. Myers, eds. pp. 161–191. New York: New York University Press.

Weinreich, U., W. Labov, and M. Herzog. 1968. Empirical Foundations for a Theory of Language Change. *In* Directions for Historical Linguistics. W. Lehman, ed. pp. 95–188. Austin: University of Texas Press.

Woolard, Kathryn A. 1985. Language Variation and Cultural Hegemony: Toward an Integration of Sociolinguistic and Social Theory. American Ethnologist 12:738–748.

14

Monoglot "Standard" in America: Standardization and Metaphors of Linguistic Hegemony

MICHAEL SILVERSTEIN

The evidence of societal plurilingualism is everywhere about us, on urban public transportation, in classrooms, wherever service-sector personnel are encountered, and on lettuce farms and across vast tracts set aside as reservations. Yet, since we live in a nation-state perpetually trying to constitute of itself an officially unified society with a uniform public Culture, one of the strongest lines of demarcation of that public Culture is linguistic, in the form of advocacy of or opposition to something that, in keeping with terminologized usage, I shall call The Standard. It is obvious that advocacy of The Standard has, in certain contexts, posed problems for those for whom the linguistic realm should be but a special case of their more widely-held, or generalized, longings for an ideal pluralism, or egalitarianism, or even free-market consumerist smorgasbordism as a construction of the American sociopolitical *telos*. And it should also be obvious that, once debate is focused on linguistic issues in terms of The Standard versus whatever purportedly polar opposites, then the fact that the situation is conceptualized in terms of The Standard indicates what we might term its hegemonic domination over the field of controversy, no matter what position is taken with respect to it.

Indeed, we might say that we live in a society with a culture of monoglot standardization underlying the constitution of our linguistic community and affecting the structure of our various and overlapping speech communities. I want to explore some of the dimensions of this culture of monoglot Standard, and to show how the essentially sociopolitical problems for societal plurilingualism present themselves in its terms. In this, the work is part of the linguistic anthropology of modern American society.

I have been using several terms in technical senses; these need definition, or at least characterization. Anthropologists speak of a culture (with a small c) as a way of orienting themselves to a structure of symbolically-enactable values implicit in the organization and interpretability (significance) of social action, that is, of interpersonally consequential behavior and thought. Hence, a culture of monoglot standardization (or Standard) can be demonstrated by showing the ways that this ideal underlies people's understanding of linguistic usage in their community, how it lies behind, or is presupposed by, the way people understand sociolinguistic behavior to be an enactment of a collective order (social or "natural" or divine or whatever). Societies have cultures, and societies are, in this sense, gradiently cohesive as groups of people.

One aspect of society-hood is being a speech community: sharing a set of norms or regularities for interaction by means of language(s). It was in this sense that Benjamin Lee Whorf ([1941]1956:138) coined the term "Standard Average European" for that set of regularities in linguistic usage, particularly "fashions of speaking" about things, that were common in gradiently characterizable degree across all of Western Europe and many parts of Central and Eastern Europe as well. A speech community need not have only one "language," then, in the normal understanding of this term.

By contrast, a linguistic community, such as the kind we refer to a culture of standardization, is a group of people who, in their implicit sense of the regularities of linguistic usage, are united in adherence to the idea that there exists a functionally differentiated norm for using their "language" denotationally (to represent or describe things), the inclusive range of which the best language users are believed to have mastered in the appropriate way. There may be no actual historical individual who, in fact, does; that is not the point. It is allegiance to the concept of such a functionally differentiated denotational norm of usage, said to define the "best" speakers of language L, that marks membership in a specific linguistic community for language L, and a sense of continuity with others in it. Note that speakers of Arabic belong to a single linguistic community—with properties somewhat the inverse of Whorf's European case—by virtue of equivalent local functional differentiation (in conditions we call 'diglossia' [Ferguson 1959; 1968]) of all the dialectal forms of Arabic from Koranic and Classical Arabic, which are usable by the "best" speakers of Arabic in appropriate situations as the denotational code *par excellence*, the mode of correct or truthful communications about what is apprehensible in God's universe. Yet, of course, there are many different speech communities—especially of the dialectal sort—in which Arabic linguistic community members take part. And, it should be recalled, both types of community, speech community and linguistic community, are gradient notions, the characteristics of which interact in specific ways in different sociohistorical conditions.

Standardization, then, is a phenomenon in a linguistic community in which institutional maintenance of certain valued linguistic practices—in theory, fixed— acquires an explicitly-recognized hegemony over the definition of the community's norm. People defer—on grounds varied as a function of their positions in the community, to be sure—to the authority of such institutions to articulate the community's norm. Hence, "best" users of the language, that is, at least, those who would be "best," strive to achieve this Standard linguistic practice, the control of which as part of the functionally differentiated norm becomes an index of "best speakerhood." As Leonard Bloomfield (whose centenary we celebrate this year) in effect noted in 1927, the Saussurean or Durkheimian linguistic norm is a universal condition for linguistic communities, while the existence of Standards is very much a function of having hegemonic institutions, such as those that control writing/printing and reading as channels of exemplary communication with language, the operation of which in a society establishes and maintains the Standard. So much so, Bloomfield pointed out, that people who speak Standardized languages (note: not, necessarily, people who speak Standard) often cannot even conceive of there being a linguistic norm in our technical sense—and hence, for them, a "language" as opposed to a "dialect" or "patois" or whatever—for languages lacking the institutionalized paraphernalia of Standardization, such as enforcement of a conventionalized writing system, or explicit communication (e.g., through schools) of a tradition of normative grammar. Even though such languages may be highly and transparently articulated into a set of context-specific registers, bespeaking subtle regularities of usage, may manifest all the communicative properties of one's own language, and may be sociohistorically specific to a cultural tradition identifiable in all other ways, still, to many speakers of standardized languages, non-standardized ones do not quite seem to be "real" languages, which, ironically enough, are for them thought to come in "naturally" standardized conditions of "objectively" distinct systems of norms.

There is, obviously, an enormous complexity to the functional diversity of language in the several American speech communities. The linguistic community of American monoglot Standard English can thus be situated in several dimensions of contrast simultaneously. For example, with respect to what Gumperz (1968:383) has called the "dialectal" (including sociolectal) variability of English linguistic usages comprehended in the partition into speech communities, Standard is endowed with claims to superiority as a "superposed" register for use in those contexts of interaction that count in society. In this sense, Standard is, as it were, the absence of "dialect," and its superiority as such is seen to emerge from its positively-specifiable attributes. With respect to the existence of plurilingualism in the nation-state, Standard English is differentiated from mere norm-governed languages (frequently not recognized as languages, as I noted above), from non-written norm-governed languages (even worse), and from languages the local forms of which are defined in relation to heterochthonous norms (even Standards), e.g., New World Spanish or French seen in relation to Castillian or Parisian insofar as understood to be Spanish or French, respectively. In this sense, Standard English becomes the unifying emblem of nation-statehood insofar as linguistic community is swept up into participation in its cultural expression.

In all these respects, the culture of Standard is aggressively hegemonic, dominating all these linguistic situations with an understanding of other linguistic us-

ages as locatable only in terms of Standard. There is thus always an interested ideology that rationalizes these sociolinguistic situations with a metaphoric model
for interpretation, in which a variant of the cultural drama of standardization acts
itself out. It is not the particular side of any issue that concerns us here, so much
as the characteristics common to and implicit in the structuring of various arguments about such issues. Let us look at a couple of examples.

We find, for example, the pro-Standard free-market economistic variant articulated by Milton and Rose Friedman in their book, *Free to Choose* (1980:25):

> No one decided what words should be admitted into the language, what the rules of
> grammar should be, which words should be adjectives, which nouns.
> . . .
>   How did language develop? In much the same way as an economic order develops
> through the market—out of the voluntary interaction of individuals, in this case seek-
> ing to trade ideas or information or gossip rather than goods and services with one an-
> other. One or another meaning was attributed to a word, or words were added as the
> need arose. Grammatical usages developed and were later codified into rules. Two par-
> ties who want to communicate with one another both benefit from coming to a com-
> mon agreement about the words they use. As a wider and wider circle of people find it
> advantageous to communicate with one another, a common usage spreads and is codi-
> fied in dictionaries. At no point is there any coercion, any central planner who has power
> to command, though in more recent times government school systems have played an
> important role in standardizing usage.

If we concern ourselves not with either the factuality or coherence of the points
made in this text, but with what it tells us about the view of language from within
the American culture of standardization, three general properties emerge in the
specifics, all relevant to my discussion further on.

First, the argument about the historical emergence of codification or standardization as a social process is displaced to the plane of the functional utility of language as a means of representation or instrument of denotation. How Standard
becomes the mode of optimal denotation is the central issue of the exercise of explanation. Note, by the way, that other than the classificatory terms alluding to
(normative) grammar, namely *noun* and *adjective*, the entire discussion of lan-
guage-as-denotational-instrumentality is cast in terms of words and word meanings, in other words the very folk view of language as a grammarless collection of
nomenclature—word-as-forms standing-for things-as-content—that Saussure
(1916:97, 158) and Boas (1911:67–73) long ago set in perspective as folk rational-
izations. In fact, generalizing from their insights, the modern, semiotic study of
the functional grounding of language and its structures, predicts that folk views
about the functions of language will characteristically center on the functional capacity of words and expressions as the salient, formulable interest of native speakers in their language (see Silverstein 1979, 1981, 1985a for discussion and references), one of those functions particularly emphasized in our folk linguistic
tradition being denotation.

Second, note that in this argument the social processes of communication are naturalized in two specific ways, and hence doubly anchored by reduction to a non- or prelinguistic realm of things: individual practical rationality seeking some kind of optimal contractarian "fit" individuals can negotiate freely among themselves for the coding relationship between linguistic words and the extralinguistic "reality" they represent, but do not affect. The history of standardization is, in this view, the process of contractarian search for "a common agreement" about the denotational value of words, the right fit naturally being acceded to by "a wider and wider circle of people" purely for (presumably economically important) convenience. This process of cumulative individual "rational choice" to participate in the "wider and wider circle of people" (namely, aggregate of individuals) using words with particular denotational values, seems to have no basis in structures of authority or "linguistic division of labor" (Putnam 1975), nor social consequences other than whatever flows indirectly from the ease of informational coding postulated to underlie and to motivate the process. These two forms of naturalization, then, anchor the processes of standardization in something outside of the social organization of language use itself, namely in psychological properties and propensities of the individual users, and in properties and things to be denoted that are independently in the world "out there." Standardization, with its accompanying codification, is really the long-term consequence of the first set of factors "solving" the functional problem presented to language as a system of denotation by the second set of factors.[1]

Third, this argument, having naturalized, as it were, the processes of standardization, presents the rise of social phenomena with "power to command" over language, such as "government school systems" (and, we might argue, dictionaries that are part of the institutional paraphernalia), as merely the natural, or rational, endpoint in concrete institutional form, of the otherwise timeless forces of denotational optimization. So institutions of standardization are created as merely the endpoints of the natural, evolutionary working of the "invisible hand," the better to effectuate what is already going on in more informal, non-institutional terms. Institutions in this sense are also "natural" phenomena in that they respond to needs already and independently present in the processes they affect/effect, but presumably help the individuals caught up in such process the better and perhaps more efficiently to realize the *telos* to which they are in any case already tending. The rhetoric of naturalization has thus moved to the justification of undeniably social institutions as aids to the realization of every individual's natural linguistic project.

Compare now a discussion that starts from opposite predispositions to value the effects of monoglot standardization, and which is couched in a different metaphorical framework for naturalization. The physicist Freeman Dyson (1979:223–24) puts his model and its rationale biologically, where the lesson of the evolution of species gives the proof of the functionality of his position valuing the greatest diversity of dialect and language:

In biology, a clone is the opposite of a clade. A clade is a group of populations sharing a common origin but exhibiting genetic diversity so wide that they are barred from inter-breeding. A clone is a single population in which all individuals are genetically identical. Clades are the stuff of which great leaps forward in evolution are made. Clones are evo-lutionary dead ends, slow to adapt and slow to evolve. Clades can occur only in organ-isms that reproduce sexually. Clones in nature are typically asexual.

All this, too, has its analog in the domain of linguistics. A linguistic clone is a monoglot culture, a population with a single language sheltered from alien words and alien thoughts. Its linguistic inheritance, propagated asexually from generation to gen-eration, tends to become gradually impoverished. The process of impoverishment is easy to see in the declining vocabulary of the great writers of English from Shakespeare to Dickens, not to speak of Faulkner and Hemingway. As the centuries go by, words be-come fewer and masterpieces of literature become rarer. Linguistic rejuvenation requires the analog of sexual reproduction, the mixture of languages and cross-fertilization of vocabularies. The great flowering of English culture followed the sexual union of French with Anglo-Saxon in Norman England. The clade of Romance languages did not spring from Latin alone but from the cross-fertilization of Latin with the languages of the local barbarian tribes as the empire disintegrated. In human culture as in biology, a clone is a dead end, a clade is a promise of immortality.

Are we to be a clade or a clone? This is perhaps the central problem in humanity's fu-ture. In other words, how are we to make our social institutions flexible enough to pre-serve our precious biological and cultural diversity? There are some encouraging signs that our society is growing more flexible than it used to be. Many styles of behavior are now allowed which thirty or forty years ago were forbidden. In many countries where minority languages were once suppressed, they are now tolerated or even encouraged. Thirty-five years after my visit to Llandudno, I stayed at the house of a friend in Cardiff, the capital city of the English conquerors in Wales, and I was happy to see that the chil-dren of my Bengali-speaking host were learning Welsh in the Cardiff city schools. Since they were already fluent in English, Bengali and Arabic, they took Welsh in stride, with-out difficulty. These children were displaying in a spectacular fashion the gift of cultural and linguistic plasticity with which nature has endowed our species. So long as we con-tinue to raise such children, we shall be in no danger of becoming a clone.

As can be seen, cultural flowering follows upon linguistic health, measured in terms of vocabulary, the folk denotational units of language. The unhealthy, "clone"-like state of a language is, for Dyson, reflected in the purported vocabu-lary-size of various writers, presumably at the apex of language use in their re-spective linguistic communities, and hence an index of the potential of the lan-guage in which they write. And the processes of recommended linguistic "clade" formation seem to rest on some kind of intermixture, of "cross-fertilization" be-tween languages, or more particularly between the speech, in each case, of a na-tion/race of "Culture" and one that, in the English and more generally Western European folklore, is considered more on the order of "local barbarian tribes," such as "Anglo-Saxon" vis-à-vis French, Celts vis-à-vis Romans, Welsh vis-à-vis English, etc. Notions of hybrid robustness in such linguistic husbandry seem to be underlying. Hence, again here, social institutions are to foster that robust state of speech by being made "flexible enough to preserve our precious biological and cultural diversity," as for example teaching the local language—here, Welsh in Cardiff—alongside the official and standardized one. (What goes for distinct languages goes, of course, for local dialect vs. Standard language even more.)

It is easily seen that in each of three respects, both the Friedmans' and Dyson's accounts of monoglot language standardization have certain recurrent general themes, despite the differences of their metaphoric models of language standardization or its opposite. They both displace the problem onto the functional plane of word denotation, seeing this as the problem of language *par excellence*. They both "naturalize," as I have termed it, the processes of standardization or diversification as ones that play themselves out with reference to aggregates of individuals, the advantages or disadvantages to whom of the one or the other course of events—wider circles of people with whom one can communicate, enhanced ability to produce literary masterpieces, linguistic/cultural vigor, etc.—are at issue. Through such naturalization, extralinguistic properties or attitudes of individuals can be read in and from their participation in standardization/diversification processes. Hence, third, both these approaches rationalize the existence or operation of social institutions promoting, authorizing, or enforcing standardization/diversification as potentially enhancing, perfecting, or enabling the individual to achieve personal consonance with the "natural" tendencies advocated.

It is noteworthy as a confirmation of the cultural nature of views of standardization/diversification that some set of variants of one or more of these themes, similarly internally coherent (or at least mutually reinforcing), appears again and again in the hundreds of articles in newspapers and magazines, advertisements for Standard-related services and products, letters to the editor, advice columns, etc., that I have been collecting and examining for the last several years.[2] The sheer number of these items alone, particularly in the major source for systematic collection, The Chicago *Tribune*, during the period in question demonstrates that the culture of standardization is a dominant mode in which the society is articulating itself to itself.

More particularly, we can discern in the corpus a very focused and socially locatable construal of Standard English in relation to all other possible forms of speech. It is what I would term the *commoditization* of Standard English and, in relation to it, of alternative forms of speech—language use, in short swept up into the brisk commerce of personal socio-economic identity. In any cultural ideology of language, to be sure, it is expectable that language use become an objectified focus of rationalization, an explicit object of the actors' subjectivities and their intersubjective understandings communicable as social thought. But more than this, we discover an *objectualization,* as I have called it (Silverstein 1984), of language and its use, in which language acquires a "thinginess" such that the properties language takes on are continuous with those of other objects in the culture. Hence, linguistic forms and their deployability-in-context can take on the characteristics of sometimes alienable, sometimes inalienable possessions and their personally-controlled display or even bestowal. Such objectualized language becomes an important adjunct to all other forms of indexicals of identity, and indeed becomes metricized—turned into a gradient measurable—in relation to them, an indexable as well as indexical in a culture that literalized the enactment of the metaphor of personal values. As a commodity, Standard English in particular can be made the object of a brisk commerce in goods-and-services for which experts make themselves available (authorities or connoisseurs in the humanistic social fields, therapists/doctors or technicians in the scientific ones, etc.) and advertisers become focal personnel of personal decision-making to acquire the desired commodity for a price. Witness to all this, reporters have become bearers of the glad tidings of availability to the concerned market, secondarily repeating the advertising messages as a surrogate "educated public" through which news of the commodity's availability is being spread.

What I am suggesting is that the traditional "*questione della lingua*" that we have always had in the United States is being transformed by a culture of language use, in particular of Standard English usage, that is changing both as to the kinds of social communication its enactment makes possible, and as to the locus of concern and enactment, the locus, as it were, of the cultural "action." From the material examined, it appears that the commoditized sense of Standard and the anxieties revealed in practical discourse about it have moved rather decidedly into the institutional setting of corporate business—where commoditization is indeed the mode of construing culture. It is the setting in which plying one's product or profession has become sometimes indistinguishable from displaying one's personal value. Briefly put, it is the world of yuppiedom.[3]

In this, as in any institutional sphere, culture manifests itself through enactable figures, inscribing tropes of "praxis," or pragmatic tropes, in the very communicative modalities of social action. Possession-of-Standard vs. lack-of-Standard, it seems, is being made culturally enactable through tropes of personal value or worth, where lack-of-Standard is gradiently negative with respect to gradiently positive possession-of-Standard. As we shall see below, though there are many specific commercial and non-commercial variants on this theme, they all turn possession-of-Standard into a realizable asset that can be achieved so as to increase overall personal value in one or another recognizable symbolic paradigm. Lack-of-Standard, by contrast, is a lack only against a background assumption that Standard is "natural" if not neutral in some sense (recall here the Friedmans' Just-So story). And indeed, this naturalization of the commodity that people are able to acquire becomes a key leitmotif underlying specific advocacies of Standard.[4]

How does this process manifest itself? Let us examine the materials with a focus on the three aspects of cultural construction of language as a problem I have introduced above. Let us see thereby that general forces of culture are at work here in a specific sociohistorical setting of institutions that are increasingly formative of contemporary American life.

First, let us take the issue of referential displacement. If language basically names things "out there," it becomes important to name them correctly, that is, not too few distinctions, not too many, but to get it, like Goldilocks, ju. . .st right. Standard English, it turns out, does just that, or at least does so better than anything else available as a variant. As the playwright Ossie Davis put it on Ted Koppel's *Nightline* on September 3, 1986,

> it's absolutely essential that there is a distinction between one thing and another, and those distinctions can only be expressed in a language that is capable of discerning the difference between one thing and another. . . . [I]f we lose the value of the words we use, then we can't clearly describe what it is we want to describe. . . . [T]ruth is absolutely essential to the practice of [life], and if we lose truth, we lose our sense of direction. . . . Language is the road map of experience, and if we tell ourselves lies and let ourselves be misguided we can go off the edge and never come back.

Adds George Will:

> Confusion creeps into language on tiny little cat feet like the fog, and before long you're in a fog. . . . [T]he issue here really is truth, our capacity to accurately describe [—uh oh, Mr. Will, a split infinitive confounding Truth!—] real states of the world. . . . It's really the slovenliness, the small incremental carelessness that bothers me most.

One might as well be listening to post-Baconian Puritan preachers talking about the road to salvation, for truthfulness, a form of referential cleanliness, is indeed next to Godliness. Hence the moral indignation, indeed outrage, that various writers can work themselves up to venting about non-Standard linguistic practices. And on the other hand, we must, as modern, rational people, defend that language that gives us access to the unvarnished, non-euphemistic, "scientific-objective," as it were, Truth. The values of technology, how science manifests itself in the corporate world of commoditization, are indeed on the same side as those of religious fervor, just as they were in seventeenth century England.[5]

It is Standard as Logos: numerous columnists and other occasional writers, with zero actual expertise, devote great numbers of column inches to talking of the "obfuscations" of truthful reality evidenced in social dialects, chic or trendy usages, and so forth. In one way or another, every report on what become from this point of view variants of "good, clear, Standard English" is presented in compatible language, in which non-Standards of the 'dialect' [= geographical dialect] or ethnic [e.g., Black] English variety are denotationally impoverished with respect to the more "truth-full" Standard, and technical jargon, such as lawyers' English, or economists', or other scientists' English are hyper-rich—nitpicking, if you will—with respect to Standard.

Thus, note that every popular presentation of regional accents, especially phonological variation, portrays the defects of the accent, with respect to Standard, as the cause of "confusion" and lack of "clarity." Indeed, "clarity" of expression is foremost among the rationalizable attributes of Standard, as our quoted disquisition on Truth demonstrated, and threats to that clarity come in ethnic-, regional-, gender-, and class-based deviations from it. *The New York Times*, for example (W. K. Stevens, *NYT* 21/VII/85, p.14), notes that

> Mr. Labov tells of a New York family that was sharply criticized by the neighborhood children for giving their son a girl's name. The name was Ian, which is how the children all pronounced Ann.

Again, note the theory underlying the charming reports that abound in the press where a particular phonological "accent" is the topic (and generally the cause of someone's making a bundle by writing a joke-book on it). Generally, the theme is the charm of the humor in confusion, as demonstrated by the puns induced between the "accented" pronunciation and how the written form of a word would be read off in Standard spelling pronunciation:

> "Ah speck yore paved with me." [I expect you're peeved with me.]
> "He made a heir at second base." [He made a(n) error at second base.]
> "Yew main to tell me yew paid four dollars for that quart of pint."
> [You mean to tell me you paid $4 for that quart of paint?]
> (quoted from "Larnin' the lingo fer trip to Taxes," by K. Biffle, Chicago *Tribune*, 18/VI/85, sec.5, pp. 1,5)

Such devices underscore the fact that for the population in the culture of Standardization, accented, positively-marked deviations have something of the quality of *malapropisms,* which are, of course, embarrassing even if charming gaffes in self-presentation as someone able to speak seriously and clearly.

But this serious and (lexically) clear speech can go too far, as in what is termed "Econspeak" in one report ("The only patter that matters in Washington," Bill Neikirk, Chicago *Tribune*, 7/XI/85), or lawyers' language ("It's perfectly clear: lawyers obfuscate," H. Witt, Chicago *Tribune*, 9/X/84, sec.2, p.9). Like a linguistic Frankenstein-monster, technical terminology and patterns of (lexical) expression are seen to have gone wild, outwitting or at least hampering humans who use them. Language, in this sense, can outwit its users; verbally splitting hairs with too much technical terminology can render us the unwilling but helpless sorcerer's apprentices awash in misguided thought.[6] At the same time, there is a sinister side to the *purposeful* use of bejargoned language, governmentese and other forms of obfuscation, "cover-up" language, which is reported as a crime against *truth,* and thus a crime against what we might term the "Standard reality" of rational persons-in-the-street.[7] Professionals, thus, doctors, lawyers, bureaucrats, are being subjected to courses and tutorials that show them how to write and speak with "cleaner, simpler, more vivid" language—like stripping away encrusted and nonfunctional muck, one supposes, as we see always in toothpaste, mouthwash, shampoo, and other such advertisements, or perhaps a form of linguistic *Bauhaus* modernism to renovate the mansions of the mind. Such language will be closer, of course, to one's ideas of generalized Standard, which surely, the argument goes, suffices to get across even the most complex concepts, if, that is, they are clean, and clear, and honestly to be communicated.

This valorization of the "just right" denotational Standard by having the "just right," accentless pronunciation and "just right" lexical expression by no means occurs in a culturally-construed social vacuum. Indeed, an elaborate consciousness of the nature of variability-around-the-Standard informs the material I have examined and the social processes of definition and differentiation of types of linguistic variants. In the particular social sector for which the greatest commoditization of Standard seems to have taken place, the urban paraprofessionals and rapidly-upwardly-mobile professionals, a "story," as it were, has to be fashioned *about the commodity* as an item of social transactions, giving it values that emerge in native social theory from objectifications of the pragmatics of linguistic usage of Standard and variant forms of language. This is what we would term a *folk meta-pragmatics*, an aspect of the constant, ongoing semiotics of language use: as for any form of social behavior that operates through pragmatic codes, it is the means of the participants' coming-to-grips with the problem of construing the effectiveness and meaningfulness of the events in which they (and here, we) take part. For language as a pragmatic (indexical) code in SAE linguistic communities, as I have elsewhere argued (Silverstein 1979, 1985a, 1985b), the folk meta-pragmatics generally consists of two kinds of semiotic movements: folk-extensionalization of indexical (pragmatically enacted) distinctions through the code of denotation, and folk-intensionalization of the distinctions among the deflected—or denotationally recoded—duplex sign-complexes (leading to what Barthes (1967:41–42) calls "refunctionalization" for objects of utility in general) that remotivates the indexical code as a schema of representation of (naturally) iconic value. The use of now denotationally-linked indexicals becomes emblematic of one's relation to the commodity and its sphere of values.

The first semiotic movement is the apprehension of some usage-marked differentiation of situation through forms and categories of a denotational code. In this way, the denotational code is seen to "extend," i.e., point directly to, the particular situational differentiation in question; the use-marking thus differentiates something that is construable as independently "out there" in the situation (were it not; we could not extend it denotationally, could we now?). The second semiotic movement is finding some motivation in the relationship of use-marking sign to its correlatively indexed situational differentiation by seeing an analogous property or set of properties, predicable of both, that shows why the one stands for the other. As is readily apparent, both of these movements are "naturalizing" in just the sense we introduced earlier; the one understands the situational differentiations to have existed independent of the use-marking that seems to enact it, while the other finds that the use-marking is "natural" for the particular situational differentiation as so apprehended because there is some common property, or at least likeness, about the use-marking and the situational differentiation. These semiotic movements of interpretation and construal, moreover, operate in both directions, in the ongoing processes of production and comprehension of our own and of others' social behavior.

The use in context of what are apprehended as forms of Standard English versus any variant forms of English, or of Standard English versus another language can thus become such a pragmatic code, in folk terms at least initially the "how" rather than the "what" of saying something.[8] But immediately one wishes to "place" use of Standard vis-à-vis such alternative uses, one comes across other social facts of variation that comprise the situational differentiations enacted by the usage of one kind of form over another, facts of social identity of speakers and hearers in situations of use of language, facts of differential influence or power correlative with such social differentiation in society, and facts about participants' commitment to ideals that construe such societal differences as good or bad (holy or evil, etc.). And, as such a pragmatic code of the "how" of interacting socially, use of Standard (vs. alternatives) is subject to the semiotic processes of folk-extensionalization and folk-intensionalization that seem to be inherent in its apprehension by its users. By such processes, social differentiations can be displaced onto linguistic differences in usage—specifically seen as differentiations around the denotational linguistic norm of Standard English—and these latter can be perceived as a guide to and natural basis for the social differentiation that they index.

Now given that the indexed social differentiations involving standardization revolve around social stratification and hierarchy of one sort or another, and given that in our fiercely egalitarian and individualistic mode of apprehending the various codes of social stratification we tend to construe such indexables as coordinated clusters of positive properties, nonsociologically-valorized symbolic attributes, of individual people—given these in our cultural construal of linguistic usage, the situating of Standard in our culture of standardization becomes understandable. Valorized as an instrument of maximally clear denotational communication, and indexically associated with those to whom its use has made accessible highly-valued characteristics, Standard English becomes a gradiently possessible commodity, access to which should be the "natural," "rational" choice of every consumer equal-under-the-law (God's and the country's), and lack of which can be seen in this symbolic paradigm as a deficit, much like vitamin deficiency (in the natural, physiological variant), or lack of a good wardrobe or proper facial make-up or freshened body odors for personal attractiveness (in the self-expression variant), or an affliction of poor background hindering one's ability to blend into the corporate background (in the Cultural, etiquette-like variant). I believe that this is a key distinction between the culture of Standard, as we have it most highly manifest in the noted social sector in America (and elsewhere, like Great Britain, to a lesser extent), and other kinds of cultural dimensions of linguistic stratification (e.g., diglossia; caste/estate ranked-dialects; socially identifiable registers, asymmetrically distributed and accessible; etc.). The naturalization of Standard at present is such, that its possession becomes a measure of (good old American) freedom, freedom to achieve professionally, personally, and, as expressed by a number of speech consultants, psychologically. Freeing people from unwanted and unsightly ("unsoundly"?) accents, bad expressions, etc. frees their true inner selves, their "real" selves, as it were: Be all that you can be; join the army of Standard-bearers! It's *both* natural *and* patriotic. Standard is our manifest destiny.

We can observe how these processes operate to re-valorize and transform a *dialectal* difference into a *superposed symbolic = (emblematic)* differentiation. They operate according to the logic of metaphorical or analogical (iconic) schemata that give the contextual parameters of code use (here, who uses the dialectal variant in what contexts to whom about what) an essential connection to the forms of the code, seen denotationally, in a schema or model of explaining (etiologically or causally) why such-and-such type of person uses such-and-such type of language in said act of code use. Observe how the Queen's English Society valorizes RP ('Received Pronunciation') with respect to geographical dialect variants, thus in effect drawing all these recognized geographical *dialects* together in a culturally *superposed* schema of variation with respect to the RP norms, the non-availability of all the elements of which to any person or group in the overall schema of differentiation becoming their deficit with respect to the Standard that has a rational basis in some identifiable characteristic:

Yorkshire miners: "defiantly talk among themselves in the local dialect" [defiant provincialism];
Welsh: "sound liltingly conciliatory";
Ulster Irish: "sound blustery" [cf. 'Windy City'?];
West Country people: "purr" [less than sophisticated; kitten-like];
Bristolians: "mysteriously add an 'l' to various words" [superfluousness of irrational];
East Anglians: "wheedle" [ungentlemanly; tricky];
Cockneys: "sound cheeky," "thick" [impertinent and stupid];
Liverpudlians: "just think of the Beatles" [!].
(source: [AP] M. Eliason, Chicago *Tribune*, 9/V/85, sec.1, p.25)

What we have here is nothing less than a schema of negatives in characterological terms, serving ultimately as a model for grounding and explaining dialect speech as a function of something about these people as individuals, by comparison to the unspoken positive virtues of those who speak the (neutral) Queen's English.

The very same phenomenon is found in the United States, where, however, there is some variability in the sources as to how a complete schema is to be reconstructed out of the observations that symbolically ground social and geographical localizations. So, we are told in the *New York Times* (W.K. Stevens, 21/VII/85, p. 14), perpetuating the East Coast variant of the myth of a "General American English" (the mythical embodiment of Standard[9]), that what Mr. Labov calls 'television network' or 'Standard' American English . . . is commonly spoken in the West by white members of all social classes.

Yet, sources from the Far Western state of California, and from the Midwest, clearly recognize that social class, urban vs. rural identity, etc. differentiate Standard speakers from others in those regions, and that they speak a geographically locatable variant with respect to Standard. Of course, many people in the eastern part of the United States attribute this "generalized" American to the Midwest or the Far West, particularly California, no doubt in an emblematic map of where the "true" America can be found to be embodied in these United States. Thus, why, in our sources, does the phonetic accent of New Yorkers "grate," and that of the Southerner bespeak mental slowness? Note here, too, the totemistic transfer of the social emblem cast in essentially individualistic characterological-personality terms onto language as what we might term a folk-etiological theory.

Again, many women construe differences in Standard-possession somewhat differently from men, though the general asymmetry in the direction of

women : men :: less-Standard : more-Standard

holds for people in the culture of Standard, thus explaining for them why, as is quoted in my data, "Women often lack punch in their speech . . . sound[ing] apologetic or unsure" (D. Solis, "A good accent is not accent to some people," *Wall Street Journal*, 22/VII/86, p. 1). The "apologetic" or "unsure" self-presentation of women is located in relatively less Standardized usage, which mediates their femaleness![10]

The situation of Standard English with respect to other languages also takes on the character of a linguistic totemism, here projecting the values of nationality as seen by speakers onto the linguistic expression of them. A Chicago *Tribune* editorial writer seeks to

examine *why* English words are so widely used in French[.]

Clearly, one reason is that English is so flexible. It is a kind of linguistic putty; it can be squeezed into any shape required and used to fill in all kinds of gaps in other languages. One cannot do that with French because it is too—well, French.

One reason why English is so adaptable is that it is so nonexclusive; speakers of English have always been ready to borrow useful words from any language.

Note how those values of self-perception of Americans vs. the French that were already established in the mythology of Benjamin Franklin in Paris—ingeniousness, ingenuousness, practicality, etc.—are projected onto the difference between the English and French languages. The adaptable welcoming, and, indeed, "natural" egalitarianism of American self-image vs. its opposite (observe the strong connotation of pretense and artificiality about French/the French) become overall attributes of the respective languages as instruments of denotation. And given how this ethno-ethnology engages with linguistic ideology as it construes another highly-regarded standard language, it is easy to see the route for various some-times vitriolic attacks on the various non-English languages the existence of which in communities in the United States obtrudes into the consciousness of op-ed piece and letter writers in our newspapers through political issues like funding for bilingual education, balloting, etc. The same kind of construal of Standard vs. non-Standard English gets applied, mutatis mutandis, in the wider field of English vs. other forms of linguistic self-presentation.[11]

There is, then, a construal of Standard English with a neutral, emblematic value centered in the unity and identity of the nation-state, that does not easily distin-guish between the dialects/sociolects-around-the-Standard and any other-lan-guages-around-the-Standard in its analysis and advocacy. Indeed, the processes of such emblematization, as I have argued a form of Barthian "refunctionalization" of denotational value, are common to social forms in all societies, and hence, in particular, to languages everywhere; that they do not make the analytic distinc-tions we do from our linguistic perspective is to be expected. What seems to be distinctive of the current cultural scene, however, is the emergence, at the very epi-center of Angst about Standard, of new mechanisms that, in "dealing with" the in-tensely experienced Standard-deficit, have the semiotic effect of commoditization, shaping the terms in which English *per se* is valorized as well. How vivid is the metaphor of language as our very "currency" of communication:

> In economic theory, bad money drives out the good. In linguistic theory as well, bad lan-guage is clearly capable of driving out good language. (Bill Neikirk, "Econspeak," Chicago *Tribune* 7/XI/85, sec. 5, p. 2)

Hence, we would suppose, the necessity for certain controls or stimulated market-correctives to deal with this debasable medium (one wonders what the linguistic monetarist would do!).

There has been emerging, then, a new kind of hegemony over Standard, closely tied to the world of American business, where its primary target audience is found, and whose language, as it were, it speaks. The authoritative discourse about Standard in relation to alternative variations comes in the form of numbers of new companies marketing products and services in recognizable cultural idioms: not just (old-fashioned) books, but up-to-the-minute cassette courses on gram-mar, vocabulary, oral diction, etc. for self-help to achieve personal transformation before the Standard; private and group "therapy" or "courses" in eliminating or masking (perhaps to become a verbal Charles Atlas?) what are considered non-Standard phonological and other patterns, combining aspects of psychotherapy, self-help groups for sharing afflictions (Accents Anonymous?), and extra-credit courses in practical or applied science (or even acting); consultancies on matters linguistic, as a mode of rationalized corporate efficiency in personnel management and image, for which linguistic standardization is a matter of interpersonal quali-control. Once-upon-a-time "elocution" teachers (drawing upon an idiom of connoisseurship in personal arts) have been fashioned into the personnel of companies of "helping professionals," (cf. private, outpatient medicine in "health maintenance organizations [HMOs]"). For an upscale fee, of course, such authoritative professionals will eradicate the deficiencies people may have in spoken and written Standard, emphasizing what we might call "corporate Standard," that is, Standard as the essential medium of corporate survival and personal success. Their names, such as Grammar Group, Creative Speech Interests, Inc., Speech Dynamics, bespeak the world they are attempting to dominate. These are wizards of the accent and of the vocabulary, of punctuation, intonation, and hypercorrect grammar, ministering like social workers or even physicians to "patients," as many characterize those "afflicted" with poor, i.e., non-Standard or non-English, linguistic habits. (Speech pathologists, indeed!)

There *is* a market. From the fraction of "Dear Abby" and "Miss Manners" space devoted to matters of grammar, usage, pronunciation, etc. in my collection of data, it is clear that there is much concern with such issues. And if, unlike the various newspaper pundits, actual experts on linguistics take positions about these matters that bespeak a so-called "permissive" stance[12]—leading directly, many believe, to such things as bilingual programs and worse!—corporate America, America, Inc., does not, nor do its entry-level but upwardly mobile white collars, nor especially the cheerleaders for those values of which, in this context, Standard becomes the emblematic focus. And if corporate America has decided that the public schools, with all their permissiveness, are not supplying it with the kind of linguistic product it needs/wants, it is certainly not going to put up with the situation, nor are entrepreneurial corporate folk going to resist filling the bill. So there is money to be made by selling the commodity in question, in the paradigm of remediation, a demand for which can be generated and maintained by using the engines of that very Satan the ayatollahs of Standard most despise and complain about as the ruination of the purity of Standard—advertising![13]

Such is the emerging hegemony over commoditized Standard English in America, spurred on by the chorus of William Safires, Edwin Newmans, John Simons, and so forth in the public media.

And if that is the case for the way monoglot Standard is situated with respect to other forms of what are termed "English" within the linguistic community, think of how this particular social formation deals with the facts of plurilingualism within the political borders of the United States at the present time. It must spell itself out in legal/political terms, seeking to motivate assertion or reassertion of Standard English by means of equating deficit-for-Standard (through, e.g., non-English mother tongue, and non-Standard version of that, to boot!) with blockage of access to the kinds of ideologically demanded "equality"—of protections, opportunities, etc.—that the courts have been (some would say, have notoriously been) trying to assert for some period of time. Hence, the arguments have to be mounted *as functional* ones, ones of *enablement* of particular non-Standard English-speaking groups, or *enablement* of the entire polity (and hence, the legitimate interest of the state to intervene against unbridled freedom) by espousing or denouncing state-supported/encouraged/restrictively enforced/franchised unilingualism (in Standard English or some other norm/standard) or plurilingualism.

It is clear that English-only amendments speak to this issue at state (currently) and potentially national levels of political organization. With reference to the populations at the economic fringes of American society, being slowly mobilized into it, these remind one of the kind of edicts about language characterized by R.F. Inglehart and M. Woodward (1967) in their classic study of "Language Conflicts and Political Community." As they point out, when such measures are taken by a dominant group in power during the phase of transition to mobility of the dominated in the system of stratification, political conflict seems to be the regularity. Yet the rationalization by which, as Katherine Woolard discovered in her study of the California referendum, people of seemingly liberal consciousness and goodwill voted overwhelmingly for the establishment of English as the official state language, can be nicely encapsulated from the ideology we have already seen, namely that access-to-[Standard] English is *direct* access—free of community-internal political bosses, etc.—to the "truths" that elections, in the fairyland of American civics ideologies, are said to be about. English gives each individual the equality under the law, somehow.

Note further that bilingual education programs, rationalized when they were passed as something to *speed* or at least increase the efficiency of mainstreaming of minority groups, have both a group-internal and an official interpretability. On Indian reservations where I have discussed the issue, it is a matter of giving the fruits of Standardization, and its paraphernalia, to the local language. To a certain extent, we can see this reading in much of the bilingualism literature written by minority linguistic community members. That is, the success of the program in officialdom's terms would be the failure of the program in group-internal terms. But note that the arguments in the larger and dominant community *pro* and *con* cannot really face up to the group-internal reasons for having such education in the first place. Instead, the argument between the *pros* (who are accused by Secretary Bennett and his assistants of being exactly that, pros, and hence economically—do we smell a whiff of corruption on the scholarly breath?—not disinterested and so disingenuous in their opinions/conclusions) and the *cons* may, indeed, I would say, must be read in terms of culture of Standard: can the virtues attributed to the educated person—the speaker of, or aspirant to, English Standard, be gotten through study by means of some other system of communication? What are the ultimate consequences of having/not having access to the paraphernalia of Standardization—in this case, the educational establishment—for the group(s) in questions? Are we exercising the state's legitimate interests in one or another form of resolution, or are we thereby preserving equality of opportunity in the laissez-faire sense? Since monoglot Standard is a *cultural emblem* in our society, it is not a linguistic problem as such that we are dealing with.

Hence, note the folly of my colleagues in the *LSA*, who ask the membership to vote on (the metaphor is wonderful!) the following resolution:

RESOLUTION

Whereas several states have recently passed measures making English their "official state language," and

Whereas the "English-only" movement has begun to campaign for the passage of similar measures in other states and has declared its intention to attach an official language amendment to the U.S. Constitution, and

Whereas such measures have the effect of preventing the legislature and state agencies and officials from providing services or information in languages other than English,

Be it therefore resolved that the Society make known its opposition to such "English-only" measures, on the grounds that they are based on misconceptions about the role of a common language in establishing political unity, and that they are inconsistent with basic American ideals of linguistic tolerance. As scholars with a professional interest in language, we affirm that:

The English language in America is not threatened. All evidence suggests that recent immigrants are overwhelmingly aware of the social and economic advantages of becoming proficient in English, and require no additional compulsion to learn the language.

American unity has never rested primarily on unity of language, but rather on common political and social ideals.

History shows that attempts to impose a common language by force of law usually create divisiveness and disunity.

It is to the economic and cultural advantage of the nation as a whole that its citizens should be proficient in more than one language, and to this end we should encourage both foreign language study for native English speakers and programs that enable speakers with other linguistic backgrounds to maintain proficiency in those language along with English.

Such wide-eyed innocence—perhaps coming from the referentialist/structuralist dogma—about what is really at stake for the groups concerned with language in relation to a culture of monoglot Standardization embarrasses me and makes me realize that perhaps my high-school math teacher was right when he said that language is too important to be left to the linguists.

Acknowledgments and History

A text of shorter compass was read as "Standardization and metaphors of linguistic hegemony" in the session "Language and Political Economy, I" at the annual meeting of the American Anthropological Association held in Philadelphia, 6 December 1986. I thank Hy Van Luong and James Collins for the invitation to participate, and the discussants of the session, John Comaroff and Jane Hill, for their oral comments. Written comments by James Collins, Paul Friedrich, Thomas Kochman, and Elizabeth Mertz have been very useful to keep in mind in the process of revision. A longer version, somewhat reoriented, was given as "Monoglot 'Standard' in America" at an interdisciplinary symposium, "The politics of language in multilingual societies" at the University of Maryland (Baltimore County) sponsored by the department of Modern Languages and Linguistics on 8 May 1987. For the opportunity to present that version, and for making my visit to the UMBC campus very pleasant, I thank Judith Morganroth Schneider of that department. Discussion with Brian Weinstein and Frank Anshen, two other participants in that symposium, has been especially helpful in further revision. For some of the technical terminology, readers may wish to consult various articles in *Semiotic Mediation*, ed. Elizabeth Mertz & Richard Parmentier (Orlando, Fla.: Academic, 1985).

Notes

1. As such, the reconstruction of this process in economistic terms is of the genus of what I would term, after Boas ([1887]1940:643) "evolutionary" thinking on this temporally bounded sequence of events, rather than "historical" thinking. Evolutionary thinking sees such processes as the natural outcome of the spatio-temporally located interaction of universally-applicable functional laws affecting phenomena and thus explaining such phenomena as an expectable instance of what is predictable on reductively explanatory grounds. Historical thinking sees such processes as having a non-reducible structure immanent in the processes themselves, the dimension of contingent causality in which crucially involving factors specific to instances of moments of the overall processes. Viewed this way, even modern biological "evolutionary" theory is "historical" thinking, according to its most articulate inside philosopher (Gould 1986). And, increasingly, the microphysics of quantum cosmogony seems to be heading in the direction of true historical thinking.

2. Except for days when I am out of town, I have been systematically scanning the *Tribune* daily, clipping articles about language, articles that contain a significant focus on linguistic or related issues, advice—personal and etiquette-couched—including "Dear Abby" and "Miss Manners" and, more recently, "Ask Ann Landers," letters to the editor, op-ed pieces, cartoons, etc. Relying further on exposure to a wide variety of the popular press, I have clipped anything of similar nature that I have come across, e.g., American Express brochures, local "learning center" commercial "course" descriptions in self-improvement (the 20th century Yuppie equivalent of the 19th century workingman's athenaeum/institute/extension school), magazine articles in general circulation press, etc. All of my examples are excerpted from this collection, which I use regularly in teaching undergraduate language in culture and society courses at The University of Chicago in order to bring the message, as it were, back home.

3. As James Collins (p.c.) has pointed out to me, it is probably no coincidence that the locus of this development of our culture of standardization is in the social sector of people whose dependence on educational credentials and similar paraphernalia of personal, upwardly mobile accomplishment would appear to be most central to social identity in the socioeconomic stratification, or of heightened pointedness in those institutional settings in which they live. This is very much reminiscent of the heightened "linguistic insecurity" of the lower middle class as calibrated in Labov's (1966; 1972) early 1960s data; presumably, similar segments of the population, articulated more on a national scale, are being mobilized into the ranks of yuppiedom.

4. In fact, this naturalization of Standard, already the hegemonic form of language in the United States, realizes the discourse of its own hegemony, just as we might expect; for then "natural" Standard continually validates power of groups and institutions that "naturally" have—and, ideologically, ought to have—control of the hegemonic discourse in such a culture of standardization. The discourse of advocacy is probably not unrelated to the coeval quest on the part of the target audience for "naturalness" in achieving the wholesome, good consumerism in life that has historically emerged from 1960s counter-cultural wholegrainism, now that corporate interests have gotten hold of such a set of themes. Language falls into step as just one more area where buying (into) the hegemonic line's product becomes nature's way. Interestingly, the anti-monoglot advocacies, such as those in favor of plurilingual educational policies, etc., frequently naturalize their arguments also (cf. Freeman Dyson as quoted above) in a form of cultural-linguistic conservationism—preservation of every linguistic snail darter in the face of "big" culture's dominant homogenization—that is as unnatural on the face of it as any inference can be, from the lessons of biological evolution about extinction of species.

5. See Silverstein 1985b:247–48 for a discussion of this point, with references, in the context of a discussion of Friends' Plain Speech.

6. See Labov's article (1969) on "The Logic of Non-Standard English" for a counter against this kind of "cognitive deficit" argument with respect to Black non-Standard. Thus, as is important to my point about the "just right" quality of Standard, note that both degrees of deviation from Standard—purported lack-of-conceptual-differentiation, as well as hyper-"intellectualization," i.e., hyperterminologization (Havránek 1964:6–9) and hyper-syntacticization—are seen to victimize people who use them. It should be noted that to answer this kind of argument purely at the level of demonstrating denotational adequacy either misconstrues the sociocultural basis for the argument (see Kochman 1974) and unwittingly takes it at face value, or pointedly tries to take it as "scientific" in spirit, but then straight-facedly buys into its premises in the folk view of language as purely denotational instrument.

7. Recall here the notion that there is such a Standard-bearing person-in-the-street as one of the defining allegiances of members of a linguistic community with a culture of standardization. This naturalization of Standard reality has taken many forms: such popular misinterpretations of Whorf's (1956) writings as Stuart Chase's (and note that he wrote a foreword to the collection), such dark visions as George Orwell's, such movements as Count Korzybski's General Semantics movement, and such self-styled religions as Scientology (nee Dianetics) are all oriented to linguistic and hence cognitive therapeutic, bespeaking a construal of language as a clothing for clear thinking about an obvious reality that governmentally and technologically controlled denotational forms can transform for ill or for good. (Note the etymologically original sense of *idéologie*, by the way, invented by Destutt de Tracy as a product of the Enlightenment.)

8. This is a rather common folk conceptualization of the notion of *style*, it should be noted, and it is probably no accident that in the culture of commoditization of Standard the term *lifestyle* recurs in many sources. When erstwhile *fashion* is turned into lifestyle we can understand the rather pointed commoditization of the "how" of self-presentation as a self conscious fashioning (pun intended) of a style as an individual's prerogative.

9. The idea that Standard is embodied in actual speakers of some particular dialect may well be grounded in and facilitated by a process attending to language in the following way. Where speakers who perceive themselves to be deficient with respect to Standard in partic-

ular forms perceive/conceptualize either (a) the absence of those "deficiencies" in some other dialect, or (b) their correspondence in some positively valorized form in some locatable dialect, whether cumulatively (arithmetically) or by structural salience (with some differential weightings), this may be taken to "be" Standard. The location of or construal of *which* dialect as such an embodiment, however, is clearly not a linguistic process *tout court;* our data show that it is a matter of just the sort of emblematic construal of social differentiation described in the body of our discussion.

10. See Silverstein 1985b:234–41. Note the formulation of P. Smith (1979:113), who observes that there is a distinction that appears to be involved here between Standard usage and perception of such usage as prestigious:

> much of the foregoing data has been summarized by the comment that women regularly employ the use of more *socially prestigious* speech than men (Labov 1970; Trudgill 1975). Sociolinguists usually use the term prestige in one of two ways, to mean either (i) the value of a way of speaking for upward social mobility (Weinreich 1963), or (ii) the avoidance of stigmatized speech variables. It may be that the use of standard speech accomplishes both of these conditions at once, but this begs the crucial question of how the standard, defined on linguistic grounds, acquires its *evaluative* connotations. It certainly poses problems for the traditional sociolinguistic view that speech simply reflects underlying social reality, for women, despite their more standard speech, do not enjoy a prestigious position in society compared to men. In short, *prestige* cannot be used interchangeably with *standard* in sociolinguistics, for the linguistic varieties that are socially advantageous (or sigmatized) for one group, may not be for another. That is, the evaluative connotations of speech cannot be assessed independently of the people that use them.

We might see this disparity as a *reflection* of the semiotic processes of extensionalization + intensionalization = (rationalized) emblematization, expressed in individual characterological/self-presentational terms. Though reflecting a perception of status asymmetries in institutional contexts between women and men, the very language of women as compared with that of men is isolated as a locus of why femaleness enacted in identifiable linguistic terms entails lower status, less power, etc., where male speech is taken to be an embodiment of Standard.

11. There is a nonprofit membership organization called "U.S. English," of which former Senator S.I. Hayakawa is Honorary Chairman, whose literature claims that "Its purpose is to restore the English-only ballot, and to limit bilingual education to a transitional role" by such means as a U.S. Constitutional amendment "designating English the official language of the United States," though of course, in the absence of case and administrative law relating to "official" language, which would develop only over a lengthy period of adjudication, the effective connection between the two things is not in fact obvious. Some of the connotative political penumbra of the movement's prose, however, is revealed in the specific phrases used, such as "foreign languages in competition with our own," "the special interest groups pressing for language separatism," etc. Note further that the proposed amendment (actually introduced in the Senate by Hayakawa in 1981, and apparently in the current 1987 House session by Representative Robert Fairchild [D., Arkansas], whose state has declared English to be the "official language" of the state) says, simply, "The English language shall be the official language of the United States," thus introducing the presumably interpretable (now vacuous) concept of "official language" vis-à-vis other languages, but silently assuming, one imagines, that Standard represents English. What, for example, would be the fate of government-sponsored programs in the "bilingual" mode for regional, class, and ethnic dialect speakers under this amendment? Since the Chairman of this orga-

nization is, as Hayakawa reassures the addressees of his direct-mail solicitation, "Dr. John Tanton, a practicing physician and well-known leader of many civic causes," we would not necessarily expect sociolinguistic expertise to frame its concerns. (Note the image of the doctor, the "practicing physician," at the helm of this monoglot juggernaut, by the way, much like one of the strong and recurrent images in terms of which Standard is authoritatively commoditized for its market.)

12. Grounded professionally in Boasian cross-cultural comparatism, and self-consciously and pointedly limiting its structural study to what we would call the central referential-and-predicational form of grammar (from phonology through sentence-structure), technical linguistics in America in the recent period has preached the doctrines of equivalence and effability: that all language structures are complete and sufficient as referential-and-predicational instrumentalities, and that anything expressible in one language can be expressed in any other, only the formal organization (including the structural complexity and specificity) and the respective means of expression differing (e.g., a word in one language may be translatable only by a grammatically complex phrase in another). But the public, including otherwise educated scientists and scholars, have taken such technical beliefs, when articulated about, for example, Standard vs. non-Standard dialects (in the technical sense, again) *none of which has a claim to superiority from the strictly referential-and-predicational doctrine of completeness plus effability* to be, from its culturally valorized understanding of Standard vs. "dialect," at least non-advocacy of Standard, and at most advocacy of "anything goes." But the naivete of American linguistics as a real-life interest group that has tried simply to constitute itself discursively as "scientific" expertise according to its internal understanding of the subject matter, rather than according to the culture that valorizes scientific expertise on *subject matters that are defined by the sociosemiotic processes of interested human action and power*, all the while attempting to speak to/influence society's interest in the latter, have been, in effect, its undoing and revalorization as itself an expectedly "liberal" (if not libertine!) interest group, looking out for its own interests in linguistic diversity in the same way that social workers are said to be a poverty or welfare lobby hell-bent on preserving their field of operation as a vital economic interest. See "Battle on Bilingual Education," from AP, in Chicago *Tribune* 19/III/87, sec. 1A, p. 33; cf. Kochman 1974 and n. 6 supra. Any inclusive semiotic analysis of language and its structure would avoid this.

13. An analysis of the mode of presentation of the commoditized Standard in relation to other forms of speech is to be completed. A sampling of materials is available from the author on request.

References

Barthes, Roland. 1967. *Elements of Semiology*. [trans. A. Lavers and C. Smith] New York: Hill & Wang.

Bloomfield, Leonard. 1927. Literate and Illiterate Speech. *American Speech* 2:432–39.

Boas, Franz. 1940. [1887] The Study of Geography. In *Race, Language, and Culture*, F. Boas, pp. 639–47. New York: Macmillan.

———. 1911. Introduction. In *Handbook of American Indian Languages*. Bureau of American Ethnology, Bulletin, no. 40, pt. 1, ed. F. Boas, pp. 1–83. Washington, D.C.: Government Printing Office.

Dyson, Freeman J. 1979. *Disturbing the Universe*. New York: Harper and Row.

Ferguson, Charles A. 1959. Diglossia. *Word* 15:325–40.

———. 1968. Myths about Arabic. In *Readings in the Sociology of Language*, ed. J.A. Fishman, pp. 375–81. The Hague: Mouton.

Friedman, Milton and Rose. 1980. *Free to Choose: A Personal Statement*. New York: Harcourt, Brace, Jovanovich.

Gould, Stephen Jay. 1986. Evolution and the Triumph of Homology; or Why History Matters. *American Scientist* 74:60–69.

Gumperz, John J. 1968. The Speech Community. In *International Encyclopedia of the Social Sciences*, vol. 9, ed. D.L. Sills, pp. 381–86. New York: Macmillan/Glencoe: Free Press. [*s.v.* Linguistics]

Havránek, Bohuslav. 1964. The Functional Differentiation of the Standard Language. In *A Prague School Reader on Esthetics, Literary Structure, and Style*, ed. P.L. Garvin, pp. 3–16. Washington, D.C.: Georgetown University Press.

Inglehart, R.F. and M. Woodward. 1967. Language Conflicts and Political Community. *Comparative Studies in Society and History* 10:27–45.

Kochman, Thomas. 1974. Standard English Revisited, or Who's Kidding/Cheating Who(m)? *The Florida FL Reporter* 12 (Spring/Fall):31–44, 96.

Labov, William. 1966. *The Social Stratification of English in New York City*. Washington, D.C.: Center for Applied Linguistics.

———. 1969. The Logic of Nonstandard English. *GURT 1969*, 1–31.

———. 1972. *Sociolinguistic Patterns*. Philadelphia: University of Pennsylvania Press.

Putnam, Hilary. 1975. The Meaning of "Meaning." In *Philosophical Papers*, vol. 2, *Mind, Language, and Reality*, ed, H. Putnam, pp. 215–71.

Saussure, Ferdinand de. 1916. *Cours de Linguistique Générale*. Lausanne-Paris: Payot.

Silverstein, Michael. 1979. Language Structure and Linguistic Ideology. In *The Elements: A Parasession on Linguistic Units and Levels, April 20–21, 1979*, ed. P. Clyne et al. pp. 193–247. Chicago: Chicago Linguistic Society.

———. 1981. The Limits of Awareness. *Working Papers in Sociolinguistics*, no. 84. Austin: Southwest Educational Research Laboratory.

———. 1984. The 'Value' of Objectual Language. Paper presented at symposium, "The Division of Labor in Language and Society," American Anthropological Association Annual meeting, Denver, Colorado.

———. 1985a. The Functional Stratification of Language and Ontogenesis. In *Culture, Communication, and Cognition: Vygotskian Perspectives*, ed. J. Wertsch, pp. 205–35. New York: Cambridge University Press.

———. 1985b. Language and the Culture of Gender: At the Intersection of Structure, Usage, and Ideology. In *Semiotic Mediation: Sociocultural and Psychological Perspectives*, ed. E. Mertz and R.J. Parmentier, pp. 219–59. Orlando, Fla.: Academic Press.

Smith, Philip M. 1979. Sex Markers in Speech. In *Social Markers in Speech*, ed. K.R. Scherer and H. Giles, pp. 109–46. Cambridge: Cambridge University Press.

Whorf, Benjamin L. 1956 [1941]. The Relation of Habitual Thought and Behavior to Language. *In Language, Thought and Reality: Selected Writing of Benjamin Lee Whorf*, ed. J.B. Carroll, pp. 134–59. Cambridge, Mass.: MIT Press.

15

The Grammar
of Consciousness
and the Consciousness
of Grammar

JANE H. HILL

Sociolinguistics should be a tool for the exploration of the role of human linguistic capacities in the dynamic of the world system. However, while both the political economic study of the world system and the structuralist study of language have made important advances in recent years, there has seemed to be little possibility of uniting them. In the present paper I propose one avenue toward such a union, using tools for the investigation of the practice of speaking developed by Mikhail Bakhtin and V.I. Voloshinov.[1] Their work suggests the shape of a theory of the linguistic foundations of consciousness, that lens that, in Marxist political economic thought, focuses the material and symbolic historical dynamic within the acting subject. I will illustrate this possibility through a brief study of the Mexicano (Nahuatl or Aztec are other names for this language) usage found in peasant communities in the Malinche Volcano region of Tlaxcala and Puebla in central Mexico.

The Malinche Volcano is a Mexicano-speaking (or, more properly, a bilingual) island in a Spanish sea. The maintenance of the Mexicano language there among people who have been in intimate contact with Spanish speakers for nearly 500 years would seem to be a textbook example of the symbolic dimension of peasant conservatism. However, as I hope to show in this paper, we find, in fact, that Mexicano usage on the Malinche is not single-mindedly conservative. Instead, its speakers have drawn upon the resources of Spanish in complex ways. Their usage today constitutes an ongoing negotiation with the symbolic power of Spanish; the form of their practice in this negotiation is closely related to the structural position of individuals in the material sector.

In terms of human geography, the Malinche Volcano region has been identified by Nutini and Isaac (1974) as an area of sloped-terrace rainfall maize agriculture which is surrounded by irrigated cash-crop agriculture in the Valley of Puebla-

Tlaxcala. Members of the Malinche towns (which range in population from a few hundred people to as many as 20,000) hold their lands privately; communal land, whether held by the towns or held under the Mexican government's *ejido* or collective farm system, constitutes only a small proportion of the area under cultivation. Lastra and Horcasitas (1979) in their linguistic survey of the state of Tlaxcala have confirmed that the Malinche region can also be defined by a uniquely high proportion of Mexicano speakers. The people of the Malinche constitute themselves as a region; this self-definition is symbolically warranted in myths like that of the Pillo, who brought water to the towns and, with the help of the ants, entered the earth and turned into a powerful being who was able to defeat the evil "government of Puebla" (the largest city of the region). At his death, the Pillo ordered that his body should be divided into pieces, and each piece wrapped in its own shroud and buried in a principal town of the Malinche:

1.   . . . *ic San Pablo del Monte, La Resurrección, ic San Luis Teolocholco,*
     In San Pablo del Monte, La Resurreccion, in San Luis Teolocholco,

     ic Huamantla, nochi in nonqueh pueblohtin que in tōcazqueh in īnacayō
     in Huamantla, in all of those towns that they would bury his flesh

     cada in īpedazo de īnacayō ye mortaja.
     each piece of his flesh already in its shroud.

The work of struggle against the "city"—the Spanish-speaking world with its market economy—begun in mythic times by the Pillo continued. Throughout the 19th century the Malinche was the locus of ongoing peasant banditry, which was shaped during the early years of the Mexican Revolution into an effective guerrilla force. This force was not, however, fortunate in its alliance with other peasant groups. Its most important leader, General Domingo Arenas, was assassinated by elements of the Zapatista army (to this day Malinche people believe that the murder took place on Emiliano Zapata's order, and they remember his army as a band of vicious thieves).

The people of the Malinche region define themselves as cultivators—*campesinos*. It is important to note at the outset, however, that a substantial proportion of the adult male population of the region is involved in regular wage labor, largely in small independent factories. While there is a good deal of controversy in the political economic literature about the structural position of populations like that of the Malinche, my own view is that the facts are best handled within the framework developed by the Mexican anthropologist Arturo Warman, who treats a similar population in the state of Morelos as a "peasantry" (Warman 1980) which has maintained relative autonomy from the capitalist sector. Warman argues that such populations live within a separate "peasant mode of production," and have bargained, albeit on increasingly unfavorable terms, with the capitalist sector (and particularly with the state) to retain their autonomy. They return to the capitalist sector that *sine qua non* of peasant status, a fund of rent, which includes a complex sum of low wages in the capitalist sector, wages largely expended within that sector, and also includes support within the communities of a labor force upon which that sector can draw. This support includes not only the provision of subsistence, but also provision to the capitalist sector of physical access to the labor force, including education (schools are built by cooperative labor), transportation (roads are also built cooperatively, and bus systems are local private enterprises), and the provision (also through cooperative work) of the plumbing and electrical systems that make it possible for women to run households with little help from men, and that bring in the acculturating forces of national and regional mass media. Warman believes that this contribution of the peasant mode of production to the development of the Mexican capitalist sector is a fundamental one; Mexican industrialization, he argues, is "made of corn" (Warman 1980:176).

One result of the very unfavorable balance of negotiating power between the peasant sector and the national capitalist sector has been an extraordinarily complex involution of social and economic systems within the peasant communities. These systems are characterized by emphasis on maize, a semi-sacred subsistence crop, the cultivation of which is so uneconomic in modern Mexico that it has been largely abandoned by other sectors. Economic exchange within the community is dominated by systems of reciprocity and redistribution; recent studies, such as that of Olivera on Tlaxcalancingo (1967), show that three-fifths of community income goes into this "ritual" sector. This sector includes the system of *compadrazgo*, or ritual kinship, which, along with blood kinship, structures reciprocity and is extraordinarily elaborated in the Malinche region (Nutini and Bell 1980; Nutini 1984). Redistributive exchange is structured through the system of *mayordomías*, graded ranks of stewardships of holy images. Both *compadrazgo* and *mayordomía* are seen within the towns as "sacred" duties, but they can be easily seen to have an economic function. It is certainly not, however, one that yields a net profit to the participants, and in the Malinche region a man usually ends his ritual career, as Eric Wolf put it, "old and poor." But this ritual sector, in spite of the fact that it drains resources from the towns into the capitalist sector through ritually required expenditure, is fundamental in structuring access to subsistence resources of the communities.

In order to sustain the involuted system of maize cultivation and ritually regulated exchange, Warman has shown that the peasant sector must borrow tools from the capitalist sector. Warman was particularly interested in use by peasants of commercial credit, which in Mexico is available through state banks for investment in cash-crop cultivation. In Morelos, peasants use the profits from such capitalized cash cropping to prop up the money-losing maize cultivation system. On the Malinche, probably the most important material borrowing from the capitalist sector is that of wages. Rothstein (1974) has shown that in the Malinche town of San Cosme Mazātecochco, most surplus from wages is turned to the buttressing of a man's position as a cultivator—toward investment in land, in fertilizers, in herbicides, and in cash-crop ventures, the profits of which can be turned toward continuing maize cultivation.

In the symbolic sector, the principal instrument that the peasant sector has appropriated and turned toward the maintenance of its involuted autonomy is the Spanish language. Mexicano and Spanish have been given sharply differentiated symbolic significance. Spanish is the language of money and the market, of the city, of evil personages in myths, and of social distance. To speak Spanish to a fellow townsman can be an aggressive denial of intimacy; the use of Spanish to outsiders to the region, regardless of their ethnicity, registers social distance in that context as well. Spanish is also the language of obscenity and of "nonsensical" drunken speech. But, in line with Brown and Gilman's (1960) proposal that expressions of social distance will also be expressions of power, Spanish elements have been refunctionalized within the Mexicano language as markers of the "power code," the register of Mexicano through which important men mark their identity, and through which even men who are not *principales* (men of high rank in the ritual hierarchy) mark their discourses as profound and authoritative. (I use the term "men" on purpose; women hardly use the hispanicized Mexicano power code.)

In contrast to the symbolic position of the Spanish language and elements borrowed from it into Mexicano, which mark power and distance, Mexicano is par excellence the language of intimacy, solidarity, mutual respect, and identity as a *campesino*. Mexicano is required at major community rituals such as the sealing of the vows between new *compadres*, or the blessing of newlyweds. Obscene "inverted greetings" in Mexicano are used by young men to test the ethnicity of strangers encountered on the roads; the return of the correct Mexicano comeback is a password allowing entrée into the town. Mexicano is the language of eating and drinking together, and even when guests at a party are speaking Spanish, they will often call loudly for more food and drink, or offer toasts, in Mexicano. The discourses of cultivation are considered particularly characteristic of Mexicano, and are often used by informants to illustrate the essential nature of the language.

The reader can immediately see that this functional balance between Spanish and Mexicano is potentially fraught with contradictions. A speaker manifesting hispanicization in the "power code" is always vulnerable to being seen as expressing social distance and "outsiderness" to his town, or as expressing the arrogance and lack of respect thought to be characteristic of Spanish speakers. Within Mexicano usage, Spanish, essential to expressing the status of men and the seriousness of their discourses, can be seen also as a source of pollution from the capitalist sector. Even in the speech of cultivators who are fully committed to the community and its complex organizations, one can observe a struggle against this ambivalence of Spanish forms. In the usage of factory workers, who are perhaps of all inhabitants of the Malinche those who are most exposed to the structural contradictions of the regional situation, one can see the escalation of this ongoing struggle into a ferocious purism that threatens the validity of the Mexicano power code; indeed, purism is precisely turned to the struggle for power between factory workers, who are beginning to show signs of becoming a classical *evolué* sector, and the *principales,* who adhere to what is thought to be the "traditional" way of life of the towns, with cultivation and selfless community service the way to a respected old age. Bartra (1978) has suggested that in the negotiation for peasant autonomy the balance has now tipped in favor of the capitalist sector, which has refunctionalized the community support of factory workers from a fund of rent into a wage supplement, such that these workers must be considered not a peasantry, but a rural proletariat that does not control a means of production. On the symbolic side, we might suggest that the Spanish-speaking capitalist sector has succeeded in refunctionalizing Mexicano purism, latent in Mexicano communities for hundreds of years (cf. Karttunen and Lockhart 1976), into a weapon through which the symbolic bulwark of peasant autonomy, the Mexicano language, can be attacked. The attack may succeed, for the lexical resources to satisfy purist demands for a *legítimo mexicano*—a pure Mexicano, without Spanish influence—no longer exist, and are precisely most lacking among the most purist group, young and middle-aged factory workers, who spend much of their lives in a Spanish-speaking environment.[2]

The concept of "consciousness" in Marxist thought would seem to provide an analytical locus at which the material and the symbolic sides of human adaptation could be linked. However, the classical work on consciousness, such as that of Lukács (1968), gives little attention to what people actually say and do and often even denigrates such attention as "empiricism." The form of conciousness is derived on a priori theoretical grounds, and the ideal "vanguard leaders" of the proletariat function as "practitioners" much as Chomsky's "ideal native speakers" function as the bearers of linguistic competence—they are theoretical abstractions, far from the behavior of real human beings. The program for the study of language suggested by Bakhtin and Voloshinov, which, particularly in the work of Voloshinov, is grounded in a Marxist structural analysis of human interaction, offers the possibility of an alternative—a rigorously empirical investigation of the "practice" of language, which will be a window on consciousness, whether peasant, bourgeois, or proletarian. This program admits the systemic aspects of language, as well as the study of usage.

For Bakhtin and Voloshinov, the central structural element of a new kind of language study (which their translators usually call "translinguistics" (cf. Todorov 1981; Bakhtin 1980 [1935]) is the "voice," and the theoretical possibilities for the juxtaposition of "voices" is the central problem of translinguistic study. A single utterance can combine a variety of voices in an intertextual polyphony or dialogue, in which both ideology and the language system function as constraints on combination. It is important to emphasize that the study of the language system remains fundamental to translinguistics. The language system of linguistics is the context-free, relatively permanent, "centripetal" side of language, the domain of "monologue," which can exploit the language system in order to constrain the possibilities for discourse. This monologic voice is somewhat similar to the "ideal native speaker," the locus of competence, but it is an active voice, using the systemic side of language as a resource for the practice of dominance. Added to this "linguistics" is the central translinguistic domain, the context-bound, shifting, responsive, intertextual, "centrifugal" production of meaning in language, which is found prototypically in the negotiations of a dialogue on equal terms, and not in monologic dominance. In dialogue as well, both conflicting ideologies and the systemic constraints of grammar are resources for the combination of voices.

In Bakhtin's analyses, the systemic unit is the context-bound utterance of the voice, the "word." In his study of the poetics of Dostoevsky, Bakhtin classifies this "word" into three major types. The first, the direct word, is "aimed directly at its object," and constitutes a claim of "semantic authority" by the speaker over that object (Bakhtin 1973 [1929]:164). A speaker whose usage is dominated by the direct word, a word to which he attributes only referential and propositional value, constructs a monologue that is ideologically consistent within itself and permits no challenge. This "direct word" of translinguistics is perhaps closest to the "word" of linguistics. The structuralist claim that language systems "admit of no positive terms" (as Saussure put it), but contain units that gain their meaning or positivity exclusively by their structural relations within the system, is a linguistic account of the ideological consistency of the monologue.

The second type of translinguistic word is the objectivized word. Instead of treating an object directly, the objectivized word makes an object of the word of another voice, through typifying it or through assigning it to a particular "character," according to a scheme proposed by an author. Most instances of represented and reported speech that have the function of "sketching character" are assigned by Bakhtin to the category of objectivized words. They are still a part of monologue, not of dialogue, since to objectify or typify another's word requires a dominant authorial voice, which makes these objects and types serve its own ideology.

The third type of translinguistic word is the "double-voiced" word. This is oriented toward another person's word, but without objectification or typification, just as in egalitarian dialogue speakers engage each other's voices. Bakhtin divides the double-voiced word into three subtypes. The first two are "passive." These include stories where the author speaks through the voice of some character; such speech often becomes an example of the monologic direct word. The second "passive" subtype includes parody and irony, which also tend to become part of an ideologically controlling, monologic voice, if the words that are parodied are allowed no independence or resistance against the author.

The last subtype is the "active" word. Here, the word of the other "exerts influence from within" (Bakhtin 1973 [1929]:164). Examples of this type include genuinely dialogic relationships between voices, in "hidden dialogue" and in polemic, in which words exhibit what Bakhtin calls a "sidelong glance" at the words of others. Here, the word of the other can resist and interrupt the authorial voice, and their relationship can be a struggle for dominance, with the embedded voice having a good chance at victory.

While Bakhtin and Voloshinov took as their principal research site the study of reported speech in the novel, Bakhtin notes specifically that multilingual communities would be appropriate sites for translinguistic investigation.

> Dialogical relationships are possible among linguistic styles, social dialects, etc., if those phenomena are perceived as semantic positions, as a sort of linguistic Weltanschauung, i.e., if they are perceived outside the realm of linguistic investigation (Bakhtin 1973 [1929]:152).

Bakhtin himself treated this research possibility only briefly, as in his discussion of the influence of the heteroglossic 16th-century marketplace on the poetic technique of Rabelais (Bakhtin 1968[1940]), or in his brief discussion of the moment of choice faced by Russian peasants between the multiple languages (each representing an ideological stance) in their environment, mentioned in "Discourse of the Novel" (Bakhtin 1980[1935]). But it seems clear that the perception among speakers that a symbolic code is also a "position" must be shaped by the material forces of power; what can be done with this perception will then be shaped by the systemic forces of ideology and of grammatical practice.

Let us begin our analysis of the practice of speaking in Malinche Mexicano, using Bakhtin's system, with a passage uttered at the beginning of a traditional story by a 40-year-old cultivator from San Miguel Canoa. The speaker is already beginning his rise in the religious hierarchy of his town, and has had an important *mayordomía* that took enormous amounts of time and money. Don Otilio cultivates just over a hectare of land, and supplements this subsistence base with wage work as a construction worker in the city of Puebla during the agricultural off seasons. He cultivates only maize, and sells maize about twice a year to raise a bit of cash, in spite of the loss sustained thereby. The passage cited in example 2 below is the beginning of the story of the Pillo and is filled with symbols of militant peasant autonomy. Yet, because it is a serious story, it is appropriate for Don Otilio to load its introduction with Spanish loan words, even though, in general, traditional stories of this type display a low frequency of Spanish loans (about half that seen in "power code" registers). Spanish loans are underlined.

2. *Nicmolhuilīz cē <u>cuento</u> de in nēc <u>antepasado</u> ōcmihtahuiliāyah in*
    I will tell a story of that ancestor (that) they used to tell

    tocohcoltzitzīhuān nēca <u>tiempo</u> ōmo<u>vivir</u>huiliaya īpan Malīntzīn cē,
    our grandfathers (about) that time when there lived on the Malinche A,

    cē <u>persona</u> ītōca ō<u>cnombrar</u>ohqueh Pillo.
    a person his name they named him Pillo.

In this example the Mexicano morphological and syntactic system is intact and dominates the Spanish loans. While loan nouns can receive Mexicano inflectional and derivational affixation, here, since there is no occasion for use of possessives, diminutives, and the like on the loan nouns they appear without any affixes, but with Mexicano determiners and demonstratives such as *cē* (one) and *nēc(a)* (that). Spanish loan nouns never receive Mexicano absolutive suffixes (most Mexicano nouns include, in the nonpossessed form, a root and an "absolutive suffix"-*tl, -tli,* or -*li,* for example, *tempāmi-tl* [wall-absolutive], *tōch-tli* [rabbit-absolutive]). This is a loan-incorporation strategy that is quite common in the languages of the world, which Markey (1983) has called "marking reversal." The "marked" loan nouns are rendered "unmarked" by being assigned to a "marked" noun class, the small class of nouns in Mexicano, such as *chichi* (dog), which do not appear with absolutive suffixes. The verbs *vivir* (to live) and *nombrar* (to name) are here fully incorporated into Mexicano, being affixed with theme formatives and person and aspect markers precisely as if they were Mexicano words. Complex sentence elements, such as *nēca tiempo ōmovivirhuiliaya* (that time [when] there used to live), are formed by adjunction rather than exhibiting the Spanish complementation and relativization markers such as *que,* which appear in some Malinche usage (as in example 6 below). The use of Spanish loans of this type occurs even in the speech of Mexicano "monolinguals" (more properly "incipient bilinguals," [cf. Diebold 1961]); the speaker in example 2 speaks Spanish haltingly, with a good deal of interference from Mexicano, as will be illustrated below in example 7.

In Bakhtin's terms, the Spanish loan words in the passage above are examples of the "direct word." They have two values, a referential one and a "semantic position," that of representing seriousness and power, which is wholly determined within the Mexicano system; the same words would certainly not be particularly potent within a Spanish discourse. That is, they are fully dominated by a "Mexicano" voice, and turned to its purpose. However, we can see in other passages uttered by this same speaker moments in which the latent ambivalence of such usage is brought to the surface, and the Mexicano voice is forced to address directly the problem of its dominance. This can be seen in the passage in example 3. Here, the speaker is a little drunk, and he has been reflecting on his poverty and the "sacrifices" of life as a cultivator, particularly the problem of coping with the steep slopes of the volcano Malinche. At the urging of an interviewer, he turns to a discussion of the female spirit of the mountain:

3. *Mihtahulia in nēca Malīntzīn, cmopialia in nēca arete, huān*
   it is said of that Malinche that she has those earrings, and

   nēca, nēca, nēca collares. In tehhuān tquiliah, 'īcolālex in
   those, those, those necklaces. As for us we say, 'her necklaces the

   Malīntzīn.' Quin-, quinmopialia, cualtzīn, mopetlānaltīa, in nēca
   Malinche. Them-, she has them, beautiful, she shines, that

   Malīntzīn. Cualtzīn quinmopialihticah, in nēca īcolālexhuān, huān
   Malinche. Beautiful she is having them, those her necklaces, and

   nēca īpīpilōlhuān cualtzīn.
   those her earrings beautiful.

Here, at the beginning of the passage we see a wholly characteristic use of Spanish loans, *arete* (earring[s]) and *collares* (necklaces). The variation in pluralization of inanimate nouns is typically Mexicano, and the use of the Spanish suffix *-es* on *collares* illustrates one of the rare instances of a borrowed affix; *-s, -es* have been added to the Mexicano repertoire of plural suffixes for use on Spanish loan nouns. However, the speaker suddenly changes his approach to these words, noting that *tehhuān* (we) would say a different form—*īcolālex* (her necklaces)—which exhibits a Mexicano possessive marker and phonological nativization of the loan word, including the plural marker [īkolāleš]. In line 4, he further nativizes the form by adding the Mexicano plural suffix for possessives, *-huān*. In line 5, *arete* is replaced by a fully Mexicano form, root and all, *īpīpilōlhuān* (her earrings). These nativized forms are clearly not simply referential "direct words." Instead, they establish a Mexicano "semantic position." In Bakhtin's system, they are double-voiced words of the "active" type, uttered by the Mexicano voice with what Bakhtin called a "side-long glance" at their Spanish alternatives. This passage is not simply a description of the beautiful and seductive Malinche, but a translinguistic battlefield, upon which two ways of speaking struggle for dominance. Bakhtin comments on this capacity for words to shift their position in mid-speaking:

> the interrelationships . . . in a concrete living context have a dynamic, not a static character: the interrelationships of voices within the word can change drastically, a single-directed word can transform itself into a hetero-directed one, the inner dialogization can be intensified or weakened, a passive type can become activated, etc. (Bakhtin 1973[1929]:165).

A second kind of evidence, in addition to the kind of backtracking and reframing seen in example 3, of the representation of the practices of peasant consciousness in speaking can be found in hesitations, stammering, and other failures of fluency, and in violation of systemic constraints on code-switching proposed by Gumperz (1982). An example of this type can be seen in example 4. Here, an elderly cultivator, a full *principal* of his town of San Lorenzo Almecatla on the edge of the Malinche region, discusses how his son was attracted into a shady business deal, which was in conflict with his community responsibilities and which eventually led to his murder.

4. *Huán ōquinōtzqueh de . . . ser tesorero īmināhuac, neh acmo ōniccāhuaya*
   and when they called him . . . to be treasurer with them, I no longer gave permission

   porque lo mismo ōyec presidente.
   because that same person was (municipal) president.

   (He was invited to be treasurer of the local community bus lines, a sure route to gaining wealth through embezzlement.)

In this passage, we see a code switch, between the verb *ōquinōtzqueh* (they called him) and its complement, *de ser tesorero* (to be treasurer), violating

Gumperz's Verb-Verb Complement Constraint (1982:88), which states that code switching will not take place between the two. In general in Malinche usage, this constraint makes an excellent test for assigning a Spanish complement phrase to the category of fully incorporated "borrowing." However, we know that Malinche speakers always emphatically reject Spanish infinitives such as *ser* as "not Mexicano"; this kind of form is particularly accessible to sanction as "mixing." In Bakhtin's terms, we can analyze this example as a struggle (and note the hesitation represented by the ellipses) between a "voice" of corrupt local politicians, speaking in the Spanish of civil government and profit-making commerce, and the Mexicano, peasant, communitarian voice of the narrator. Here, the "Spanish" voice is powerful enough to break through systemic constraints on its appearance, and we see Spanish *ser* instead of Mexicano *yēz* (to be).

If cultivators such as Don Otilio in example 3 and Don Gabriel in example 4 face a struggle with the ambivalent place of the Spanish they have turned to the purposes of Mexicano, we might imagine that the struggle would become particularly acute in the usage of factory workers. Factory workers face a number of problems in the successful presentation of a "Mexicano" identity that will warrant their access to community resources. These resources, distributed through the community ritual sector, are a vital backstop to factory-worker participation in a particularly oppressive and insecure wage labor market, which often denies them legally mandated benefits and minimum wages, and in which they experience frequent layoffs. During layoffs (and even when employed) they are hard-pressed for basic subsistence, and they maintain themselves and their families through the loans that circulate among *compadres,* and the redistribution of high-quality food that takes place in the system of feasting organized through the *mayordomías.* But the identity of factory workers is ambivalent. They can often devote little time to cultivation, relegating these tasks largely to women, children, and the elderly in their families. They find it almost impossible to participate fully in the *mayordomía* system. Since they spend most of their time out of town, they have less opportunity than do cultivators to keep their political fences mended within the town. While the towns value endogamy, factory workers often meet and marry the sisters and daughters of workmates who come from other towns; these women often do not even speak Mexicano (although they usually try very hard to learn it). Such wealth as they have, which comes through wages, is wealth acquired in a "universalistic" sector; the wealth of a cultivator, acquired on his lands (even though lands are privately held, the towns consider the lands "their own" and fiercely defend against acquisition of land by outsiders), is "particularistic"—his access to land and water is possible because he is a *mexicano*, a *campesino*, a *puebleño* (member of the town). The increasing permeability of the towns, because of improved transportation and the penetration of mass media, is a matter of great concern; members of the towns are often quite hostile to outsiders (a hostility that culminated in the murder of three students from Puebla by men of San Miguel Canoa in 1968).[3] Thus, factory workers, in contrast to cultivators, face special problems in authenticating their identity as "member of the town."

The ability to use the Mexicano language is an important badge of such an identity, and here as well factory workers face special problems. Education, particularly for boys, is held to be very important in the towns, and parents often speak in Spanish to children during the school years in order to help them succeed. This means that in late adolescence and early adulthood, many young men are relearning Mexicano as a "first-and-a-half" language. However, a young man who goes to work in a factory spends an enormous amount of time outside the town arena where he might consolidate his Mexicano competence, in an environment—the workplace—where Indian identity is often fiercely stigmatized. Mexicano is used in the workplace only for teasing and joking at the expense of the butt, who is temporarily assigned the identity of a *cuāxepoh* (stupid Indian, literally "grease-head," perhaps related to American English *greaser,* "Mexican"). Thus, workers experience intense pressure toward the local vernacular Spanish norm and are not exposed to as many counterpressures from Mexicano as are cultivators. The two groups exhibit different patterns of bilingualism. Cultivators are likely to exhibit Mexicano interference in Spanish, while workers exhibit the opposite pattern. In example 5 we see this in the speech of a 30-year-old factory worker:

5. *Amo nicpia* pleito, *siempre* niviviroa en paz *ica in notahtzin huan*
   Not I have lawsuits, always live in peace with my father and

   nonantzin huan ica nos-, nopilhuan.
   my mother and with my-, my children.

Here, the frequency of Spanish borrowings is not particularly unusual. However, a Spanish systemic voice dominates. For instance, this speaker does not exhibit contrastive vowel length, as in Mexicano, but has simply a pattern of stress alternation borrowed from Spanish. We also see lexical and morphological penetration. The form *ica* (usually *īca* [with]) is the Mexicano instrumental, not the form for marking accompaniment, which is *īnāhuac*. In the last word, we can see the Spanish agreement pattern appear as the speaker adds *-s,* the Spanish plural, to the Mexicano possessive prefix *no-* (my), in order to make it agree with *pilhuan* (children); he immediately corrects this slip.

Assimilation to Spanish in the usage of young factory workers is also apparent in the syntax of complex sentences, illustrated in example 6 in the usage of a 26-year-old factory worker from the same town as that of the speaker in the previous example.

6. *Pues neh niquimati de que Malintzin cah—como se dice* vivo?*—yoltoc!*
   Well I   I know   that Malinche is—how does one say alive?—alive!

   Yoltoc, huan cerro non, cah sagrado según no imaginación, verdad, de que
   alive, and mountain that, is, sacred according to my imagination, right, that

personas que yahueh ompa quinequi mohuetziz di ipan de que ipan tepetl
people who go there she wants him to fall from on it who on the mountain

yahui, zan yenon.
goes, just that.

Here, again, we notice the absence of vowel-length contrast, and the obvious problem with lexical resources faced by such speakers. In addition the speaker uses the Spanish *que* to form embedded, rather than adjoined, complement and relative clauses. *Que* embeds the complement of the expression of propositional attitude, *según no imaginación* (according to my imagination [understanding, belief]). *Que* also forms the relative clauses, *personas que yahueh* (people who go), and *que ipan tepetl yahui* (who go on the mountain). This speaker is also having difficulty keeping verb number agreement straight, changing from plural *yahueh* (go) to singular *mohuetziz* (will fall) and singular *yahui* (goes). A hispanicized use of Mexicano *cah* (to be in a place) also occurs: here, it is calqued (loan-translated) on Spanish *está*, which can be used for "is in a place," but can also be used to link nouns and predicate adjectives. In Mexicano, we would find *in Malīntzīn, yōltoc* or *yōltoc in Malīntzīn* (the Malinche is alive), without *cah*. Note also that the speaker in example 6 has failed to use the Mexicano adjunctor *in* before the noun *Malintzin* in the first line, as Mexicano would require. This is almost certainly due to the pressure of stigmatization of the use of *in* in Mexicano-ized Spanish.

The pattern in example 6, of interference from Spanish into Mexicano syntax, can be contrasted with the opposite pattern, seen in example 7, a Spanish utterance by Don Otilio, the cultivator of examples 1, 2, and 3.

7. *Como ejemplo ahorita yo, yo es mi tio este señor, ya para mis hijos*
   For example now I, I is my uncle this man, now for my children

   ya se ve ihcōn cē su abuelito.
   now is seen thus one their grandfather.

Here, we find Mexicano lexical interference in *ihcōn* (thus) and *cē* (one). We see interference from Mexicano possessive morphology in the expression *cē su abuelito* (one their grandfather), calqued on Mexicano *cē īncohcoltzīn* (or *cē īmiabuelito*) [one their grandfather]). Perhaps most interesting, however, is the calqued relative clause *yo es mi tio este señor* (this man who is my uncle), a loan translation from Mexicano *neh notio nin señor*, with the addition of the Spanish copula *es* to adjoin *neh and notio.*

These examples show the intrusion of Spanish ways of speaking into the Mexicano usage of young wage laborers. While both cultivators and factory workers exhibit Spanish loan words, the Mexicano voice of most cultivators, while struggling with the ambivalence of Spanish loans, has at least the syntactic and morphological tools to dominate the loan words and turn them to its own purposes. In the usage of most factory workers, however, particularly the young, the Spanish voice has clearly moved into a more dominant position, occasionally penetrating even the morphological system of Mexicano. A highly hispanicized and calqued Mexicano is an inadequate filter for the pressure toward relexification and language shift that young factory workers face.

Members of the community, including factory workers themselves, see the Spanish in the Mexicano speech of such young men as "refunctionalized." Instead of serving as an elegant metonym of authority and prestige, it is seen as a symptom of pollution from the Spanish-speaking world. That is, this Spanish is seen as "Spanish," and a threat to Mexicano identity. In the face of this problem, factory workers often become ferociously purist, particularly as they reach middle age and come into competition with men who in their adult careers have taken the cultivator-ritual participation route to the control of community resources. While all Malinche speakers are capable of purism (as seen in example 3), I have encountered the fully developed purist repertoire only among middle-aged factory workers, who subject other speakers to vocabulary tests, challenge their usage as "mixed" in conversation, focus very self-consciously on selected syntactic phenomena such as noun-number agreement, and argue that no Mexicano usage which now occurs in the communities has any validity, because it is not *legítimo mexicano*. Many factory workers have developed their purism as a weapon to be deployed in a struggle for power; they challenge as "mixed" the hispanicized usage even of prestigious *principales*. Such challenges are often successful, even when the grammar of the challenger is of the type seen in examples 5 and 6 or 8 below, because people are, in general, self-conscious about lexical items, but are not attuned to (or at least do not have an appropriate set of discourses for commenting upon) grammatical structures.[4]

Space does not allow illustration of all of the different kinds of purist discourse, so I illustrate only one type, the challenge of "mixed" usage, as shown in example 8. The challenger is a 60-year-old factory worker, who has lived most of his life in Mexico City, visiting his home town only on weekends. Now retired in the town, he has invested capital saved from wages in political contributions which have brought him the CONASUPO (the national farm-product purchasing agency) maize brokerage for his town. While this is not a "traditional" route to power in these communities, Don Leobardo has become a figure to be reckoned with. In order to work in his town, my husband and I had to seek his permission, even though he held no official position other than the corn brokerage. An American graduate student working in the town asked Don Leobardo's permission to record our conversation with him, and it was given. We went to his house with our Mexicano-speaking interviewer. Don Leobardo was drinking with his cronies, all important men. In conversation, he exhibited purism as a tool of dominance, challenging the identity of the young interviewer by attacking even such seemingly innocent hispanisms as place names and personal names. This is seen in the following brief excerpt:

8. DL: *In teh, ticmah, quenin motoca, non, non tlatzintli, campa titlacat?*
         As for you, do you how your name, that, that land, where you are born?

         Ticmah? Tlen, tlen motoca?
         Do you know? What, what your name?

   I: *Quēnin ītōca in tlālticpac?*
         How its name the earth?

   DL: *Quen itoca in ca-, campa tiviviroa in teh?*
         How its name where, where you live you?

   I: *Pos ihcōn ītōca, San Miguel Canoa.*
         Well thus its name, San Miguel Canoa.

   DL: *Entonces ye morrevolveroh.*
         Then now it is mixed up.

   I: *Ah.*

   DL: *Entonces yocmo igual.*
         Then it's no longer the same.

In this passage, it is evident that Don Leobardo's Mexicano has become a virtual pidgin. He calques even routine expressions on Spanish, saying, for instance, *quenin motoca* (How your name) instead of universal Mexicano *tlen motōca* (What your name). In the first utterance, he does not, in fact, mean *motōca*, (your name), but *ītōca* (its name). He has forgotten to prefix the antecessive marker *ō-* to the past tense verb *-titlacat* (you were born). The form *morrevolveroh* (it is mixed up) should be *morevolveroa*, or perhaps *ōmorevolveroh* (it was mixed up). Don Leobardo, like the speakers in examples 5 and 6, lacks the long-short vowel contrast. His Mexicano is so bad that the interviewer has some difficulty understanding him, and requests clarification. However, his performance is received with complete seriousness by his fellow townsmen, and also by the interviewer, who is fully aware of his power. Fortunately, after scoring several purist points, Don Leobardo grew friendly and eventually became one of our most helpful supporters.

Confronted with the possibility of this kind of linguistic terrorism, many young people prefer not to speak Mexicano, except in contexts where it is absolutely required. The interviewer stood up to Don Leobardo's attack because it was his job to speak in Mexicano, even to hostile strangers to whom one would normally speak Spanish. Thus, purist rhetoric joins other pressures in driving Mexicano into an underground, often secret, solidarity code. Don Leobardo is "speaking Mexicano," but the Spanish origin of his purist voice is clearly apparent in the form of his usage, and its result, discouraging the use of Mexicano, is entirely in line with national policy. And, of course, Don Leobardo is in no position to tell anyone how to say "San Miguel Canoa" in *legítimo mexicano;* as far as we know, there is only one native speaker of Mexicano on the Malinche, the scholarly Don Amado Morales of Santa Catarina Ayometitla, who owns dictionaries and grammars of this language. The Spanish voice that uses Don Leobardo as its mouthpiece can also be heard in the cities, where we were often told that there was no point in studying Malinche Mexicano because it was so broken down and his-panicized. The failure of this purist voice to provide an alternative derives also from a national policy that provides no indigenous-language educational materi-als in the Malinche region.

The debate over the structural position within the world system of populations like that of the Malinche Volcano has been conducted almost exclusively in mate-rialist terms. Only Arturo Warman has seen the importance of studying the "sym-bolic flow"—the "words and ideas [which] actually connect the modes of produc-tion and shape their relations toward the inside and toward the outside" (Warman 1980:304). In this paper, I hope I have shown that attention to language can shed important light on the nature of consciousness, the symbolic practice of a struc-tural position. Close examination of usage and structure in the speech of the peo-ple of the Malinche reveals several points of interest. First, it shows that the peas-ant use of Mexicano, far from being conservative, is a dynamic and highly creative endeavor which draws widely on the symbolic resources of its environment. Second, it shows that there are important differences between different kinds of people who all "speak Mexicano." These differences in linguistic practice suggest that the delicate balancing act of "peasant autonomy" is beginning to fail; the con-tradictions within the material sphere, as well as the contradictions within the sym-bolic sphere, seem to be yielding a shift in which the capitalist sector and its Spanish voice are gaining the upper hand. Interestingly, the linguistic data are eas-ier to interpret than the economic data. While Bartra (1978) proposes that Mexican "peasant" populations are in fact a rural proletariat, in contrast to the argument of Warman and Stavenhagen that they constitute a "peasant mode of production," it is in fact very difficult to test whether or not an institution like the stewardship of the saints has been refunctionalized and brought under domination by the capital-ist sector, or whether it is still structurally shaped within an autonomous peasant mode.[5] But the structuralist tools of the linguist give a much clearer picture of the relative dominance of "Mexicano" and "Spanish" voices, and provide access to a structural index that might be consulted with profit by political economists.

Notes

Acknowledgments. Work on Mexicano has been sponsored by the National Endowment for the Humanities (NEH-RO-20495-74-572), by the American Council of Learned Societies, and by the Penrose Fund of the American Philosophical Society. I would like to thank Naomi Quinn, Gillian Feeley-Harnick, Alice Ingerson, and the other participants in the symposium on Language and Consciousness at the Spring 1985 Annual Meeting of the American Ethnological Society for their comments on this paper; responsibility for error is, of course, my own.

1. It has become customary to include a discussion of whether Voloshinov's *Marxism and the Philosophy of Language* (1973[1930]), with its great article on reported speech, was

really written by Bakhtin. My own view is that until the question is definitively settled (and currently I believe it is not), we should give credit to both scholars. In the present paper I have neglected the terminological categories of Voloshinov's work in favor of those developed by Bakhtin in *Problems of Dostoevsky's Poetics*, (1973[1929]), but the two treatments of the interactions of the word are closely related. The theoretical foundations of the treatment in Marxism are detailed in the Voloshinov work; in Bakhtin's treatment, they are not (scholars like Todorov have emphasized Bakhtin's eclecticism).

2. This is not the only refunctionalization of Mexicano symbolic values by the Spanish-speaking sector. The Mexican state has "folklorized" (Jaulin 1979) Mexicano speech, turning it into a source of handy lexical vehicles for indigenist patriotism. It is interesting to note that one of the main expressions of this, the giving of Mexicano personal names such as *Xochitl* (Flower) and *Cuauhtemoc* (Eagle Descended) (the name of the last ruler of the Mexica Aztec) to children, has penetrated the Malinche, being currently popular among the best-educated young couples. Many local priests strongly oppose such names, and I know of at least one case where a couple took advantage of the town priest's brief absence at a conference to have a more liberal-minded visitor baptize their child. Mexicano surnames such as *Xaxalpa* (Sandy Place) and *Tecxis* (Land Snail) are common on the Malinche.

3. No Malinche people seem to be involved in collective class action. The sort of sporadic violence represented by the Canoa incident, was over land between towns, and a high level of interpersonal violence are the major manifestations of the structural contradictions facing Malinche people. Like Mexicano-speaking people elsewhere in Mexico, they do not see themselves as "tribal," and have not formed an "Indian Council," the kind of organization that has emerged among some other indigenous groups with the blessing of the ruling PRI party. Very few Malinche factory workers are members of unions, and many people who have been involved in factory work see their major political outlet as being the official national peasant organization, the CNC.

4. Both Sapir and Whorf addressed the question of what kinds of categories in language might become the object of conscious consideration; Boas, of course, believed that patterning in language was generally inaccessible to consciousness. However, Sapir noted that both scholars and bilinguals were often quite conscious of linguistic categories of all types. The degree of "consciousness" of a linguistic category is quite possibly related to the kinds of social use that are made of that category. While in general lexical usages seem to be particularly accessible to stereotyping, phonological usages and grammatical usages have also become sociolinguistic markers (as in r-less and negative-concord versus r-ful and negative-polarity varieties of American English).

5. Perhaps the most detailed treatment of this problem is found in Greenberg (1982), where data from homicide are used to explore the structural function of the *cargo* system among the Chatino of Oaxaca.

References

Bakhtin, Mikhail M. 1968[1940]. Rabelais and His World. Cambridge, MA: MIT Press.
———. 1973[1929]. Problems of Dostoevsky's Poetics. Ann Arbor, MI: Ardis.
———. 1980[1935]. The Dialogic Imagination. Austin: University of Texas Press.
Bartra, Roger. 1978. Capitalism and the Peasantry in Mexico. Latin American Perspectives 9:36–47.
Brown, Roger, and A. Gilman. 1960. The Pronouns of Power and Solidarity. *In* Style in Language. T. Sebeok, ed. pp. 253–276. Cambridge, MA: The Technology Press.

Diebold, A. Richard. 1961. Incipient Bilingualism. Language 37:91–110.

Greenberg, James. 1982. Santiago's Sword. Berkeley: University of California Press.

Gumperz, John. 1982. Discourse Strategies. Cambridge: Cambridge University Press.

Jaulin, Robert. 1979. Del Folklore. *In* La Des-Civilización. R. Jaulin, ed. pp. 85–90. México: Editorial Nueva Imagen.

Karttunen, Frances, and James Lockhart. 1976. Nahuatl in the Middle Years. University of California Publications in Linguistics 85.

Lastra de Suárez, Yolanda, and Fernando Horcasitas. 1979. El Náhuatl en el Estado de Tlaxcala. Anales de Antropología 16:275–323.

Lukács, Georg. 1968. History and Class Consciousness. Cambridge, MA: MIT Press.

Markey, Thomas L. 1983. Change Typologies: Questions and Answers in German. Studies in Language and Literature in Older Germanic Dialects. B. Brogyany and T. Krommelbein, eds. (forthcoming)

Nutini, Hugo G. 1984. Ritual Kinship: Ideological and Structural Integration of the Compadrazgo System in Rural Tlaxcala. Princeton: Princeton University Press.

Nutini, Hugo G., and Betty Bell. 1980. Ritual Kinship: The Structure and Historical Development of the Compadrazgo System in Rural Tlaxcala. Princeton: Princeton University Press.

Nutini, Hugo G., and Barry L. Isaac. 1974. Los Pueblos de Habla Náhuatl de la Región de Puebla y Tlaxcala. México: Instituto Nacional Indigenista.

Olivera, Mercedes. 1967. Tlaxcalancingo. Instituto Nacional de Antropología e Historia, Departamento de Investigaciones Antropológicas, Publicación No. 18. México.

Rothstein, Frances. 1974. Factions in a Rural Community in Mexico. Ph.D. dissertation. University of Pittsburgh.

Todorov, Tzvetan. 1981. Mikhaíl Bakhtine, Le Principle Dialogique Suive de Écrits du Cercle de Bakhtine. Paris: Editions du Seuil.

Voloshinov, V. N. 1973[1930]. Marxism and the Philosophy of Language. New York: Seminar Press.

Warman, Arturo. 1980. "We Come to Object": The Peasants of Morelos and the National State. Baltimore: Johns Hopkins University Press.

About the Book and Editors

The Matrix of Language introduces students and other readers to recent debates in the study of language and culture. The articles in this anthology, selected for their readability, present a range of methodological approaches and well-known case studies that illustrate the interconnection of language, culture, and social practice. The editors' introductory essays compare and contrast specific approaches in four broad areas: language and socialization, gender, the ethnography of speaking, and the role of language in social and political life. The book is a valuable introduction in linguistic anthropology and sociolinguistics courses and a resource for anyone exploring the relation of language to psychology, political theory, feminist studies, and literature and folklore.

Donald Brenneis, professor of anthropology at Pitzer College, is the former editor of *American Ethnologist*. **Ronald K.S. Macaulay** is professor of linguistics at Pitzer College.

Contributors

Richard Bauman is Distinguished Professor of Folklore at Indiana University.

A. L. Becker is professor emeritus of linguistics and anthropology at the University of Michigan

Ruth A. Borker was teaching in the Sociology/Anthropology Department at Randolph-Macon Women's College at the time of her death.

Penelope Eckert is associated with Xerox-PARC, Palo Alto, and teaches in the Department of Linguistics at Stanford University.

Steven Feld is professor of anthropology at the University of California, Santa Cruz.

Shirley Brice Heath is professor of English and linguistics at Stanford University.

Jane H. Hill is professor of anthropology and linguistics at the University of Arizona.

Judith T. Irvine is professor of anthropology at Brandeis University.

José E. Limón is professor of English at the University of Texas.

Daniel N. Maltz is an independent scholar in Lynchburg, Virginia.

Fred R. Myers is professor of anthropology at New York University.

Elinor Ochs is professor of applied linguistics at U.C.L.A.

Bambi B. Schieffelin is professor of anthropology at New York University.

Michael Silverstein is Samuel N. Harper Professor of Anthropology, Linguistics, and Psychology at The University of Chicago.

Ruth Smith is assistant professor in the Department of Speech Communications at Purdue University

Carolyn Taylor is assistant professor of speech communication at the University of Illinois, Champaign-Urbana

Credits

Chapter 2: Shirley Brice Heath, "What No Bedtime Story Means: Narrative Skills at Home and School," *Language and Society* 11 (1982). ©1982 Cambridge University Press. Reprinted with the permission of Cambridge University Press.

Chapter 3: Reprinted from Elinor Ochs, Ruth Smith, and Carolyn Taylor, "Detective Stories at Dinnertime: Problem-Solving Through Co-Narration," *Cultural Dynamics* 2 (1989) by permission of Sage Publications Ltd.

Chapter 4: Steven Feld and Bambi B. Schieffelin, "Hard Words: A Functional Basis for Kaluli Discourse," in *Analyzing Discourse: Text and Talk*, ed. Deborah Tannen (Washington, D.C.: Georgetown University Press, 1981). Reprinted by permission.

Chapter 5: Daniel N. Maltz and Ruth A. Borker, "A Cultural Approach to Male-Female Miscommunication," in *Language and Social Identity*, ed. John J. Gumperz (New York: Cambridge University Press, 1983). Reprinted with the permission of Cambridge University Press.

Chapter 6: Elinor Keenan (Ochs), "Norm-Makers, Norm-Breakers: Uses of Speech by Men and Women in a Malagasy Community," in *Explorations in the Ethnography of Speaking*, 2d ed., ed. Richard Bauman and Joel Sherzer (New York: Cambridge University Press, 1989). Reprinted with the permission of Cambridge University Press.

Chapter 7: Penelope Eckert, "The Whole Woman: Sex and Gender Differences in Variation," *Language Variation and Change* 1 (1989). ©1990 Cambridge University Press. Reprinted with the permission of Cambridge University Press.

Chapter 8: A. L. Becker, "Biography of a Sentence: A Burmese Proverb," reproduced by permission of the American Anthropological Association from *Text, Play, and Story* (1984). Not for further reproduction.

Chapter 9: Richard Bauman, "'Any Man Who Keeps More'n One Hound'll Lie to You,'" in *Story, Performance, and Event: Contextual Studies of Oral Narrative*, ed. Richard Bauman (New York: Cambridge University Press, 1986). Reprinted with the permission of Cambridge University Press.

Chapter 10: José E. Limón, "Carne, Carnales, and the Carnivalesque: Bakhtinian Batos, Disorder, and Narrative Discourses," reproduced by permission of the American Anthropological Association from *American Ethnologist* 16:3, August 1989. Not for further reproduction.

Chapter 11: Donald Brenneis, "Grog and Gossip in Bhatgaon: Style and Substance in Fiji Indian Conversation," reproduced by permission of the American Anthropological Association from *American Ethnologist* 11:3, August 1984. Not for further reproduction.

Index